KU-166-078

The Hamlyn Encyclopedia of
SNOOKER

EXIT
EMBASSY WORLD SNOOKER
EMBASSY WORLD SNOOKER

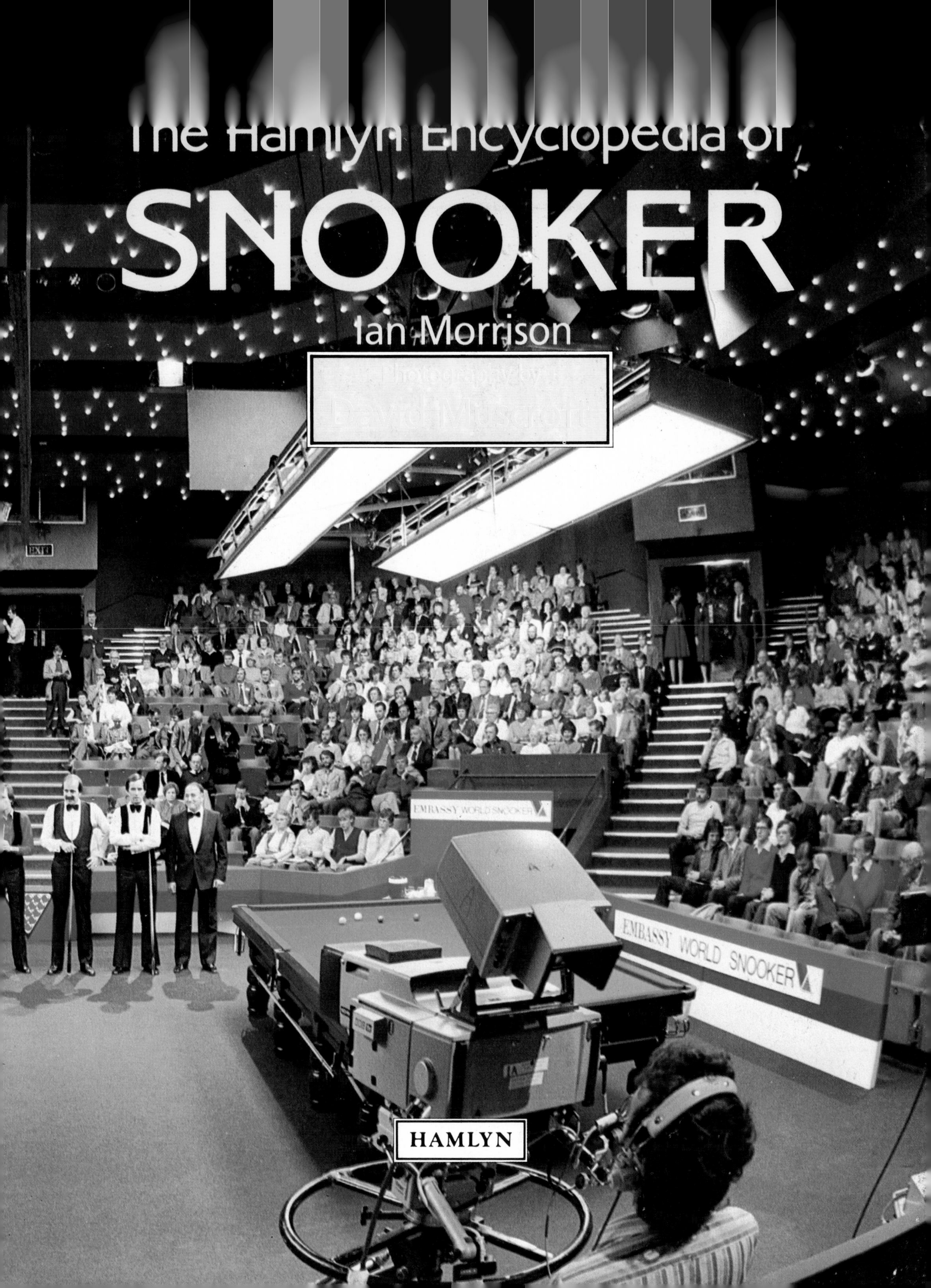
The Hamlyn Encyclopedia of
SNOOKER
Ian Morrison
Photography by
David Muscroft
EMBASSY WORLD SNOOKER
EMBASSY WORLD SNOOKER
HAMLYN

Prepared and typeset by Peter MacDonald, Twickenham
Designed by Grahame Dudley

First published in 1985 by
The Hamlyn Publishing Group Limited
Bridge House, 69 London Road
Twickenham, Middlesex TW1 3SB
and distributed for them by
Octopus Distribution Services Limited
Rushden, Northamptonshire, England

Second impression 1986
Revised and updated 1987

ISBN 0 600 55604 2

Printed and bound by Graficromo s.a., Cordoba, Spain

Acknowledgements

The author and publishers gratefully acknowledge the help and co-operation of the following in the preparation of this book: Bernard Franks and Roy Stobbs, former secretaries of the Billiards and Snooker Control Council; David Ford, the current secretary of the B&SCC and all his staff at their Leeds headquarters; Arthur Raison, secretary of the Billiards and Snooker Referees' Association; and all players, referees and officials, the world over, who kindly provided information for the compilation of this encyclopedia.

All photographs were supplied by David Muscroft (Ad. Lib. Photo Agency) with the exception of those on pages 28, 48, 64 (both), and 128 (top left) which were supplied by the Billiards and Snooker Control Council, that on page 65 which was loaned by Mrs Kingsley Kennerley, and that on page 112 by the Mansell Collection.

To Les Dodd,
without whom I would never have been
interested in snooker in the first place

Introduction

by Dennis Taylor
1985 World Professional Snooker Champion

Over the last fifteen years or so, the game of snooker has emerged from relative obscurity to become one of the most popular of all pastimes, for players and spectators alike. Some of the credit for this must of course go to the television companies, whose excellent coverage of the major snooker tournaments has brought this colourful game into homes up and down the country, at home and abroad, to an audience many of whose members have never lifted a cue. But the snooker circuit is not by any means a media invention: the game has a history, with elegant conventions, its own legendary figures and famous incidents; those who play the game now are continuing a tradition that goes back to India in the last century and beyond, to when a form of billiards was played on the lawns of the French aristocracy.

As professional players we all welcome the increase in popularity that the game has undergone – not simply because the rewards are greater, but because the contests are tougher, the pressures more intense and the matches often more exciting as a result. A good number of young players, who might otherwise have gone very different ways, have been attracted into the sport and are building brilliant careers. These are lively times, and it seems certain that over the next few years snooker will continue to increase in popularity all over the world.

This encyclopedia gives a detailed insight into the sport, and I am sure it will provide enjoyment as well as information for anyone who wants to learn more about the fascinating game of snooker.

Dennis Taylor
Blackburn, July 1985

Amateur

Although the world championships and national championships are still referred to as amateur championships, the word 'amateur' no longer exists in the eyes of the governing bodies, the Billiards and Snooker Control Council (B&SCC) or the International Billiards and Snooker Federation. There are two categories of players – professionals and non-professionals.

In 1970 the World Professional Billiards and Snooker Association (WPBSA) broke away from the B&SCC, and they recognized professional players only. Thus a professional was deemed to be a player who was a member of the WPBSA – other players were then known as non-professionals.

On 27 November 1972, a few hours after the Football Association passed a resolution abolishing the word 'amateur' from their sport, the B&SCC did the same. The new resolution was to come into force on 1 July 1973.

Restrictions on prize money won by amateurs also disappeared in 1972; there are now no restrictions on their earnings whatsoever. The lifting of these restrictions resulted in the introduction of more open events.

Up until then, the competitions a top-class amateur could take part in were few and far between: he was generally restricted to his own area. Open events, played all over the country, gave amateur players the opportunity to play alongside professionals. And also it gave less successful professionals the opportunity to compete regularly.

The first amateur to win a four-figure sum from a snooker tournament was Doug Mountjoy who took the £1,000 first prize in the inaugural Pontins Open in 1974. There are many open events in which high-class amateurs can compete regularly, most of them carrying first prizes around £1,000-£2,000.

A gifted amateur can earn good money from these events. For instance, Steve Newbury, accepted as a professional in 1984, won £8,000 as an amateur in 1983 – he earned nowhere near that sum in his first professional season!

The WPBSA abandoned its application scheme in 1985 and introduced two Professional Ticket tournaments in which points, and merit points, were awarded based on performance. The leading eight players at the end of the two tournaments were invited to join the professional ranks for the 1985-86 season. The number of Ticket tournaments was increased to four in 1986 when, again, the top eight players were invited to join the professional ranks, along with the winner of the English Amateur title. The appropriate number of lowest ranked professionals at the end of the season lose their membership of the WPBSA.

See also English Amateur Championships
World Amateur Championships

Assembly Rooms

The present-day Derby Assembly Rooms were built in 1977. They stand on the site of the former Assembly Rooms building, which was used only as a dance-hall. The new premises are used

One of England's best-known amateurs, George Wood – among jubilant Vic Harris supporters after Harris had beaten Wood in the 1981 English amateur final

for a variety of events, ranging from film shows to live entertainment, from an annual beer festival to the recording of the BBC *Best of Brass* programme. Now an established home of professional snooker, the venue has also staged squash tournaments in the past. The impressive tiered accommodation makes it an attractive proposition for snooker spectators, and the great hall can hold in the region of 1,500 of them.

The first major snooker event to be held at the Assembly Rooms was the 1980 British Gold Cup. Alex Higgins was a popular winner of that first trophy, and delighted the audience with breaks of 135 and 134 in consecutive frames. When the Yamaha International Masters succeeded the British Gold Cup in 1981, the new tournament continued to have the Assembly Rooms as its home.

Snooker lost the support of Yamaha in the 1984-85 season, but a sponsor was found for a new tournament. The Dulux British Open took place at the Assembly Rooms, and thus ensured that Derby maintained its connection with the sport.

Association of Billiards and Snooker Referees

The Association of Billiards and Snooker Referees was founded in September 1977, with Len Oldham as its fi st chairman and Arthur Raison as its first secretary. Len Oldham has since died, and his position has been filled by Ernie Smith of Coventry. But Arthur Raison continues his work as the association's secretary from his Birmingham base.

The idea of the association was mooted by Stan Brooke and Len Oldham many years prior to its actual formation. Since 1977 it has introduced greater uniformity in the examination of referees and, in conjunction with the Billiards and Snooker Control Council, has brought about standard interpretation of the rules of the games.

Bill Werbeniuk – the first recipient of the Snooker Writers' 'Personality of the Year' award

There are approximately 500 members of the association, either as direct members, or via local County Billiards and Snooker Associations.

Association of Snooker Writers

Formed in 1981, the Association of Snooker Writers held its first full meeting during the 1982 Benson and Hedges Masters tournament at the Wembley Conference Centre.

The founder members of the Association were:
Alex Clyde (*New Standard*)
Ted Corbett (*Daily Star*)
Clive Everton (*Guardian/Sunday Times*)
Sydney Friskin (*The Times*)
Janice Hale (*Daily Telegraph/Observer*)
Terry Smith (*Daily Mirror*)

The Association conducts its business under the chairmanship of Clive Everton, with Janice Hale as secretary. One of its prime functions is to make annual awards to snooker personalities. The annual presentation is regarded as snooker's Oscar night. The first presentation evening was held at the Redwood Lodge Country Club Bristol in September 1983, and the same venue staged the second awards night in 1984. The awards were taken over by the WPBSA in 1985 (*see* WPBSA).

The recipients of the Association's awards have been:
1983 Player of the Year: Steve Davis
Personality of the Year: Bill Werbeniuk
Services to Snooker Award: Mike Watterson

1984 Player of the Year: Steve Davis
Personality of the Year: Dennis Taylor
Services to Snooker Award: Clive Everton
Special Trophy: Mike Green (retiring secretary of the WPBSA)

Attendances

Unlike many other sporting events, attendances at snooker matches are rarely recorded. It would in any case be pointless to compare attendances of one match against those at another because one match may consist of a single session whereas another may consist of four sessions. In the case of the latter, the four attendances would constitute the match attendance.

The record attendance for any one session at a professional tournament in Great Britain was in the first round of the 1983 Benson and Hedges Masters at the Wembley Conference Centre when 2,876 watched the Bill Werbeniuk-Alex Higgins match (which Werbeniuk won 5-4).

Because of its capacity, the Wembley Conference Centre has been responsible for the leading attendances in Britain. There have, however, been some other notably large attendances, as follows:

☆ The 1972 Park Drive tournament play-off match at Belle Vue, Manchester, between Alex Higgins and John Spencer attracted a crowd of 2,000. This was believed to be the first 2,000 crowd at a competitive snooker match in Britain. Spencer won 5-3.

☆ Crowds of 2,000 or more for a session are the exception rather than the rule. But in 1982, Tony Meo and Steve Davis attracted crowds of that order on their first visit to the Thai-Nippon Stadium in Thailand.

☆ The lowest known paying attendance for a match involving two professionals in tournament play was in 1982. The first round match between Jim Meadowcroft and Bernard Bennett in the Professional Players' Tournament at Birmingham attracted a paying audience of *one*!

☆ The 1975 Pontins Open final between Ray Reardon and Patsy Fagan attracted a crowd of 1,500. This was surprising in view of the fact that the match started at 10.30 a.m.

Australia

It was an Irishman named Henry Upton Allcock who was responsible for taking the games of billiards and snooker to Australia. A billiard table manufacturer, he emigrated to Australia in the mid-18th century, and it was not long before he was continuing his successful trade in his new homeland.

The demand for his product was high, and in order to stimulate further interest in the game he brought some of the leading professional billiards players over from England to give exhibition matches. In 1887 the English professional Frank Smith Senior arrived in Australia and introduced the game of snooker. It is believed that Smith learned the game from one of the sport's pioneers – John Roberts Junior.

One of the most famous names in the two sports in Australia at that time – and for many years after – was Lindrum. The first member of that famous family to come to prominence, Fred Lindrum, was the Australian professional billiards champion at the turn of the century. He was eventually succeeded as champion in 1908 by his son Fred Junior, who, in turn, was succeeded by his nephew Horace Lindrum in 1934. Fred Senior was also the father of one of the greatest billiards players the world has ever seen – Walter Lindrum.

But it was Horace who was the best of the snooker-playing Lindrums. Very talented, he was first seen in Britain in 1936 when he met Joe Davis in the final of the world professional championships. He led Davis 27-24 at one point. But in the end Davis showed his class and came back to win 31-27.

Lindrum lost in the final to Davis twice more, in 1937 and 1946. But in 1952 he finally succeeded in becoming world champion when he beat Clark McConachy in a two-man championship, to become the only Australian ever to win the title.

Between the end of Lindrum's career and the beginning of Eddie Charlton's, the Australian scene was dominated by two men – Norman Squire and Warren Simpson. The Australian billiards championships date back to 1920 but, surprisingly, the first snooker championships were not held until 1953. Warren Simpson became the first champion when he beat Robert Marshall in the final. Seventeen years later he was the surprise finalist in the world professional championships.

The competition was held in Australia in 1970 for the first time. Eddie Charlton was one of the fancied competitors, but in the semi-finals Charlton and Simpson were drawn together, and it was Simpson who sprang a surprise by winning 27-22. The final saw Simpson up against John Spencer, but Spencer proved too strong for the Australian, winning by 37-29.

It is Eddie Charlton, however, who has been the leading Australian professional during recent years. Apart from holding the Australian professional championship from 1964 to 1984 (except 1968) Charlton has won very little in major championships. But despite this, he is regularly among the big earners, and never far away from the major tournaments.

Eddie Charlton held the Australian professional title every year from 1964 to 1984, with the exception of 1968

The world title eluded him on the three occasions he reached the final. In 1968 he lost to John Pulman, in 1973 to Ray Reardon, and in 1975 to Reardon again, when he was involved in an epic final. The Welshman eventually won the best-of-61 frame match by just one frame.

Three amateur players that deserve special mention are Frank Harris, Max Williams and Ron Atkins, who all finished runner-up in the world amateur championship.

As in Britain, snooker in Australia is gaining in popularity and is beginning to attract television audiences. The longest professional snooker event in Australia, the Winfield Masters, is the Australian equivalent of the BBC's *Pot Black*. The tournament attracts leading professionals from all over the world, and in 1983 the format was altered to a traditional knockout format.

There was a threatened split in Australian professional snooker in 1984, but fortunately the Australian Professional Players' Association (dominated by Eddie Charlton) and the new Australian Billiards and Snooker Association settled their differences. A new body, the Australian Professional Players' Association (Billiards and Snooker) Limited, was formed as the accepted Australian professional body. Ian Anderson was elected chairman, with Eddie Charlton as vice-chairman.

Australian Professional Championship

Most national professional championships have had mixed lives. The Australian championship is no exception.

It was revived in 1984 when the World Professional Billiards and Snooker Association announced its £1,000-per-entrant sponsorship of national championships, and also as a result of sponsorship from Tooheys brewery. This was the first time the championship had been contested since 1978, and Eddie Charlton won the title he had last won six years earlier.

Charlton's long reign as champion ended in 1985 when John Campbell beat him 10-7 in the final. Charlton missed his first final since taking the title in 1964 when Warren King and John Campbell contested the 1986 final. King won 10-3. King beat Charlton 10-7 to retain his title in 1987.

Australia – Results (finals)

National snooker championship

1953 W. Simpson beat R. Marshall
1954 W. Simpson beat F. Edwards
1955 E. Pickett beat J. Harris
1956 R. Marshall beat W. Simpson
1957 W. Simpson beat R. Marshall
1958 F. Harris beat W. Simpson
1959 K. Burles beat F. Harris
1960 K. Burles beat R. Marshall
1961 M. Williams beat L. Rahilly
1962 W. Barrie beat J. Lyons
1963 F. Harris beat W. Barrie
1964 W. Barrie beat F. Harris
1965 W. Barrie beat A. Cuffe
1966 M. Williams beat R. Atkins
1967 M. Williams beat R. King
1968 M. Williams beat R. Meares
1969 W. Barrie beat M. Williams
1970 M. Williams beat H. Andrews
1971 M. Williams beat G. Miller
1972 M. Williams beat B. McLass
1973 M. Williams beat B. McLass
1974 J. Condo beat J. Campbell
1975 R. Atkins beat F. Thomas
1976 R. Atkins beat L. Heywood
1977 R. Atkins beat J. Bonner
1978 K. Burles beat R. Atkins
1979 J. Campbell beat J. Bonner
1980 W. King beat J. Giannaros
1981 W. King beat J. Campbell
1982 J. Giannaros beat W. King
1983 G. Lackenby beat A. Campbell
1984 G. Wilkinson beat A. Campbell
1985 J. Bonner beat P. Tarrant
1986 G. Miller beat P. Hawkes
1987 P. Hawkes beat R. Farebrother

Most wins: 8 – Max Williams
Most finals: 9 – Max Williams
Highest break: 119 – R. Atkins (1986)

Australian Open

1954 W. Simpson beat F. Edwards
1955 Not held
1956 Not held
1957 W. Simpson beat N. Squire
1958 Not held
1959 Not held
1960 F. Davis (England) beat K. Burles

Ladies' Championship

1975 Fran Lovis beat Marion Westaway
1976 Fran Lovis beat Lesley McIlrath
1977 Fran Lovis beat Lesley McIlrath
1978 Fran Lovis beat Ann Depac
1979 Fran Lovis beat Lesley McIlrath
1980 Lesley McIlrath beat Fran Lovis
1981 Lesley McIlrath beat Ann Green (née Depac)
1982 Megan Fullerton beat Lesley McIlrath
1983 Fran Lovis beat Linda Lucas
1984 Megan Fullerton beat Fran Lovis
1985 Linda Lucas beat Megan Fullerton

Australian Junior Championship

1979 G. Jenkins beat D. Ida
1980 D. Jones beat G. Jenkins
1981 L. Higgins beat R. Leighton
1982 R. Leighton beat D. Keygan
1983 N. Vasic beat M. Jobson

See also Australian Professional Championship
Winfield Australian Masters

Warren King – one of Australia's professionals who challenged Eddie Charlton's supremacy

B

Balls

Present-day snooker and billiards balls are made of resin composition, which has proved to be an economical and acceptable substitute for the old ivory balls. Ivory had been used in ball-manufacture from the early days of snooker, and remained popular until the mid-1920s, when it was superseded by resin composition. Ivory had replaced wood at the beginning of the 19th century, and had it not been for an American, John Wesley Hyatt, the ivory ball would probably have been in use much longer. It was Hyatt who invented celluloid in the 1860s, and this invention was used in the manufacture of billiard balls.

It took some years from the manufacture of the first 'artificial' balls, however, for them to become adopted officially. The breakthrough came in 1926, when composition balls became the approved type for the English amateur championships. The following year they were accepted by the professionals.

Originally less than two inches in diameter, the first 2-inch billiard balls were seen in 1830, when table manufacturer John Thurston started supplying them with all his tables.

The modern ball must be 52·5mm (2¹⁄₁₆ inches) in diameter, with a tolerence of +0·05mm to -0·08mm. Each ball in a full set must be of equal weight, with a tolerance of three grams per set. The 2¹⁄₁₆-inch diameter ball has been the regulation size ever since the rules of snooker were first drawn up.

John Wesley Hyatt – inventor of the composition ball

Barron, Jonathan
Jonathan Barron is in the record books as the only person to have won the English amateur snooker championship three years in succession – and he is likely to remain the only player to perform that feat. The recent trend is for the winner of the title to apply for professional status. That was not the case in Barron's day; in fact he never joined the professional ranks. He first hit the headlines in 1963 when he became the second man, after Mark Wildman, to score a century break on television. The leading amateur in the early seventies, he appeared in his first national final in 1962, when he lost to Ron Gross 11-9.

Barron's first success in the amateur championship came in 1970, when he beat the northern champion Sid Hood 11-10 in a close final. The second leg of the hat-trick was achieved in 1971 when he beat Doug French, again in a close match, 11-9. And he completed the hat-trick by gaining sweet revenge over Ray Edmonds in 1972, in what was yet another close contest at 11-9.

Winning the national title gave Barron the right to enter the world amateur championships, which he did in 1970, when they were held in Edinburgh. He went on to win the final, beating Sid Hood (whom he had beaten in that year's national final). On his way to the world title he lost only one match – a group match – to Ireland's Jack Rogers.

As national champion in 1972, he again went to the world championships, and once again he did not have too far to travel, as they were held in Cardiff. However, he could not retain his title, but lost in the semi-final to the man he had beaten in the English amateur final – Ray Edmonds.

Barron hails from Mevagissey in Cornwall, and is quite content playing in the local league. He has resisted the temptation to compete at the top level since his glory days in the early seventies, and decided to concentrate his efforts on his curio shop overlooking the harbour at Mevagissey.

Career highlights
World Amateur Champion 1970
English Amateur Champion 1970, 1971, 1972

Baulk
Baulk is the area of the table between the bottom cushion and the baulk-line. The baulk-line is drawn parallel to the bottom cushion and 73·66cm (29 inches) away from it. No balls are placed in the baulk area at the beginning of a game except the cue-ball, which must be placed in the 'D' at the start of a game.

Baynton, Maureen
Undoubtedly one of the leading female players of the post-war years, Maureen Baynton won a record eight national titles at snooker and seven at billiards. That list would have been even longer had she not taken a nine-year spell out of the game.

Born in Peckham, Maureen Barrett (as she was then) was schoolgirl champion in 1947 at the age of ten, and from there she progressed into the senior ranks. Her first national title came in 1954 when, as a 17-year-old, she won the women's amateur snooker championship for the first time. The following year she was both national billiards and snooker champion. She won both titles in the same season on six occasions, the last time being in 1968, the year in which she turned professional. But

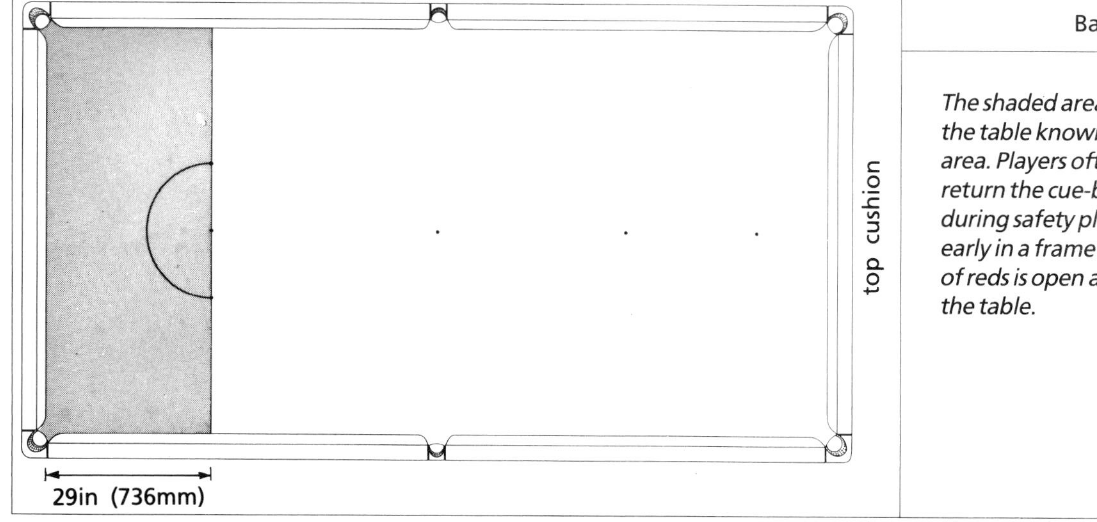

Baulk

The shaded area is the part of the table known as the baulk area. Players often aim to return the cue-ball into baulk during safety play, especially early in a frame when the pack of reds is open at the top end of the table.

unfortunately, financial guarantees did not materialize; disillusioned with the sport, Maureen went into retirement.

She returned to snooker in 1976, reverting to her amateur status, and since her return has remained one of the better players on the women's circuit, although she has to contend with the increasingly high quality of players from Britain, Australia and Canada.

Maureen Baynton is very excited at the future prospects of the women's game, which could well have seen a second member of the Baynton household join the women's snooker circuit: 19-year-old daughter Wendy is a competent player – she was coached by Jack Karnehm – but she decided not to follow in her mother's footsteps and is pursuing a business career instead.

Career highlights

- National Amateur Snooker Champion 1954-56, 1961-62, 1964, 1966, 1968
- National Amateur Billiards Champion 1955-57, 1961, 1964, 1968
- Pontins Women's Champion 1979
- World Open Championship (runner-up) 1983

BCE International

See Fidelity Unit Trusts International

Belgium

In 1984 there were fewer than 12 full-sized billiard tables in the whole of Belgium. Three years later there were 22 clubs in Brussels alone, and more than 200 in the entire country, as Belgians made the rapid switch from carom (pocketless billiards) to snooker.

The country had produced world-beaters at carom – for example Raymond Ceulemans and Ludo Dielis – but it was not until such stars as Steve Davis, Alex Higgins, Jimmy White, Terry Griffiths and others took part in the first BCE Belgian Classic in 1986 that the country became hooked on snooker. The television viewing figures outnumbered those for the country's national sport, cycling – and that is a considerable achievement.

Terry Griffiths beat Kirk Stevens 9-7 in the final of the inaugural Classic but, because of a clash of dates with the new Matchroom League in 1987 and the failure to attract the leading players, the second Classic was cancelled. However, this has not dampened the enthusiasm of the Belgian public, and more and more of them are taking to the sport daily.

Benson and Hedges Irish Masters

The only major snooker tournament held in a bloodstock sales ring, the Benson and Hedges Irish Masters is very much at home in the surroundings of the 744-seater Goffs Sales Ring (the world's fourth largest), at Kill, County Kildare, not far from Dublin. Held there every year since the first tournament in 1978, the event is well supported and receives television coverage from Radio Telefis Eireann. First prize money has risen from £1,000 in its first year to over £29,000.

Since the event changed from a round-robin style competition to a knockout event in 1981, Terry Griffiths has reached three finals. Perhaps his best win was in the 1982 final, when he beat Steve Davis 9-5 for his third consecutive victory. When the pair met in the final again two years later, Davis gained revenge with a 9-1 win.

Davis himself has reached four finals, and his only reversal was that defeat by Griffiths. His third win, also 9-1, was in 1987. This time the loser was his stablemate Willie Thorne, for whom it was a second successive defeat in the final.

The break record in the Masters is held by Davis who compiled a 133 against Eddie Charlton in 1983, which beat his own championship best of 128 set the previous year. The 1983 event was notable not only for Davis's record break: it was also the tournament in which Irishman Dennis Taylor introduced his now famous spectacles to the snooker world.

Benson and Hedges Masters

Regarded by many of the leading professionals as the game's most prestigious tournament after the world professional championships, the Benson and Hedges Masters was first contested in 1975. On that occasion ten of the world's leading players were invited to take part in the tournament sponsored by the giant tobacco firm, Gallaher. The first Masters event was held at the West Centre Hotel, Fulham, and the first champion, John Spencer, collected a cheque for £2,000.

The tournament was not a resounding success in its first year, largely because of its location, and in its second year it was moved into the city, to the New London Theatre. This time it was more successful, and Ray Reardon beat Graham Miles in the final to gain some consolation for his previous year's defeat by Spencer.

Reardon was in the final again for the third successive year in 1977, but, sadly for him, he could achieve only the runner-up position once more. This time he was defeated by an unknown Welshman named Doug Mountjoy, who had been a professional for only a couple of months, after having won the world amateur title. Mountjoy was invited into the tournament as a late replacement, and proved his ability by defeating John Pulman, Fred Davis and Alex Higgins (all former world champions) on his way to the final.

For the first time since the Masters was introduced four

Benson and Hedges Irish Masters: Results (finals)

1978 J. Spencer (England) 5
D. Mountjoy (Wales) 3

1979 D. Mountjoy (Wales) 6
R. Reardon (Wales) 5

1980 T. Griffiths (Wales) 9
D. Mountjoy (Wales) 8

1981 T. Griffiths (Wales) 9
R. Reardon (Wales) 7

1982 T. Griffiths (Wales) 9
S. Davis (England) 5

1983 S. Davis (England) 9
R. Reardon (Wales) 2

1984 S. Davis (England) 9
T. Griffiths (Wales) 1

1985 J. White (England) 9
A. Higgins (Ireland) 5

1986 J. White (England) 9
W. Thorne (England) 5

1987 S. Davis (England) 9
W. Thorne (England) 1

Most wins: 3 – Terry Griffiths
3 – Steve Davis
Most finals: 4 – Terry Griffiths
4 – Steve Davis
Highest break: 133 – Steve Davis (1983)

Benson and Hedges Masters – Results (finals)

1975 John Spencer (England) 9
Ray Reardon (Wales) 8
1976 Ray Reardon (Wales) 7
Graham Miles (England) 3
1977 Doug Mountjoy (Wales) 7
Ray Reardon (Wales) 6
1978 Alex Higgins (Ireland) 7
Cliff Thorburn (Canada) 5
1979 Perrie Mans (South Africa) 8
Alex Higgins (Ireland) 4
1980 Terry Griffiths (Wales) 9
Alex Higgins (Ireland) 5
1981 Alex Higgins (Ireland) 9
Terry Griffiths (Wales) 6
1982 Steve Davis (England) 9
Terry Griffiths (Wales) 5
1983 Cliff Thorburn (Canada) 9
Ray Reardon (Wales) 7
1984 Jimmy White (England) 9
Terry Griffiths (Wales) 5
1985 Cliff Thorburn (Canada) 9
Doug Mountjoy (Wales) 6
1986 Cliff Thorburn (Canada) 9
Jimmy White (England) 5
1987 Dennis Taylor (Ireland) 9
Alex Higgins (Ireland) 8

Most wins: 3 – Cliff Thorburn

Most finals: 5 – Alex Higgins

Highest break: 147 – Kirk Stevens (1984)

years earlier, in 1978 Ray Reardon failed to reach the final. He could only reach the semi-finals, where he lost to Alex Higgins, the eventual winner.

The tournament moved to a new home in 1979 – the Wembley Conference Centre, its present home. Perrie Mans of South Africa beat Cliff Thorburn and Ray Reardon before going on to beat Alex Higgins in the final, thus becoming the first overseas winner of the title. In his quarter-final with Eddie Charlton, Higgins established a new tournament record break of 132.

With the move to the new venue, the tournament started attracting crowds which broke British attendance records. The 1980 final between Alex Higgins and Terry Griffiths was watched by over 2,300 people. Griffiths won a fairly one-sided affair, the highlight of the final being his clearance of 131 – just one short of Higgins's championship best.

The following year's final was a repeat confrontation, but this time Higgins gained his revenge. Griffiths, however – in scoring a 136 break in the final – did deprive him of the championship top break. The two semi-finals were spectacular affairs, with both Higgins and Griffiths trailing 5-1 and 5-2 to their respective opponents, Cliff Thorburn and John Spencer, before both won 6-5.

In 1981 the Benson and Hedges Masters said goodbye to Fred Davis, who had competed in the tournament every year since its inception. Immensely popular with television audiences, Davis had a moment of glory, beating Kirk Stevens 5-4 in the first round, before finally bowing out to Terry Griffiths.

Griffiths appeared in his third successive final in 1982, but

Terry Griffiths, four times Benson and Hedges finalist

suffered defeat at the hands of Steve Davis who won his first Masters title.

Because of its popularity, both live and on television, the first prize money went up dramatically in 1983 from £8,000 to £16,000. The number of invited players rose also, from 12 to 16 (it had been increased from 10 to 12 in 1981). A crowd of over 2,800 witnessed the Bill Werbeniuk-Alex Higgins first round clash. Higgins, leading at one point by 3 frames to 0, eventually succumbed to the big Canadian who came back to win 5-4.

Another Canadian, Cliff Thorburn, took the title. He beat Ray Reardon, who was appearing in his first final since 1977; both sessions of their match attracted over 5,000 spectators. The top break of the tournament was 128, and was recorded by the man who seems to make a habit of knocking in big breaks in the Masters – Terry Griffiths.

Crowds were slightly down for the live matches in 1984, but the competition still attracted good television viewing figures. Jimmy White won his biggest cheque to date when he took the £35,000 first prize, but the tournament really belonged to Kirk Stevens. After eliminating Steve Davis in an earlier round, Stevens scored a maximum 147 break in his semi-final with White. His efforts brought him £11,500 for that break alone.

Cliff Thorburn and Doug Mountjoy – both past Masters champions – contested the 1985 final which the Canadian won. Thorburn became the first man to win the title three times when he beat Jimmy White 9-5 the following year, as the crowds continued to pour into the Wembley Conference Centre.

The highlight of the 1986 event was the quarter-final between Steve Davis and Willie Thorne. Thorne made a 138 clearance to level the match at 2 all, the Masters' highest break apart from the 147 from Kirk Stevens; but Davis responded with a 122 clearance in the next frame. Thorne drew level again with a 110 break, and Davis took the last frame to win 5-4.

In 1987 Alex Higgins, finding some of his old sparkle, succeeded in reaching his fifth final, but he lost to his fellow Irishman Dennis Taylor, who collected the £51,000 first prize.

Billiards and Snooker Control Council

Although professional players are sporting superstars these days, it is to the grass roots that the Billiards and Snooker Control Council (B&SCC) devotes a great deal of its interest. The professionals split from the B&SCC in 1971 and now has no control over the professional game. Its main functions are to make and revise the rules of billiards and snooker, to certificate referees all over the world, to keep official break records, to keep championship records, and to organize English national competitions for amateur players.

Membership to the B&SCC is available either through a club, or as an individual. The membership fee for clubs is nominal. Only affiliated members or members of affiliated clubs may take part in national competitions.

The first meeting of the council took place on 31 January 1885, when professional billiards players and billiards traders decided to form an association. Originally named the Billiards Association, it was formed at a meeting at the Andertons Hotel, London, on 14 February 1885. The prime reason for forming the association was to formulate the rules of billiards. The first set of snooker rules was published by the association in 1900.

In 1908 the Billiards Control Club was formed, and their function was to organize championships. The Control Club merged with the Association in 1919 to become the Billiards Association and Control Club. In January 1971 the name was changed to incorporate the word 'snooker' for the first time. Lord Lonsdale, who was responsible for giving the Lonsdale Belt to boxing, was a one-time president of the Billiards Association and Control Club. The president in 1987 is television commentator Ted Lowe, and the chairman is Stanley Brooke. One of the longest-serving officials of the council was Len Oldham, who gave in all 26 years' service and became chairman in 1971. He resigned the following year to become full-time secretary. He retired on his 65th birthday in 1978 and was made a vice president in 1982. He died the following year.

To obtain details of membership contact: The Secretary, B&SCC, Coronet House, Queen Street, Leeds, West Yorkshire, LS1 2TN

Billiards and Snooker Foundation

The Billiards and Snooker Foundation was formed in 1969, and is jointly sponsored by the Billiards and Snooker Control Council and the Billiards and Snooker Trade Association. Two members of each body sit on the committee of the Foundation, and the majority of the funds comes from the trade. Traders in billiards and snooker goods make a mandatory contribution as well as a contribution based on UK sales.

The aim of the Foundation is to teach young people under the age of 18 the basic skills of billiards and snooker. Before they can be taught however, it is vital to have qualified coaches. To achieve this, the National Coaching Scheme was introduced, also in 1969.

Players at both billiards and snooker can apply to go on courses at the Lilleshall Sports Centre, and once suitably qualified, they can organize coaching 'schools' in their own area. The Foundation reimburses coaches for their out-of-pocket expenses as well as paying them for their teaching time.

Television commentator Jack Karnehm acts as the National Coach for the foundation.

Billiards and Snooker Trade Association

The Billiards and Snooker Trade Association plays a very important role in the development of both sports at grass-roots level. They are joint sponsors, and chief financial backers, of the Billiards and Snooker Foundation, which is responsible for the high level of coaching within the sport.

In addition, the Association uses a Code of Practice which has been approved by the Office of Fair Trading, and all members of the association are bound by that code. The game benefits generally as standards are maintained and improved.

The Association agreed to sponsor the English Amateur Billiards Championship for the first time in 1986-87.

Break

In snooker, the word break has three meanings. First, it is the term used to define the opening shot in a frame, although in this instance it is often referred to as a 'break-off.'

Second, it is a sequence of scoring shots. And finally, it is the term used to define the points value in a sequence of scoring shots. For example, a break may consist of potting one red ball followed by one black ball. The value of the break is then one for the red and seven for the black – a total of eight.

A break can be made by just potting one ball. All breaks come to an end when a player fails to pot the object-ball, or he plays a foul shot.

See also Breaks
Maximums

Joe Johnson, now professional, is the former holder of the record break by an amateur – 140, made at the TUC Club, Middlesbrough, in 1978

Breaks

First century break: the first century break by a professional, as recognized by the Billiards Association and Control Club, was by Canadian Con Stanbury at Winnipeg in 1922, when he recorded a break of 113.

First recorded maximum: The first record of a maximum 147 break was by 'Murt' O'Donoghue at Griffin, New South Wales in 1934. Not being in tournament conditions it was not ratified as an official record. The first maximum by an amateur, as recognized by the BACC, was by Canadian Leo Levitt in 1948, at the Windsor Billiards and Bowling Club, Montreal.

First official maximum: On 22 January 1955 Joe Davis recorded the first official maximum break, in an exhibition match against Willie Smith at the Leicester Square Hall, London.

Other official maximums:

1965 Rex Williams against Mannie Francisco in Cape Town.
1982 Steve Davis against John Spencer in the Lada Classic.
1983 Cliff Thorburn against Terry Griffiths in the world professional championships at Sheffield.
1984 Kirk Stevens against Jimmy White in the Benson and Hedges Masters at Wembley.

First maximum in tournament play: John Spencer recorded a maximum in the 1979 Holsten Lager tournament at Slough, but it was not ratified as an official record because the pockets were oversize. Spencer's 147 beat Ray Reardon's record of 146 set in the 1972 £2,000 Park Drive Tournament.

First televised maximum: Steve Davis – as above. This was the first break to be covered in its entirety by television cameras, although BBC Wales once, when filming a documentary, caught the closing stages of Ray Reardon compiling a maximum. While John Spencer was compiling his maximum in the Holsten Lager tournament in 1979, the break was missed because the cameraman had gone off for lunch.

First televised century break: Mark Wildman of Peterborough scored the first century break to be seen on television in 1962, when taking part in an amateur event.

First total clearance: Sidney Smith recorded the first official total clearance in 1936, with a break of 133. Murt O'Donoghue, at Wellington, New Zealand, in 1929 made the first known total clearance, but his break of 134 was never ratified as official.

1,000 century breaks: In March 1970 at Sydney, Horace Lindrum scored his 1,000th century break in public, to become the first player ever to reach this milestone.

Other notable breaks:

☆ Kingsley Kennerley, in 1939 compiled a century break which was the first by an amateur to be officially recognized.

☆ During a match with Tony Knowles at Huddersfield in 1986 John Parrott followed a 101 clearance with total clearances of 133 and 136 – all within four frames.

☆ Paul Dawkins of Barry became the youngest player to make a total clearance in April 1986: 143 in the heats of the British under-19 championships. He was 15 years 163 days old.

Kirk Stevens scored a maximum break against Jimmy White in 1984

☆ Martin Clark was officially credited with a new record break by an amateur when he made 141 during the 1986 Home International championship.

☆ Ronnie O'Sullivan compiled a 117 break at the Barking Snooker Centre in November 1986: he was aged 10 at the time.

☆ The highest break in a *bona fide* league match in Britain is 139 by Colin Moreton. He compiled his break in 1987 while playing for Accrington Snooker Club 'A' against Lee Street of the Accrington Elite 'B' team in the Riley East Lancashire league. It surpassed the 12-month-old record established by Andrew Weeks by one point.

☆ In 1965 Rex Williams beat Joe Davis's 19-year-old world championship record of 136 with a break of 142 against John Pulman. Bill Werbeniuk, in a match with John Virgo 14 years later, equalled Williams's record.

☆ The current world championship record is Cliff Thorburn's 147, set in 1983, when his opponent was Terry Griffiths.

☆ Willie Thorne holds the record for the most maximums in a career with over 30 to his credit – all in practice matches. His highest break in competition play is 143.

☆ Tony Drago of Malta established a new record break for the world amateur championships in his match against Christian d'Avoine of Mauritius in 1984. His break of 132 beat the previous championship best of 127 held by current Irish professional Eugene Hughes.

☆ At Minehead in 1978, David Taylor made three consecutive frame clearances of 130, 140 and 139. And in 1982, professional Jim Meadowcroft made four consecutive clearances of 105, 115, 117 and 125.

Notable break records of Joe Davis:
During his career, the legendary Joe Davis compiled 687 century breaks at snooker and 87 billiards breaks in excess of 1,000. The following are some milestones in his snooker career.
1928 Compiled his first century break in public, against Fred Pugh at Manchester.
1930 Davis scored the first ever century break in the world professional championships.
1939 Against Alec Brown, in London, he compiled the 100th century break of his career.
1946 During the world championships he compiled six century breaks. Two of them were in the final against Horace Lindrum when he scored 133 and 136 to break the championship record *twice*.
1950 He came close to the first maximum with a 146 against Canada's George Chenier.
1951 On 16 July playing in an exhibition match he compiled breaks of 103, 128 and 134 in consecutive frames.
1953 Against Jackie Rea, in London, Davis compiled the 500th century break of his career.
1955 At the Leicester Square Hall he compiled the first official maximum break.
1965 Davis scored the 687th – and final – century break of his career.

See also National Breaks Competition.

British Open

See Dulux British Open

Brown, Alec

To many present day snooker followers the name Alec Brown means very little. His list of career highlights may not be all that impressive, but Alec Brown was responsible for an important addition to the rules of billiards and snooker. A tough competitor, he hailed from Piccadilly and spent 33 years as a professional before arthritis ended his career. But it is for one incident that he will be remembered. Playing Tom Newman in the Daily Mail Gold Cup at Thurstons Hall in 1938, he found the cue-ball buried among the pack of reds after a successful long pot. He was snookered on all the colours, and, to make matters worse, he found he could not satisfactorily 'bridge' to play the shot. So, out of his pocket, he produced a cue the length of a fountain-pen, and proceeded to play the shot; referee Charlie Chambers ruled it a foul stroke and awarded seven points to Newman.

Brown protested at the penalty; after all, there was nothing in the rules stating how long – or short – a cue must be. Nevertheless, Chambers ruled that the stroke was not within the spirit of the game. Immediately after the incident the Billiards Association and Control Club amended the rules to state that the minimum length of a cue must be three feet.

Until the bombing of Thurston's during the war, the Alec Brown affair was the most explosive incident to have occurred at the hall.

Career highlights
News of the World Champion 1951

Burroughes and Watts

Billiard table manufacturers Burroughes and Watts were highly regarded for first-class craftmanship of their goods, and second-hand Burroughes and Watts billiard tables are much sought-after items.

Kirk Stevens – losing finalist to Silvino Francisco in the 1985 Dulux British Open

Canada's most successful professional, Cliff Thorburn, celebrates after winning the world title in 1980

The company was formed in 1836 and had premises in Soho Square. Shortly afterwards they moved from their original premises to No. 19 Soho Square which housed the company's offices and showrooms. Their famous match-room, with seating for 150, was added at the end of the century.

In addition to manufacturing high-quality tables and accessories, historically Burroughes and Watts have endeavoured to promote billiards and snooker in many different directions.

They were responsible for bringing top Australasian players Clark McConachy and Walter Lindrum to Britain: Lindrum was on contract to the company for a retainer of £60 per week – a large sum for the 1930s. Also at that time they sponsored female players Joyce Gardener and Ruth Harrison in an effort to promote the women's game.

Burroughes and Watts were also responsible for the development of the junior game, and in 1922 they organized, and staged, the British boys' under-16 championship; the title was won by Walter Donaldson. Also in 1922, the company staged the first major professional snooker match in London, when Arthur Peall played Joe Brady.

Further diversification saw them become publishers of several billiards journals, notably *Billiards Monthly*.

The company had branches in most major cities up and down the United Kingdom at the turn of the century, as well as in Canada and South Africa. The manufacturing side of their operation moved from Soho Square to Bow towards the end of the century.

In 1951 Burroughes Hall was chosen to stage the world amateur billiards championship which was revived after 13 years. And, following the closure of the Leicester Square Hall in 1955, Burroughes was the only venue for championship play in London until the early sixties.

The famous hall closed in 1966; shortly afterwards the controlling interest in the company was sold to the Hurst Park Syndicate, and its repair side was acquired by the Lancashire-based E.J. Riley and Company, out of which was born the Riley Burwat company.

Campbell, John

A former Australian amateur champion, John Campbell turned professional in 1982 but it was not long before he had assumed the mantle of Australia's top player. This was in 1985, when first he beat Eddie Charlton in the Winfield Australian Masters, losing to Tony Meo in the final, then he inflicted another defeat upon Charlton in the final of the Australian Professional Championship – a title Charlton had held for many years.

Campbell followed that success with good results in all the following season's ranking tournaments and came within striking distance of a place in the top 16, in fact reaching 18th place.

He reached the Crucible stage of the world championship that season and progressed to the second round, beating former champion Ray Reardon at the first hurdle. However, he lost to Willie Thorne in the next round.

He slipped down the rankings a couple of places in 1986-87, but maintained his Embassy performance, reaching the Crucible once more before losing to Silvino Francisco in the opening round.

John Campbell and Warren King have emerged from the shadow of Eddie Charlton and in 1986 the pair of them contested the Australian professional final – the first time for many years that Charlton was not one of the participants. King was the winner, but the emergence of both these players means that the state of Australian snooker looks healthy for the future.

Career highlights
Australian Professional Champion 1985
Professional Players' Tournament (quarter-final) 1983
Winfield Australian Masters (runner-up) 1985
Australian Amateur Champion 1979

Canada

Organized snooker in Canada did not exist at all until the late seventies. Since then, this pool-playing nation has become a force to be reckoned with on the professional snooker circuit, and in players like Cliff Thorburn, Kirk Stevens and Bill Werbeniuk it has competitors who can compete at the highest level. For many years, though, snooker in Canada was restricted to the 'money matches' which attracted a lot of hustlers.

Despite Canada's recent explosion on to the professional scene, it was a Canadian, Con Stanbury, who was the first overseas player to compete in the world professional championships. He arrived in Britain for the 1935 championships and stayed in the country until his death some 40 years later. He was never quite a world-class player because he tended to play snooker like pool. But nevertheless he was the first Canadian to make an impact on the sport.

The first Canadian to attain true world status was George Chenier. He has also been one of the few players who could claim to be world class at both snooker and pool. The pinnacle of his snooker career came in 1950, when he established a new world record break of 144. His record stood only four weeks until broken by Joe Davis – who, as it happens, was playing Chenier at the time!

Chenier was North American snooker champion from 1948 until his death in 1970. His one and only attempt at the world title was in 1950, when he lost to Fred Davis in the semi-final.

Snooker tables in Canada are renowned for their 'generous' pockets, and consequently 147 breaks are not too rare in the country – Cliff Thorburn is reputed to have made over 20 of them. But the first 147 in Canada was made at the Windsor Billiards and Bowling Club, Montreal, on 24 November 1948 by Leo Levitt.

Canada, like all countries, suffered because of snooker's dormancy in the fifties and sixties and it was not until the early seventies that the country produced another player capable of competing at the highest level. That person was Cliff Thorburn. Outstanding in his own country, Thorburn lacked experience against other world-class players. In 1971, however, he got his chance when Rex Williams, Fred Davis and John Spencer toured Canada. Thorburn fared well, and two years later he proved himself in the world championships when he beat Dennis Taylor before narrowly losing, by one frame, to Rex Williams. Since then Thorburn has appeared in three world finals, winning the title once, after an epic battle with Alex Higgins in 1980.

Thorburn was joined on the professional circuit in Britain by Kirk Stevens and Bill Werbeniuk, and the three of them won the World Team title for Canada in 1982.

The upsurge in popularity of the sport in Canada in the seventies led to the introduction of the Canadian Open. First held in 1974, its home was the noisy National Exhibition Centre in Toronto. The event attracted many of the world's leading players, and was also responsible for the introduction of many top-class amateurs who later made the grade as professionals – Kirk Stevens and Tony Meo being just two.

Because of the ever-increasing professional calendar in Britain, the Canadian Open was discontinued after the 1980 event which, ironically, was the first outside broadcast of a snooker event in the country.

The birth of the Canadian Open also led to the instituting of the inaugural Canadian amateur championships in 1979 and, in 1983, the first official Canadian professional championships – although several unofficial championships had been held since the end of the Open in 1980.

As a result of Canada's new standing in the snooker world, the 1982 world amateur championships were held in Calgary, and were won by Welshman Terry Parsons. In the final Parsons played Canadian Jim Bear, who led 5-1 at the end of the first session, and 7-5 at the end of the second before losing 11-8. This was Canada's best performance in the championships.

Jim Bear and his brother John are two of Canada's many professionals. But despite the number of Canadians who are members of the WPBSA, the one-time challenge by Canadians to the top players has waned in recent years. Bill Werbeniuk has slipped out of the top 16, as has Kirk Stevens, who has been enduring troubled times away from the table. Only Cliff Thorburn has succeeded in maintaining the Canadian challenge, in spite of a slight drop in his ranking position.

Canadian Amateur Championship – Results (winners)

1979 J. Wych	**1985** A. Robidoux
1980 Jim Bear	**1986** G. Natale
1981 R. Chaperon	
1982 B. McConnell	
1983 A. Robidoux	
1984 T. Finstad	

Canadian Open

The Canadian Open used to be held during the Canadian National Exhibition week in Toronto. It was first held in 1974, but was contested for the last time in 1980; it was discontinued as a result of the English season starting earlier, and thus clashing with the September timing of the Canadian event.

Cliff Thorburn won the inaugural open in 1974 – his first of four victories. He beat Dennis Taylor 8-6 in the first final, the losing semi-finalists were Graham Miles and Alex Higgins.

Higgins liked this event. He appeared in every semi-final, and in three successive finals. His first final appearance was in 1975, when he beat John Pulman 15-7. The event that year was memorable for the number of big breaks – over 20 century breaks were compiled. It also saw a young amateur reach the semi-finals: that amateur was Willie Thorne, who had had an excellent quarter-final win over John Spencer.

Another amateur, in the person of Canadian Bernie Mikkelsen, reached the semi-finals in 1976; but he crashed out 9-1 to Higgins, who nevertheless could not emulate his previous year's success, going down 17-9 to John Spencer in the final.

Higgins rediscovered his winning ways in 1977, when he gained revenge over Spencer in the final. The event could not be staged in the National Exhibition Centre, but was played in a very hot marquee instead. Another new young star emerged: this was 18-year-old Kirk Stevens, who led Ray Reardon before eventually losing 5-3, but his name was firmly implanted in the minds of those who witnessed his brave performance.

Continuing its reputation for providing new talent, the 1978 event saw the emergence of yet another youngster – Tony Meo. He had a memorable semi-final victory over Alex Higgins and then led Cliff Thorburn 10-6 in the final, before allowing the Canadian to gain a 17-15 victory.

Kirk Stevens came close to his first final in 1979, but lost 9-7 in the semi-final to Terry Griffiths. In the final Griffiths met Thorburn, who won his third title in a best-of-33 frame match that went the full distance.

The last Canadian Open was held in 1980, and its name changed to the Canadian National Exhibition Open. There was a touch of irony in the fact that the last playing of the event should be the first one to receive television coverage – it was, as it happens, the first outside broadcast of any snooker competition in Canada.

The four semi-finalists were the same players as in 1979, and the final was also a repeat, but this time Cliff Thorburn had an easier task in overcoming Terry Griffiths to win his fourth and last title.

Canadian Open Championship: Results (finals)

1974 C. Thorburn (Canada) 8
D. Taylor (Ireland) 6

1975 A. Higgins (Ireland) 15
J. Pulman (England) 7

1976 J. Spencer (England) 17
A. Higgins (Ireland) 9

1977 A. Higgins (Ireland) 17
J. Spencer (England) 14

1978 C. Thorburn (Canada) 17
T. Meo (England) 15

1979 C. Thorburn (Canada) 17
T. Griffiths (Wales) 16

1980 C. Thorburn (Canada) 17
T. Griffiths (Wales) 10

Most wins: 4 – Cliff Thorburn
Most finals: 4 – Cliff Thorburn
Highest break: 146 – John Spencer (1977)

Canadian Professional Championships

The first official Canadian professional championships were held in 1983. Although several unofficial championships have been held over the years, the previous most prestigious event was the Canadian Open, which disappeared in 1981.

The successful Canadian world team trio of Kirk Stevens, Cliff Thorburn and Bill Werbeniuk was expected to dominate the new championship. But Werbeniuk did not take part in 1983, and Thorburn was eliminated 9-6 in the semi-final by the little-known Frank Jonik. Stevens was the only one of the trio to make the final, and he only just scraped through in his semi-final against the previous year's world amateur finalist, Jim Bear. In the final Jonik came within a whisker of causing another major upset before losing to Stevens 9-8.

Held during the Canadian National Exhibition at Toronto, this tournament must have been played in one of the noisiest environments of any major snooker championship...a simulated tank battle taking place within earshot of the players!

The event was to have been replaced in 1984 by the Canadian Masters, but the failure to secure a sponsor resulted in the Masters being cancelled, and the championships were therefore held for the second time. This time Cliff Thorburn fared better, winning the final, easily, against Mario Morra. Since then Thorburn has remained the most consistent Canadian professional, winning the title again in 1985 and 1986.

Canadian Professional Championships – Results (finals)

1983 K. Stevens 9
F. Jonik 8
1984 C. Thorburn 9
M. Morra 2
1985 C. Thorburn 6
R. Chaperon 4

1986 C. Thorburn 6
J. Wych 2
1987 C. Thorburn 8
J. Bear 4

Highest break: 128 – Jim Bear (1983)

Car Care Plan World Cup

See Tuborg World Cup

Chalk

The purpose of chalk on the tip of a cue is to prevent miscueing. It was first used around 1820, and within 15 years was widely used by the majority of players. It became popular as a result of the efforts of John Carr of Bath. Carr was the marker (scorer) for billiard room owner John Bartley, and Bartley was one of the first exponents of the screw-shot. Carr made a small fortune selling the 'special' chalk which he claimed would enable anybody to perfect Bartley's special shot. It was, of course, just ordinary chalk!

American chalk is used by the majority of players today.

Chamberlain, Sir Neville

Sir Neville Chamberlain – not to be confused with the Prime Minister of the same name – occupies an important place in snooker history. It was as a 19-year-old, while serving with the 11th Devonshire Regiment in India in 1875, that Chamberlain is credited with the invention and naming of the game when he referred to a fellow officer as a 'snooker' after the latter had missed an easy pot. The term 'snooker', was at that time, the slang word for a new recruit at Woolwich Barracks.

Chamberlain – full title Colonel Sir Neville Francis Fitzgerald Chamberlain, KCB, KCVO – was born on 13 January 1856. Educated abroad and at Brentwood School, Essex, he joined the army in 1873 and served with the Devonshires for three years. He subsequently served in the Central India Horse Guards and was on the staff of Sir F. Roberts throughout the Afghan War, during which he was wounded, and was awarded a bronze star. He also served during the Burma campaign and the South African War. At the time of his retirement in 1916 he had been the Inspector General of the Roya' Irish Constabulary for the previous 16 years. He was knighted in 1900.

Champion of Champions

After his first snooker venture with the Dry Blackthorn Cup, boxing promoter Mike Barrett tried snooker promotion again in 1978 with the *Daily Mirror*-sponsored Champion of Champions event at the Wembley Conference Centre.

The event was held on just one day. The four contestants,

Bartley's Billiard Room in Bath, where it is believed that chalk was first used on the tip of the cue in the 19th century

Patsy Fagan, Ray Reardon, Alex Higgins and Doug Mountjoy, attracted an 1,800-strong crowd who were treated to a Reardon-Higgins final which the Welshman won. In between matches two youngsters played exhibition frames to keep the crowd entertained. The two youngsters were Terry Whitthread and Jimmy White.

The event was not held the following year, but returned in 1980 when it moved to a new venue, the New London Theatre in Drury Lane. The anticipated crowds did not attend, which turned the venture into a financial disaster.

Ten players took part in two round-robin groups, with the two winners meeting in the final. The format came in for criticism from the players, who had to play dead frames. Doug Mountjoy beat John Virgo 10-8 in the final of what turned out to be the last Champion of Champions tournament.

Champion of Champions: Results (finals)

1978 R. Reardon (Wales) 11
A. Higgins (Ireland) 9

1979 Not held

1980 D. Mountjoy (Wales) 10
J. Virgo (England) 8

Highest break: 128 – Steve Davis (1980)

Eddie Charlton with a devoted fan – the dog used to bark whenever Charlton appeared on television

Charlton, Eddie

Known as 'Steady Eddie', Eddie Charlton has been one of the sport's most consistent performers since 1970, since when he has appeared in two world professional championship finals as well as making six semi-final appearances. Between 1976 and 1984 he figured in the top ten of the WPBSA's ranking list every year – only Ray Reardon can also stake such a claim.

Charlton hails from New South Wales, and, although he started playing snooker at the age of nine, he went down the mines after leaving school. That all came to an end in 1963, when he turned professional at the late age of 33. The following year he won the Australian professional championship for the first time.

Australia's outstanding player since the mid-1960s, he held the Australian professional title every year from 1964 to 1984 except 1968, when he lost to the late Warren Simpson. This two-decade reign ended in 1985 when he was beaten 10-7 in the final by John Campbell.

Charlton's first visit to Britain was in 1968, when he came to challenge John Pulman for the world title; Pulman won 39-34. The following year the championships were conducted as a knockout competition, but Charlton did not return to Britain.

The championships were held in Australia in November 1970, however, and Charlton was one of the favourites for the title. In the semi-final he was matched against fellow Australian Warren Simpson. Charlton's record against Simpson was such that he was clear favourite, but Simpson sprang a major surprise, winning 27-22: this was only the second time he had beaten Charlton in six years. Charlton's next defeat by a fellow Australian on level terms was ten years later, when John Campbell beat him at the City Tatts Club in Sydney in 1980.

Charlton has played in the world championships ever since, and he has the amazing record of having beaten somebody in every championship except those of 1974 and 1981, when he fell to John Dunning and Doug Mountjoy respectively, at the first hurdle.

It is surprising that, despite his consistency over the years, he has not won a major title in Britain and, apart from the world championships, he has not reached a major final. His two world championship finals have both ended in defeat by Ray Reardon, in 1973 and 1975.

Charlton does, however, claim one world crown – that of World Match-Play Champion. The event was held in Melbourne in 1976, and Charlton beat Ray Reardon for the title. The event was scheduled to be held again, but never was; Charlton therefore claims to be the holder of the title!

Expert at both billiards and snooker, he has come close to winning the world professional billiards title on three occasions, but was beaten in the finals by Rex Williams in 1974 and 1976 and by Mark Wildman in 1984.

The holder of the highest competitive break record (141) in Australia, Charlton also holds the break record for the BBC television *Pot Black* series. His break of 110 in 1973 has never been bettered; in fact, there were only two other instances of a century break being made. He certainly liked the 'quick-fire' format of the *Pot Black* series: he won the event on three occasions, was runner-up once, scored the highest break in three series, and was awarded the programme's Personality Award in 1981.

Keen on all sport, he was fanatical as a youngster and devoted the same degree of professionalism to all the sports in which he competed as he does to snooker. He played senior grade soccer for over 10 years, and in 1950 was a member of the Swansea Belmont crew that won the Australian surfing championships. He also excelled at speed rollerskating, athletics, cricket and boxing. But the proudest moment of his sporting career came in 1956 when he and his brother Jim carried the Olympic torch as it made its way to Melbourne for the opening ceremony of the XVIth Olympiad.

Over the years Charlton's snooker activities have extended beyond the competitive game. His snooker circus used to take the game across the vast Australian continent and he, along with other leading players, would treat people in the remote areas of Australia to the delicate skills of the sport they would never normally have had a chance of seeing.

He has also been involved in the promotional side of the sport and was involved in the promoting of the 1970 and 1975 world professional snooker championships held in Australia. In more recent times he has been involved in the promotion of the Winfield Australian Masters. For his services to the sport Eddie Charlton was awarded the Australian Order of Merit in 1980.

His place among the world elite may have slipped in recent years, and indeed he dropped out of the top 16 in 1986 for the first time since the rankings were introduced. A further disastrous season in 1986-87 saw him slip even further and he ended in 26th place – his lowest ever position. He has also been dethroned as Australia's top player with the emergence of John Campbell and Warren King, but any player who takes on Charlton still finds him a tough competitor and a difficult man to beat.

Career highlights

- World Professional Snooker Championship (Runner-up) 1968, 1973, 1975
- World Professional Billiards Championship (Runner-up) 1974, 1976, 1984
- World Professional Match-Play Champion 1976
- *Pot Black* Champion 1972, 1973, 1980
- Australian Professional Champion 1964-67, 1969-78, 1984

Chenier, George

While Canadian snooker flourishes thanks to the likes of Cliff Thorburn, Kirk Stevens, and Bill Werbeniuk, it is to another man that the sport of snooker in Canada owes its existence. That man was George Chenier – the first Canadian snooker player to be considered as world class.

As with many of his compatriots, it was at pool that Chenier excelled, but he gradually became more interested in snooker. In 1949 he was considered to be one of the world's best snooker players, yet very few had heard of him, let alone seen him, outside his own continent.

Joe Davis was certainly made aware of his presence in Bermuda in 1949 when they met in a best-of-81 frame match. Davis won 41-30, but Chenier's performance was as good as, if not better than, most of Davis's fellow professionals back home were capable of giving.

Although he kept his roots in Canada, Chenier travelled to England for the 1950 world professional championships. After beating Peter Mans (Perrie's father) he lost to Fred Davis in the semi-final. This was his only attempt at the world title.

That same year he established a new world record snooker break of 144 at the Leicester Square Hall. But four weeks later while he was playing Joe Davis, he saw his record taken from him as Davis registered a new record of 146.

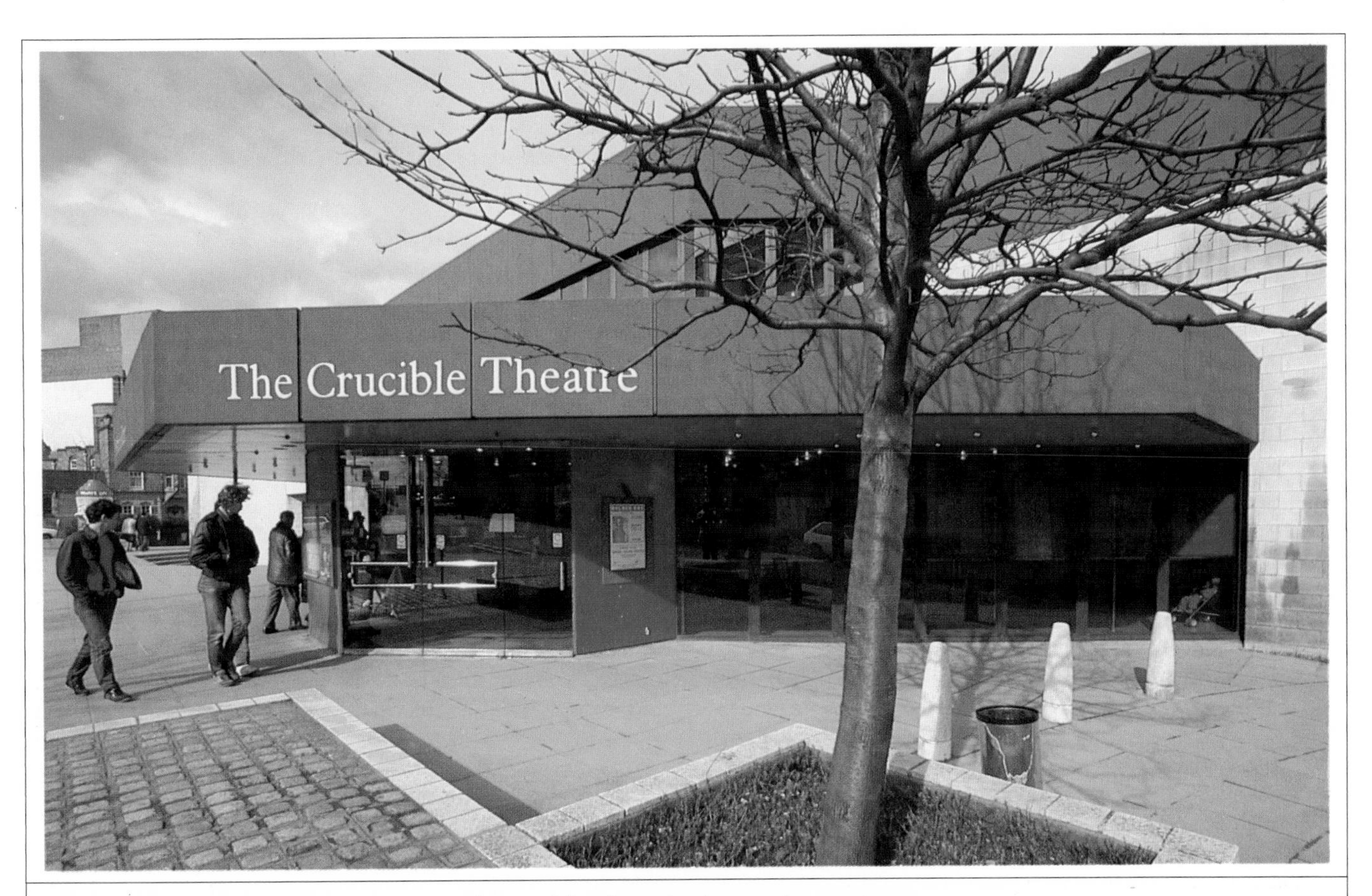

The outside of snooker's most famous home

Assembling the special lighting at the Crucible Theatre in readiness for the world championships

Chenier died of a heart attack in 1970 at the age of 63. He was at the time the North American snooker champion – a title he had held since 1948.

Career highlights
North American Snooker Champion 1948-1970

China
Barry Hearn has said that China is the biggest potential growth area on earth for snooker. His first-hand knowledge of how popular the sport could become there derives from a visit he paid them in 1987, when he took his seven players plus Rex Williams to compete in the BAT sponsored Kent Cup. Prior to this, and following tours of other Far Eastern countries – Thailand, Hong Kong, Singapore and Malaysia – Hearn had arranged for Steve Davis and Dennis Taylor to play an exhibition in Canton in 1986. The first ever professional snooker match to take place in China aroused so much interest that there was little trouble in arranging the Kent Cup, with its £100,000 prize money, for the following year.

The proposed five hours television coverage of the event, which was held in the 6000-seat Peking Sports Stadium, was increased to more than 10 hours and the viewing audiences were estimated at one thousand million. Willie Thorne won the first prize, beating Jimmy White 5-2 in the final, and he delighted the huge audience with a break of 126 in the final frame.

If only a small proportion of those who watched the Kent Cup on television take up the sport, there will soon be a lot of snooker tables in China, and Barry Hearn's prediction could well prove to be accurate.

Clare, E.A. & Son Ltd.
Now part of the large and strong Clare-Padmore-Thurston group, Clare's commenced business as billiard table manufacturers in November 1912. It was then that Edward Arthur Clare, who had served his apprenticeship with the Liverpool firm of billiard table manufacturers J. Ashcroft & Co, established his business.

The company opened its first billiard hall in the mid-1920s, and within a short period it owned eight halls.

Current chairman Norman Clare, son of Edward, joined the company in 1930 as a 16-year-old, and on his 21st birthday the company changed its style to E.A. Clare & Son. Edward Arthur Clare died in 1963 at the age of 81 – and he was still working up to five days before his death.

That same year the company had the chance to acquire the major shareholding in Thurston's, which it did with Norman Clare being appointed chairman. The Birmingham firm of Thos. Padmore & Sons joined the group in 1966 to make it one of the largest billiard table manufacturers in the world.

They manufacture a full range of tables ranging from miniatures to modern and traditional full-size tables. In addition they have an excellent repair and maintenance service, and their fitters fly all over the world to erect tables.

Cloth
The cloth on a billiard table is the subject of great respect, and its manufacture is indeed a highly skilled operation. As many as ten different types of wool are blended to make a pile of wool necessary to spin the yarn for a piece of billiard cloth. Each type of wool is blended for a specific purpose, and manufacturers closely guard the secrets in what is called their 'Blend Book.'

Since the first world war, finest West-country wool has been used in the manufacture of the cloth. Prior to that, the highest-quality cloths were made from the wool from flocks of Hungarian sheep. These sheep, however, were slaughtered during the first world war to feed the starving.

With West-country wool being used for cloth manufacture, Gloucester has become the home of the industry; the leading manufacturer is Strachan and Company, based in Stroud. They make the high-grade West of England cloth.

Making a billiard table cloth involves spinning the yarn on extra wide looms. The yarn is woven into a piece of cloth 3m (120 inches) wide and approximately 70m long. It then goes through a process known as 'fulling' or 'milling', which shrinks the cloth to a width of about 2m (72 inches), and a length of approximately 50m. The purpose of the next process is to raise the pile of the cloth so as to form the nap. The nap is then expertly cut to the correct height. The nap on the cloth, when laid on the table, should always run from the baulk end of the table to the spot end. The nap plays an important part in the game of snooker; players have to make allowances for it when playing certain shots, particularly when playing acute-angled shots into the centre pockets. To see the effect of the nap one has only to run the hand along a piece of velvet or similar material. When run one way the 'pile' appears to be standing up, and when run in the opposite direction it appears to be lying down.

Maintenance of cloths, once fitted, is imperative, and they should be regularly ironed and brushed.

In 1923 the Manchester firm of Reddaway & Company manufactured a new 'napless' cloth called the 'Janus' cloth. Made out of cotton rather than wool, it had no nap and was reversible. Many leading professionals of the day liked the cloth, which was very fast, because they could accumulate big breaks on it. But it was not practical for everyday club use: it quickly became dirty and greasy, and was easily dented if anything was dropped on it. Consequently it went out of fashion in the late thirties.

It is believed that green was chosen as the colour of the cloth so as to simulate grass – billiards, in its original form, used to be played outdoors. It is not known when the first billiard table cloth was used, but the accounts of the first Duke of Bedford in 1664 reveal that he paid £15 to a joiner for a billiard table, and £3 8s 9d. (£3·44) for 6½ yards of green cloth to cover it.

Coral United Kingdom Open
See Tennents United Kingdom Open

Crucible Theatre
The Crucible Theatre in Sheffield is regarded as snooker's Wembley, although the world professional championship is the only snooker event held there. The theatre throws open its doors to the vast army of snooker followers for 17 days every April for the world championships, but for the remainder of the year it stages plays and concerts.

The Crucible runs its own repertory company – the third largest in the country – and puts on five or six productions per year. The main theatre seats 1,013 people.

The idea of housing the world championships at the Crucible came from Mike Watterson's wife. Watterson used to promote the world championships, and his wife put the suggestion to him after she had been to the theatre to watch a play there. Watterson being a local lad, the idea appealed to him, and in 1977 the world championships were held at their new home.

The first winner of the world title at the Crucible was John Spencer. And until Steve Davis laid the bogey in 1984, no champion had successfully defended his title there.

One of the greatest moments in the Crucible Theatre's sporting history – and indeed snooker's history – came on Saturday 23 April 1983, when Canadian Cliff Thorburn recorded the first ever maximum break in the world championships.

The Crucible Theatre and the Embassy World Championships are synonymous. It is hard to imagine the championships ever being played at a different venue. And indeed, following Embassy's announcement in 1985 that they will be sponsoring the world championships for a further six years, the Crucible is assured of being the tournament's home until 1990 at least.

By definition, a crucible is a utensil used for melting and fusing metals together. The theatre is appropriately named – during those 17 days' snooker at the Crucible in April each year the game of snooker is certainly in a melting-pot.

Cue

From the 15th century to the turn of the 19th century, billiards had always been played with a mace – a stick like a golf club. Around 1800 the straight cue was developed and became more popular, although the mace was still used by some players. The design of the cue at that time was very little different than the present day model. It did not, however, have a tip on it. That followed a few years later when a French political prisoner, Capt. Mingaud, developed a tip out of leather. Around the 1820s Messrs. Thurston's made cues from a variety of woods: Brazil wood, pear tree, maple sycamore, satinwood, lime, teak, and many more. Today's cues are made of Canadian maple and South American hardwoods like ebony and rosewood.

Captain Mingaud – inventor of the leather cue-tip

The cue has three distinct features. There is the butt, which is the larger end of the cue. There is the tip, the end of the cue which strikes the cue-ball. And there is the shaft – the tapered part of the cue between the butt and the tip. To give the cue balance, the butt is loaded with lead. Since the introduction of the cue its design has changed very little. The biggest change, which came in the mid 1970s, was mass production of the two-piece cue. The cue is in two pieces and screwed together in the middle before use to provide a normal 'one-piece' cue. The effect of this is that it makes the carrying of cues far simpler. Popular with many players today – amateur and professional – the first world champion to win the title with a two-piece cue was John Spencer in 1977. Following on from the two-piece cue, the latest design has been to add an even longer piece to the butt-end of a two-piece cue to give an extended cue – useful for playing shots with the rest or the spider. The average length of the present day cue is approximately 4 feet 10 inches (147cm) and that has departed very little from the length when first seen over 170 years ago.

Although the rules of snooker state that 'the cue shall be not

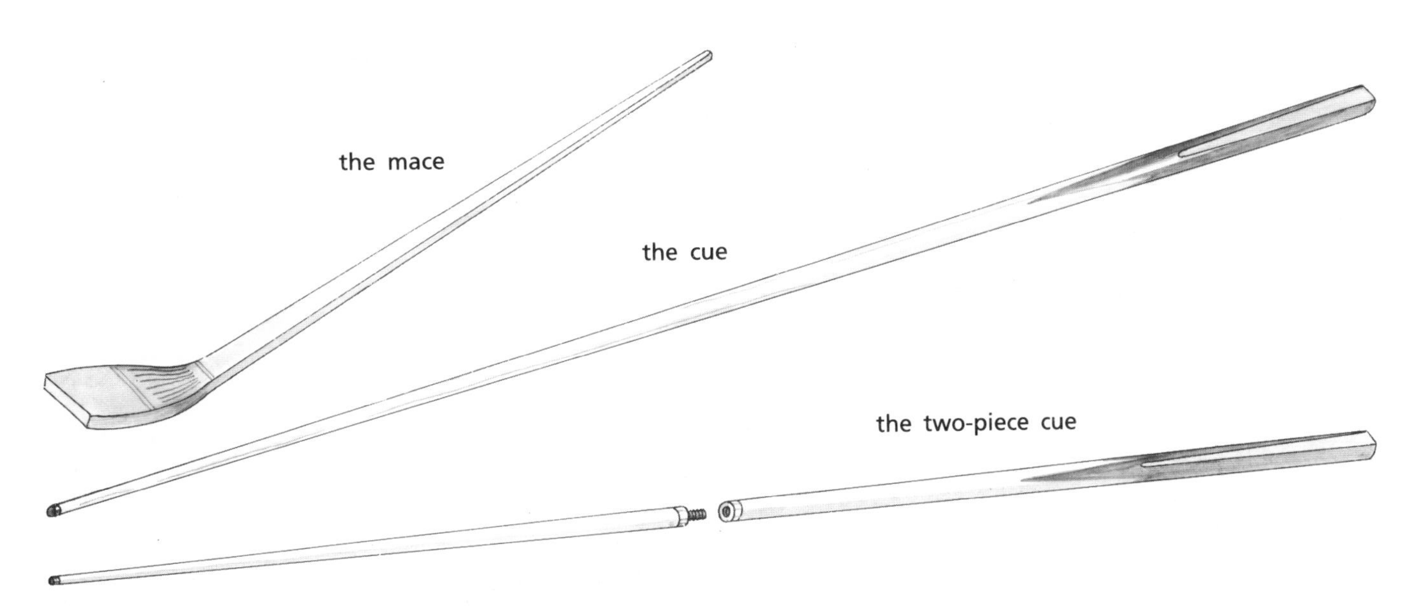

less than 3 feet (910mm)', it is very rare to see a cue that small. The rule was introduced in 1938 after Alec Brown of Piccadilly produced a miniature cue from his pocket with which to play a difficult shot from the pack of reds. The match, against Tom Newman at Thurston's, caused a great deal of controversy. There were no rules stipulating the length of the cue at the time, but referee Charlie Chambers ruled that the shot was not played within the 'spirit' of the game and awarded a foul with seven points to Newman. After that the Control Council changed the rules, stipulating that the minimum length must be three feet.

A studious looking Fred Davis

Cue-ball

The cue-ball is the white ball, and it must remain on the table at all times. If it leaves the table, or enters a pocket, then it is a foul stroke and the player who made the shot is penalized.

Until 1958 it was legal to play the 'jump shot' – that is, to make the cue-ball jump over another ball – but this is now a foul stroke. For further details of penalty values for such an offence see *Foul*.

Davis, Fred

Fred Davis is the last link between pre-war snooker and the present-day, and how fortunate the snooker world has been to have seen Fred as part of the 'new' game that was born-again in the seventies. He is a great ambassador for the game, a gentleman and good sport; the ever-smiling face of Fred Davis is always welcome in snooker halls.

Born in Whittingham Moor near Chesterfield in August 1913, Fred was 12 years younger than Joe, and because of their age difference the pair of them shared very little of their childhood. But Fred was motivated by Joe's success and was determined to emulate him. Without any coaching from Joe, Fred never did quite equal his more illustrious brother, but certainly joined him as one of the game's leading figures – a position he has held for many years.

Fred Davis's first major title was the National Under-16 title in 1929. Later that year he turned professional and went on to win the junior professional billiards title three years in succession. Short-sightedness was a big problem, however, and the wearing of spectacles made the game difficult for him. He had no alternative but to seek some new solution to the problem, and this he did by introducing the famous swivel-lens spectacles which subsequently became the saviour of many short-sighted snooker players.

Living in the shadow of Joe as a professional, he was hoping to give a good account of himself in his first world championship in 1937, but he lost to Welshman Bill Withers. Joe, showing his supremacy, restored family pride by defeating Withers 30-1 in the next round of the competition.

Joe and Fred met in the world final just once – in 1940 – and the pair of them treated the spectators to one of the greatest matches of all time. Joe won, but by only one frame in the best-of-73 frame match.

Fred spent over five years away from the sport because of army service during the war, but in 1947, after Joe's retirement from serious competition, Fred was given the ideal opportunity to replace his brother as world champion. Up against the lone Scot, Walter Donaldson, Davis started favourite, but Donaldson was showing real fighting spirit and Davis could not break through. Consequently, for the first time since the introduction of the championships in 1927, a member of the Davis family was not world champion. Fred Davis made amends in 1948 when he beat Donaldson, and again he beat him to win the title in 1949 and 1951; a slight hiccup in 1950 led to Donaldson taking the title back, temporarily.

In 1974 he suffered a second heart attack (the first was in 1970) but he still came back to reach that year's world championship semi-final, where he lost to Ray Reardon.

In recognition of his services to English snooker, Davis was made captain of the England team that competed in the 1979 and 1980 world team championships; he led them to second place behind Wales in the inaugural competition in 1979.

Even after achieving so much within the sport he still had one ambition left, and that was to win the world billiards title. His first billiards success was the junior billiards title in 1929, and in 1980 he fulfilled his final ambition when he beat Rex Williams for the world title to become only the second man, after his brother Joe, to win the world professional titles at both billiards and snooker.

Taking part in fewer tournaments these days, Davis has moved from his Stourport farm to Denbigh, North Wales, not far from Llandudno, where he lived in the mid-fifties when his wife ran a hotel in the town. When he does venture out to compete he knows that he will have the crowd on his side; he is that well-loved no matter where he plays.

Fred can certainly claim to have been the second best player around in Joe's heyday, for he was the only person to beat him on level terms. In fact he beat him on four occasions. Since the rebirth of the sport in the seventies, he has enjoyed every minute of it. His main concern is that the game should be fun, and he has the personality to achieve this.

Fred Davis was awarded the OBE in 1977 for his services to billiards and snooker.

Fred Davis: Career Highlights
- World Professional Snooker Champion 1948-49, 1951
- Professional Match-Play Snooker Champion 1952-56
- World Professional Billiards Champion 1980 (twice)
- United Kingdom Professional Billiards Champion 1951
- News of the World Champion 1958, 1959
- Australian Open Champion 1960
- National Under-16 Billiards Champion 1929

Davis, Joe

Over the years the arguments have raged as to whether George Best was as good as Tom Finney. Or whether Muhammed Ali was as good as Joe Louis. In snooker that same question is asked about Joe Davis and his namesake Steve.

Naturally, questions of that nature can never be answered. Joe's record of winning 15 world titles spread over 20 years is certainly an outstanding feat in the world of sport. On the other hand, Steve's record of winning the title four times in the present snooker climate could be considered to be its equal. One thing that cannot be disputed is Joe's prodigious contribution to the game, in that he gave snooker, almost single-handedly, an air of respectability. At the time when billiards was in its prime, Joe Davis decided to learn the subtleties of snooker. In very little time he had mastered the game – and that was before most other people had played it, or understood it. He did, as he said, 'merely commercialize' snooker.

Joe Davis was born in Whitwell, Derbyshire (the house still stands today, and a plaque commemorates his birth there) on 15 April 1901. At the age of 13 he was the Chesterfield and District amateur billiards champion; at 18 he turned professional, and in his first professional match he beat Albert Raynor. He figured in his first world billiards championship in 1922 but was eliminated by the defending champion Tom Newman.

It was around this time that Davis's keen interest in snooker was developing, and in 1926 he played a significant part in getting the Billiards Association and Control Club to agree to stage a world snooker championship.

Davis became the first champion in 1927, and he won the sum of £6 10s (£6·50) for beating Tom Dennis in the final at Camkin's Hall in Birmingham. That title was to remain in Davis's possession until he retired from world championship play in 1946. In that time he played 34 matches in the championship and won them all. The nearest he came to defeat was in the 1940 final, when his brother Fred held him to 37-36. The world billiards title followed the year after his first snooker success, and he went on to win it on four occasions in all.

After leaving the world championship scene Davis continued to play in exhibition matches and handicapped events but, as had happened with John Roberts Junior before him, his continued presence on the snooker scene inevitably devalued any competition in which he did not participate. Nevertheless, his reputation still made him one of the best-known sportsmen of his day.

Davis was one of the original directors of the new Leicester Square Hall, which was opened in 1947. Like its predecessor Thurston's, the new hall became the 'home' of snooker. Joe Davis gave some of his best performances there, and none bet-

A rare picture of Joe Davis holding a two-piece cue

A study of the perfect player – Joe Davis in 1933

ter than on 22 January 1955, when, playing Wille Smith, he recorded the first ever official maximum break of 147. It was, however, over two years before the break was eventually ratified by the BA&CC. The reason for this delay was that at that time professionals played a rule which the BA&CC did not recognize. (It stated that a player could make his opponent play again after a foul stroke.) Consequently Davis's first application for ratification of the record was refused. He made a second application in 1957, and at a meeting of the BA&CC on 7 February that year they refused it again. But at a meeting the following month they recognized the record at the third time of asking.

Record breaks constantly fell Davis's way. He made his first snooker century against Fred Pugh at Manchester in 1928, and his 500th against Jackie Rea in 1953. By the time he had retired in 1964 he had made 687 snooker century breaks and 83 billiard breaks of 1000 or more. He broke the world record snooker break on five occasions: first in 1937 with a break of 137, then in 1938 (138), 1947 (140), 1950 (146) and finally with his maximum in 1955. He also broke the world championship break record several times and was, in 1935, the compiler of the first century in the championships.

A one-time chairman of the Professional Players Association, Joe Davis was also heavily involved with raising money for charity, and in recognition of this he was awarded the OBE in 1963. He lived to see snooker enter its greatest phase when the world championship moved to the Crucible Theatre in Sheffield. Ironically, it was while watching his brother Fred's epic world championship semi-final with Perrie Mans in 1978 that Joe collapsed from the illness that was, a short while later, to claim his life. He returned to London from Sheffield and subsequently underwent a six-and-a-half-hour operation. He never fully recovered from that, and on July 10, 1978 he passed away while convalescing in Hampshire. In his will Davis left nearly £85,000 – a small sum compared to what he would have earned from the sport today, but large in comparison to the £6·50 he collected for winning the first world title. He left his revered cue, which he bought for just 7s 6d (37½p), to his son Derrick, who arranged for it to be displayed at the Eccentric Club.

Dubbed by a *Daily Mail* cartoonist 'the Sultan of Snooker' and 'the Emperor of Pot', Joe Davis was indeed the king. To a certain extent his superiority held back the sport for many years, but without him there would probably not have been a world championship, among many other things.

Career highlights
World Professional Snooker Champion 1927-40, 1946
World Professional Billiards Champion 1928-30, 1932
News of the World Champion 1950, 1953, 1956

Davis, Steve

Just as soccer had Pele, cricket had Bradman, boxing had Ali and horse racing has Piggott, snooker has its own supreme superstar in Steve Davis.

Britain's most highly paid sportsman, it is his dedication that has taken him to the top of the ladder in his chosen sport. Perhaps strangely, Romford-born Davis won neither national junior nor senior amateur snooker titles although he did beat Ian Williamson to win the national under-19 billiards title in

Joe Davis relaxing on the Thames

1976. His snooker playing started in 1969; he was 12, and his father Bill encouraged him to play while they were on holiday at a Pontins holiday camp. Bill Davis, a good standard club player with the Plumstead Common Working Men's Club, soon had Steve playing at the club upon their return from holiday.

His mother Jean, a school-teacher, was not altogether enthusiastic about his new-found pastime, and insisted that he continue his education; he obtained five GCE O-level passes and had commenced A-level studies. She had an idea that he might join the the Civil Service, or become a banker.

While still at school Steve Davis used to work on Saturdays to get some extra pocket money together. He first worked in a butcher's shop and then a greengrocer's – the latter paid 28p per hour – and these were the only jobs Davis ever had. The A-levels were abandoned when Steve left school at 17, seeking to play snooker full-time.

His big break came in 1976. By this time he was playing regularly at the Romford Lucania club. In March that year the club was bought by Barry Hearn, who immediately spotted the potential of Davis and signed him under contract. Hearn brought leading professionals to the Lucania to challenge the youngster. He turned professional in September 1978, but the previous 13 months saw Davis close his amateur career in spectacular fashion. In August 1977 he registered the first maximum break of his career when playing Ray Martin in a practice match at the Plumstead Common club – the previous day he had made clearances of 139 and 133! He was quickly selected for the England team in the Home International championship. He won the Working Men's Club & Institute Union snooker title, and was beaten by the nine-times winner Norman Dagley in the billiards final. A member of the winning London team in the inter-counties championship, Davis then went on to beat Tony Meo 7-4 in the final of the Pontins Open at Prestatyn. He made his last amateur appearance in the final of the Lucania Pro-Am, which he won for the third time by beating current professional Vic Harris.

As a professional Davis's first win was a repetition of his Pontins Open success. This time, instead of receiving 30 points per frame he was conceding 30, but he still managed to win the title by beating amateur Jimmy White in the final. Davis remains the only player to have won the title when conceding 30 points per frame to his opponent in the final.

The first time he came to the attention of the wider public was in the following year's world professional championships at the Crucible Theatre. He had to fight through the qualifying rounds, but he then beat Patsy Fagan and the defending champion, Terry Griffiths, before losing to eventual finalist Alex Higgins. It was at about this time that Davis was gaining another reputation – as a space invaders addict. This reputation caused Alex Higgins to quip, when asked about Steve: 'Steve? Steve who? Is he that video games player?'

Before 1980 was out Davis had won his first major professional title, beating Higgins in the final of the Corals United Kingdom Professional Championship at Preston. From then on, the Steve Davis story has been little else but one success after another. He followed his Coral win with victory in the Wilson's Classic at Bolton less than a week later, beating Dennis Taylor in the final.

Five individual titles and the world team title came Davis's way in 1981, but the most cherished, naturally, was his first world title which he won by beating Doug Mountjoy in the final at the Crucible.

He added four more major individual titles to his list of successes the following year. In addition he won the inaugural world doubles title with Tony Meo, and the *Pot Black* and Pontins Professional titles. But if 1982 brought more honours for Steve Davis, it also brought him one of the biggest shocks of his career – and one of the biggest in the history of the sport. Up against new professional Tony Knowles in the first round of his world championship defence, Davis slumped to a 10-1 defeat. There were also defeats in the final of the Benson and Hedges Irish Masters and the Lada Classic (both times to Terry Griffiths). Naturally the pundits were all too ready to say that he was over the top. The following year he won back his Irish Masters, Lada and world professional titles, and also won the Jameson, Scottish Masters, Tolly Cobbold Classic, world doubles for the second year running and the world team title. Having won the latter, Davis simultaneously held all three world professional titles – singles, doubles and team.

In 1984 he won his third world title after an epic battle with Jimmy White; he also won five other major titles that season and his winnings soared to a record £150,000 for that one season alone.

The 1984-85 season started as the previous one had ended, Davis winning the first two major tournaments, the Scottish Masters and the Jameson International. He had also secured the Coral UK Open and English Professional titles by the time the world championship came round, and when he raced to a 7-0 lead over Irishman Dennis Taylor he looked set to win the title for a fourth time. However, Taylor came back and won the title on the final black in the most dramatic moment ever seen at the Crucible.

The Davis machine continued to roll on, and before the year was out he had avenged that defeat by Taylor with a 9-8 win in the final of the Rothmans Grand Prix; he then beat Willie Thorne by two frames in the final of the Coral UK Open, and Thorne was also his victim in the final of the Dulux British Open. He then went into serious practice for the world championship and reached yet another Crucible final, but Yorkshireman Joe Johnson, with an astonishing display of determination, won his first title by 18 frames to 12.

In contrast to other seasons, the 1986-87 season was three ranking tournaments old by the time Davis won his first major event, the Tennents United Kingdom Open. But his victory over Neal Foulds in the final was a personal milestone, as his career earnings from prize money alone passed the £1 million mark. Another title followed when, partnering Tony Meo, he won the world doubles; then Davis went on to win the next ranking tournament, the Mercantile Credit Classic.

Fired up as always for the world championship, Davis reached his third successive final in 1987. His desire to win was greater than ever and, despite another spirited performance from Joe Johnson in a repeat of the previous year's final, Davis held on to win his fourth title.

In 1986-87 Davis retained his number one ranking comfortably, and his winnings for the season amounted to a record £322,814. This has not diminished his appetite for winning, and all the signs are that as long as he can pick up a snooker cue, second best will never be good enough for Steve Davis.

Career highlights

World Professional Snooker Champion 1981, 1983, 1984, 1987
Jameson International Champion 1981, 1983, 1984
Coral United Kingdom Professional Champion 1980, 1981, 1984, 1985

Steve Davis, the master cueman, doing what he does best...

Yamaha International Masters 1981, 1982
Dulux British Open 1986
Tennents United Kingdom Open 1986
Mercantile Credit Classic 1987
Rothmans Grand Prix 1985
Lada Classic 1983-84
Benson & Hedges Masters 1982
Benson & Hedges Irish Masters 1983-84, 1987
Tolly Cobbold Classic 1982-84
English Professional Champion 1981, 1985
Langs Scottish Masters 1982, 1983, 1984
Hofmeister World Doubles 1982, 1983, 1985, 1986 (with Tony Meo)
World Cup 1981, 1983
WMC&IU Snooker Champion 1978
Pontins Open 1978, 1979
National Under-19 Billiards Champion 1976

Donaldson, Walter

One of the original 'grinders', Walter Donaldson was a careful, steady player, but at the same time was one of the greatest long-ball potters the game has seen.

Born in Coatbridge, he was the first Scottish-born player to join the élite of the snooker world. He won the national junior under-16 billiards championship in 1922 at the age of 15, and the following year he turned professional. Unfortunately he was playing in the same era as Joe Davis. Donaldson made a living from the game but was unable to topple Davis when it came to tournament play.

His first venture into the world professional snooker championships was in 1933, when he reached the semi-final only to lose to Davis, 13-1. He did not compete again until 1939.

During the war he was out of the sport for five years while serving in the army, but his return saw him vying with Fred Davis for the world number one position. Joe Davis had retired from championship play in 1946, the same year that Donaldson established a new official world record break of 142. Fred Davis and Donaldson met in the 1947 world championship final, and it was up to Fred to maintain the family tradition – the name Davis had been on the world championship trophy since 1927. But it was not to be: Donaldson won 82-63. They met in the final the following year and this time Davis won. Davis beat Donaldson again in the 1949 final, but in 1950 it was the latter's turn to win. They met again in 1951 and Davis edged in front to take a 3-2 lead in their battle for world championship wins.

After the split in the professional ranks in 1952, the Professional Billiard Players' Association organized its own 'world championships' known as the Professional Match-Play championships. Davis and Donaldson contested the 1952, 1953 and 1954 finals – but Donaldson lost all three.

He retired from competitive play in 1954, but maintained contact with the sport. He died at his home in Buckinghamshire in 1973, at the age of 66.

Career highlights

World Professional Snooker Champion 1947, 1950
World Professional Snooker Champion (runner-up) 1948-49, 1951
World Professional Match-Play (runner-up) 1952-54
National Under-16 Billiards Champion 1922

...and enjoying life away from the table

Drago, Tony

When Tony Drago left the amateur ranks to become Malta's only professional snooker player in 1985, he had a string of successes and records to his name. He was, the previous year, the youngest ever winner of the Maltese amateur title at 18. And when he went to Dublin for that year's world amateur championship he started as one of the favourites. Sadly, the safety play of this exciting and naturally gifted potter let him down, but he did leave Ireland as the holder of a new championship record break of 132.

In his first year as a professional Drago enjoyed wins over Eddie Charlton in the Rothmans Grand Prix and Mark Wildman in the Coral UK Open. He ended that first season ranked 37th but he climbed to 32nd in 1987 after a memorable tournament in the Tennents UK Open. He saw off Rex Williams in the 3rd round with a match-winning 103 break, and in the next round he beat John Virgo 9-6. On his first visit to the table in the opening frame he equalled the championship record of 141. Willie Thorne was his next opponent, and Drago beat him for the second time during the season, having eliminated Thorne from the BCE International. Steve Davis was the next obstacle in Drago's way, but the way he was playing, he feared nobody.

He raced into a 3-0 lead before Davis won the next four in a row. The lead then alternated between Davis and the Maltese player and they went into the final frame level at 8-all. Drago built up a 54-1 lead, but then let Davis in. The three-times world champion missed the blue with his last red. Drago had an easy yellow with the rest but nerves got to him and he missed it. Davis had no difficulty in tidying up the match and entering the semi-finals. Drago picked up £9,000 for his efforts, but, more important, he gained the experience of knowing how to handle such a situation.

Drago is certainly an exciting player to watch, and an exciting prospect. His speed around the table is reminiscent of that of Jimmy White and Alex Higgins. Sadly, he often gets homesick and then returns to Malta. Hopefully he will get over that, and British fans will more regularly be treated to his enormous skills.

Career Highlights
Tennents United Kingdom Open (quarter-final) 1986
Maltese Amateur Champion 1984

Dress

Snooker was a game for gentlemen, and thus it was that formal wear became the usual apparrel in which either billiards or snooker was played. The game has maintained its long and fine tradition of smart dress by both players and referees, and the upholding of that tradition has helped the sport's image, particularly in the early days of television. It was a rare sight to see such well dressed, clean cut sportsmen, and it was on this image that – to some extent – its success has been built.

Although the Billiards and Snooker Control Council has no set rules regarding dress, the World Professional Billiards and Snooker Association does have its own dress regulations. And one area in which it is particularly strict concerns the wearing of ties and bows. Because the number of players appearing without such attire was on the increase, in 1982 they made it compulsory for every player, unless he could provide a certificate

It is not only the players who dress well – not orthodox, but this snooker jumper is certainly original

Both Steve Davis and the sheepdog have their eyes on the Dulux British Open Trophy

from a doctor before each tournament, endorsed by a medical officer appointed by the WPBSA.

The WPBSA insist on players wearing a lounge suit for morning and afternoon sessions, and an evening suit for an evening's session of play. More and more players are moving away from the traditional black attire, but the whites, reds, and other bright colours are still acceptable providing the player looks smart.

Dry Blackthorn Cup

The Dry Blackthorn Cup was held just once, in 1977, but it was a first on two counts. It was the first time the Wembley Conference Centre had been used for a snooker tournament, and it was the first tournament promoted by Mike Barrett, better known these days for his Frank Bruno promotions.

The prize money was £4,350, which was a record for a one-day tournament. Four players – Patsy Fagan, John Spencer, Alex Higgins and Ray Reardon – competed, and played in a knockout tournament with two semi-finals and a final, which was won by Fagan.

The Wembley Conference Centre was then, as it is today, a good venue, and a crowd of around 1,500 watched the day's play. As well as the high-class snooker that players of their calibre could be relied on to produce, those watching were hoping to see a maximum 147 break. A considerable incentive – a prize of £50,000 – awaited the player who could achieve this in the course of the competition.

Dry Blackthorn Cup: Result (final)

1977 P. Fagan (Eire) 4
A. Higgins (N. Ireland) 2

Highest break: 77 – Ray Reardon

Dulux British Open Championship

The Dulux British Open started life as The British Gold Cup in 1980. The 16-man event had three trade sponsors, E. J. Riley, Strachas, and the Composition Billiard Ball Supply Company. Alex Higgins beat Ray Reardon 5-1 in the final played at the Derby Assembly Rooms.

When Yamaha Organs entered the sport in 1981 their tournament, originally called the Yamaha Organs Trophy, replaced the Gold Cup and, like its predecessor, was held at Derby.

The original format saw 16 players split into four groups whose members played one another on a round-robin basis over the best of three frames, with the top four progressing to a knockout stage. The first Yamaha title went to Steve Davis who beat David Taylor, appearing in only his second major final.

Davis retained the title in 1982 with a masterly display in the final against Terry Griffiths, winning 9-7 thanks to the help of a tournament-equalling record break of 135. The format remained unaltered in 1983 and Ray Reardon took the £12,000 first prize, beating Jimmy White 9-6, after trailing 6-4.

The last Yamaha in 1984 saw a change of format once more with all matches being the best-of-three. The 27 qualifiers played round-robin matches in groups of three. The nine winners than played in three more groups, and the three finalists also played round-robin matches. Steve Davis, Dave Martin and John Dunning made up the final trio. Both Davis and Martin beat Dunning and in the deciding match Davis beat Martin 3-0 to win the title for the third time.

When Dulux took over the event in 1985 it reverted to a straightforward knockout format and it became a ranking tournament.

Through their Paints Division, ICI invested £250,000 in the tournament in the first year and the first prize was snooker's first ever £50,000 prize. The inaugural final was between South African Silvino Franciso and Canadian Kirk Stevens...and it was Francisco's Bank Manager who ended up the happier of the two!

Scot Murdo McLeod dumped the defending champion Francisco in the fourth round a year later, and Steve Davis went on to beat Willie Thorne 12-7 in the final.

The fourth round was again the graveyard of the defending champion in 1987 as Davis lost 5-4 to John Virgo, a semi-finalist the previous year. The final, as the previous year, was contested by two members of the Barry Hearn stable – Jimmy White and Neal Foulds. They helped to swell the Matchroom kitty by £96,000 with White taking the top prize of £60,000.

Dulux British Open Championship – Results (finals)

1980 A. Higgins (Ireland) 5
R. Reardon (Wales) 1
1981 S. Davis (England) 9
D. Taylor (England) 6
1982 S. Davis (England) 9
T. Griffiths (Wales) 7
1983 R. Reardon (Wales) 9
J. White (England) 6
1984 1. S. Davis (England)
2. D. Martin (England)
3. J. Dunning (England)
1985 S. Francisco (South Africa) 12
K. Stevens (Canada) 9
1986 S. Davis (England) 12
W. Thorne (England) 7
1987 J. White (England) 13
N. Foulds (England) 9

Most wins: 4 – Steve Davis
Most finals: 4 – Steve Davis
Highest break: 145 – Dave Martin (1986)

E

Earnings

Since snooker became a television sport, snooker players have achieved 'superstar' status, and with this has come the appropriate high earnings. Major championships now carry first prizes of £50,000 or more, which makes snooker a glamorous sport. But as far as most of the professionals are concerned, that is not the whole story.

Steve Davis is by far the greatest earner the sport has known, and his income is in the million-pounds-a-year bracket. That does not come from prize-money alone, but is supplemented by television appearances, endorsements to manufacturers, and a lucrative exhibition deal with a brewery. However, Davis is the exception when it comes to earnings, and many professionals have to supplement their winnings with outside jobs.

The average prize winnings for all professionals in the 1986-87 season was just over £21,000. But if you ignore the top 16 earners then that average drops dramatically to £7,900; 82 professionals won under £10,000 for the season, and 21 collected no prize money at all. Most players engage in exhibition matches to supplement their incomes, and their income from these varies depending upon the stature of the individual player. A top-class professional who has received plenty of television coverage can earn up to £2,500 for a night's work. A professional never seen on television would be lucky to pick up £100 for a similar display – assuming he could get the work in the first place.

The following tables show how far the sport has progressed since the 1975-76 season. The top ten money winners from major tournaments in that season are given, and by way of comparison, the top ten from the 1986-87 season are also shown. The number of major tournaments on which the figures are based rose from three to sixteen.

Winning wherever they go – looks like Las Vegas is as profitable as the Crucible Theatre for Steve Davis and Barry Hearn

Earnings 1975-76

1. Ray Reardon	£9,000
2. Alex Higgins	£2,250
3. Graham Miles	£1,550
4. Eddie Charlton	£1,500
5. John Spencer	£1,350
Fred Davis	£1,350
7. Perrie Mans	£1,000
8. Dennis Taylor	£825
9. John Pulman	£675
Rex Williams	£675

Willie Thorne's prize money for the season was just £125.

1986-87

1. Steve Davis	£322,814
2. Jimmy White	£225,758
3. Neal Foulds	£172,093
4. Dennis Taylor	£160,201
5. Willie Thorne	£152,839
6. Cliff Thorburn	£109,784
7. Tony Meo	£102,092
8. Joe Johnson	£101,153
9. Alex Higgins	£99,825
10. Terry Griffiths	£84,883

(These figures do not include special 'break' prizes)

Steve Davis took his career winnings past the £1 million mark in 1986 when he won the UK Open.

Ray Edmonds, deep in concentration

Edmonds, Ray

Ray Edmonds has been playing snooker at the highest level, amateur and professional, since the sixties, but it was only in the eighties that he became a household name. Although he has an excellent playing record, mostly as an amateur, he is now well known for his role as a member of the ITV snooker commentary team, where his vast experience is highly valued.

His playing career goes back a long way – to 1961, in fact, when he reached the final of the English amateur championship, which he lost to Alan Barnett. He built on that experience to win the title eventually, in 1969, by beating Jonathan Barron (which thwarted Barron's chances of winning four successive titles).

Edmonds himself appeared in three successive finals, in 1972, 1973 and 1974, and after defeats by Barron and Marcus Owen, he won his second title in 1974 beating Patsy Fagan.

Finishing runner-up in the 1972 championship meant that Edmonds was eligible to compete in the world amateur championships in Cardiff. He could only finish second in his qualifying group, but nevertheless he still qualified for the semi-finals, where he scored a memorable 8-6 win over Barron (who had beaten him in that year's amateur championship final). In the final Edmonds had an even more memorable victory. Up against South African Mannie Francisco he lost the first six frames but showed his great fighting spirit by coming back to win 11-10. He successfully defended his world title in 1974 beating Welshman Geoff Thomas in the final in Dublin, but in Johannesburg in 1976 he failed to make it a hat-trick when Malta's Paul Mifsud eliminated him in the quarter-final.

Having won the CIU championship on two occasions – in 1971 and 1972 (he is one of only two men since the war to win the title in successive years) – and represented England in 21 Home International Championship matches (more than any other player except John Hargreaves and Sid Hood) he left his illustrious amateur career behind him to turn professional in 1978. Unfortunately, his successes in the professional ranks nowhere near match those of his amateur days. An expert at both billiards and snooker, Edmonds reached his first world professional billiards championship final at the Hatton Garden Billiard Centre in 1985 after three previous semi-final appearances. He beat Norman Dagley (also appearing in his first final) 3-1. His best professional snooker result was in 1981 when he reached the semi-final of the English professional championship at the Haden Hill Leisure Centre, Sandwell, near Birmingham, before losing 9-0 to Steve Davis.

One-time manager of a painting and decorating business, Ray Edmonds hails from Lincolnshire and spent many years in the Skegness area before settling in Cleethorpes, Humberside, where he opened his own snooker centre.

Career highlights

- World Professional Billiards Champion 1985
- World Amateur Snooker Champion 1972, 1974
- English Amateur Snooker Champion 1969, 1974
- English Professional Snooker Championship (semi-final) 1981
- WMC & IU Snooker Champion 1971, 1972

Eire

Billiards has been played in the Republic of Ireland since the turn of the century, and in Joe Nugent it had one of the leading amateur players of the day. His record of finishing runner-up in the English amateur billiards championship on three occasions was no mean feat in those days.

The next Eire player of outstanding ability was Seamus Fenning, who won his national snooker title on five occasions. He also won the billiards title six times, and won a total of eight All-Ireland titles.

Had Charles Downey not been resident in England, he would surely have won the national title more than once, but that was more than compensated for when he won the coveted English amateur snooker title in 1952.

The Republic has eight professionals at present, including, in Eugene Hughes, a potential star of the future. British junior billiards and snooker champion in 1975, he won two national titles and was holder of the record break in the world amateur championships before he turned professional in 1981. Since then he has proved himself to be a tough competitor to beat

Republic of Ireland Amateur Snooker Championships – Results (finals)

1927 T.H. Fayrey beat M.H. Walker
1931 J. Ayres*
1933 S. Fenning beat J. Ayres
1934 Not held
1935 S. Fenning*
1936 Not held
1937 P.J. O'Connor*
1938-1939 Not held
1940 P. Merrigan beat S. Fenning
1941-1946 Not held
1947 C. Downey beat P. Merrigan
1948 P. Merrigan*
1949 S. Fenning*
1950-1951 Not held
1952 W. Brown beat S. Fenning
1953 S. Brooks beat W. Brown
1954 S. Fenning Beat J. Redmond
1955 S. Fenning beat W. Brown
1956 W. Brown beat S. Fenning
1957 J. Connolly beat G. Gibson
1958 G. Gibson beat F. Murphy
1959-1960 Not held
1961 W. Brown beat F. Murphy
1962 J. Weber beat G. Buffini
1963 J. Rogers beat G. Hanway
1964 J. Rogers beat G. Buffini
1965 W. Fields beat J. Grace
1966 G. Hanway beat J. Rogers
1967 P. Morgan beat J. Rogers
1968 G. Hanway beat T.G. Hearty
1969 D. Daley beat J. Rogers
1970 D. Sheehan beat P. Thornton
1971 D. Sheehan beat J. Weber
1972 J. Rogers beat D. Sheehan
1973 F. Murphy beat J. Bannister
1974 P. Burke beat P. Miley
1975 F. Nathan beat J. Weber
1976 P. Burke beat L. Watson
1977 J. Clusker beat F. Murphy
1978 E. Hughes beat N. Lowth
1979 E. Hughes beat D. Sheehan
1980 D. Sheehan beat E. Hughes
1981 A. Kearney beat P. Miley
1982 P. Browne beat R. Brennan
1983 J. Long beat P. Ennis
1984 P. Ennis beat J. Long
1985* G. Burns beat K. Doherty
1986 G. Burns beat D. McKiernan
1987 K. Doherty beat R. Nolan

Most wins: 5 – Seamus Fenning

* Records not kept

David Taylor – winner of the English amateur title in 1968

and has edged his way towards the top twenty in the world rankings. Hughes is joined in the professional ranks by Paddy Browne (at 17 the youngest winner of the Eire title, in 1982), Pascal Burke, Tony Kearney, Billy Kelly, Dessie Sheehan, Paul Watchorn and 1970s star, Patsy Fagan.

The Republic of Ireland could boast another professional in 1985, although he represented Australia rather than his native country: Eire-born Paddy Morgan emigrated to Australia after winning national titles in the late sixties, and subsequently turned professional. Now based in England, Morgan claims to be the only professional snooker player to have been a bus conductor in three countries – Ireland, Australia and England!

Paddy Morgan and Pascal Burke have achieved the best-ever placings for their country in the world amateur snooker championships when they reached the semi-final stage in 1968 and 1974 respectively.

Southern Ireland has staged one of the professional season's big events – the Benson and Hedges Irish Masters – since 1978. The event, held in Goffs sales ring at County Kildare, attracts a top-class field of professionals who are not involved in qualifying matches for the world professional championships – the Irish Masters is the last big event before the Crucible.

See also Irish Masters
Irish Professional Championships

English Amateur Championships

One of snooker's long-established competitions, the English amateur championships have been contested since 1921, although their forerunner – the amateur snooker championships – were first held in 1916. The first matches were held at Orme's Hall, Soho Square, on Monday 28 August 1916. The entry fee was just 10s 6d (52½p).

It is the pinnacle of any amateur player's career to win the final of the amateur championship, and today around 850 hopefuls set out on that long road each season.

That figure of 850 is a far cry from the 26 entrants who contested the first championships in 1921. In those early days each match except the final was played over three frames and the aggregate scores of those frames counted towards the eventual result. The final was held over seven frames. M. Vaughan beat S.H. Fry 384-378 in the 1921 final; he would have been victorious on frames as well, because he won 4-3. The highest break of the competition was 27 – by Fry. The current record break, 138, was made by Tony Chappel in the 1984 competition, playing against fellow Welshman Wayne Jones. Perhaps surprisingly, the first century break in the championships did not come until 1962, when Geoffrey Thompson broke the barrier with a 115 break.

The aggregate-score method of deciding matches remained in force until 1926. That year, F.T.W. Morley lost in the final even though he won four of the seven frames; after that the outcome was decided on frames.

As the number of entrants in the competition rose in the post-war years, the event was reorganized regionally, split into northern and southern sections. The two winners would then meet in the final of the championship.

The winning of the English amateur championship was regarded as the stepping-stone to greater glories – namely, the professional scene. It is interesting to note that since 1962 only two of the English amateur finalists – Jonathan Barron and George Wood – have not applied for professional status. All the others have applied, and been accepted.

England international Jonathan Barron has one of the best records in the championships, and his three successive wins are likely to remain unsurpassed for many years because of the present-day trend for a player to apply for professional status after winning the title.

The first amateur champion subsequently to make an impact on the professional game was Kingsley Kennerley, champion in 1937 and 1940. Rex Williams, the 1951 champion, went on to make an impact in the professional game at both billiards and snooker; Williams was the youngest winner of the title until 1979, when Jimmy White assumed that record. But since then many former champions have gone on to achieve success in the professional game. Terry Griffiths, Ray Reardon, John Pulman and John Spencer, however, are the only winners of the amateur championship to have gone on to win the professional world title.

The Bristol-based table manufacturers BCE became the first trade sponsors of the championship in 1983, and in 1985 the World Professional Billiards and Snooker Association assisted with sponsorship. BCE, however, signed a deal with the B&SCC in 1986 that will ensure their support until at least 1991 both for the Amateur Championship and their Grand Masters Championship, for over-50s, inaugurated in 1986-87.

See also Amateur

English Professional Championships

As a result of the World Professional Billiards and Snooker Association's agreeing to give grants amounting to £1,000 per entrant to national professional championships, the English professional championship was revived in the 1984-85 season. In addition to the WPBSA grants, the Suffolk brewers Tolly Cobbold sponsored the event. Cobbold's abandoned their highly successful Classic in order to direct their energies into this new project.

The English professional title had only once been contested prior to 1985, and that was in 1981. Steve Davis beat Tony Meo in the final at the Haden Hill Leisure Centre, Sandwell. The £4,000 first prize was not in keeping with the prize money of other sponsored events at the time, and consequently the championship was discontinued until revived under the sponsorship of Tolly Cobbold.

Steve Davis was the second winner of the title, easily beating Tony Knowles 9-2 in the final. Davis had a fairly easy passage to the final, except in the semi-final, where he met Tony Meo, whom he had beaten in the only other final four years earlier. Davis had to come back from 8-7 down to win 9-8. Meo succeeded Davis as champion when he won his first major professional tournament.

English Professional Championships: Results (finals)

1981 S. Davis 9 A. Meo 3
1982-1984 Not held
1985 S. Davis 9 A. Knowles 2
1986 A. Meo 9 N. Foulds 7
1987 A. Meo 9 L. Dodd 5
Most wins: 2 – Steve Davis
Highest break: 139 – Tony Knowles (1985)
139 – John Virgo (1987)

English Amateur Championships – Results (finals)

The Amateur Snooker Championship

1916 C.N. Jaques

1917 C.N. Jaques

1918 T.N. Palmer

1919 S.H. Fry

1920 A.R. Wisdom

English Amateur Championships

1921 M.J. Vaughan 384
S.H. Fry 378

1922 J. McGlynn 423
C. Cox, Jun 301

1923 W. Coupe 432
E. Forshall 337

1924 W. Coupe 413
H.G. Olden 333

1925 J. McGlynn 392
W.L. Crompton 308

1926 W. Nash 383
F.T. Leaphard 356

(1921-1926 played aggregate scores over seven frames)

1927 O.T. Jackson 4
A.W. Casey 2

1928 P.H. Matthews 5
F. Whittall 4

1929 L. Steeples 5
F. Whittall 4

1930 L. Steeples 5
F. Whittall 1

1931 P.H. Matthews 5
H. Kingsley 4

1932 W.E. Bach 5
O.T. Jackson 3

1933 E. Bedford 5
A. Kershaw 1

1934 C.H. Beavis 5
P.H. Matthews 2

1935 C.H. Beavis 5
D. Hindmarch 3

1936 P.H. Matthews 5
C.H. Beavis 3

1937 K. Kennerley 6
W.H. Dennis 3

1938 P.H. Matthews 6
K. Kennerley 1

1939 P. Bendon 6
K. Kennerley 4

1940 K. Kennerley 8
A. Brown 7

1941-1945 Not held

1946 J. Pulman 5
A. Brown 3

1947 H. Morris 5
C.A. Kent 1

1948 S. Battye 6
T. Postlethwaite 4

1949 T.C. Gordon 6
S. Kilbank 4

1950 A. Nolan 6
G. Owen 5

1951 R. Williams 6
P. Bendon 1

1952 C. Downey 6
J. Allen 1

1953 T.C. Gordon 6
G. Humphries 5

1954 G. Thompson 11
C. Wilson 9

1955 M. Parkin 11
A. Nolan 7

1956 T.C. Gordon 11
R. Reardon 9

1957 R. Gross 11
S. Haslam 6

1958 M. Owen 11
J. Fitzmaurice 8

1959 M. Owen 11
A. Barnett 5

1960 R. Gross 11
J. Price 4

1961 A. Barnett 11
R. Edmonds 9

1962 R. Gross 11
J. Barron 9

1963 G. Owen 11
R. Gross 3

1964 R. Reardon 11
J. Spencer 8

1965 P. Houlihan 11
J. Spencer 3

1966 J. Spencer 11
M. Owen 5

1967 M. Owen 11
S. Hood 4

1968 David Taylor 11
C. Ross 6

1969 R. Edmonds 11
J. Barron 9

1970 J. Barron 11
S. Hood 10

1971 J. Barron 11
D. French 9

1972 J. Barron 11
R. Edmonds 9

1973 M. Owen 11
R. Edmonds 6

1974 R. Edmonds 11
P. Fagan 7

1975 S. Hood 11
W. Thorne 6

1976 C. Ross 11
R. Andrewartha 7

1977 T. Griffiths 13
S. Hood 3

1978 T. Griffiths 13
J. Johnson 6

1979 J. White 13
D. Martin 10

1980 J. O'Boye 13
D. Martin 9

1981 V. Harris 13
G. Wood 9

1982 D. Chalmers 13
M. Bradley 9

1983 A. Jones 13
J. Parrott 9

1984 S. Longworth 13
W. Jones 8

1985 T. Whitthread 13
J. McNellan 4

1986 A. Harris 13
G. Grennan 9

1987 M. Rowing 13
S. Lanigan 11

Most wins: 4 – P. Matthews, M. Owen
Most finals: 5 – J. Barron, R. Edmonds
P. Matthews, M. Owen
Highest break: 138 – A. Chappel (1984)

Steve Davis during the 1985 English professional championship, which he won for the second time

Equipment

To play a game of snooker the players need a table, some balls and a cue. These items are covered individually in this book, but other ancillary pieces of equipment are described here.

The **triangle** is normally wooden, and is used by the referee for setting up the red balls in a pyramid before a game.

Because of the size of a billiard table it is not always possible to play every shot with a traditional cue, because of the inaccessibility of the cue-ball. The following cueing aids are, however, made available to the players.

The **rest** is used for playing those shots that are just out of reach with the normal cue.

The **half-butt** is, perhaps, the most difficult piece of equipment to use. It is approximately 3m (9 feet) in length, and is accompanied by a cue of similar length. It is used for shots that are nearly a table's length away, and, because of its length, makes accurate control of the cue-ball difficult.

The **spider** is used for a shot which is in any case difficult to reach, and additionally there is another ball close to the cue-ball, necessitating a bridge for the shot to be played.

The spider and (right) the extended spider in use

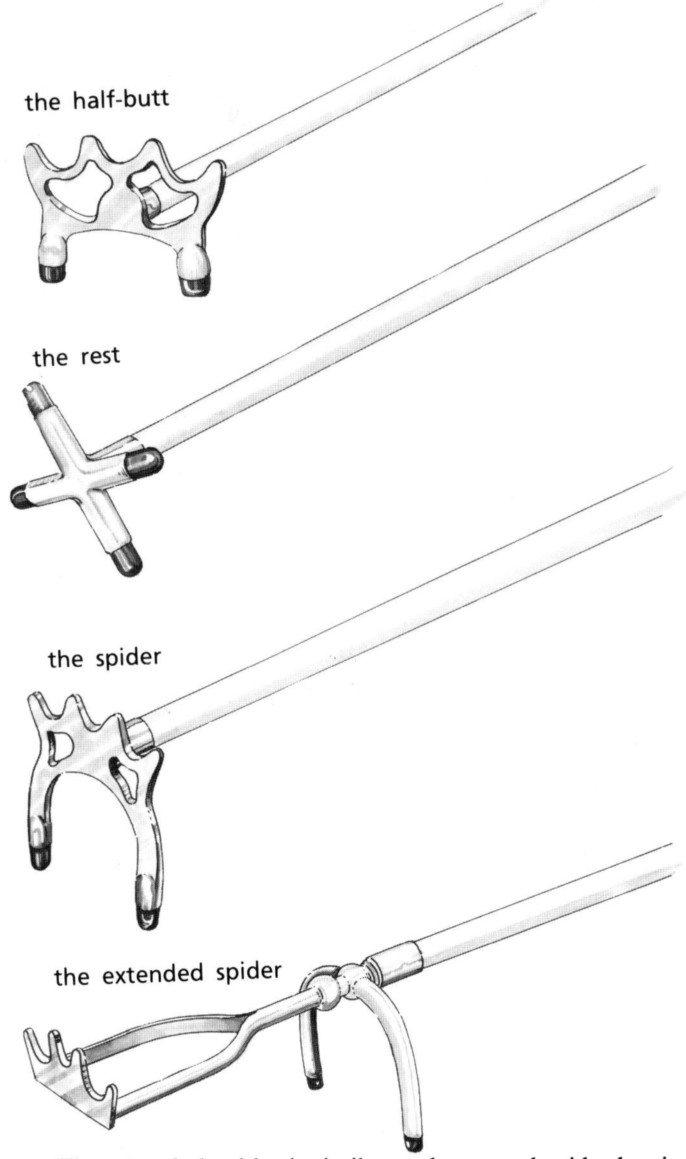

The **extended spider** is similar to the normal spider but is used when the cue ball is surrounded by other balls and it is impossible to make a normal bridge to play the shot.

Once the referee has passed the equipment to the player, it is then the player's responsibility to look after it. If he drops it on the table and interferes with any of the balls, he shall be penalized as if he had played a foul shot.

Everton, Clive

Editor of the monthly journal *Billiards and Snooker* since December 1966, Clive Everton has remained loyal to the sport, and has been an important member of the snooker fraternity during its growth period. He gained a B.A. Honours Degree in English from Cardiff University and took up a teaching post in Halesowen. From there he went into journalism, and became a hockey, tennis, badminton and squash correspondent. But he always had a love of billiards and snooker, and enjoyed playing both sports, as well as reporting on them.

The Billiards Association placed a great deal of faith in Clive Everton when they appointed him editor of their magazine in 1966, but this faith was fully justified. The magazine eventually became *Snooker Scene* of which Everton remains the editor; he is also the snooker correspondent for *The Guardian* and *The Sunday Times*. He is also the proprietor of snooker's other leading magazine, *Cue World*. In addition, he is a very valued and knowledgeable member of the BBC commentary team.

As a player, it is in billiards that Everton has excelled. Winner of the boys' under-16 title in 1953, he went on to win the under-19 title three years later. He won the Welsh billiards title five times, and was runner-up on four occasions, but he never managed to win the English amateur title, despite reaching no fewer than five finals.

He took part in every world amateur billiards championship from 1971 until his turning professional in 1981, and reached the semi-finals twice – in 1975 and 1977.

Since joining the professional ranks, Everton's success has been limited to reaching the quarter-final stage of the world billiards championships in 1982 and 1983. And on the snooker front he can claim little success – a victory over Patsy Fagan to reach the second round of the 1982 Professional Players' Tournament is perhaps his best result.

Apart from his journalistic talents, he was responsible for the revival of the British boys' championships in 1968; the under-16 championship had not been held for the previous six years.

Career highlights

- National Snooker Pairs Champion 1977 (with Roger Bales)
- National Under-16 Billiards Champion 1953
- National Under-19 Billiards Champion 1956

Exhibition Matches

Exhibition matches have always been a part of the snooker scene, although their role and purpose has changed in the post-war years. In the forties and fifties, when competitive tournaments were considerably fewer than today, leading professionals like Joe and Fred Davis, Walter Donaldson, Willie Smith and others used to engage in exhibition matches. The exhibitions were often week-long events and were very competitive affairs, with large sums of money at stake. Most exhibition matches in that era were held at Thurston's Hall, which subsequently became the Leicester Square Hall. But some players took their 'shows' around the provinces, and some even ventured abroad to display their talents.

Today, the exhibition match has a totally different purpose. Professionals and leading amateurs are engaged in competitions for most of the season, but when there is a lull in their programme most of them like to take part in relaxed fixtures whereby the professional can play against several club players in one night. The crowds pay to be entertained with large breaks, good banter, and a series of trick shots at the end of the evening – and most professionals provide all this. They are generally good value for money, but the fee can vary from £100 up to perhaps £2,500 per night or more.

Fagan, Patsy

Hailed as one of the most exciting players of the mid-seventies, Patsy Fagan's fall from glory was as dramatic as his rise to fame.

One of 12 children, he was born in Dublin, but has spent

most of his snooker-playing days in London. A resident professional at one of the Ron Gross Snooker Centres, he first came to prominence in 1974 when he reached the final of the English amateur championship, where he was to lose to Ray Edmonds.

Two years later he made an impact on the championship again when he created a tournament record break of 115.

Having failed to reach the 1976 final, Fagan decided to turn professional. He started 1977 with the first maximum of his career – on his 25th birthday in January, (against Dave Gilbert at the Clapton Bus Garage Social Club). Before the year was out he had become the first United Kingdom professional champion – his first major win as a professional. In the final he beat fellow first-year professional Doug Mountjoy to take the £2,000 first prize at the Blackpool Tower Circus.

A great break-builder, he picked up another £2,000 cheque a couple of weeks later when he won the Dry Blackthorn Cup at the Wembley Conference Centre – the first snooker tournament to be played there. He fell at the first hurdle in defence of his United Kingdom title in 1978, but managed to reach the quarter-final of that year's world championship. To reach that stage he was engaged in a memorable first-round match with fellow Irishman Alex Higgins, which Fagan won 13-12.

In the quarter-final he lost to Fred Davis. That is the nearest the Dubliner has come to the world title, and indeed, apart from reaching the last eight of the 1979 United Kingdom championship, he has not progressed that far in a tournament since, although the 1985 world championship indicated a change in Fagan's fortune. After beating Willie Thorne in the first round he narrowly lost to Ray Reardon in the second.

The first sign of his decline came in 1979 when he suffered a shock first-round defeat in the world championships; his conqueror was an 'unknown' by the name of Steve Davis.... Since then it has been a downhill slide for Patsy Fagan. To add to his problems he suffered a twitch which prevented him from playing with the rest. He has, however, remained on the professional circuit, and snooker spectators everywhere would be glad to see the popular Irishman among the winners again.

Career highlights

English Amateur Championship (runner-up) 1974
United Kingdom Professional Champion 1977

Families

Snooker, like any other sport, occasionally sees members of one family excel. The following are some of the better-known families who have enjoyed a long and/or successful association with the sports of snooker and billiards.

Agrawal

In 1983 Subash Agrawal reached the final of the world amateur billiards championship, only to lose to fellow Indian Michael Ferreira. Twelve months later Subash's brother, Omprakash – known as O.B. – went one better, beating the defending champion Terry Parsons of Wales in the final of the world amateur snooker championships in Dublin. In winning the title, O.B. became the first player from outside England or Wales to win the title.

Bear

Canadian brothers Jim and John Bear are both current professionals. John was accepted as a professional in 1980, and Jim in 1983. Since they both became professionals they have never met in a major tournament in Britain. They did, however, meet in the quarter-final of the Canadian professional championships in 1983; Jim won 9-5.

Patsy Fagan

Jim was Canadian amateur champion in 1980, and at the world championships on home soil in 1982 he threw away a 7-1 lead in the final and lost to Welshman Terry Parsons.

Charlton

It is a fact, little known outside Australia, that Eddie Charlton has a brother who is a professional snooker player, and a son who is attempting to follow in his father's footsteps.

Eddie's broher Jim is a publican in Newcastle, New South Wales, and confines his snooker playing to his own country. Eddie's son Edward also plays only in Australia.

Jim took part in his first major tournament for some time in 1984, when he competed in the reborn Australian Professional championship. He suffered an early exit, however, being defeated 6-1 in the first round by Robbie Foldvari.

Eddie Charlton has achieved success the world over, and full details of his career are given elsewhere in this encyclopedia.

The Charlton family is well known in Australia thanks to the Eddie Charlton Snooker Circus. Eddie, Jim, Edward, Jim's son Garth, and fellow Australian professional Ian Anderson tour the country, taking their sport to a nation which, because of its sheer vastness, would otherwise not be able to witness live snooker matches.

Collins

George Collins was a 19th-century billiards player, and his daughter Eva was one of the first women to play the sport in public.

Eva's brother Frank was a renowned coach and referee in the early part of the 20th century.

Davis

Fred and Joe Davis are undoubtedly the best-known pair of snooker and billiards-playing brothers ever known; but it was Joe – the elder – who became a sporting legend.

Unbeatable, he was world professional snooker champion from 1927 until the time of his retirement from world championship play in 1946. He was also three times world professional billiards champion.

Fred also held both titles, the snooker on three occasions, and the billiards on two occasions. The latter title did not come his way until 1980 when, at the age of 66, he defeated reigning champion Rex Williams to fulfil a life-long ambition.

Joe and Fred met in the 1940 world snooker final, and this was the nearest Joe ever came to defeat in the final: Fred came within one frame of victory, but Joe was the eventual winner by 37 frames to 36.

Still competing at the highest level, Fred Davis is one of the most popular and respected members of the sport and his name – like his late brother's – will be always remembered among the snooker fraternity.

Foulds

When Geoff and Neal Foulds qualified for the final stages of the 1983 Coral United Kingdom championship at Preston they became the first father and son to compete in the final stages of a major professional snooker tournament.

The eagerly anticipated meeting between the two never materialized as both suffered first round defeats. The pair of them have, however, twice met in competitive play: in the final of the London championships when Geoff showed his paternal superiority by defeating Neal 4-3, on the final black, and in the 1986 English Professional Championship when Neal won 9-4.

Francisco

In 1983, Peter Francisco attempted to become the third member of the Francisco family to join the professional ranks, but his application was deferred by the WPBSA because he still had six months national service in the South African navy to serve. The following year, however, he was accepted, and thus followed in the footsteps of his father Mannie and uncle Silvino.

Mannie and Silvino have been prominent members of the South African billiards and snooker scene for many years, both as amateurs and now as professionals. Mannie won 13 South African billiards titles and six snooker titles. Silvino won three billiards and four snooker titles, while the latest addition, Peter, has won three snooker titles.

Mannie was runner up in the world amateur billiards championship in 1971, and the following year was runner-up in the world snooker championships. In the 1976 snooker championships, Mannie and Silvino met in the quarter final. Silvino won 5-1: the first time he had defeated his brother in a tournament.

In the professional ranks, it is Silvino who has the better record and in the 1984-85 season he won his first major tournament, the Dulux British Open. But Mannie has not played professionally outside his native South Africa.

Gray

Harry Gray lost to Fred Lindrum in the final of the 'native-born' Australian billiards championship in 1887. Both men produced famous sons.

Fred was the father of Walter, and Harry the father of George. George Gray and Walter Lindrum both became 'greats' of Australian billiards.

Harveson

Another father-and-son combination. English-born Cecil Harveson went to settle in South Africa before the first world war, and became a professional billiards player. His son Ronny also became a professional.

Kwok

New Zealand brothers Dale and Glen Kwok have dominated their national amateur snooker championships in the 1980s. Glen was 1981 champion; Dale was champion in 1982 and 1983, and Glen regained the title in 1984. The pair of them have both competed in the world amateur championships, although never in the same year. Dale took part in 1978 and 1984 while Glen competed in 1982.

Lindrum

The name Lindrum is identified with billiards and snooker in the same way as that of Davis. And in a way, because the family goes back through three generations of billiards players, it is an even more distinguished name than Davis. Fred Lindrum I was the first of the billiard-playing Lindrums, and it was he who took the family from their Plymouth (England) home to Australia in 1838. His son Fred II was also a keen player, and was the father of Walter and Fred III. These two both took to the sport, but it was Walter who became one of its outstanding players.

The greatest billiards player ever, Walter Lindrum holds the record for the highest official break – 4,137 – and was winner of the world professional championship on the two occasions he entered it.

The other member of the family was Horace, nephew of Walter. It was to snooker rather than billiards that Horace turned, and he proved himself among the world's greatest players in the 1930s and 1940s. Four times world professional snooker finalist, he lost on three occasion to Joe Davis before eventually winning the title by beating Clark McConachy in the two-man competition in 1952.

Mans

Peter Mans and his son Perrie hold the distinction of being the only father-and-son combination to have both reached the quarter-final stage of the world professional snooker championships.

Peter, South Africa's first professional, reached the last eight in 1950, where he lost to Canadian George Chenier. Perrie has reached the quarter final stage on three occasions, and was, in 1978, the beaten finalist.

Peter Mans died in 1975.

Owen

Brothers Gary and Marcus Owen won the English amateur championship between them on no fewer than five occasions, and appeared in a further two finals.

Both outstanding as amateurs, it was Gary who won the first world amateur snooker championship in 1963; three years later he retained the title. Both eventually turned professional, and Gary reached the world professional championship final in 1969, only to lose to John Spencer.

Gary and Marcus played each other on many occasions, but their most famous meeting was in the second round of the 1974 world professional championships. Marcus (representing Wales at the time) defeated Gary (who by then had emigrated to Australia, and was representing his new country) 15-8.

Father and son, Geoff (left) and Neal Foulds

Roberts

Although John Roberts Junior and Senior were both billiards players, they should not be overlooked here because of their vast contribution to, and domination of, the sport in the 19th century. John Senior, from Liverpool, contested the first world billiards championship (as it was then billed) at St James's Hall in February 1870. He was beaten by William Cook, but John Roberts Junior restored family honour by taking the title from Cook two months later.

The championship was conducted as a challenge competition in those days, and John Junior held the title on and off until 1885. He so excelled at the sport that his reputation was comparable with that of Joe Davis during the latter's heyday in the 1920s and 1930s.

Robinson

The two leading New Zealand players of the 1970s were father and son, Herbie and Russell Robinson.

Herbie was the New Zealand billiards champion four times, and in the 1976 final he had the rare distinction of beating his son – the only instance of father and son meeting in a national championship final.

Smith

Frank Smith Senior is generally credited with taking the game of snooker to Australia when he emigrated in 1887. His son, Frank Junior, later went on to become Australian professional champion.

Fatalities

Snooker and billiards, fortunately, are two of the safest of all games to play, and accidents are a rarity. However, there have been recorded instances of fatalities occurring during billiards or snooker matches.

In 1926 a boy called Spencer died from injuries sustained while playing billiards at the Western Counties Institution at Starcross, Devon. He was accidentally hit in the eye with the cue and died later in the Royal Devon and Exeter Hospital.

Raymond Priestly of Melbourne died while trying to play the 'shot of a lifetime' in January 1979. Suspended upside-down over the table, hanging by his legs from the rafters, he slipped, crashed head first on to the concrete floor, and died.

The only known case of a duel fought with billiard balls took place in France in the mid-19th century when two Frenchmen, Messieurs Lenfant and Mellant, fell out over a game. They agreed to duel by throwing a ball at each other in turn. Lenfant lost when hit in the forehead; he died instantly.

Fidelity Unit Trusts International

The success of advertising and sponsorship is often difficult to evaluate. However, in the case of Irish whiskey distillers Jameson, the measure of their success in snooker sponsorship was easily gauged right from the start: within 12 months of their sponsoring the first Jameson International tournament in 1981, sales of their product in Britain rose by over 50 per cent.

The first major tournament of the season open to all professionals, the Jameson was highly regarded on the professional circuit. The value of its first prize – £30,000 in 1984 – possibly has some bearing on that! It also carried world ranking points and was, in fact, the first tournament after the world championships to receive ranking points status. It was also the first major snooker tournament to be covered at length by Independent Television – this was their response to the BBC's coverage of the world championships.

The first tournament saw the emergence of a new star in the person of Dave Martin, who, on his way to the semi-finals, eliminated such notable colonials as Eddie Charlton and Bill Werbeniuk. In the semi-finals it was a different matter, as Irishman Dennis Taylor gave him a 9-1 drubbing. Taylor's opponent in the final was Steve Davis, who had just edged Alex Higgins out 9-8 in their semi-final. The final saw Taylor receive the medicine he had given to Martin – he was whitewashed 9-0. Titleholder Davis went out in the quarter-finals at the Derby Assembly Rooms in 1982. He lost to David Taylor, the man he had beaten at the corresponding stage in 1981 – sweet revenge for Taylor, who remains the only man ever to have beaten Davis in the competition.

Taylor went all the way to the final – his third final appearance in major competitions. Sadly for him, he could only win his third runner's-up prize. The victor was Tony Knowles, who could now get rid of the label 'the man who beat Steve Davis 10-1', which he had been carrying since that famous upset in that year's world championships. At last he had won a major professional title, and had earned an identity of his own. To rub salt into Taylor's wounds, Knowles also deprived him of the break prize in the final, with a break of 114.

A change of venue to the Eldon Square Recreation Centre, Newcastle, saw Steve Davis regain the title in 1983 with a 9-4 final victory over Cliff Thorburn. He also took advantage of the final, just as Knowles had done the previous year, to win the break prize, with a 120 break. Davis won his third title in four years in 1984 when he beat Tony Knowles 9-2 in the final, but the break prize went to the youngster Neal Foulds, who compiled a championship record 140.

That was the last Jameson-sponsored event; Goya replaced them in 1985 and the event was re-named the Goya Matchroom Trophy. Cliff Thorburn took the £35,000 first prize after a 22-frame battle with Jimmy White at Trentham Gardens, Stoke-on-Trent, winning 12-10 after trailing 7-0 and then 10-8.

Thorburn was expected to retain the title the following year when it was sponsored by BCE and called the BCE International – but Londoner Neal Foulds had different ideas and beat Thorburn 12-9 in the final to win his first major tournament. One great moment from the tournament was John Spencer's 134 break in the pre-televised stage.

The 1987 event is being sponsored by Fidelity Unit Trusts.

Fidelity Unit Trusts International: Results (finals)

1981 S. Davis (England) 9 D. Taylor (Ireland) 0	**1985** C. Thorburn (Canada) 12 J. White (England) 10
1982 T. Knowles (England) 9 D. Taylor (England) 6	**1986** N. Foulds (England) 12 C. Thorburn (Canada) 9
1983 S. Davis (England) 9 C. Thorburn (Canada) 4	**Most wins:** 3 – Steve Davis
1984 S. Davis (England) 9 T. Knowles (England) 2	**Most finals:** 3 – Steve Davis 3 – Cliff Thorburn

Highest break: 140 – Neal Foulds (1984)

Fisher, Allison

Despite being still a teenager, Allison Fisher has dominated women's snooker since 1985. She is the best female snooker player ever seen and, with the new professional ticket series that allow membership to the WPBSA, she stands every chance of becoming the first female professional snooker player to play alongside her male counterparts. She is certainly good enough.

She hails from Sussex, and first played on a full-size table when she was 12. A year later she was the only female player in the Lewes League. Allison left school with five O-levels but firmly set her heart on playing snooker.

Unbeatable by other women, she won the 1985 Women's World Amateur Championship and then, when the sport went open, she won the world title again in 1986, beating Sue LeMaich 5-0 in the final. She showed her dominance by only dropping one frame in the entire competition. When she beat Mandy Fisher (no relation) 5-1 to win the UK Women's Championship at Leicester later in the season, the single frame won by her namesake was, again, the only one she dropped.

She completed a notable season by winning the B&SCC Women's Championship, and her 103 break in the final was the first century break in a women's tournament.

Her domination of the women's game is greater than Steve Davis's of the men's. Given the chance, Allison would dearly love to compete against male professionals regularly. The way the system works at present, that day could be approaching.

Career highlights
- Women's World Champion 1986
- Women's World Amateur Champion 1985
- National Amateur Champion 1985
- United Kingdom Women's Champion 1987
- B&SCC Women's Champion 1987

Fisher, Mandy

Cambridgeshire-born Mandy Fisher has been one of the leading female players of the 1980s. A very stylish player, Mandy has also been involved in the administration of the game, as she was once the secretary of the Women's Professional Billiards and Snooker Association.

She first came to prominence in 1980 when she won the Pontins title, and the following year she reached the final of the women's world open at Thorness Bay on the Isle of Wight. She lost to seasoned campaigner Vera Selby that day, but in beating Ann Johnson and Fran Lovis on the way to the final she served notice of her potential.

In 1983 she became the first woman to reach the last 128 of the English amateur championship before being eliminated 4-1 by David Pugh of Birmingham. But the 1983-84 season was to bring greater glories for Mandy Fisher. Winner of the newly instituted National Express Grand Prix, she won a total of £14,000 in prize money during the season – a sum bettered by only 16 of her male counterparts.

As well as being the overall winner of the grand prix, she won two of the five rounds and reached the final of two others. In her match with Grace Nakamura in the Basingstoke round, she recorded a break of 62 – the highest ever break by a woman in tournament play. It has since been beaten by Allison Fisher, and Stacey Hillyard, the latter becoming the first woman to make a century break. In the past couple of years Mandy has had to step aside and watch her namesake Allison dominate women's snooker.

Career highlights
- World Open Championship (runner-up) 1981
- United Kingdom Women's Championship (runner-up) 1987
- National Express Grand Prix (Overall champion) 1984
- Pontins Women's Champion 1980

Foul

There are many ways in which a foul shot may be deemed to have been played. The following is a list of the principal ways in which penalty points can be incurred. In all instances the penalty awarded is the value of the ball 'on', or four points, whichever is greater.

☆ Failing to hit the object-ball with the cue-ball: Penalty value – four points or the value of the colour, whichever is greater.

☆ Striking an incorrect object-ball with the cue-ball: If the object-ball is a red and the cue-ball hits one of the colours, then the penalty value is four points or the value of the colour hit.

If the object-ball is a colour and the cue-ball strikes a red or a wrong colour, then the penalty value is four points or the value of the object-ball, or the value of the colour hit, whichever is greatest.

☆ Potting the white ball: The penalty value depends on the colour of the object ball – it is four points, or the value of the colour if the latter is greater.

☆ If a player causes the cue-ball to jump over another ball without first striking the object-ball, then this is deemed a foul and carries a minimum four-point penalty.

☆ If, in the referee's opinion, the striker has failed to use the best of his ability to make contact with the object-ball, then the appropriate penalty will be awarded. The non-striking player can then, if he wishes, have the cue-ball returned to its original position, and make the offending player take the shot again.

☆ A penalty of four points is incurred if the cue-ball is played while any of the balls is still moving from the previous shot.
☆ If the cue-ball is hit more than once in any one action this is a foul. Minimum penalty – four points.
☆ If a striker plays a shot with both feet off the ground this is also a foul. Minimum penalty – four points.
☆ Any player taking his shot out of turn is penalized a minimum of four points.
☆ If, in taking a free ball, the striker causes his opponent to be snookered on the free ball, then the striker is penalized four points. This does not apply if only the pink and black balls are left on the table.
☆ A push shot is deemed to have been made when the tip of the cue is still in contact with the cue-ball when this makes contact with the object-ball, or it is still in contact with the cue-ball once this has commenced its journey. Such an offence is penalized by the value of the object-ball that is 'on' at the time – subject to the minimum of four points.
☆ Should the striker take a shot and one of the coloured balls is incorrectly spotted, then the shot is deemed to be a foul. The penalty value of the foul is four points or the value of the object-ball (not the incorrectly spotted colour) at the time.
☆ In the event of a player touching any ball with anything other than the tip of his cue he shall be penalized. The penalty value is four points or the value of the object-ball, or the value of the ball touched, whichever is greatest.
☆ Any ball that is forced off the table, no matter in what circumstances, renders the apppropriate shot a foul. The penalty is the value of the ball that leaves the table, subject to a minimum of four points.
☆ If, after potting a red ball, a player should commit a foul before nominating his colour, he shall be assumed to have been taking the black, and will have a seven-point penalty awarded against him.

In all instances of penalty points being awarded, they are added to the non-offending player's score. He may, after his opponent has played a foul shot, ask him to play again.

If more than one foul has been committed during one shot then the one carrying the highest penalty value will be awarded against the offending player.

All foul shots carry a minimum penalty of four points.

See also Cue-Ball
Free ball
Object-ball
Push Shot

Foulds, Geoff

What better way to spend your 44th birthday than playing Steve Davis in the first round of a major professional snooker championship! That is exactly what happened to Geoff Foulds in the first round of the 1983 Coral United Kingdom Championship at Preston. And Davis – a former team-mate of Geoff's in the England amateur team of 1977-78 – showed no birthday goodwill as he beat Foulds 9-1.

On the adjacent table, Geoff's son Neal was playing David Taylor. This was the first time father and son had reached the final stage of the same major professional tournament. Sadly, Neal suffered the same early exit as his father – Taylor beat him 9-4.

They are currently, without doubt, the finest father-and-son combination around, and have been for some time. A long-standing challenge to any other father-and-son combination has not yet been taken up.

Geoff, an England international on ten occasions, is a much respected coach, operating from his Ealing Snooker Club base; his expertise has been much sought after by many youngsters – most of all by his own son. To a certain extent Geoff's own game suffered because of the time he devoted to Neal, but this will seem a reasonable investment if Neal's great potential fully materializes.

Because of his experience, Geoff Foulds was employed as the technical adviser to the BBC Television series *Give us a Break* in 1983, and he played most of the shots seen on the screen.

Career highlights
Pontins Open (runner-up) 1980

Foulds, Neal

Neal Foulds was tipped as the man to succeed Steve Davis as snooker's number one figure. That was quite a forecast to make about a then new 20-year-old professional, but Foulds seems to be carrying that burden well as, in just four years as a professional, he has risen to number three in the world.

Modest, level-headed and sensible, his image and attitude are both right for the game. A lot of credit for that, and for his success on the table, goes to his father Geoff and coach Ron Gross. Geoff Foulds, also a professional player, made a lot of personal sacrifices in order to further Neal's game. Those sacrifices have paid dividends as Neal is now regarded as one of the world's best players.

Born in Perivale, Middlesex, Neal started playing snooker at the age of 11. At that time he wore spectacles, but now wears contact lenses. He left school with two O-levels, but all he wanted to do was play snooker. In 1982, when 18, he won the national under-19 snooker title, beating his great adversary John Parrott in the final. He won international honours with England later that year and in 1983 was accepted as a professional by the WPBSA. At the end of his first professional season he had moved into 30th position in the rankings, thanks largely to a second round appearance in the world championships at the Crucible. Here he lost to Doug Mountjoy, but that was after a memorable 10-9 win over Alex Higgins in the first round, in which the youngster showed great calmness and composure in front of the television cameras.

His second full season started off in style. He won £3,750 for the highest break (140) in the Jameson International, and he then picked up valuable ranking points after reaching the semi-final of the Rothmans Grand Prix. Following fine wins over Willie Thorne and Tony Knowles, his hopes were eventually dampened when Dennis Taylor beat him in the semi-final.

Steve Davis beat Foulds in the first round of the 1985 Embassy, but he had gained enough experience to show that he was going to be a force to be reckoned with. In 1985-86 he was regularly among the ranking points, but his previous successes were totally eclipsed by a magnificent season in 1986-87, when he jumped to third in the rankings.

He won his first major tournament, the BCE International, and then lost to Steve Davis in the final of the Tennents United Kingdom Open. He was also runner-up, to Jimmy White, in the Dulux British Open. Foulds started the 1987 world championship as one of the favourites, and when he was matched with defending champion Joe Johnson in the semi-final he was still favourite to reach his first final, but Johnson was in form and won 16-9.

Now a member of the Barry Hearn stable, Foulds looks likely to win the world title one day; he certainly has youth on his side. He may even prove to be Steve Davis's successor – as predicted by no less an authority than Davis himself.

Career highlights
- BCE International Champion 1986
- National Under-19 Snooker Champion 1982
- Pontins Professional Champion 1987
- Pontins Open Champion 1984
- Pontins Junior Champion 1980

Frame

A frame is completed once all the balls are finally potted, or there is a foul shot on the final black ball (assuming the black needs to be potted to decide the frame). It can also be terminated upon one player conceding the frame to his opponent.

The number of frames that make up a game vary greatly. A game can consist of a single frame – as is the case in most leagues up and down the British Isles – or it can be the best-of-35 frames, which is the case in the world professional championship final.

The final of the 1947 world professional championship was the best-of-167 frames; 'only' 145 were completed, however, as Fred Davis beat Walter Donaldson 84-61.

See also Game

Francisco, Mannie

The elder brother of Silvino, Mannie Francisco is also a professional snooker player although he rarely competes outside his native country. South African amateur snooker champion on six occasions, and billiards champion on 13 occasions, he turned professional in 1978 because of the strain on the amateur sportsman in South Africa.

Although he is a professional, Francisco is not a member of the WPBSA, and consequently is not eligible to take part in tournaments organized by them. It is in his home country, however, that he has enjoyed his considerable successes.

He won his first South African snooker title in 1959, and the following year he won the first of his 13 billiards titles. As a result of his success at billiards, he represented South Africa at the world amateur championships on five occasions between 1960 and 1971. His best placing was second to Norman Dagley in the final play-off group in the last of those years.

Francisco also took part in the world amateur snooker championships on two occasions. The first, in 1972, saw him reach the final, where he lost 8-7 to Ray Edmonds after leading 6-0 and then 7-2.

His other appearance in the championships saw him lose to his brother Silvino in the quarter-finals in 1976; this was the first time he had lost to Silvino in tournament play.

Although he has failed to gain a great deal of recognition worldwide, the name of Mannie Francisco will be immortalized in the record books. It was Mannie whom Rex Williams was playing, at Johannesburg in 1966, when Williams became the second man to register an official 147 break. Mannie's participation in competitive play has been considerably curtailed as a result of his choosing to stay in South Africa, but he now has the added interest of watching the development of his son Peter, who has recently been accepted as a member of the WPBSA. Mannie Francisco himself has now almost abandoned billiards and snooker for bowls.

Career highlights
- World Amateur Snooker Championship (runner-up) 1972
- World Amateur Billiards Championship (runner-up) 1971
- South African Amateur Snooker Champion 1959, 1964, 1965, 1966, 1971, 1975
- South African Amateur Billiards Champion 1959, 1961-66, 1968-71, 1974, 1977

Francisco, Peter

When Peter Francisco was accepted in 1984 as a member of the WPBSA he became the third member of the famous South African family to join the professional ranks. Peter's father Mannie, one time runner-up in the world amateur championship, was a professional before him and Peter joined Mannie's brother, Silvino, on the professional circuit.

His first season was a series of disappointments and he finished a lowly 59th in the rankings. But a season later he had jumped 33 places thanks to reaching the last 16 of three ranking tournaments. His best result was a 5-4 win over Jimmy White in the Dulux British Open.

Peter started the 1986-87 season by collecting four ranking points from the first tournament of the season, the BCE International at Trentham Gardens. After beating Mark Wildman and Alex Higgins he reached his first ranking tournament quarter-final by beating Canadian Marcel Gauvreau in the 5th round. In the quarter-final he met uncle Silvino and the youngster gained a splendid 5-3 win and set up a semi-final match with Cliff Thorburn. He allowed the Canadian to build up a 4-0 lead but pulled back to 7-7 before Thorburn won the last two frames for a 9-7 win.

Those four points helped Peter move up the rankings to 18th, just ten places below Silvino. If he continues improving at the same rate as he did in his first three seasons as a professional, their positions could well be reversed in the near future.

Career highlights
- BCE International (semi-final) 1986
- South African Amateur Snooker Champion 1981-83
- South African Amateur Billiards Champion 1983

Francisco, Silvino

A professional since 1978, former oil company executive Silvino Francisco came to Britain for the first time in 1982. His goal was the world professional championship. Despite two impressive qualifying round wins of 9-0 and 9-1 over Chris Ross and Paddy Morgan respectively, Francisco was 250-1 to win the title. These were fair odds of course, bearing in mind that he was little known outside South Africa. But victories in the competition proper over Dennis Taylor and Dean Reynolds set those odds tumbling as he prepared to meet Ray Reardon in the quarter-final. The 'fairy-story' ended there, for Reardon put Francisco out of the competition; but since that day, the name of Silvino Francisco has been well known by the British public, and he has been a regular member of the professional scene in Britain.

Born in Cape Town of Portuguese descent, 39-year-old Silvino is the younger brother of fellow professional Mannie Francisco. The pair of them were outstanding amateur players. In terms of success, Mannie had the better record of the two in their amateur days, although Silvino did win four South African snooker titles and three billiards titles. One of Silvino's greatest moments from his amateur days came in the 1976 world amateur championships. He reached the semi-final,

Silvino Francisco – now South Africa's number one player

where he lost to eventual winner Doug Mountjoy. But in the quarter-final he beat his brother Mannie – the first time he had beaten him in competitive play.

Silvino has made steady progress since his United Kingdom debut in 1982, and he started the 1984-85 season just outside the exclusive top 16 in the world rankings, in 17th place. His rise in the rankings was aided by his reaching the quarter-final of the 1983 Jameson International (at which stage he lost 5-1 to Steve Davis.)

Having reached the semi-final of the Jameson in 1984, losing to Tony Knowles, Silvino Francisco enjoyed the best moment of his professional career in 1985 when he lifted his first major title, the Dulux British Open. A great semi-final win over Alex Higgins and victory over Kirk Stevens in the final saw him pocket the game's then biggest first prize of £50,000.

Silvino Francisco had a troubled time following his Dulux win when, following comments about his opponent in a national newspaper, he was fined £6,000 and had two ranking points deducted. Six months later, however, the money and points were returned after a successful appeal.

Since then, he has struggled to find his form on the table and, although he won the South African professional title, the nearest he has come to success in Britain was in the 1986 Rothmans Grand Prix, when he reached the semi-final.

Career highlights

- Dulux British Open Champion 1985
- South African Amateur Snooker Champion 1968, 1969, 1974, 1977
- South African Amateur Billiards Champion 1972, 1973, 1975

Free Ball

The free ball rule in snooker, introduced in 1919, is one that confuses many people, but is quite simple. If, after a foul has been committed, (a) the cue-ball is snookered, or (b) the object-ball can be seen and hit by a direct shot, but cannot be directly hit on both its outside edges, the referee shall declare a free ball. The non-offending player has the option of making his opponent play again or, if he wishes, he may take the shot himself. If the latter, he may take any ball on the table. The ball he takes will be treated as if it was the ball 'on' and receives points to the value accordingly. If, for example, he takes a blue when he would normally be required to play a red, then the blue – if potted – would count as one point and the break would continue with a shot at a colour.

Game

A game of snooker consists of a pre-determined number of frames. In order to achieve a positive result it is normal to make each game consist of an odd number of frames, so that a tie is not possible.

In some tournaments, however, games are played over two frames, and the aggregate scores at the end of the two frames decide the winner. This system is less common in top-level snooker, as it is difficult to separate two good players. Who wins in the end is a matter of luck.

In most major championships the number of frames per game increases as the tournament progresses. For example, in the 1985 world championships the qualifying games were played over the best of 19 frames. The first-round games were the same, but second-round and quarter-final games were the best of 25 frames. The semi-finals were the best of 31 frames, and the final itself was the best of 35.

Ganley, Len

Born in Lurgan, near Belfast, referee Len Ganley moved to Burton-on-Trent in 1971. He only visited Britain to spend a ten-day holiday with his sister – and stayed.

A fully qualified referee in Ireland, he discovered that his qualifications were not recognized in England. But it was not long before he became recognized by the Billiards and Snooker Control Council; he obtained his Grade 'A' certificate in 1979, and is now a full-time referee – finding it more to his liking than the milk-roundsman and bus-driving jobs he had when he first arrived in Burton.

A leading player in the Lurgan/Lisburn and Belfast League, Ganley continued playing when he moved to England, and won the Burton and South Derbyshire snooker title twice. His highest break was 136.

As a referee he has enjoyed many cherished moments, not least the 1983 world professional championship final between Steve Davis and Cliff Thorburn. But the game that gave him the most pleasure was the 1983 Coral United Kingdom Championship final between Alex Higgins and Steve Davis, when Higgins came back – apparently from the dead – to snatch a dramatic victory.

Ganley's talents as an actor have also been fully exposed: he was the referee seen crushing the snooker ball in a Carling Black Label lager advertisement on television, which also featured those two other stars of the silver screen, John Spencer and Terry Griffiths.

Gardner, Joyce

Hailed as the first lady of snooker, Joyce Gardner was the driving force behind the women's game in the 1940s and 1950s. Seven times national professional womens billiards champion, and four times beaten snooker finalist, Joyce made her name as a great exhibition player after the war.

She used to compete against, and frequently beat, her male counterparts in matches to raise money for charity. In all, she raised in excess of £250,000 for various charities; on one occasion in the 1940s, in her role as compère of an event, she auctioned a bottle of whisky, and it fetched the staggering sum of £1,100!

Joyce was born in Gloucester, but moved to London at an early age. Her billiards and snooker talent was soon spotted

Neal Foulds

Len Ganley

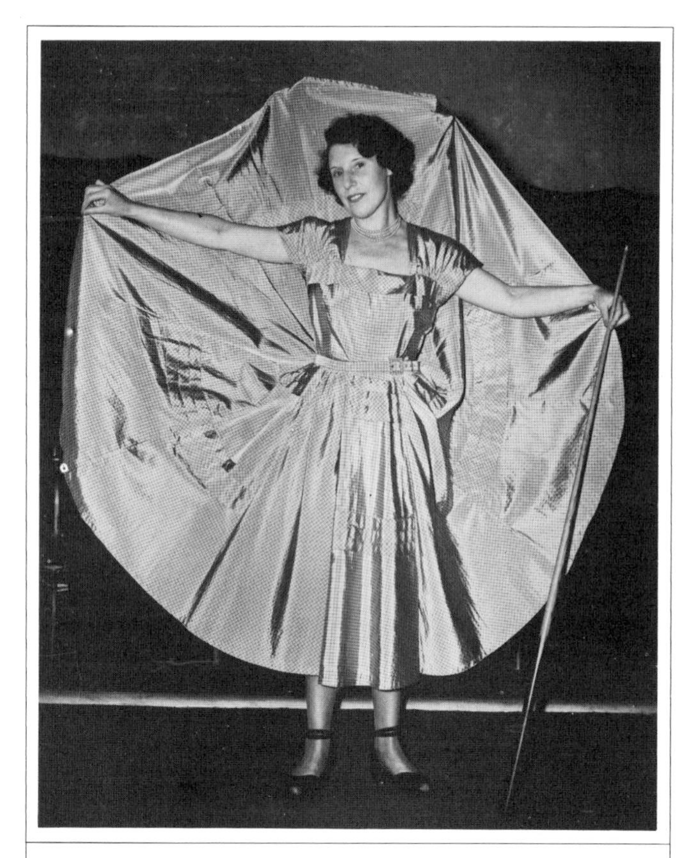

Joyce Gardner: the dress was 12 yards around the hem

and, at the age of 20, she turned professional, aided by a contract from Burroughes and Watts.

She won her first national professional billiards title in 1931. She lost the title to Ruth Harrison in 1934 but regained it in 1935, and held it until 1939. Her best snooker break was 82, and best billiards break, 318.

In 1946 Joyce became the first woman to compère the world professional snooker championship. She was also the first woman to commentate on snooker for BBC radio, and was the first billiards or snooker player – male or female – to have her portrait hung in the Royal Academy.

As the sport – and women's billiards and snooker in particular – declined in the sixties, Joyce Gardner maintained her professional status and, at the time of her death in August 1981, she was the only female member of the World Professional Billiards and Snooker Association.

Career highlights

National Professional Billiards Champion 1931-33, 1935-38

Gold Cup

The Daily Mail Gold Cup was regarded by many as more prestigious than the world title itself. The *Daily Mail*, previously sponsors of two billiards gold cup tournaments, transferred their allegiance to snooker in the 1936-37 season and sponsored the 15-week long event.

The event took the leading players of the day around the country, playing each other in a round-robin competition. They were handicapped, with Joe Davis playing off scratch each time and having to concede as many as 45 points per frame. In addition there was a sealed handicap for each match, which was not revealed until the conclusion of the tournament. There were no cash prizes, but the winner received the prestigious gold cup, and there were other prizes consisting of silver tea services, wireless sets and similar goods.

Daily Mail Gold Cup – Results

1937	Ist J. Davis	2nd H. Lindrum
1938	1st J. Davis	2nd W. Smith
1939	1st Alec Brown	2nd S. Smith
1940	1st Alec Brown	2nd S. Lee

Goya Matchroom Trophy

See Fidelity Unit Trusts International

Griffiths, Terry

The snooker career of Terry Griffiths was relatively late in developing. He was 25 when he appeared in his first Welsh amateur championship final in 1972, where he lost to Geoff Thomas. But, between then and 1978, when he turned professional, he enjoyed an outstanding amateur career.

He went on to gain revenge over Thomas by defeating him in the 1975 final to win his first Welsh title, and in 1977 and 1978 he was a double English amateur champion. His victories over Sid Hood and Joe Johnson respectively were easy wins, and Griffiths was starting to attract a lot of attention.

His international career saw him lose just two matches in 14 Home International matches for Wales – Willie Thorne of England and Scotland's Eddie Sinclair being his only conquerors. As Welsh champion, Griffiths took part in the 1976 world championship in Johannesburg, which was won by his compatriot Doug Mountjoy. Griffiths fell at the quarter-final stage to Jimmy van Rensburg of South Africa, just as an all-Welsh final was becoming a distinct possibility.

Griffiths was looking forward to the world championships again in 1978, but current professional Steve Newbury put paid to those ambitions by beating him in the quarter-final of that year's Welsh championships. At the time he could not have known what a favour Newbury was doing him – but Griffiths immediately turned professional as a result of not being able to go to the world championships – and within a year he had won the world professional championship.

In fact his first professional tournament was the 1978 Coral United Kingdom Professional Championship, and he was poised to spring a surprise when he led former world champion Rex Williams 8-2 in their qualifying round match; but Williams came back, in an amazing recovery, to win 9-8.

Griffiths did, however, spring many surprises in the world championships at the Crucible. He beat Bernard Bennett and current television commentator Jim Meadowcroft in the qualifying tournament. And then he enjoyed victories over three former finalists – Perrie Mans, Alex Higgins and Eddie Charlton; the last of these was a classic encounter that went on into the early hours of the morning.

In the final Griffiths beat Irishman Dennis Taylor, who was also searching for his first title, to become the fourth man after Joe Davis (in the first year of the championships), John Spencer and Alex Higgins to win the title at his first attempt. He also became the fourth man after John Pulman, John Spencer and

Ray Reardon to win the English amateur title and then the world professional title. After this world championship success, his son, who was a keen Ray Reardon fan, asked his father: 'Does this mean you're as good as Ray Reardon now?'

Before 1979 was out Griffiths had become the Coral UK finalist, and was a member of the Welsh team that won the world team cup.

Griffiths started 1980 with victory in the Benson and Hedges Masters, and followed this up with the first of three consecutive Benson and Hedges Irish Masters titles. A second world team title came as Wales beat Canada in that year's final. Griffiths was also the subject of Eamonn Andrews' famous words 'This Is Your Life' in 1980.

Apart from his Irish Masters and Pontins professional titles, 1981 was one of near misses and runner-up positions in the Coral UK championship, Benson and Hedges Masters and World Team Classic.

His best year followed in 1982, when he gained impressive victories in the Coral, Lada Classic and Irish Masters. But between then and the end of 1984 a string of runner-up positions in the Welsh professional championships, Hofmeister World Doubles, Benson and Hedges Masters (twice), Yamaha International, Tolly Cobbold Classic and Benson and Hedges Irish Masters followed. A *Pot Black* win in 1984 and a Pontins Open success the previous year were his only successes during that period.

Surprisingly, since his world championship win Griffiths has performed poorly at the Crucible, not progressing past the quarter-finals. Steve Davis beat him 13-10 in the second round in 1980, and again 13-9 the following year in the quarter-final.

Apart from retaining his Welsh Professional and Pontins Professional titles in 1986, Griffiths failed to reach the semi-final stage of any of the ranking tournaments in 1986-7 but is so methodical a player that, despite lean times on paper, he can never be treated lightly.

If he had not decided to follow careers as a blacksmith, postman, bus conductor and insurance salesman, Terry Griffiths could possibly have been a successful rugby player. At school he played in the same team as famous Welsh internationals Phil Bennett and Derek Quinnell.

Career highlights

- World Professional Snooker Champion 1979
- Coral United Kingdom Professional Champion 1982
- Benson & Hedges Masters Champion 1980
- Lada Classic Champion 1982
- Benson & Hedges Irish Masters Champion 1980-82
- World Cup 1979-80
- Pontins Professional Champion 1981
- Pontins Open Champion 1983
- BCE Belgian Classic Champion 1986
- Pot Black Champion 1984
- Welsh Professional Champion 1985-86
- English Amateur Champion 1977-78
- Welsh Amateur Champion 1975

Terry Griffiths

The Guildhall, Preston: Steve Davis in action during the Coral UK Professional Championship

Guildhall, Preston

Owned by the Preston Borough Council, the Guildhall was opened in November 1972. The building houses two theatres: the Charter Theatre which has seating for 800, and the Grand Hall, with a seating capacity of 2142.

Sporting events are held in the Grand Hall, and snooker is just one of the many sports held there. In addition there is boxing, wrestling, tennis, table tennis, badminton, and indoor bowls which, like snooker, has received television coverage. The first snooker tournament to be held at the Guildhall was the Coral United Kingdom Professional Championship in 1978. It is still the home of the tournament today, although under different sponsors.

It was in that event, in 1980, that Steve Davis won his first major professional title. And in the 1982 and 1983 tournaments the sport saw two of its best-ever finals. In 1982 Terry Griffiths came from 15-13 down against Alex Higgins to win 16-15. The following year the final again went to its maximum 31 frames; this time it produced a change of fortune for Higgins as he came from behind to beat Steve Davis. But what a recovery he had to stage – Higgins trailed 7-0 at the end of the first session, but fought back to win the match 16-15.

One of the larger snooker venues, the Guildhall attracts good crowds which create a superb atmosphere, and this makes it a popular venue with players and spectators alike.

Guinness World Cup

See Tuborg World Cup

H

Hallett, Mike

After gaining his first international honours in 1978, Mike Hallett, in August 1979, put in his application for professional status. He was duly accepted, and nobody was more surprised, or delighted, than Hallett himself.

As an amateur he was a model player, but the big titles always eluded him, with the exception of the national under-16 title which he won in 1975. He was a stylish player, despite the lack of major honours, and the England selectors recognized this when they picked him for the Home International series in 1978.

Further glory was to fall on Hallett when he put defending champion Dennis Taylor out of the 1986 world championship at the first hurdle. But all that was eclipsed by his marvellous run in the 1986 World Doubles championship at Northampton when he and Scottish prodigy Stephen Hendry went all the way to the final before losing to three-times winners Steve Davis and Tony Meo.

The 1986-87 season ended with the Humbersider reaching the top 16, thanks largely to a magnificent world championship in which he reached the quarter-final before losing to Neal Foulds.

Career highlights

- World Professional Snooker Championship (quarter-final) 1987
- English Professional Championship (semi-final) 1986
- Hofmeister World Doubles (runner-up) 1986 (with Stephen Hendry)
- National Under-16 Snooker Champion 1975

Mike Hallett, a professional for nearly ten years

Handicapping

The purpose of handicapping, whether in a club tournament or a pro-am event, is to make all matches evenly balanced, so that they will last their allotted number of frames.

When assessing handicaps at club level the best player is normally placed on scratch (zero), or sometimes given a minus handicap. The other players receive a start commensurate with their skills. It is possible for a good professional, or even a top-class amateur, to concede 100 points per frame and still win... the author was on the receiving end of such a defeat once, administered by current professional Les Dodd.

In pro-am events the professionals concede points to their amateur rivals. The amount of the handicap is fixed for each event, but varies from one to the next. It can be as low as four points per frame, or as high as 30, but it normally depends on how many frames make up a game. The Pontins Spring Open imposes a 25-point-per-frame handicap on the invited professionals, and a 21-point handicap on the uninvited professionals.

One of the best cases of mis-handicapping must surely have been at the City Tattersalls Club, Sydney, in 1979, when Australian amateur Leon Heywood challenged British professional Graham Miles. Miles conceded 21 points and Heywood went on to compile a 147 break, so that the eventual score read Heywood 168, Miles 0.

Another classic case of mis-handicapping was in the one and only Sunday Empire News handicap tournament in 1948. The handicaps for each game were put in a sealed envelope and only opened at the end of the game. In the final Fred Davis beat his brother Joe by one frame – the first time he had beaten him without a handicap. To everyone's amazement, when the envelope was opened *Joe* received two frames, and thus *won* by one frame!

Hearn, Barry

Barry Hearn had very little involvement with snooker until November 1974 when, as Financial Director of Kendall House Investments, his company purchased the 17 Lucania Snooker Halls. Hearn was appointed chairman of Lucania and in March 1976 he set eyes on Steve Davis. Davis walked into one of the Lucania halls to play snooker, Hearn spotted him – and the rest is legend.

His first venture into snooker management saw him take Steve Davis, Geoff Foulds and Vic Harris under his wing. He used to send them – all exceptional amateurs – around the various Lucania halls helping younger players. Foulds and Harris are no longer with Hearn, but Steve Davis was joined as one of the 'Matchroom' professionals by Tony Meo in 1981, Terry Griffiths in 1982 and more recently by Dennis Taylor, Neal Foulds, Willie Thorne and Jimmy White.

A very shrewd businessman, Hearn has arranged lucrative endorsement deals for his players, and at the same time has made his own future financially secure. He sold 16 of the 17 Lucania Halls to Riley Leisure for £3·1 million in 1982. He retained the Romford club which he has since turned into the Romford Snooker Centre, and the old matchroom has been turned into a luxury night club called – The Matchroom.

Now a director of Rileys, Hearn is aiding the growth of the sport abroad, particularly in the Far East, by organizing tournaments involving his star players.

Born in Dagenham, Essex, Hearn is a director of the World Professional Billiards and Snooker Association. He did not play snooker as a youngster, but these days you cannot keep him off the table. His personal best break is 57 – one of just two occasions he has broken 50 in competition play. But that, he said, '...warranted a lap of honour.'

Hendry, Stephen
Since winning his first Scottish amateur title in 1984 at the age of 15, Stephen Hendry, from Dalgety Bay, has broken a string of records. He was the youngest winner of the Scottish amateur title, and then became the youngest qualifier for the world amateur championship and then the youngest winner of the Scottish professional title, which made him the youngest ever winner of a national professional title. In 1986, while only 17, he became the youngest competitor in the world professional championship and towards the end of the year, and still under 18, he became the youngest finalist in a professional tournament when, with partner Mike Hallett, he reached the final of the world doubles before losing to seasoned campaigners Steve Davis and Tony Meo.

Hendry has the perfect stance and his natural ability can be compared with Steve Davis's and Jimmy White's when they were his age. His records are certainly as impressive as those of Davis and White when they were 17, and few will argue that he will emulate them and go on to greater glories – Willie Thorne and Steve Longworth, who both lost to Hendry at the Crucible in 1987, will testify to that; another is Joe Johnson, the defending champion, who only just beat the young Scot in the quarter-final of the 1987 world championship.

The son of a West Lothian fruiterer, Hendry is a very marketable commodity himself; the setting up of Stephen Hendry Snooker Limited showed tremendous foresight, as he has the potential to be the biggest ever earner in the sport's history.

Career highlights
- Winfield Australian Masters 1987
- World Professional Snooker Championships (quarter-final) 1987
- Hofmeister World Doubles (runner-up) 1986 (with Mike Hallett)
- Mercantile Credit Classic (semi-final) 1987
- Scottish Professional Champion 1986-87
- Scottish Amateur Champion 1984-85

Higgins, Alex
Just as the thousands used to flock through the turnstiles at Old Trafford to watch the skills of Belfast-born George Best, so they now flock through the turnstiles at the Crucible Theatre, the Spectrum Arena, Hexagon Theatre and the rest to watch the skills of another of Belfast's famous sons – Alex Higgins.

Best's and Higgins's lives have followed similar patterns, which have attracted more attention than their sporting skills at times. But Alex Higgins is the biggest box-office attraction in the world of snooker, and few will argue with the title of 'People's Champion', as he proclaimed himself after winning his second world crown in 1982. Such was his popularity in 1982 that he was voted runner-up to Daley Thompson in the BBC's annual 'Sports Personality of the Year' competition.

If he had had his own way, and sufficient dedication, Alex Higgins would have been a professional jockey instead of a

Barry Hearn's 'Magnificent Seven'. From left to right: Willie Thorne, Jimmy White, Dennis Taylor, Neal Foulds, Terry Griffiths, Tony Meo and the 'founder member', Steve Davis

snooker player. He had been playing snooker since the age of 11 at the Jampot Club, not far from his council house home in Abingdon Street, Belfast, where he lived with his three sisters; but he left home at the age of 14 to join the Eddie Reavey racing stable. At that time he weighed just 7½ stone, but in the two and a half years he was with Reavey his weight shot up to 11 stone and he left without enjoying a ride in public.

He moved to London and worked in a paper-mill for a while, and it was then that he took up snooker again, in the Soho billiard halls. He returned to Ireland and started playing in the Belfast and District Snooker League. He played for the City YMCA Club captained by George Connell, and it was on the table at Connell's home, in 1965, that Higgins compiled his first century break. In 1968 he won both the Northern Ireland and All-Ireland amateur titles.

He returned to England as a professional in 1971 to live in the tough snooker-schooling area around Manchester, and the following year, at just 23 years of age, became the youngest-ever world professional champion.

In his first world championship he came through the qualifying competition to beat favourite and former champion John Spencer in the final at the Selly Oak British Legion in Birmingham – a far cry from the scene of his second world championship win ten years later.

His style of play was fast and exciting, and he was a breath of fresh air to the sport. His unique style certainly did much to increase its popularity. The controversies of Alex Higgins seem to be well remembered and documented, but it cannot be denied that he has enjoyed great success on the snooker table. In addition to losing world championship appearances, to Ray Reardon in 1976 and to Cliff Thorburn in a classic final in 1980, Higgins appeared in every Benson and Hedges Masters final between 1978 and 1981, winning in the first and last of those years. And victories in the Tolly Cobbold Classic (twice), the British Gold Cup, Pontins Open and Canadian Open (twice) have all helped to make him one of the biggest money-winners on the professional circuit.

Another tournament which Higgins seems to have dominated is the United Kingdom professional championships. He has appeared in four finals since 1980, winning just one – but that one produced one of the best wins of his career. Up against Steve Davis in the 1983 final, Higgins had been having a bad year. His form had dropped dramatically, highlighted by defeats by Dave Martin in the Jameson International and Mike Watterson in the Professional Players Tournament, and he had suffered domestic problems. By the time the UK championships came around a reconciliation with his wife Lynn was on the cards and she attended the final. But it all seemed to be going wrong for the Ulsterman as Davis romped into a 7-0 first session lead. Higgins came back, though, to record a memorable 16-15 win.

It had been 18 months since he had won the world crown at Sheffield, amidst scenes of great emotion as he insisted that his wife Lynn and daughter Lauren enter the arena to share his moment of triumph. Between then and the UK championship success he had endured a great deal of personal stress. But this latest victory had the sweet smell of success about it in more ways than one.

His best result since that win was in the 1984 World Doubles championship when, teamed up with Jimmy White, he beat Cliff Thorburn and Willie Thorne to lift the title, thus deposing Steve Davis and Tony Meo who had held the title for the previous two years.

The hottest property in snooker, Scotland's talented youngster, Stephen Hendry

Despite being a member of the winning Ireland team in the World Team Cup in 1985, 1986 and 1987, Higgins has not won a major individual title since the 1983 Coral United Kingdom Championship. He reached the final of the 1984 Coral UK Open, but lost to Steve Davis. He reached two finals in 1986-87, but neither competition attracted more than 16 entrants. He lost to Cliff Thorburn in the final of the Scottish Masters and then to fellow Irishman Dennis Taylor in the Benson and Hedges Masters at Wembley. But he collected a cheque for £28,000 which helped swell his earnings for the season to nearly £100,000.

However, the season was marred by an incident involving a WPBSA official during the Tennents United Kingdom Open at Preston. Higgins was fined by local magistrates, and further fined a total of £12,000 and banned for five tournaments by the WPBSA.

In view of the severity of the punishment, he was determined to go out on a winning note in the 1987 world championship, before his enforced ban, but Terry Griffiths beat him in the last 16.

Alex Higgins has had several skirmishes with the authorities during his illustrious career, but on his day he is one of the finest players in the world. Fortunately for other players, his performance is erratic. Irrespective of how he plays, Higgins is still the biggest box office draw in the game and, wherever he appears, fans pour in by their hundreds to see the 'People's Champion'.

Alex Higgins – even the cleaning of his cue is done with such determination!

Career highlights
- World Professional Snooker Champion 1972, 1982
- Benson & Hedges Masters Champion 1978, 1981
- Coral United Kingdom Professional Champion 1983
- Tolly Cobbold Classic winner 1979-80
- British Gold Cup winner 1980
- Hofmeister World Doubles Champion 1984 (with Jimmy White)
- World Cup 1985-87
- Irish Professional Champion 1983
- Pontins Professional Champion 1980
- Pontins Open Champion 1977
- All-Ireland Amateur Champion 1968
- Northern Ireland Amateur Champion 1968

Hillyard, Stacey

Only 13 years of age at the time, Stacey Hillyard caused a sensation at the 1983 women's world open at Brean Sands when she eliminated number five seed, and 1981 runner-up, Mandy Fisher in the final 32 of the competition. She was defeated in the next round by Julie Islip, but the schoolgirl from Christchurch, Dorset, could hardly have imagined what the next 18 months had in store for her.

At the Hertford Sporting Club, Coventry, the following October she lifted the women's world amateur title, beating Canadian Natalie Stelmach 4-1 in the final. And more was to come: on 15 January 1985, she set the snooker world alight by becoming the first woman to make a century break in competitive play. And she was still under 15 years of age!

Her magical break was made against 45-year-old Linotype operator Bill Scorer in the Walter C. Clark League, Premier Division, in Bournemouth. It took 15 minutes and totalled 114 by the time the 5 foot 5 inch (1.65m) Stacey had potted the last black. Not only was it the first women's century, it was also the first in the Walter C. Clark League.

A pupil at Highcliffe Comprehensive School in Dorset, she is so modest that she never told any of her fellow pupils about her achievements in the world of snooker. An exciting player in the mould of Jimmy White, she maintains that she had three ambitions within the sport. She has now fulfilled the first. The second is to become the first woman to compile a 147 break, and the third is to be the first woman to win a world championship – against the men.

Career highlights
- Women's World Amateur Champion 1984
- B&SCC Ladies Championship (runner-up) 1987

Hofmeister World Doubles

Before 1982, no serious attempt had been made to play doubles within the professional game since back in 1947, when Joe Davis and Walter Donaldson used to play Fred Davis and John Pulman in exhibition matches. Not daunted, however, the brewers Hofmeister agreed to sponsor a new world doubles championship in 1982. With promoters, sponsors and the television companies looking for something different, here was the perfect opportunity.

The world doubles is now an attractive and welcome part of the professional calendar, but it did well to survive its first year. The National Recreation Centre at Crystal Palace was chosen as the venue. The playing conditions were far from ideal and the place itself was difficult to reach. The latter was emphasized by the sparseness of the audiences – just 67 people attended the first session of play, which saw such notable names as Terry Griffiths, Doug Mountjoy, Kirk Stevens and Jim Wych in play.

Steve Davis and Tony Meo encountered very little difficulty on their way to winning the first title. The final itself against Griffiths and Mountjoy was one of their easiest matches – they won 13-2. This win for Davis gave him a unique treble as it meant he was the holder of all three professional world titles – individual, team, and now doubles. Davis and Meo also won the break prize with their combined break of 193 during their semi-final match with Tony Knowles and Jimmy White.

A move to the Derngate Centre, Northampton, in 1983 saw the competition enjoy the success it deserved. Unlike the previous year's contest, this one was well supported by the public.

Davis and Meo retained their title, and yet again they found the path to victory an easy one. The final was another one-sided affair in which they disposed of Tony Knowles and Jimmy White 10-2. Once again they won the combined break prize with a new championship best of 196, which included a 140 clearance by Davis in the 9-1 semi-final drubbing of Eddie Charlton and Bill Werbeniuk.

The Derngate Centre hosted the event for the first time in 1983 and the change of venue proved unlucky for Davis and Meo as they lost to the eventual winners, Alex Higgins and Jimmy White, in the semi-final.

Alex Higgins – speaking with conviction

It was, however, back to winning ways for Davis and Meo in 1985, but only after coming from behind to win their quarter-final against the strong pair of youngsters Neal Foulds and John Parrott. In the final Davis and Meo beat the surprise package of the tournament, Ray Reardon and Tony Jones.

In a tournament that they have made their own, the two Londoners swept all aside once more in 1986 to win the title for the fourth time out of five attempts. Furthermore, they added the championship record combined break of 217 to their list of records. The latest pair to feel the full force of the 'Dynamic Duo' were Mike Hallett and youngster Stephen Hendry, but they were not good enough for the more experienced pair on the day.

Hofmeister World Doubles Championships – Results (finals)

1982 S. Davis & T. Meo (England) 13
T. Griffiths & D. Mountjoy (Wales) 2
1983 S. Davis & T. Meo (England) 10
T. Knowles & J. White (England) 2
1984 A. Higgins (Ireland) & J. White (England) 10
C. Thorburn (Canada) & W. Thorne (England) 2
1985 S. Davis & T. Meo (England) 12
R. Reardon (Wales) & T. Jones (England) 5
1986 S. Davis & T. Meo (England) 12
M. Hallett (England) & S. Hendry (Scotland) 3

Most wins: 4 – Steve Davis & Tony Meo
Most finals: 4 – Steve Davis & Tony Meo
Highest break: 217 – Steve Davis & Tony Meo (1986)

Home International Championships

In 1969 Wales met England in an international match at Port Talbot. This was the first official amateur international and its success lead to the introduction of the Home International Championships the following season.

England beat Wales 10-8 in that first match, full details of which are as follows (England names first):

Jonathan Barron beat Doug Mountjoy 3-0
Ray Edmonds beat Terry Parsons 3-0
Sid Hood lost to John Ford 1-2
Pat Houlihan lost to Mario Berni 0-3
Colin Ross beat Aubrey Kemp 2-1
Geoff Thompson lost to Alwyn Lloyd 1-2

The second year saw the Republic of Ireland join England and Wales to form a three-team championship. Each nation played one match on home soil, and the first winners were England.

In the 1971-72 season Scotland made it a four-nation tournament, and again England were the winners.

The competition enjoyed a tremendous boost in 1978 when holiday firm Pontins stepped in to sponsor it. Playing matches throughout the season at different venues was a great drain on the funds of the national bodies. Pontins agreed to sponsor the

Home International Championship tables

1970-71
1. England 4 pts
2. Wales 2 pts
3. Eire 0 pts

1971-72
1. England 5 pts
2. Wales 4 pts
3. Scotland 3 pts
4. Eire 0 pts

1972-73
I. England 5 pts
2. Wales 5 pts
3. Scotland 2 pts
4. Eire 0 ots

1973-74
1. England 5 pts
2. Wales 4 pts
3. Eire 2 pts
4. Scotland 1 pt

1974-75
1. Wales 6 pts
2. England 4 pts
3. Scotland 2 pts
4. Eire 0 pts

1975-76
1. Wales 6 pts
2. England 4 pts
3. Scotland 2 pts
4. Eire 0 pts

1976-77
1. England 6 pts
2. Wales 4 pts
3. Scotland 2 pts
4. Eire 0 pts

1977-78
1. Wales 6 pts
2. England 4 pts
3. Scotland 2 pts
4. Eire 0 pts

1978
1. England 8 pts
2. Wales 5 pts
3. Scotland 4 pts
4. Eire 3 pts
5. Isle of Man 0 pts

1979
1. England 10 pts
2. Wales 7 pts
3. Eire 6 pts
4. Scotland 4 pts
5. N.Ireland 3 pts
6. Isle of Man 0 pts

1980
1. Wales 10 pts
2. England 8 pts
3. Eire 5 pts
4. Scotland 4 pts
5. N.Ireland 3 pts
6. Isle of Man 0 pts

1981
1. Wales 8 pts
2. England 6 pts
3. Scotland 6 pts
4. Eire 4 pts
5. N.Ireland 3 pts
6. Isle of Man 1 pt

1982
1. Wales 8 pts
2. England 7 pts
3. N.Ireland 5 pts
4. Scotland 4 pts
5. Eire 3 pts
6. Isle of Man 1 pt

1983
1. Wales10 pts
2. England 8 pts
3. Scotland 5 pts
4. N.Ireland 3 pts
5. Isle of Man 2 pts
6. Eire 2 pts

1984
1. Wales 9 pts
2. England 7 pts
3. Scotland 7 pts
4. N.Ireland 4 pts
5. Eire 3 pts
6. Isle of Man 0 pts

1985
1. Wales 10 pts
2. England 6 pts
3. N. Ireland 6 pts
4. Eire 4 pts
5. Scotland 4 pts
6. Isle of Man 0 pts

Junior winners: England

1986
1. England 10 pts
2. Wales 5 pts
3. N. Ireland 5 pts
4. Scotland 5 pts
5. Eire 5 pts
6. Isle of Man 0 pts

Junior winners: Wales

Most wins (team): 9 – Wales

Most wins (individual): 35 Alwyn Lloyd (Wales)

Highest break: 141 – Martin Clark (England) 1986

championships which were – and are still today – played during the Autumn Festival of Snooker at their Prestatyn camp in North Wales.

The Isle of Man, in 1978, became the fifth nation to join the championships, and the following year the present-day complement of six nations was completed when Northern Ireland joined.

England and Wales have dominated the series. Not only have they won between them all 17 championships contested to the end of 1986, they have both occupied the first two places in the final league table each season.

Scotland, in 1984, were the first nation to offer anything like a serious challenge to the top two, when they held both England and Wales to a draw. Their star performer was 15-year-old Stephen Hendry, the youngest-ever Scottish amateur champion.

Six players make up each team, and each one plays one opposing team member in each match. Each game is the best of three frames, and the aggregate frames are added together to calculate the result of each match. All six nations play each other once in a league system.

The highest possible match score is 18-0, but no team has ever won by this margin. There have been two instances of a 17-1 scoreline however: In 1970-71 when Wales beat the Republic of Ireland and in 1981 when England beat the Isle of Man.

A Junior Home International Championship was introduced in August 1985 and played at Hemsby, near Great Yarmouth. The following year Heysham, near Morecambe, became the new home of the senior event.

Hong Kong

The Far East is one of the growth areas of snooker, and Hong Kong has a prospect capable of one day joining the professional ranks in the person of Gary Kwok Kwan Shing. Gary Kwok and his team-mate Cheung Che-Ming became the first representatives of their country to take part in the world amateur championships when they went to Calgary in 1982. And Gary came away from the championships having earned a great deal of praise. In the strong group that contained eventual winner Terry Parsons, Gary lost only one match – and that was to Parsons. He was just edged out of a quarter-final place, but had done enough to make people aware of his name – even if they could not pronounce it!

He did not fare as well in the 1984 championships, although he still left his mark on them. One of only two men to beat the eventual winner, O.B. Agrawal of India, he also compiled a break of 129 – the second highest ever in the world amateur championships.

Gary Kwok left the championships early, saying he had business commitments back home, and forfeited his last match against England's Chris Archer. He is a versatile person and most probably did have business commitments, being the manager of a snooker hall, an actor, and a television horse-racing commentator.

Barry Hearn took his professionals Steve Davis, Tony Meo and Terry Griffiths as well as Doug Mountjoy to Hong Kong in 1983 and they, together with Cheung Che-Ming and Stanley Leung, contested the inaugural Camus Hong Kong Masters (Camus are cognac distillers). Mountjoy beat Griffiths 4-3 in the final at the Queen Elizabeth Stadium, but it was Griffiths who stole the limelight with a 140 break in the final – the highest break ever seen in Hong Kong.

The four Britons returned for the tournament in 1984, and brought with them Jimmy White and John Parrott. The tournament was a new style eight-man straight knockout, and the shock of the first round was Jimmy White's 3-1 defeat by Gary Kwok. Kwok lost to Mountjoy in the semi-final, who in turn lost to Steve Davis in the final.

The enlarged five-man Matchroom team, plus Tony Knowles, took part in 1985 and the following year the new complement of seven members of the Hearn stable, plus Canadian Cliff Thorburn, competed in the fourth Camus Masters, won by Willie Thorne.

The Hong Kong Billiards and Snooker Association was formed in 1979 and in 1985 the country opened the largest snooker club in the world, with 113 tables.

Hong Kong: Results

Hong Kong Open Snooker Championship

1981 Kwan-Shing Kwok beat Che-Ming Cheung
1982 Kwan-Shing Kwok beat Che-Ming Cheung

Camus Hong Kong Masters

1983 Doug Mountjoy (Wales) 4 beat Terry Griffiths (Wales) 3
1984 Steve Davis (England) 4 beat Doug Mountjoy (Wales) 2
1985 Terry Griffiths (Wales) 4 beat Steve Davis (England) 2
1986 Willie Thorne (England) 8 beat Dennis Taylor (Ireland) 3

Hughes, Eugene

A professional since 1981, Eugene Hughes was born in Blackrock, County Dublin, and in 1985 he moved his base to Kings Cross, London in a move similar to that made by Patsy Fagan some ten years earlier.

Shortly after establishing his new base, Hughes reached the quarter-final of the newly instituted Dulux British Open, where he lost to fellow Irishman Alex Higgins. This quarter-final appearance followed up his remarkable semi-final appearance in the Jameson International a few months earlier. The Jameson, which gave Hughes the biggest payment of his professional career, with a cheque for £10,000, saw him beat Doug Mountjoy 5-1, Ray Reardon 5-1 and Willie Thorne 5-2 before losing to Steve Davis 9-3 in the semi-final.

He tends to be a slow and deliberate player, but his style has won him many honours. He was the national under-19 billiards and snooker champion in 1975, and three years later he won the first of his two national snooker titles; he also became the All-Ireland snooker champion in 1979.

Having won his national title in 1978, Hughes was eligible to compete in that year's world championships in Malta. He failed to qualify for the quarter-finals, as indeed he did when he competed in the 1980 championships at Launceston, Australia. He did, however, leave those championships as the new holder of the record break – 127 – in the world amateur championships – a record that was to hold until beaten by Tony Drago in 1984.

He turned professional in 1981 and later that year he added to his 20 amateur international appearances when he represented the Republic of Ireland as a professional in the State Express World Team competition.

Hughes first came to prominence as a professional when he reached the quarter-final of the 1983 Professional Players Tournament, enjoying good wins over Bill Werbeniuk (5-0) and Terry Griffiths (5-2) before losing to Willie Thorne in the last eight. The highlight of his professional career came when, with Dennis Taylor and Alex Higgins, he was a member of the All-Ireland team that won the World Cup competition in 1985, 1986 and 1987.

He followed this up by reaching the quarter-final of the Irish

The England team that competed in the 1981 Home International Championship at Prestatyn. Left to right: George Wood, Barry West, Ian Williamson, Bob Harris, Les Dodd, Graham Cripsey, John Hargreaves, Mike Darrington

Masters. He beat Ray Reardon convincingly five frames to nil to reach that stage, then led Steve Davis by three frames to nil before losing 5-4.

Career highlights
- Jameson International (semi-final) 1984
- BCE International (semi-final) 1986
- World Cup 1985-87
- All-Ireland Snooker Champion 1979
- Republic of Ireland Amateur Snooker Champion 1978, 1979
- National Under-19 Snooker Champion 1975
- National Under-19 Billiards Champion 1975

I

Important Dates

Although billiards was played in the days of Mary Queen of Scots, it was not until the latter part of the 19th century that the game of snooker was born. Its real growth started during the 1920s – thanks largely to Joe Davis.

The following are some important dates in the history of snooker.

1875 British Army officers stationed at Jubbulpore, India, first played the game. It is believed that one of them, Sir Neville Chamberlain, gave the name to the sport when he declared that one of his opponent's shots was a 'snooker' after he had failed to pot a relatively easy coloured ball. The word at that time was the name given to a first-year cadet at Woolwich Barracks.
1892 Billiard table measurements were standardized.
1900 The Billiards Association published a set of snooker rules.
1916 C.N. Jacques won the first English amateur snooker championship.
1919 The Billiards Association and the Billiards Control Club amalgamated.
1919 To avoid the drawn game (a not infrequent occurrence), the re-spotting of the black was introduced. The free-ball rule was also introduced.
1927 Touching ball rule introduced.
1927 Joe Davis won the first world professional championship; his prize money was just £6 10s 0d (£6·50) and he took the same trophy that today's world champions hold aloft at the Crucible.
1947 Joe Davis retired from world championship play to concentrate on exhibitions.
1952 Following a split from the BACC (Billiards Association and Control Council) the professionals formed their own Professional Billiards Players Association.
1955 Joe Davis recorded the first official maximum 147 break at Thurston's.
1963 The first world amateur championships were held in Calcutta, the winner being Birmingham fireman Gary Owen.
1964 The rift between the professionals and the BACC was healed.
1965 Joe Davis retired from public engagements.
1969 England played Wales at Port Talbot in an international match. It was the forerunner of the Home International series that started the following year.
1969 The BBC Television series *Pot Black* was born.
1970 The professionals split from the BACC yet again. This time they formed the WPBSA (World Professional Billiards and Snooker Association).
1971 The BACC changed its name to the B&SCC (Billiards and Snooker Control Council).
1976 Embassy began their sponsorship of the world professional championships.
1977 John Spencer won the first world professional championship to be held at the Crucible Theatre. He also became the first player to win the title using a two-piece cue.
1978 The 'father' and greatest practitioner of the game, Joe Davis, died at the age of 77.
1982 Steve Davis registered the first televised maximum break against John Spencer in the Lada Classic at Oldham.
1984 Steve Davis became the first man to retain his world title at the Crucible.

India

India occupies a special place in snooker history, for it was at Jubbulpore in 1875 that Sir Neville Chamberlain first used the term 'snooker' while playing a version, derived from billiards, of the modern game. Five years later the first rules of snooker were drawn up, and posted in the Ooty Club in Ootacamund.

Legendary English billiards player John Roberts Junior visited India in the early 1880s and met Chamberlain. As a result of this meeting Roberts took the game of snooker back to England – and so it all began.

The Indian Billiards and Snooker Association was formed in 1930, and the following year the inaugural national billiards championships were held; the snooker championships followed in 1939. One of the early administrators of billiards and snooker in India was M.M. Begg who, over 30 years later, was responsible for the inaugural world amateur snooker championships in Calcutta in 1963. He also put up the trophy for the winner of that tournament.

Many famous players visited India from time to time to give exhibitions. One regular visitor was Horace Lindrum who, in 1952, became the first to record a century break in the country.

As a result of having watched the likes of Lindrum, Wilson Jones emerged as India's first true world-class player – at both billiards and snooker. National snooker champion five times, he won the billiards title on a record 12 occasions, and in 1958 and 1964 was world billiards champion; he was also runner-up in between.

India has been one of the few nations to continue to produce top-class billiards players even though snooker has become the more popular of the two games in other countries. In addition to Jones winning the world title twice, Michael Ferreira won it on three occasions to give India five world billiards titles.

Until 1984, however, they had done very little in the snooker world, although Ratan Bader did hold the official world record amateur break of 122 between 1964 and 1967. In 1984 they made the breakthrough when O.B. Agrawal beat defending champion Terry Parsons to win the world amateur title in Dublin. If O.B.'s brother Subbash had won the final of the world amateur billiards championship the previous year it would have been a notable family double.

O.B. Agrawal and Geet Sethi were accepted as members of the World Professional Billiards and Snooker Association in 1985, thus becoming India's first professionals.

Indian Amateur Snooker Championship: Results (finals)

1939 P.K. Deb beat M.M. Begg
1940 P.K. Deb beat H.P. Smith
1941 V. Freer beat P.K. Deb
1942 P.K. Deb beat V.R. Freer
1943 Not held
1944 Not held
1945 Not held
1946 T.A. Selvaraj beat S. Coelho
1947 T. Sadler beat A. Wali
1948 W. Jones beat T. Sadler
1949 T.A. Selvaraj beat W. Jones
1950 F. Edwards (England) beat T.A. Selvaraj
1951 T.A. Selvaraj beat W. Reed
1952 W. Jones beat C. Hirjee
1953 L. Driffield (England) beat C. Hirjee
1954 W. Jones beat C. Hirjee
1955 T.A. Selvaraj beat T. Sadler
1956 M.J. Lafir (Ceylon) beat C. Hirjee
1957 M.J. Lafir (Ceylon) beat C. Hirjee
1958 W. Jones beat C. Hirjee
1959 M.J. Lafir (Ceylon) beat T. Cleary (Australia)
1960 W. Jones beat M. Lafir
1961 M.J. Lafir (Ceylon) beat W. Jones
1962 R. Marshall beat A.K. Basu (Australia)
1963 M.J. Lafir (Ceylon) beat T. Monteiro
1964 S. Shroff beat T. Monteiro
1965 S. Shroff beat T. Monteiro
1966 T. Monteiro beat S. Shroff
1967 S. Shroff beat T. Monteiro
1968 S. Mohan beat T. Monteiro
1969 S. Shroff beat A. Savur
1970 S. Shroff beat A. Savur
1971 T. Monteiro beat A. Savur
1972 S. Shroff beat S. Aleem
1973 S. Shroff beat T. Monteiro
1974 M.J. Lafir (Sri Lanka) beat A. Savur
1975 M.J. Lafir (Sri Lanka) beat A. Savur
1976 A. Savur beat M.G. Jayaram
1977 M.J. Lafir (Sri Lanka) beat A. Savur
1978 A. Savur beat D Subba Rao
1979 A. Savur beat G. Parikh
1980 J. White (England) beat A. Savur
1981 G. Parikh beat S. Habib
1982 O.B. Agrawal beat S. Habib
1983 M.G. Jayaram beat O.B. Agrawal
1984 G.Sethi beat beat S. Sawant
1985 G. Sethi beat S. Sawant
Most wins: 8 – Mohammed Lafir (Sri Lanka)

Inter-Counties Snooker Team Championship: Results (finals)

1974 Glamorgan 5
(G. Thomas/J. Prosser/M. Berni/J. Selby)
Lincolnshire 1
(R. Barnes/S. Hood/M. Goodwin/R. Edmonds)

1975 Greater London 9
(J. Fisher/G. Foulds/J. Beech/P. Fagan)
Cornwall 7
(J. Barron/L. Varcoe/C. Gay/I. James)
[Cornwall led 5/3 at end of 1st leg]

1976 Lancashire 'A' 9
(D. Hughes/P. Medati/J. Virgo/G. Scott)
Greater London 'A' 5
(J. Fisher/G. Foulds/J. Beech/P. Fagan)
[4/4 at end of 1st leg]

1977 Lincolnshire 9
(J. Stobie/R. Barnes/R. Edmonds/M. Goodwin)
Cornwall 3
(D. Thorncroft/C. Gay/I. James/L. Varcoe)
[Lincolnshire led 6/2 at end of 1st leg]

1978 London 9
(T. Meo/G. Foulds/S. Davis/R. Brown)
Yorkshire 2
(P. Oakley/J. Johnson/D. Rourke/R. Swift/I. Williamson)
[London led 6/2 at end of 1st leg]

1979 London 9
(G. Gibson/W. West/J. White/R. Brown)
Durham 3
(D. Martin/D. Chalmers/R. Kell/B. Jones)
[London led 5/3 at end of 1st leg]

1980 Hampshire 5
(B. Watson/N. Fairall/M. Williams/A. Micalef)
Merseyside 2
(G. Scott/B. Thorogood/E. Duggan/L. Dodd)

1981 Durham 5
(R. Kell/K. Sumpton/J. Griffin/K. Barnett)
Wessex 0
(B. Bernard/W. McGregor/T. Cavey/A. Clarke)

1982 London 5
(N. Foulds/P. Ennis/R. Brown/D. Gilbert)
Staffordshire 1
(J. Hargreaves/D. Williams/A. Woodbridge/M. Smith)

1983 Yorkshire 5
(S. Duggan/B. West/T. Emmott/P. Oakley)
Essex 3
(T. Putnam/G. Keeble/C. Archer/M. Smith)

1984 Yorkshire 5
(D. Rice/P. Oakley/B. West/T. Emmott)
Devon 4
(A. Snell/D. Walker/R. Cole/P. Edworthy)

1985 Devon 5
(A. Snell D. Walker R. Cole P. Edworthy)
Lincolnshire 0
(J. Stobie B. Watson K. Ashby J. Cundy)

1986 London 5
(G. Filtness/J. Wright/R. Connor/B. Scarlett)
Staffordshire & West Midlands 2
(A. Harris/S. James/M. Clark/J. Chambers)

1987 Kent 5
(G. Turner/C. Carpenter/A. Wix/M. Smith)
Yorkshire 3
(D. Rice/P. Smith/M. Rowing/P. Bardsley)

Most wins (team): 5 – London (including one as Greater London)
Most finals (team): 6 – London (including two as Greater London)
Most wins (individual): 3 – Roger Brown (London)
Most finals (individual): 3 – Roger Brown (London)
3 – Geoff Foulds (London/Greater London)
3 – Peter Oakley (Yorkshire)
Highest break: 85 – Jimmy White (London) 1979

Under-21 finals
(Under-19 from 1987)

1980 Essex 5
Gloucestershire 4
1981 Cornwall 5
Yorkshire 3
1982 Surrey 5
Essex 4
1983 Staffordshire 5
Devon 3
1984 London 5
Derbyshire 1
1985 East Sussex 5
North East 2
1986 Staffordshire & West Midlands 5
East Sussex 3
1987 Staffordshire & West Midlands 5
Devon 3

India's Michael Ferreira, three times world amateur billiards champion, with England's Ray Edmonds

Inter-Counties Championships

The Billiards and Snooker Control Council introduced the inter-counties team snooker championship in the 1973-74 season; the following season it introduced a similar championship for billiards. It is strictly for amateurs who are members of affiliated clubs, each affiliated county selecting a team of four playing members. Each match is played over two frames and the frame scores are aggregated. In the event of a tie, a sudden-death tie-break over one frame is played. There has only been one instance of a tie-break being required to decide the final: that was in 1984, when David Rice of Yorkshire beat Andy Snell of Devon to take the title back to Yorkshire for the second successive year.

Some of today's professional players have appeared in winning teams in the championship. The following is a complete list: Geoff Foulds, Patsy Fagan, Dennis Hughes, Paul Medati, John Virgo, George Scott, Ray Edmonds, Tony Meo, Jimmy White, Steve Duggan, Barry West, Neal Foulds, Dave Gilbert and Steve Davis.

The first final, in 1974, was played over just one leg, but between 1975 and 1979 the finals were played over two – each finalist enjoying the benefit of home advantage. After 1979 however, it reverted to a single leg, played at a neutral venue.

The B&SCC added an under-23 snooker tournament to the inter-counties championships in the 1979-80 season, which was changed to an under-21 competition and from 1986-87 to an under-19 competition. And it was in this competition in 1985 that a piece of snooker history was created when 16-year-old Alison Fisher became the first female to compete in an open national final.

International Billiards and Snooker Federation

The International Billiards and Snooker Federation (IBSF) was formed as the World Billiards and Snooker Council in 1971, changing its name in 1973. The Council was formed as a result of dissatisfaction by overseas national associations that the Billiards and Snooker Control Council (then the Billiards Association and Control Council) should be the governing body of both the English domestic game and the game at international level. Consequently, the IBSF – with a one-nation, one-vote constitution – took control of the organization of world amateur championships at both billiards and snooker.

The B&SCC remains the sport's governing body, although its main function is to organize the game in England. It has agreed to the IBSF's request that it should make no changes to the rules of either game without consulting them first.

The IBSF elects its own chairman, who remains in office for two years. But the chairman of the B&SCC is automatically a joint vice-chairman of the Federation. The secretary of the B&SCC is also secretary of the IBSF.

Countries affiliated to the Control Council are entitled to be members of the IBSF, and therefore be represented at world championships and at general meetings of the Federation.

At the end of 1984 the International Billiards and Snooker Federation had nearly 30 members, from the Sudan to Mauritius, and from Bangladesh to Zimbabwe.

International Matches

The first record of a billiards or snooker international or 'test' match dates back to 1932, when Australians Clark McConachy and Walter Lindrum beat England's Joe Davis and Tom Newman in a billiards test match.

One of the earliest international tournaments to be held outside conventional Commonwealth snooker-playing countries was in Marseilles, France, in March 1939, when former Welsh

Results of all amateur snooker international matches (except Home International)

1967
Cape Town: South Africa 1
England 3
Durban: South Africa 4
England 0
Johannesburg: South Africa 0
England 4
England won series 2-1

1973
Cardiff: Wales 9
Rest of World 9

1975
Cape Town: South Africa 2
British Isles 2
Durban: South Africa 1
British Isles 3
Johannesburg: South Africa 2
British Isles 2
British Isles won series 1-0, with two games drawn.

1977
Liverpool: England 14
Canada 4
Renfrew: Scotland 8
Canada 10
Douglas: Isle of Man 5
Canada 13
Port Talbot: Aberdare and Rhondda Leagues 8
Canada 10
Dublin: Republic of Ireland 4
Canada 6

1979
Warrington: England 9
Wales 9

1980
Milton Keynes: England 13
Scotland 5

amateur champion Tom Jones beat H.F. Smith 6-3 in the final. The first snooker test series was held in 1967, when Ray Reardon and Jonathan Barron, representing England, beat South Africa, represented by Mannie Francisco and Jimmy van Rensburg, 2-1 in a three-test series held at Cape Town, Durban and Johannesburg. In 1975 a second series was arranged in South Africa. This time Alwyn Lloyd and Ray Edmonds represented the British Isles, and the Francisco brothers – Mannie and Silvino – together with Mike Hines represented the home country. Again three tests were played, at the same venues as 1967. The first and third were drawn, but Britain won the series thanks to victory in the second test.

In between those two tests Wales played an international against the Rest of the World at Cardiff in 1973, and drew 9-9.

Canada, in 1977, made the first full-length tour by an international team, playing matches against England, Scotland, the Isle of Man, the Aberdare and Rhondda Combined League team, and a Republic of Ireland team on their way home. After losing to England in the opening match of the tour, the Canadians remained undefeated. The star of the team was a youngster named Kirk Stevens.

The Home International Championship is the most important and prestigious amateur snooker international tournament in the world.

There have been only two instances when home countries have met each other, apart from in the championships. These were in 1979, when England and Wales drew at Warrington, and in 1980, when England beat Scotland at Milton Keynes.

See also Home International Championship

Ireland

See Eire

Irish Professional Championships

Like many non-televised tournaments, the Irish professional championships have been struggling to overcome the problem of financial viability. It is a fact of life that the absence of television coverage deters the larger sponsors, and consequently the Irish national championships were in doubt in 1984-85.

Sponsored by Irish brewers Smithwick's in 1982 and 1983, the championships have endured a varied life. Jack Rea became the first holder of the title in 1947 and between then and 1982 the championships were conducted as a challenge competition; the holder used to decide who, when, and where his challenger would be for the title. Apart from a solitary defeat by new professional Jack Bates in 1952, Rea held the title until he met the young Alex Higgins in a challenge match in 1972.

Higgins successfully defended on four occasions – twice each against Patsy Fagan and Dennis Taylor. Taylor eventually beat Higgins, and then made one successful defence of the title before the eight-man knockout format was introduced in 1982.

When Taylor successfully defended the title against Fagan he played the match at the Riverside Theatre at the University of Ulster in Coleraine – the first time a match for the title had been played outside Belfast. The Riverside Theatre, with its intimate 380-seat capacity arena, was also used for the first of the new-style tournaments in 1982, in which Dennis Taylor held on to his title, beating Alex Higgins in the final. The two had been seeded straight into the semi-finals where they met

Ireland's top two players for more than a decade, Dennis Taylor and Alex Higgins, seen here before the start of the 1987 Benson and Hedges Masters at Wembley

Irish Professional Championships: Results (1982 on)

1982 Dennis Taylor 16 Alex Higgins 13	**1985** Dennis Taylor 10 Alex Higgins 5
1983 Alex Higgins 16 Dennis Taylor 11	**1986** Dennis Taylor 10 Alex Higgins 7
1984 Not held	**1987** Dennis Taylor 9 Joe O'Boye 2

Highest break: 132 – Alex Higgins (1983)

two young aspirants, Eugene Hughes and Tommy Murphy. Higgins, who came back into the tournament at the eleventh hour after earlier withdrawing, trailed 14-8 in the best-of-31 frame final. He fought back to trail 14-13 before Taylor won the next two frames to clinch the title, and the £3,300 prize money.

The tournament moved back to Belfast in 1983 and was held at the 1000-seater Maysfield Leisure Centre on the outskirts of the city. Higgins regained the title, and was clearly delighted at not only winning the title, but doing so in his home town. The event was sponsored by Smithwick's for the second time, and Higgins beat Taylor 16-11 in the final to take the £6,000 first prize money.

In his quarter-final match against Jack Rea, the 1947 champion, Higgins compiled a tournament-best break of 132.

The Irish championships were almost abandoned in 1984-85, but at the eleventh hour Strongbow – former sponsors of the Welsh professional championships – stepped in to save them. Dennis Taylor beat Alex Higgins in the final and Taylor beat his great rival when the two met again in the final a year later.

J

Jameson International

See Fidelity Unit Trusts International

Johnson, Joe

When Joe Johnson beat Cliff Wilson in the second round of the 1985 Mercantile Credit Classic, it was the Yorkshireman's first victory in four professional matches played before television cameras. Yet Johnson held the record for the highest break by an amateur (140), and that *was* made in front of the cameras – at the TUC Club, Middlesbrough, in 1978.

A grossly underrated player, Johnson has fought to overcome the psychological barrier of the television cameras, and with the victory over Wilson, and one over Warren King in the next round, that barrier had been broken.

Joe Johnson preceded Tony Knowles as national under-19 snooker champion in 1971, and in 1978 he was runner-up to Terry Griffiths in the English amateur championship. He represented England on ten occasions in the Home International Championships, and Griffiths was one of only two men to beat him. As runner-up in the English amateur championship he

One of snooker's nice guys, Joe Johnson defied all the pundits by reaching a second successive world championship final in 1987

The greatest moment in Joe Johnson's career as he holds aloft the World Championship Trophy after beating Steve Davis in the 1986 final

competed in the world event in Malta, and reached the final, which he lost to Cliff Wilson.

He turned professional in 1979 but had to wait until 1983 for his first major final. In that year's Professional Players' Tournament he beat Jimmy White, Eddie Charlton, Cliff Thorburn and Tony Meo on his way to the final. The scores in his wins over Charlton and Thorburn were 5-0 and 5-1 respectively. In the final he met the in-form Tony Knowles, and when Knowles led 6-1 Johnson was regarded as a complete no-hoper. But he pulled back and lost only narrowly by 9 frames to 8. During his fight-back he compiled a championship-best break of 135. Perhaps it was no coincidence that the event was not televised.

After that performance Johnson crept up the world rankings and into the top 16. He has remained consistent, and in 1985 reached the semi-final of the Mercantile Credit Classic before losing to Cliff Thorburn.

The world championships had always proved a stumbling block to Johnson, but in 1986 he overcame that and went on to beat Steve Davis 18-12 in one of snooker's great moments. Johnson's win gave renewed hope to many professionals, who must have thought Davis invincible, because his win was emphatic and completely different from Dennis Taylor's battle of nerves in the previous year's final.

Johnson struggled to find his form after that success, but he did spend a lot of time giving back to the sport what he had got out of it. He won a lot of friends after his world title success, but not a lot of tournaments. However, it all came good at the Crucible 12 months later when he defied all the pundits and reached his second successive final, only to lose an intriguing contest to Steve Davis.

Career highlights
- World Professional Champion 1986
- World Professional Championship (runner-up) 1987
- World Amateur Championship (runner-up) 1978
- National Under-19 Snooker Champion 1971

Junior Championships

The Billiards and Snooker Control Council organizes four junior competitions each year. They are the national under-19 championships at both billiards and snooker – generally referred to as the junior championships – and the national under-16 championships in both sports – generally referred to as the boys' championships.

The first to be held were the under-16 billiards championships in 1922. The idea for such an event came from journalist Harry Young, and it came to fruition that year when the first final was held at the Burroughes and Watts matchroom. The first champion was the now legendary Walter Donaldson.

In 1944 a new event was added to the junior calendar when, thanks to the efforts of snooker enthusiasts in Scunthorpe, the inaugural boys' snooker championships were held in the town. The first winner was future professional, and world amateur champion, Gary Owen.

Scunthorpe staged the event until 1949, when the championship, like its billiards counterpart, moved to Burroughes and Watts. That year saw the introduction of the under-19 championships for both sports.

The junior billiards championships lapsed in the early 1960s through lack of support, and when Burroughes and Watts closed in 1966 the snooker events were not held the following year. However, thanks to the efforts of current journalist,

National Under-16 Snooker Championships: Results (finals)

1944 G. Owen*
1945 R. Baker*
1946 D. Thomas*
1947 M. Knapp*
1948 R. Williams beat G. Hobbs
1949 (Scunthorpe) R. Williams*
(Burroughes and Watts) D. Lewis beat I. Cheetham
1950 M. Owen beat D. Williams
1951 M. Owen beat E. Parry
1952 M. Wildman beat D. Breese
1953 J. Board beat K. Preston
1954 D. Bond beat B. Allen
1955 P. Shelley beat P. Ferrari
1956 A. Hart beat D. Bond
1957 P. Shelley beat A. Orchard
1958 D. Bend beat D. Trevelyan
1959 J. Doyle beat P. Cox
1960 N. Cripps beat A. Matthews
1961 Not held
1962 J. Virgo beat A. Grant
1963 J. Hollis beat T. McCarver
1964 D. Clinton beat J. Hollis
1965 J. Maugham beat P. Demaine
1966 J. Terry beat R. Reardon
1967 Not held
1968 E. Stone beat A. Vincent
1969 P. Hughes beat W. Thorne
1970 W. Thorne beat S. Mays
1971 J. Mills beat R. Dean
1972 J. Mills beat T. Wells
1973 P. Bardsley beat K. Jones
1974 S. Holroyd beat D. Battye
1975 M. Hallett beat P. Hargreaves
1976 W. Jones beat D. Bonney
1977 J. White beat D. Bonney
1978 D. Adds beat M.E. Jackson
1979 T. Pyle beat J. Parrott
1980 T. Whitthread beat J. Parrott
1981 C. Hamson beat S. Ventham
1982 S. Ventham beat C. Thomas
1983 S. Hendry beat N. Pearce
1984 B. Morgan beat A. Harris
1985 B. Bunn beat M. Russell
1986 D. Grimwood beat D. Clarke
1987 J. Woodman beat M. Reevers

Most wins: 2 – Rex Williams
2 – Peter Shelley
2 – Marcus Owen
2 – J. Mills

Record break: 81 – Anthony Harris (1984)

National Under-19 Snooker Championships: Results (finals)

1949 A. Kemp beat L.R. Watt
1950 J. Carney beat R. Reardon
1951 R. Williams beat C. Wilson
1952 C. Wilson beat M. Owen
1953 C. Wilson beat M. Owen
1954 M. Wildman beat E. Parry
1955 W. McGivern beat M. Wildman
1956 E. Sinclair beat A. Hope
1957 H. Burns beat G. Wright
1958 W. West beat D. Bend
1959 D. Root beat D. Bend
1960 D. Bend beat I. Rees
1961 I. Rees beat T. Clarke
1962 A. Matthews beat T. Collinson
1963 A. Matthews beat A. Stringer
1964 J. Fisher beat R. Dolbear
1965 J. Virgo beat J. Hollis
1966 J. Hollis beat M. Colleran
1967 Not held
1968 J. Maughan beat D. Clinton
1969 J. Terry beat J. Peacock
1970 J. Terry beat W. Blake
1971 J. Johnson beat G. Grimes
1972 A. Knowles beat M. Gibson
1973 W. Thorne beat P. Edworthy
1974 A. Knowles beat P. Smith
1975 E. Hughes beat P. Bain
1976 I. Williamson beat P. Death
1977 I. Williamson beat W. Jones
1978 T. Meo beat I. Williamson
1979 J. O'Boye beat D. Gilbert
1980 T. Murphy beat K. Hayward
1981 D. Reynolds beat T. Murphy
1982 N. Foulds beat J. Parrott
1983 M. Thompson beat B. Rowsell
1984 M. Clark beat B. Rowsell
1985 W. Rendle beat M. Cadenhead
1986 B. Pinches beat J. Wattana
1987 M. Johnston-Allen beat A. Henry

Most wins: 2 – Cliff Wilson
2 – A. Matthews
2 – John Terry
2 – Tony Knowles
2 – Ian Williamson

Highest break: 100 – Neal Foulds (1982)

* Records not kept

professional player and television commentator Clive Everton, all four championships were revived in 1968, and held at Oldbury in the West Midlands. Since 1975 the championships have been organized by the Billiards Association and Control Council.

Over the years the championships have produced many great players and champions of the future. The first boys' billiards champion, Walter Donaldson, became a world champion, as did 1929 winner Fred Davis. The 1925 winner was well-known *Pot Black* referee Sydney Lee. In the post-war era, Clive Everton – to whom the championships owe so much – was a boys' billiards champion; and one of the most notable champions in the post-war years was Rex Williams, who won both boys' events in 1948 and 1949, the junior billiards title in 1949, and both junior titles the following year.

Current professionals Marcus Owen, Mark Wildman, John Virgo, Willie Thorne, Mike Hallett, Wayne Jones, Stephen Hendry and Jimmy White have all won the boys' snooker title, and Tony Meo, Tommy Murphy, Dean Reynolds and Neal Foulds have all been junior champions in recent years.

Willie Thorne has been a three-times winner of the junior billiards title, which has also been won by Steve Davis (who was never a junior snooker champion).

Ray Reardon never won the junior snooker title either, but was runner-up in the second year (1950). His fellow Welshman Cliff Wilson was, however, a two-times winner of the event.

While many champions have gone on to greater fame within the sport, the only junior champion to go on and win a senior national title in a different sport was 1960 under-16 champion Norwood Cripps, who became a national rackets champion.

Three young hopefuls arrive at Burroughes Hall for the final of the 1948-49 Under-16 Billiards Championship. Right: the eventual winner, Rex Williams, shakes hands with runner-up Jack Carney

K

Karnehm, Jack

Now a television commentator and national coach for the Billiards and Snooker Foundation, Jack Karnehm was a top-class billiards player, particularly in his amateur days. His moment of greatest glory as a player came in 1969, when he won the world amateur billiards championship which was held in his native London. This ended a memorable year for Karnehm, as he had won the English amateur billiards championship for the first time in April, then become world champion in November.

He had competed in the world billiards championships once before – in Pukekohe, New Zealand in 1964. He paid his own fare on that occasion, as he was not the automatic choice as the England number one player. As the number two, however, he went on to finish runner-up to Indian Wilson Jones. During the tournament he compiled a 392 break in just 16 minutes.

Soon after his 1969 world championship success Karnehm turned professional but made very little impact on snooker – in fact he competed in the world championships on three occasions, and not only did he fail to win a match, but he failed to win a single frame. He lost 8-0 to John Pulman in 1974, 11-0 to Dennis Taylor in 1977 and 9-0 to Roy Andrewartha in 1978.

His billiards, however, was kinder to him: he beat Rex Williams to win the United Kingdom professional title in 1980, but lost to him in the final the following year. In 1971 he was also runner-up to Leslie Driffield for the Billiards Association and Control Club's version of the world professional title. He challenged Williams for the world title in 1973, but was well beaten by over 4,000 points in their match at Chelmsford.

In 1978, Karnehm and Clive Everton joined Ted Lowe in the BBC commentary team for the world professional snooker championships at Sheffield – the first major BBC snooker venture apart from *Pot Black*. In January of the following year, Karnehm, a former chairman of the BA&CC, replaced Leslie Driffield as national coach. Since then he has been heard regularly giving his expert television commentaries.

Career highlights
- World Amateur Billiards Champion 1969
- United Kingdom Professional Billiards Champion 1980
- English Amateur Billiards Champion 1969

Kennerley, Kingsley

Kingsley Kennerley was the first English amateur snnooker champion who went on to make any sort of impact on the professional game. From 1937 to 1940 inclusive, he appeared in every final of the English amateur billiards and snooker championships, making him one of the greatest all-round amateur players. He started playing both games when he was eleven years old. The only table he could play on was at the Congleton Brass Band Club, but in order to get into the club he had to pretend he was a budding cornet player. The cornet talent mysteriously never developed – whereas the billiards and snooker talent certainly did.

In 1937 he completed the first of his two amateur billiards/snooker championship doubles, and his record break of 549 in the billiards championship stood until 1978.

After the war Kennerley turned professional, but he could never manage to scale the same heights as in his amateur days. In the post war era the shift was towards snooker, but Kennerley had a preference for billiards. He entered the world snooker championships every year between 1946 and 1953, but never got beyond the second round. The next time he entered was in 1974 when he was 60, and he lost to Jim Meadowcroft in the qualifying stages. His last appearance was in 1980.

Until the slump in the sport in the sixties, Kennerley was making a good living from exhibition matches and coaching. He was then forced to take a job away from the sport, and when the boom came in the seventies he had lost his old form.

Kennerley died suddenly at Birmingham in 1982 aged 68.

Career highlights
English Amateur Snooker Champion 1937, 1940
English Amateur Billiards Champion 1937-40

A youthful Kingsley Kennerley

Kick

A simple definition of what constitutes kick is 'when either the object-ball or the cue-ball does not travel at the anticipated angle after making contact'. Several explanations have been proposed, the most popular being that kick is caused by chalk on one of the balls. When it occurs, there is a distinctive sound as the balls collide, and both players and commentators identify this immediately.

Warren King, golden boy of Australian snooker

King, Warren

Warren King turned professional in 1982 at the age of 27, and is one of the new breed of Australian professionals who emerged to challenge Eddie Charlton as the country's top player. Australian amateur champion in 1980 and 1981, and runner-up to Joe Giannaros in 1982, King was first noticed by the wider public when selected to play for Australia in the World Team Classic in 1983. They played Canada in their opening match, and King followed Eddie Charlton's win over Bill Werbeniuk with an excellent 2-1 win over Cliff Thorburn to give Australia a 2-0 lead. They seemed poised to spring a surprise, but four successive defeats gave the match to Canada, although not before King had further left his mark on the match by taking a frame off Kirk Stevens.

He made his biggest impact on the British fans during the 1985 Mercantile Credit Classic. After narrowly beating Steve Duggan in the qualifying competition, he had an excellent victory over John Spencer in the first round, which put him into the televised stage. His first game in front of the cameras saw him beat Jimmy White. He then came up against another qualifier, Joe Johnson, who, playing his best snooker for a long time, ended King's hopes of the £40,000 first prize.

In King, many saw Eddie Charlton's successor as Australia's top player. He had his first crack at Charlton's Australian title in 1984, but lost to the Master. Then in 1986 King beat John Campbell to clinch the title and establish himself as one of the new 'Kings' of Australian snooker.

Career highlights
Mercantile Credit Classic (quarter-final) 1985
Australian Professional Champion 1986-87
Australian Amateur Champion 1980-81

English national coach Jack Karnehm (left) with fellow television commentator Ted Lowe

Knowles, Tony

Tony Knowles started playing snooker at the Tonge Moor Conservative Club, Bolton, at the age of nine. Fortunately for Knowles, his father was the steward of the club and consequently he was able to spend many hours on the club's tables. He decided when he was 18 that he was going to make a career of playing snooker, and abandoned Art College, where he was studying to become a graphic artist. His choice of profession has paid off, as Tony Knowles is now one of the biggest money winners in sport.

The late Jim Worsley – the man instrumental in bringing Alex Higgins to England in the seventies – took an interest in his early career, and saw him win the national under-19 championship at the first attempt, beating Matt Gibson of Glasgow in the 1972 final. On the morning of the final Tony compiled the first century break of his career. He won the title for a second time two years later, beating Paul Smith of Hitchen in the final.

Apart from his two junior titles, Knowles's amateur career was undistinguished. He did, however, represent England in the Home International Championships in 1978 and 1979, playing a total of nine matches and winning them all. His five wins in 1979 earned him the Player of the Series award. His biggest win as an amateur was the Pontins Autumn Open at Prestatyn that year, when he beat Dave Martin 7-0 in the final.

His first application for professional status was refused in November 1979, but the following February he was accepted as a member of the World Professional Billiards and Snooker Association. A quarter-final appearance in the United Kingdom professional championship in 1981 was his best professional performance until the 1982 world championships. Then the little-known Knowles created one of the biggest upsets in snooker history when he beat the defending champion Steve Davis. The snooker world was astounded as Knowles raced into a 4-0 lead before Davis won a single frame, and even more astounded when he ended the evening session 8-1 in front. Any talk of a Davis comeback the next day was soon dispelled as

Knowles won the first two frames of the next session to record a memorable 10-1 victory. Knowles then beat Graham Miles before narrowly losing to Australian Eddie Charlton in the quarter-final.

Later that year he managed to lose the tag of 'the man who beat Steve Davis' when he won his first major professional title, the Jameson International, beating David Taylor in the final.

His second success came the following year when he beat Joe Johnson in the final of the Professional Players' Tournament by nine frames to eight at the Redwood Lodge Country Club, Bristol. He teamed up with Tony Meo and Steve Davis in the England team to win the World Team Classic; the trio had been runners-up the previous year. He completed 1983 by finishing runner-up to Davis in the Scottish Masters, and again in the world doubles championship when Steve Davis and Tony Meo beat Knowles and his partner Jimmy White. Knowles came close to reaching his first world championship final in 1983 when he lost a cliff-hanger of a semi-final to the Canadian Cliff Thorburn. Leading 15-13, Knowles needed just one frame for victory, but he allowed Thorburn to win the last three frames and thus deprive him of his second world championship meeting with Steve Davis.

Ranked number two behind Davis in 1984, Knowles was on the wrong end of two giant-killing acts – both by the young Liverpudlian John Parrott. Having already beaten Alex Higgins, Parrott proceeded to beat Knowles in the Lada Classic at Warrington and then, a couple of months later, beat him again in the first round of the world championship at the Crucible.

A win in the Winfield Australian Masters in the summer of 1984 was followed by two lucrative final appearances in the 1984-85 season, but on each occasion he lost to Steve Davis. First he was soundly beaten 9-2 in the Jameson International, and then by the same score in the final of the English professional championship. Some consolation for Knowles in the latter was his lifting of the break prize for a break of 139.

Davis has well and truly avenged that world championship defeat: in each of the four individual finals in which Knowles has been runner-up, it is Steve Davis who has beaten him. In addition to the two mentioned above, Davis also beat him in the finals of the 1983 Scottish Masters and the 1984 Tolly Cobbold Classic.

Career highlights

- Jameson International Champion 1982
- Professional Players' Tournament Champion 1983
- World Cup 1983 (member of winning England team)
- Winfield Australian Masters Champion 1984
- Pontins Open Champion 1979
- National Under-19 Snooker Champion 1972, 1974

L

Lada Classic

See Mercantile Credit Classic

Tony Knowles...snooker rather than graphic arts

Langs Scottish Masters

The Langs Scottish Masters is the first tournament of the professional season and, despite being restricted to eight invited professionals, it carries prize money in excess of £28,000. The event was first held in the vast Kelvin Hall in Glasgow in 1981, and the first winner was 19-year-old Jimmy White. On his way to the title White beat three former world champions, Ray Reardon, Steve Davis and Cliff Thorburn, to become the youngest ever winner of a professional tournament.

A change of venue to the plush, intimate banqueting room of Glasgow's Holiday Inn saw a more enjoyable competition in 1982, and Steve Davis beat his old adversary Alex Higgins in the final to win the first of three successive Scottish Masters titles. When he won his second title the event had been moved to yet another venue, the Skean Dhu Hotel, Glasgow. On his way to that 1983 title Davis established a tournament record break with a 133.

The 1984 Masters was the first to remain at the same venue two years in succession and Davis beat Jimmy White to win his third title.

Since the era of Davis's domination, Canadian Cliff Thorburn has taken charge. He beat Willie Thorne 9-7 in the 1985 final and in the semi-final against Silvino Francisco he followed up a 133 break with a championship record total clearance of 142.

Thorburn retained his title in 1986, this time at the expense of Alex Higgins in a tense game that went its full distance. Higgins had some consolation as he compiled the top break of 131 in the final.

Langs Scottish Masters – Results (finals)

1981 J. White (England) 9
C. Thorburn (Canada) 4
1982 S. Davis (England) 9
A. Higgins (Ireland) 4
1983 S. Davis (England) 9
T. Knowles (England) 6
1984 S. Davis (England) 9
J. White (England) 4
1985 C. Thorburn (Canada) 9
W. Thorne (England) 7
1986 C. Thorburn (Canada) 9
A. Higgins (Ireland) 8

Most wins: 3 – Steve Davis

Most finals: 3 – Steve Davis
3 – Cliff Thorburn

Highest break: 142 – Cliff Thorburn (1983)

Lee, Sydney

A child prodigy at billiards in the 1920s, it is as referee of the BBC Television *Pot Black* series that Sydney Lee is better remembered. He was not a qualified referee, and when Ted Lowe asked him to become the referee of the series in 1970, he had never refereed a serious snooker match in his life. But his popularity and the respect in which he was held by the professionals made him the obvious choice.

Sydney Lee refereed in every series up to 1980, when ill-health forced him to retire. His services to the series and the sport in general were recognized when he was made the recipient of the *Pot Black* Personality Award in 1977.

Born in Streatham, Lee was a schoolboy champion in 1925, and was runner-up in the English amateur billiards championship in 1929. He went on to win the title every year from 1931 to 1934 inclusive. In between he appeared in two world amateur (then known as British Empire Championships) finals: in 1931 he lost to Laurie Steeples, but in 1933 he won the title, beating Welshman Tom Jones in the final.

He turned professional in 1935, and specialized in billiards. He was a personal friend of Walter Lindrum, which, perhaps, had some bearing on his decision to specialize in the three-ball game. But sadly, billiards went into decline shortly after Lee turned professional, and he never mastered snooker in the same way as billiards.

He competed in his first world snooker championship in 1936, losing 16-15 to Clare O'Donnell. Thereafter he competed every year, but it was not until 1947 that he gained his first victory in the championships when he beat J. Lees in a qualifying round match. His best snooker result was in 1940, when he was runner-up to Alec Brown in the Daily Mail Tournament. He was never fortunate enough to compete in the world professional billiards championships – they were not held between 1934 and 1951, Lee's prime years.

After the war Lee was resident professional at Burroughes Hall, in London, until its closure in the mid-sixties. It was here that he developed into an excellent exhibition match player and an expert coach. Many players came to him for assistance; and many of today's older professionals have at some stage sought the guidance of Sydney Lee.

Sydney was not the only member of his family to gain sporting recognition: his brother Benny was a champion skater.

Steve Davis – winner of three of the four Scottish Masters tournaments staged between 1981 and 1984

The venue of the Sunday Empire News Snooker Tournament: Sydney Lee versus Kingsley Kennerley

It is perhaps a touch ironic that, despite his preference for billiards, Lee had the distinction of being the first person to be seen playing snooker on television: in 1936 he was seen giving a demonstration over the airwaves from Alexandra Palace. The snooker world lost a great friend when Sidney Lee died in 1986.

Career highlights
- British Empire Billiards Champion 1933
- English Amateur Billiards Champion 1931-34
- National Under-16 Billiards Champion 1925

Leicester Square Hall

The most famous billiards and snooker hall in the post-war era, the Leicester Square Hall was built on the site of the old Thurston's Hall that was demolished by a German bomb in 1940. When the newly constructed hall opened on 3 October 1947, it was no longer under the proprietorship of Thurston's. It had three new directors – Bob Jelks, a table and equipment manufacturer, and famous players Joe Davis and Sidney Smith. These three took out the lease on the premises with the sole aim of promoting snooker at the hall.

Despite its change of name and ownership, the hall was still affectionately called Thurston's by most of the players. The first match at the hall saw Joe Davis beat his business partner Smith in the best of 71 frames. The next match to be staged at the hall after this was the world championship final between Fred Davis and Walter Donaldson.

However, the hall enjoyed only a short life. The building was owned by the Automobile Association, and they needed the space to extend and develop their offices; consequently the hall closed in 1955. At 10.15 p.m. on the last night, Fred Davis potted the last black, playing against his brother Joe. But it was Joe – appropriately – who won the last match at the venue; then the doors of the Leicester Square Hall were closed for the last time by manager Ted Lowe.

The following Wednesday all the equipment except the match-table was sold by auction. The match-table, acquired by the *News Chronicle* and offered by them as a prize to the winners of a five-a-side snooker tournament, was won by the Abertillery Central Club.

One week before the club closed, it was fortunate enough to witness snooker's equivalent of the first four-minute mile – a maximum break. On 22 January 1955, Joe Davis registered the first-ever 147 break, thus beating the old record of 146 set at the same venue some five years earlier by Canadian George Chenier.

The closure of the Leicester Square Hall left Central London with only one billiard hall – at Burroughes and Watts, in Soho Square.

Lindrum, Horace

A child prodigy at both billiards and snooker, Horace continued the great Lindrum tradition. Nephew of the great Walter Lindrum, he was born in 1912 as Horace Morell, but changed his name to Lindrum.

At the age of 16 he was capable of compiling a century break at snooker, and at the age of 19 he became the Australian professional snooker champion. He came to Britain for the 1936

Sydney Lee at just 11 years of age

Steve Longworth, who has held a place in the top 32 since 1986

world championships and reached the final, in which he had a formidable opponent in the shape of Joe Davis. Lindrum led Davis 27-24 at one stage and looked like being the first player to beat the great man on level terms. But it was not to be. Davis won ten frames in succession to win the title 34-27.

This was not the first – nor last – time the two met. Three years earlier they had played a challenge match in Melbourne. The prize was £100 plus all the gate money. Davis won easily, by 42 frames to 22.

Lindrum matched Davis in technique, but he did not have that same 'big match' temperement. He never beat Davis on level terms, but he did beat him on several occasions with a seven-point start.

Having arrived on British shores for the 1936 championships, he stayed for the remainder of the 1930s. His first year in Britain not only saw him reach the world final, but he established a new official record snooker break of 114. Later in the year he pushed the record up to 131 – only to see it taken from him later the same night when Sidney Smith registered a 133. The following year he made a 141 break, but this was never ratified as official. He reached his second successive world final in 1937, and again he met Davis. And again he pushed Davis all the way, before going down 32-29.

He returned to Australia during the war, and in 1941, at Penrith, New South Wales, he registered the first maximum of his career, in an exhibition match. By 1946 he was back in England and was having his third attempt at beating Davis in the world final. This was Davis's last defence of the title he had held since 1927, and a 1,000-strong audience packed into the Westminster Royal Horticultural Hall for every session of the match. Davis bowed out on a winning note, beating Lindrum 78-67 in the best of 155 frames.

Two semi-final appearances, in 1947 and 1951, saw him beaten by Walter Donaldson on each occasion, but in 1952 he was contesting the final again. Following a split in the professional ranks, the championship consisted of only two competitors – Lindrum and fellow Australasian Clark McConachy. Lindrum won 94-49, and at last the world title – albeit a hollow one – was his.

Not only did Horace Lindrum have a pleasing personality, but his style of play was a treat to watch. He retired from competition play in 1957 and became one of the world's leading exhibition players; he then came out of retirement in 1963 to take part in – and win – the Australian Open Championship. And in 1967, at the age of 55, he broke his own New Zealand break record with a break of 143.

Still playing in 1970 he did, in March that year, become the first man to record 1,000 snooker century breaks in public. Four years later the snooker world mourned the loss of the last in the long line of the famous snooker-playing Lindrum family when Horace died at the age of 62.

Career highlights
- World Professional Snooker Championship (runner-up) 1936, 1937, 1946
- World Professional Snooker Champion 1952

Lindrum, Walter

Although he was primarily a billiards player, it would be impossible to compile a snooker encyclopedia without including Walter Lindrum. Without a doubt he was the greatest billiards player who ever lived.

Born in Kalgoolie in 1898, he was the son of Fred Lindrum, the Australian native billiards champion. (Walter's brother Fred Junior was also Australian champion.) The family connection with the game went back even further: Walter's grandfather, Fred I, was also a prolific billiards player. It was Fred I who took the family to Australia from their home in Plymouth, England.

Holder of the current official world billiards break record of 4,137, Walter Lindrum beat W.J. Peall's old record of 3,304 in 1932, when, playing against Joe Davis at Thurston's, he made his record break in 2 hours 55 minutes, over three sessions.

Fast scoring, as well as high scoring, was a notable feature of Lindrum's game. In 1929, against Willie Smith, he made a 1,000 break in 36 minutes. And he once made a century break in 29 *seconds*. Another feature of his game was his sportsmanship – he never queried a referee's decision.

A natural right-hander, he learned also to play left-handed because part of one of the fingers on his right hand was missing. He made his first billiards century break at the age of 12, and by the time he was 16 he had compiled a 500 break.

He competed in only two world billiards championships, in 1933 and 1934, and won both, defeating Joe Davis each time.

Walter Lindrum never took snooker seriously – he left that to his successful nephew Horace. He retired from competition play in 1950 to concentrate on playing exhibitions, mostly for charity; one youngster who used to play exhibitions with him was Eddie Charlton.

Awarded the OBE in 1958, Lindrum collapsed and died suddenly while on holiday two years later, on 30th July 1960. His contribution to the game of snooker was very little; but his contribution to the game of billiards was immense.

Career highlights
World Professional Billiards Champion 1933-34

Longworth, Steve

Former mail-order delivery van driver Steve Longworth certainly delivered the goods when he reached the semi-final of the English professional championship in his first season as a professional in 1984-85. The 36-year-old who (like Dennis Taylor) lives in Blackburn crowned his amateur career by winning the Man of the Series award in the 1983 Home International series and followed this up by beating Wayne Jones to win the English amateur championship in 1984.

Walter Lindrum (top) – possibly the greatest billiards player ever, and Horace Lindrum (above, with Joe Davis)

His victory over Jones in the final of the English amateur, at the Commonwealth Sporting Club, Blackpool, was a formality after the end of the first session. Longworth led 6-2, and then extended the lead to 11-5 at the end of the next session. He won the required two more frames to win 13-8, and thus became the first Lancastrian since David Taylor (in 1968) to win the title.

Longworth was accepted as a professional at the third time of asking but a disastrous start to his new career resulted in his nearly giving the game up. However, his wife Madeleine talked him out of it, and it was shortly afterwards that he had his good run in the English professional championship, beating Ray Edmonds, Mark Wildman, Paul Medati and Jimmy White before losing 9-6 to Tony Knowles in the semi-final.

The following season he got into the top 32 thanks to another good run, this time in the Rothmans Grand Prix, when, after beating John Parrott and David Taylor, he reached the last 16 before losing to Kirk Stevens.

Apart from a last 16 appearance in the Tennents United Kingdom Open in 1986-87, the season had little cheer for Steve Longworth...until the world championships came around. He beat Tommy Murphy in the final qualifying round to reach the Crucible for the first time. He then enjoyed a great win over Kirk Stevens before falling to the talented youngster Stephen Hendry. The two ranking points he collected at the Crucible were enough to keep him in the top 32 for the 1987-88 season.

Career highlights
English Professional Championship (semi-final) 1985
English Amateur Champion 1984

Lowe, Ted

It is not as a player that Ted Lowe has made his contribution to snooker but as an organizer, administrator, and broadcaster. The senior BBC commentator, he has been broadcasting on the sport since 1954, and until 1978 his was the only voice heard on television commentaries.

Lowe was General Manager of the famous Leicester Square Hall from the time it opened its doors in 1947 until January 29 1955, when it was his sad duty to close the doors for the last time. He got the job at Leicester Square Hall following a meeting with Joe Davis in 1945. As secretary of the Smith's Meters Social Club, he arranged for Davis to attend the club to give an exhibition. It was then that the two of them got talking, and as Davis was a director of the Leicester Square Hall, he later invited Lowe to become its General Manager.

Fortunately, just before the closure of the Hall, Lowe was starting to carve out a career for himself in broadcasting. In September 1954, the leading sports commentator of the day, Raymond Glendenning, was scheduled to commentate on a snooker match. He was taken ill, and Lowe was called in as a late replacement. He covered the event so successfully that he became the regular snooker commentator for the BBC.

It was Lowe who devised the formula for the popular BBC *Pot Black* series. Asked by producer Phillip Lewis to submit a format for a snooker programme, Lowe came up with an idea which has changed very little since its introduction in 1969. Not only did he devise *Pot Black*, but he was responsible for getting the relevant professionals together to compete in it.

Then in 1977, while enjoying a day at Chester races, Lowe met BBC producer Nick Hunter and convinced him the Corporation ought to look at further snooker coverage, and it was under Hunter's guidance that the world professional championships were covered extensively in 1978. Until then Lowe's was the only voice heard on televised snooker commentaries,

Ted Lowe introduces the world championships at the Crucible Theatre, although the partition has other ideas...

but with the world championships held over two weeks he needed help, and it came in the shape of Jack Karnehm and Clive Everton, who joined him in the commentary box.

Lowe, brought up in the horse-racing village of Lambourne in Berkshire, has also commentated on bowls matches for the BBC, and in his organizing capacity was a founder member of both the Referees' Association and the Professional Billiard Players' Association. He was also responsible for arranging the first meeting between Joe Davis and Horace Lindrum in England. He is known as 'Whispering' Ted Lowe because of his dulcet tones behind the microphone, and his expert knowledge of the sport is acknowledged by most – including the players themselves.

Lucania Snooker Halls

The name Lucania has been synonymous with billiards and snooker for nearly 70 years. Five men, led by William and James Berry, owners of the Merthyr Tydfil Express, met in Merthyr on December 15, 1919, with the intention of forming a company with a capital of £100,000 to build, purchase, or rent suitable accomodation to convert into billiard halls, and thus meet the demands of working miners in South Wales, and of the many men returning from the war with leisure time on their hands.

Billiard halls were already popular in the area, but were attracting the wrong type of client. The new company, which intended to call itself the Welsh Billiards and Recreation Company, wanted to allow people to play billiards in comfort. By the mid-thirties the number of halls they managed was well in excess of 100. Many of them were above the shops of Burtons the tailors, who purposely built first floor accommodation on their premises for use as either billiard halls or ballrooms.

Lucania clubs were opened throughout South Wales as well as the south and west of England. But the war years brought a decline in billiards and snooker popularity, and in the fifties and sixties many of the club's tables were broken up in order to sell the slate, often for paltry sums.

The second chapter of the Lucania story started in November 1974, when Barry Hearn was installed as chairman of the Lucania group after Kendall House Investments – of which he was Financial Director – acquired the 17 remaining Lucania Halls. The increased popularity of snooker led to the opening of the first new Lucania since the 1930s, at Thornton Heath, in 1976. Since then the name Lucania has entered snooker legend as the 'birthplace' of Steve Davis.

Hearn's company sold 16 of the 17 halls to the Riley Leisure Group in 1982 and the name of the one remaining Lucania in his charge was changed to the Romford Snooker Centre.

How the clubs came to be called Lucania is not clear. There are two accounts. The first relates that the company acquired fittings from the SS LUCANIA which was torpedoed during the first world war. As a mark of respect for the sunken ship the company placed at least one item of its fittings in each of their clubs, and named them after her.

The second, more likely version is that the founders failed to agree on a name for the company at their inaugural meeting in 1919, and the solicitor present suggested that it be named after the premises in Wellington Street, Merthyr, where the meeting was being conducted. That name was Lucania Buildings.

...but Ted Lowe, a true professional, carries on regardless

M

McConachy, Clark

New Zealander Clark McConachy appeared in his first world billiards championship in 1932. He appeared in his last final in 1968 – 36 years later.

McConachy was unquestionably the greatest billiards and snooker player ever produced by his country. He was adept at both sports, although he had a preference for billiards.

In 1914, as a 19-year-old from Timaru, he won the New Zealand professional billiards title. He held it undefeated for the remainder of his career. McConachy was at his peak at the same time as those other legends – Joe Davis, Tom Newman and Walter Lindrum. In terms of trophies won, he may not have been their equal; but in skill, he certainly was. He proved his real all-round ability in 1932 when he contested both the world billiards and the world snooker finals. McConachy was defeated in both – by Joe Davis. However, the year did have some cheer for him, as he recorded the highest billiards break of his career, at Thurston's, when he made a break of 1,943.

Famous for playing in a green eye-shade, McConachy is also remembered as being the first player to make billiards breaks of 1,000 in two successive visits to the table. In 1951, nineteen years after his first attempt at a world title, he got his second chance when he met the young Englishman John Barrie in the billiards final. This time the title was McConachy's.

This was the first world billiards final since 1934 and the last until 1968. In that year Rex Williams made the trip to Auckland to challenge McConachy for his title. McConachy was now 73 years of age, and suffering from Parkinson's disease, which affected his cue arm. The pundits gave him no chance of beating the younger Williams, but he put up a tremendous fight and in the end he only narrowly lost, by just 265 points.

Owner of a billiard hall, like his father before him, he carried on playing and coaching well into his eighties. He died at home in Auckland just five days before his 85th birthday. A great ambassador for the sport, Clark McConachy was awarded the MBE in 1964.

Career highlights

- World Professional Billiards Champion 1951
- World Professional Snooker Championship (runner-up) 1932, 1952
- World Professional Billiards Championship (runner-up) 1932, 1968

McIlrath, Lesley

With Fran Lovis, Lesley McIlrath has dominated Australian ladies' snooker in the seventies and eighties. The pair of them have met in the Australian championship final on four occasions, and after losing to Lovis three times, Lesley McIlrath eventually gained revenge by winning the 1980 final. She won her second title the following year when she beat Ann Green (formerly Ann Depac) in the final.

Not only did Lesley win her first Australian title in 1980; she

'Whispering' Ted Lowe in his normal role. The senior BBC snooker commentator, he has been broadcasting on the sport since 1954, and, until the 1978 world championships, his was the only voice heard on BBC television commentaries

also registered the best win of her career that year, taking the Guinness World Open at Hayling Island. She beat off 45 challengers to take the then record prize for a ladies' event, £700, by beating Agnes Davies 4-2 in the final.

Attempting to retain her world title in 1981, she lost to Sue Foster at the quarter-final stage.

When the event was next held, in 1983, it was again Sue Foster who ended Lesley's hopes of getting the title back. This time they met in the semi-finals, and Sue Foster won 6-5, winning on the final pink.

Lesley McIlrath turned professional in 1983, and was looking forward to spending the summer of 1984 playing in Britain; in particular she was looking forward to competing in the new National Express Grand Prix. However, things did not work out as planned. Three days before the opening event at Abertillery, she underwent an appendix operation. She reached the last eight, but shortly afterwards returned to Australia disillusioned, and never competed in any more National Express events.

Career highlights
- 1976 Australian Championship (runner-up)
- 1977 Australian Championship (runner-up)
- 1979 Australian Championship (runner-up)
- 1980 World Open Champion
  Australian Champion
- 1981 Australian Champion
  Pontins Ladies Champion
- 1982 Australian Championship (runner-up)

See also Australia
Women's snooker

McLeod, Murdo

One of six Scots to turn professional in 1981, Murdo McLeod was the highest ranked of them in the 1984-85 season, having moved into the top 30 of the WPBSA rankings. Born in Edinburgh and now based at Livingstone, he has achieved his best results to date in his native Scotland. His best wins by far were the Scottish professional title in 1983 and 1985, beating Eddie Sinclair in the final on both occasions. When McLeod won the 1983 title it was the first time in three attempts that he had progressed beyond the first hurdle, and he avenged his defeat at Sinclair's hands in the final of the Scottish open championship in 1975.

McLeod has been playing snooker for a long time. He was runner-up in the Scottish amateur championship final back in 1970, losing to Dave Sneddon. Between 1975 and 1980 he represented Scotland in the Home International Championships on 11 occasions; one of his best performances was in beating current professional Dave Martin in the 1979 event. Apart from his success in the Scottish professional championship, McLeod's best professional results have been beating Willie Thorne 5-4 in the second round of the Professional Players' Tournament in 1982, David Taylor by the same score in the 1984 Lada Classic, Eddie Charlton 5-1 in the first round of the 1984 Mercantile Credit Classic, and Willie Thorne – again – 5-0 in the second round of the 1985 Dulux British Open.

Maltese National Amateur Snooker Championships: Results (finals)

1947 L. Galea beat G. Taliana	**1962** A. Borg beat M. Farrugia	**1977** A. Borg*
1948 T.B. Olivier beat V. Reginiano	**1963** A. Borg beat M. Farrugia	**1978** P. Mifsud*
1949 L. Galea beat V. Naudi	**1964** M. Tonna beat P. Grech	**1979** P. Mifsud*
1950 W. Asciak beat L. Galea	**1965** A. Borg beat W. Asciak	**1980** J. Grech*
1951 W. Asciak beat L. Galea	**1966** A. Borg beat W. Asciak	**1981** J. Grech*
1952 A. Borg beat E. Bartolo	**1967** P. Mifsud beat A. Borg	**1982** P. Mifsud beat J. Grech
1953 A. Borg beat W. Asciak	**1968** P. Mifsud beat P. Grech	**1983** P. Mifsud*
1954 W. Asciak beat J. Regiano	**1969** P. Mifsud beat W. Asciak	**1984** T. Drago*
1955 A. Borg beat W. Asciak	**1970** P. Mifsud beat P. Grech	**1985** P. Mifsud beat T. Drago
1956 W. Asciak beat A. Borg	**1971** P. Mifsud beat J. Lodge	
1957 W. Asciak beat A. Borg	**1972** A. Borg beat P. Mifsud	
1958 W. Asciak beat A. Borg	**1973** A. Borg beat P. Mifsud	
1959 A. Borg beat P. Grech	**1974** P. Mifsud beat A. Grech	
1960 A. Borg beat M. Farrugia	**1975** P. Mifsud beat J. Grech	**Most wins:** 13 – Alfred Borg
1961 A. Borg beat P. Grech	**1976** P. Mifsud*	* Records not kept

His record in the world professional championship has been poor, and in his first three attempts at the event he failed to reach the competition proper.

Career highlights
Scottish Professional Champion 1983, 1985

Clark McConachy won the New Zealand professional snooker title in 1914 and held it for the rest of his career

Malta

During the war Malta became an important British military base. As a result, British servicemen brought snooker to the island, and after the war – in 1947 – the national championships were instituted.

Malta has produced two outstanding players in Alfred Borg (national snooker champion 13 times) and Paul Mifsud (11 times champion).

Borg held the Maltese national break record of 108 for 15 years until it was twice broken in 1984 – first by Joe Grech, and then by Tony Drago, who established a new world amateur championship record of 132 in Dublin.

Malta has twice staged world amateur championships: on the first occasion the world amateur billiards championships were held at the Malta Hilton Hotel in 1971; then in 1978, the world amateur snooker championships – in which Cliff Wilson beat Joe Johnson in the final – were held at the National Sports Pavillion. During the 1971 world championships, the World Council (now the International Billiards and Snooker Federation) was formed following a meeting at the Hilton.

Paul Mifsud has been Malta's leading international player. In addition to his 19 Maltese billiards and snooker titles, he was world amateur billiards champion in 1979 and runner-up to Doug Mountjoy in the 1976 world amateur snooker championships. In 1983 Mifsud became Malta's first-ever professional, but the following year he resigned his membership of the World Professional Billiards and Snooker Association. However, Malta was not without a professional for long, because exciting prospect Tony Drago was accepted as a professional in 1985. In 1984, at 18 years of age, Drago was the youngest-ever winner of the Maltese title.

Drago went to Dublin for the world championships as one of the favourites, but his safety play let him down and he lost in the quarter-final to Englishman Chris Archer.

Drago was already well known to the Dublin crowd, as he had beaten Steve Newbury in the final of the Seiko Tallaght Open in that city earlier in the year. He was also, by the time the world championships came around, a regular member of the British amateur scene. He did not disappoint the Dublin crowd with his fine style of play, which saw him produce century breaks in successive frames, and also set up the new championship record break.

Murdo McLeod, the first Scot ever to win a match at the Crucible in the World Championships

Mans, Perrie

Perrie Mans, the likeable South African, followed in his father's footsteps when he took up professional snooker, and has gone on to become his country's best-known player. Perrie's father, Peter, was South African champion 13 times, and was the country's first professional champion. He used to play Joe Davis and, with the aid of a seven-point start, used to beat him. He showed his true potential when he reached the quarter-final of the world professional championships in 1950, before losing to Canadian George Chenier.

Perrie Mans (his real name, which he prefers, is Pierre) is from Johannesburg, and used to spend many hours as a youngster practising at one of his father's two snooker halls, the St James's Club in Jameston. In 1960, when only 19, he entered his one and only South African amateur championship, and won it. Five years later he won his first native professional title. He subsequently held the title (contested on a challenge basis) every year from then until 1981 with the exception of 1979 when he lost to Derek Mienie.

The British public were treated to the long-potting skills of the left-handed South African in the mid-seventies when he was a regular competitor on the British circuit. And his ornately decorated waistcoats made him quite distinguishable.

Invited to play in the BBC Television *Pot Black* series in 1977, he went on to win it, beating another player making his *Pot Black* début, Doug Mountjoy, in the final.

The following year Perrie Mans reached the number two position in the world, due to a memorable world professional championship, in which he lost in the final to Ray Reardon. Having beaten three former finalists – John Spencer, Graham Miles and Fred Davis – on his way to the final, he led Reardon 18-17 at one stage, but eventually lost 25-18.

His best win as a professional came in 1979 when he beat Ray Reardon, Cliff Thorburn and then Alex Higgins in the final, to win the Benson and Hedges Masters. Since those days he has slipped down the world rankings, and in 1981 dropped out of the top ten for the first time in six years. This slide down the rankings has been largely due to his spending more time back home in his native South Africa.

In the mid-seventies there was little professional opposition in his home country. That is no longer the case, and he prefers to play there rather than make the long haul to Britain to compete. In addition Perrie Mans is, along with fellow professional Jimmy van Rensburg, a promoter of snooker events in South Africa. Away from the table he is a keen pigeon fancier, and has enjoyed considerable success at that as well.

Career highlights

- World Professional Snooker Championship (runner-up) 1978
- Benson & Hedges Masters Champion 1979
- *Pot Black* Champion 1977
- South African Professional Champion 1965-77, 1980-84
- South African Amateur Champion 1960

Marathons

In the 1940s and 1950s, week-long matches in the world championships were commonplace. The 1952 world final between Horace Lindrum and Clark McConachy was the best of 187 frames (the current world championship final is contested over the best of 35 frames).

As matches vary in the number of frames played, it is impossible to say which has been the longest drawn-out. It is possible only to recall frames and sessions that have been notably long.

The longest frame on record lasted 76 minutes and was in the 1985 world doubles championship at Birmingham. It was between Les Dodd and his Canadian partner Jim Bear, who were playing Bill Werbeniuk and Eddie Charlton. Seventh seeds Charlton and Werbeniuk eventually won 5-4 but it took over five hours.

The longest frame in a singles match was in the 1980 world championship match between Cliff Thorburn and Doug Mountjoy. It lasted 69 minutes.

The 1981 world championship qualifying match between Jack Fitzmaurice and Mario Morra lasted 9 hours 8 minutes, and the last session lasted a then record, for an unbroken session, of 5 hours 20 minutes.

In the 1983 world championship Cliff Thorburn and Terry Griffiths broke the record for the longest session and the latest finish to any match in the championships. Their second round match finished at 3.51 a.m. and the final session lasted a record 6 hours 25 minutes. Thorburn's quarter-final match with Kirk Stevens lasted 6 hours 11 minutes, and finished at 2.12 a.m. This is the second latest finish, and second longest session in the championships. For good measure, Thorburn's semi-final meeting with Tony Knowles lasted 4 hours 45 minutes.

The record for the latest finish in the world championship, before the Thorburn-Griffiths clash, also involved Griffiths – against Eddie Charlton in 1979. It finished at 1.39 a.m. and lasted 5 hours 25 minutes.

Martin, Dave

Dave Martin caused a sensation and became famous overnight in 1981 when he reached the semi-final of the Jameson International at the Derby Assembly rooms. An unknown, and a professional for less than 12 months, Chesterfield-based Martin beat John Dunning, Bill Werbeniuk, Eddie Charlton and Graham Miles to reach the semi-final stage of the tournament. In the semi he met Dennis Taylor and despite crashing out 9-1, he had done enough to establish himself.

By his own admission, he made the mistake of thinking that the success and the television publicity was his passport to further success. He was wrong, however, and he now knows that no matter how successful a player is, he still has to work hard at his sport. And that is what Martin has been doing ever since.

He is never treated lightly by his fellow professionals, as he is always capable of bringing off a major surprise. And in 1984 – back at the Derby Assembly rooms – he did just that when he reached the final of the Yamaha International Masters. After playing through the qualifying competition he beat off the challenge from Australian Paddy Morgan and David Taylor in his three-man group in the competition proper before winning his semi-final group containing the experienced pair of Eddie Charlton and Ray Reardon. In the final he was in a group with Yorkshireman John Dunning, and Steve Davis. He beat Dunning for a guaranteed second place, but was no match for Davis, who beat him 3-0 to clinch the title.

Martin's professional career started in 1981 when, after two applications to turn professional had been turned down, he won a WPBSA professional ticket tournament. It was surprising to many that he was not accepted on either his first or his second applications, as he had represented his country in the Home International Championship on nine occasions, and was runner-up to Jimmy White and Joe O'Boye respectively in the 1979 and 1980 English Amateur championships. With John Spencer and Ray Edmonds he is one of the only three people to have been defeated in successive finals since the war. With D. Reed he also formed the winning combination that took the national pairs title in 1978.

Despite maintaining his position in the top 32, Martin has not got as close to winning a title as he did in 1984. But success could just be around the corner for him.

Eddie Charlton and Terry Griffiths, whose 1979 world championship semi-final was a marathon of safety play

Career highlights
- Yamaha International Masters (runner-up) 1984
- Jameson International (semi-final) 1981
- National Pairs Champion 1978 (with D. Reed)

Match

A match is an agreed number of games. At club level it is rare to have a match in which only two players are involved. Matches normally involve teams of players, and their aggregate game, or frame, scores are taken into account to decide the match result.

A good example of this is the Home International Championships. Each team consists of six players and the six competing nations play each other in a series of round-robin matches. At the end of the match the totals of all frames won by each team are added together to decide the result of the match. For example the results of the England versus Scotland match in the 1986 championships were as follows:

England		Scotland	
A. Harris	1	R. Lane	2
M. Clark	2	K. McIntosh	1
G. Grennan	2	S. Nivison	1
G. Filtness	3	B. Kelly	0
G. Wilkinson	1	J. Allen	2
R. Marshall	3	J. McNellan	0
Total	12	Total	6

There has been one occasion when the world professional championship was decided on matches. This was in 1965, when Rex Williams challenged John Pulman for the title. They played a series of matches all over South Africa; defending champion Pulman won by 25 matches to 22.

Matchroom League

The Matchroom League was the idea of Barry Hearn. His seven players, plus Cliff Thorburn, travelled around Britain and played a series of matches against each other on a League basis. The event was sponsored by Rothmans and carried a first prize of £50,000. The players all met each other once in an 8-frame match. Three points were awarded for a win and one for a draw. The League started at Torbay in January 1987 and finished at Liverpool four months later. Steve Davis won the first prize. He lost two matches, to Jimmy White and Cliff Thorburn, while runner-up Neal Foulds only lost once, to Davis. The highest break of the League was 136 by Terry Griffiths.

Final Table:

	P	W	D	L	F	A	PTS
Steve Davis	7	4	1	2	36	20	13
Neal Foulds	7	3	3	1	31	25	12
Jimmy White	7	3	2	2	27	29	11
Terry Griffiths	7	2	3	2	28	28	9
Dennis Taylor	7	2	2	3	28	28	8
Tony Meo	7	2	2	3	26	30	8
Cliff Thorburn	7	2	2	3	25	31	8
Willie Thorne	7	1	3	3	23	33	6

Perrie Mans in action, in one of his ornate waistcoats

Mans away from the table, more soberly dressed

Maximums

At one time the scoring of a maximum 147 break in snooker (15 reds with 15 blacks, followed by all the colours) was regarded as the equivalent of running a sub-four-minute mile in athletics. And in fact, the first official maximum came less than a year after Roger Bannister's historic run in May 1954. Since then, the running of a four-minute mile has become commonplace, whereas the 147 break in snooker is still a rarity.

Many players have made unofficial maximums in practice conditions. Willie Thorne and Cliff Thorburn are champions in this respect with well over 20 each (although many of Thorburn's were made on Canadian tables which have more generous pockets). The making of 'official' 147s has, however, been restricted to just five instances.

The first witnessed maximum was in Australia in 1934, when New Zealander Murt O'Donoghue recorded one. Horace Lindrum, Leo Levitt and Clark McConachy all made maximums that were never ratified because they were not on standard tables. It was, perhaps inevitably, Joe Davis who made the first official maximum, in 1955. Since then there have been four other official maximum breaks.

These five official maximums were made as follows:

22 Jan 1955
Leicester Square Hall,London
Joe Davis v Willie Smith
Exhibition match.

22 Dec 1965
Cape Town, South Africa
Rex Williams v Mannie Francisco
Exhibition match

11 Jan 1982
Oldham Civic Centre, Lancashire
Steve Davis v John Spencer
Lada Classic

23 Apr 1983
Crucible Theatre, Sheffield
Cliff Thorburn v Terry Griffiths
World Professional Championships

28 Jan 1984
Wembley Conference Centre, London
Kirk Stevens v Jimmy White
Benson and Hedges Masters

The 147 break by Steve Davis in the Lada Classic was the first in tournament play to be officially ratified as a record. The first maximum actually made in tournament play was by John Spencer in the 1979 Holsten Lager Tournament at Slough. The break was disallowed for record purposes, however, because the table had oversize pockets.

For a break to be recognized as official, it must be shown to have been made on a table with pockets of the correct size according to the templates approved by the Billiards and Snooker Control Council (see the illustrations accompanying the entries on Pockets and Templates).

Mark Boyd of Accrington (17) compiled two maximum breaks within three weeks in 1986, and with a different cue each time!

Brian Morgan of Southend was officially confirmed as the youngest person ever to compile a maximum, which he did in February 1986. He was 17 years 6 months and 17 days old at the time, two weeks younger than Tony Meo when he performed the feat in 1976.

Although 147 is regarded as the 'maximum' break, it is technically possible to register a break of 155: if a player's opponent leaves him in a free-ball situation, he may take a colour ball as a red, and then a black. With eight points already on the scoreboard, he can then continue the break with all the reds still on the table.

This has never happened officially, but Alex Higgins came close to a 155 in 1976 when, against Willie Thorne, he took all 16 'reds' but could only manage to take 10 blacks. His break was 146. Cliff Thorburn also came close to a '16-red maximum' in 1984 when he cleared up by taking all 16 reds in a match with Geoff Foulds. But again he could not manage a black with each of them, and his break was 139.

The diagrams on pages 82-83 show how Steve Davis took the final red and then continued to make his historic maximum in the 1982 Lada Classic.

Meo, Tony

In 1972 Tony Meo had to choose between staying in England or returning with his Italian parents to their homeland. Born in London, the 13-year-old decided to stay to be near his friends. That same year he took up snooker, after having played most sports but not found one which he really liked. Before long his talents were spotted, and Tooting taxi driver Bob Davis took Meo and his school mate from the Ernest Bevin Comprehensive school, Jimmy White, under his wing. The pair of them developed fast and became too big for Davis to manage, and they subsequently teamed up with London's top player of that time, Patsy Fagan, under the managership of Henry West.

In 1976 Meo, at 17, became the youngest person ever to compile a maximum 147 break when he did so against Terry Whitthread. His first big win came in 1977 when he beat professional Doug Mountjoy 5-4 in the final of the Warners Pro-Am tournament. That same year he beat White in the final of the Pontins Junior competition at Prestatyn, and in 1978 he beat two-times winner of the National Under-19 championship, Ian Williamson, to win the title.

That same year he was the discovery of the Canadian Open, of which he reached the final. He led Cliff Thorburn 10-6 at one stage before eventually losing 17-15. But his victory over Alex Higgins in the semi-final was the best win of his career so far.

He turned professional in June 1979, leaving the amateur ranks with a win over Jimmy White to take his second Warners Open final.

Dave Martin

Tony Meo

It did not take Meo long to hit the headlines as a professional. In the following year's United Kingdom professional championship – the one that gave Steve Davis his first major win – he eliminated defending champion John Virgo in the second round 9-1, but lost to Davis.

In 1981 Meo came close to winning his first major competition, but he lost to Steve Davis in the final of the inaugural English professional championship. He did, however, win that year's Winfield Australian Masters. The left-hander joined with Davis under Barry Hearn's management before the end of the year, and that served to boost his confidence.

He teamed up with Steve Davis to win the inaugural world doubles title in 1982 – Meo's first major professional win – and the pair retained it the following year. Meo beat Silvino Francisco in the final to win the Pontins professional title at Brean Sands in 1983, and proved himself a notable doubles player by winning the pairs title with Jimmy White.

He was holder of two world titles simultaneously in 1983 when, with Steve Davis and Tony Knowles, he helped England to win the World Team Classic.

That first big individual title still eluded him, but Meo came close to winning it in the 1984 Lada Classic. In the final, against Steve Davis yet again, he was leading Davis 8-7 and needed just one frame for victory. He was in a commanding position and had an easy shot on the yellow, followed by fairly easy colours to win the game and the title. It was not to be, however, as someone in the crowd distracted him by shouting out. He missed the yellow and Davis proceeded to win that, and the next, frame.

He reached number ten in the world rankings in 1984 and the following year he won his first major individual title when he beat Neal Foulds in the final of the English Professional Championship. Despite beating Les Dodd to retain the title 12 months later, Meo did not fare too well in ranking events and when he lost to John Parrott in the first round of the world championships at Sheffield, he slipped out of the top 16, the only member of the Barry Hearn troup to start the 1987-88 campaign outside that élite.

Career highlights
- English Professional Champion 1986-87
- Lada Classic (runner-up) 1985
- Hofmeister World Doubles Champion (with Steve Davis) 1982-83, 1985-86
- World Cup Champion (with Steve Davis) 1983
- Winfield Australian Masters Champion 1981, 1985
- Pontins Professional Champion 1983
- Pontins Doubles Champion 1983 (with Jimmy White)
- National Under-19 Snooker Champion 1978
- Pontins Junior Champion 1977

Mercantile Credit Classic

The Mercantile Credit Classic was first introduced into the professional calendar in 1980 as the Wilson's Classic, with northern brewers Wilsons as the sponsors. It attracted television coverage, but only on Granada television. However, when the Czechoslovakian car company Lada took over the sponsorship in 1982 the event was networked.

Lada could hardly have wished for a better start to their first year as sponsors because it was during the tournament, at the Oldham Civic Hall, that Steve Davis compiled the first televised 147 break. Only eight competitors took part in the first tournament but the fans were treated to a classic final between Davis and Terry Griffiths, which the Welshman won 9-8.

When the Lada Classic moved to its new home at the Spectrum Arena, Warrington, in 1983, capacity crowds were a key feature and from the enlarged field of 16 Steve Davis and Bill Werbeniuk emerged as the two finalists. Although it was the biggest payday of the Canadian's career he could not thwart Davis, who won his second title.

Davis retained his title the following year but only after being pushed all the way by stablemate Tony Meo, who went down 9-8. That was the final Lada event, but it certainly had some memorable moments. There was a break of 143 by Rex Williams and there was the birth of a new superstar, John Parrott, who, after beating Doug Mountjoy, Alex Higgins and Tony Knowles (5-1), had the chance to beat Davis in the semi-final. However, he lost an extremely tense contest 5-4.

Finance company Mercantile Credit stepped into the breach when Lada pulled out in 1984, and the new tournament has also enjoyed some memorable moments.

The first Mercantile was won by Willie Thorne, who took his first major title, but many of the seeded players (eight of the top 16) fell at the untelevised stage. One of the unfancied players was Joe Johnson, who reached the semi-final before losing to Cliff Thorburn, but he proved, at last, that he could play in front of the television cameras – good practice indeed for what he was to do less than 18 months later at the Crucible.

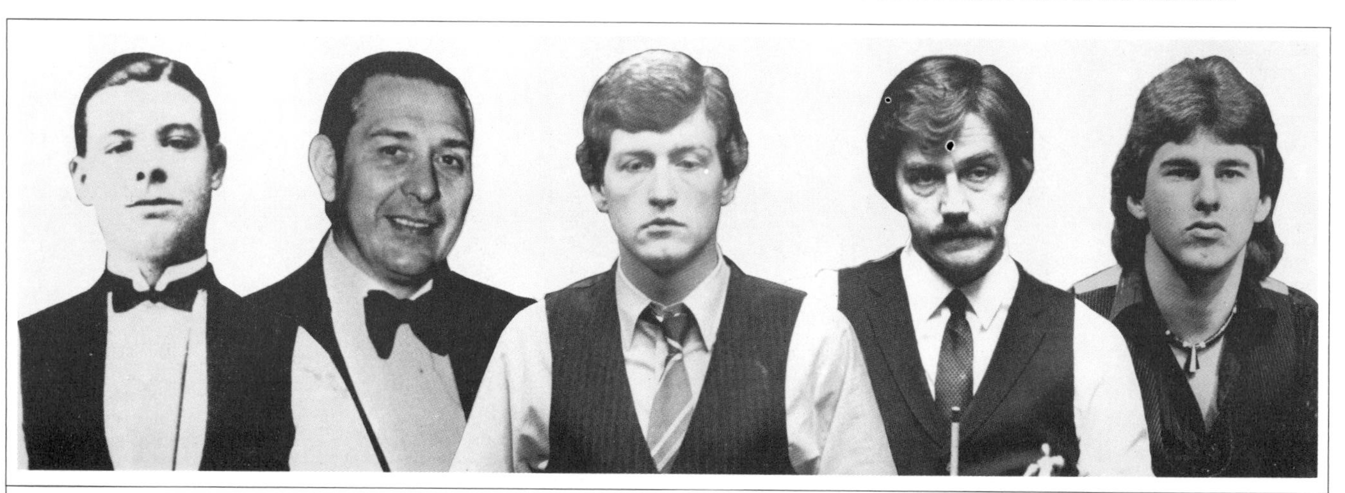

The only players to have made official maximum breaks: Joe Davis, Rex Williams, Steve Davis, Cliff Thorburn and Kirk Stevens

Willie Thorne, winner of the inaugural Mercantile Credit Classic in 1985 – his first major professional title

Jimmy White collected the £45,000 winner's cheque in 1986 after winning a thriller against Cliff Thorburn by 13 frames to 12, and that was after White forfeited a frame for arriving late for the second session – the first time since 1979 anybody had forfeited a frame for that reason.

When Steve Davis beat White, also 13-12, to win the title in 1987, he completed a unique treble as he had won the title under all three sponsors, Wilsons, Lada and Mercantile. The 1987 Classic was notable for more than the great final, it saw the emergence of two talented youngsters, both of whom had been tipped as stars of the future. One was Humbersider Dean Reynolds and the other was the Scot Stephen Hendry. Both reached the semi-final stage.

Mercantile Credit Classic: Results (finals)

1980 (Jan) J. Spencer (England) 4 A. Higgins (Ireland) 3
1980 (Dec) S. Davis (England) 4 D. Taylor (Ireland) 1
1982 T. Griffiths (Wales) 9 S. Davis (England) 8
1983 S. Davis (England) 9 B. Werbeniuk (Canada) 5
1984 S. Davis (England) 9 T. Meo (England) 8
1985 W. Thorne (England) 13 C. Thorburn (Canada) 8
1986 J. White (England) 13 C. Thorburn (Canada) 12
1987 S. Davis (England) 13 J. White (England) 12

Most wins: 4 – Steve Davis
Most finals: 5 – Steve Davis
Highest break: 147 – Steve Davis (1982)

Mifsud, Paul

By far the best billiards and snooker player produced by Malta, Paul Mifsud became the country's first-ever member of the WPBSA in 1983.

However, he decided to resign his membership in 1984 after a personal sponsorship deal fell through; he felt he could not afford to take time off work and pay his own fares to England to compete. Malta therefore lost its one and only professional.

Mifsud, from Zeebug, first attracted attention at the 1972 world amateur snooker championships in Cardiff when he won his qualifying group (which including eventual winner Ray Edmonds) without losing a match. Mifsud, however, was taken ill during the competition and was rushed to hospital with a collapsed lung. He made a speedy recovery, but was naturally weakened by his illness and was eliminated from the tournament soon after.

He did not compete in the 1974 world championship, but two years later he impressively beat defending champion Ray Edmonds and top South African Jimmy van Rensburg in the quarter and semi-finals respectively. In the final, though, he was no match for Welshman Doug Mountjoy, who won by a record 11-1 margin.

A quarter-finalist in the 1978 championship, he lost to Canadian Kirk Stevens, and in 1980 he lost at the semi-final stage to eventual winner Jimmy White. He led White 6-4 before losing 8-6. In 1982 he maintained his excellent record in the event, reaching the quarter-final stage before losing to eventual finalist Jim Bear of Canada.

It is not only at snooker that Paul Mifsud has shone. He is an outstanding billiards player as well. He has won the Maltese amateur snooker championship on 13 occasions, and the bil-

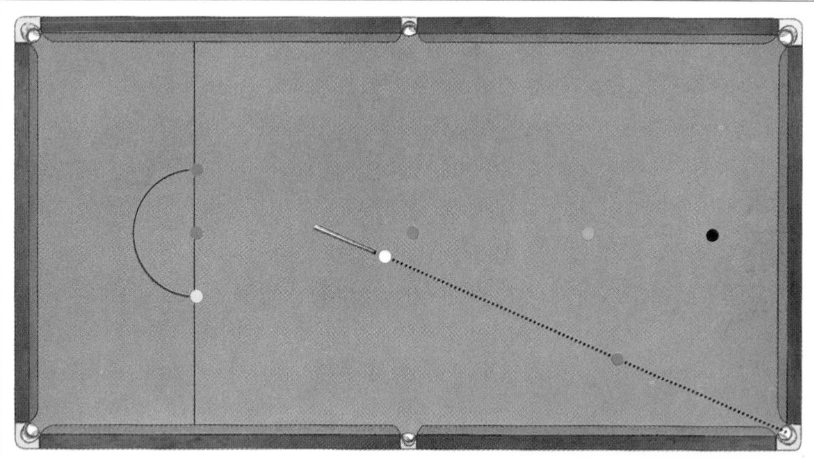

1. This was the situation confronting Steve Davis after he had potted all but one of the reds and taken a black with each one. The red went in, but the cue-ball was not in quite the right position to get him on the yellow after the black...

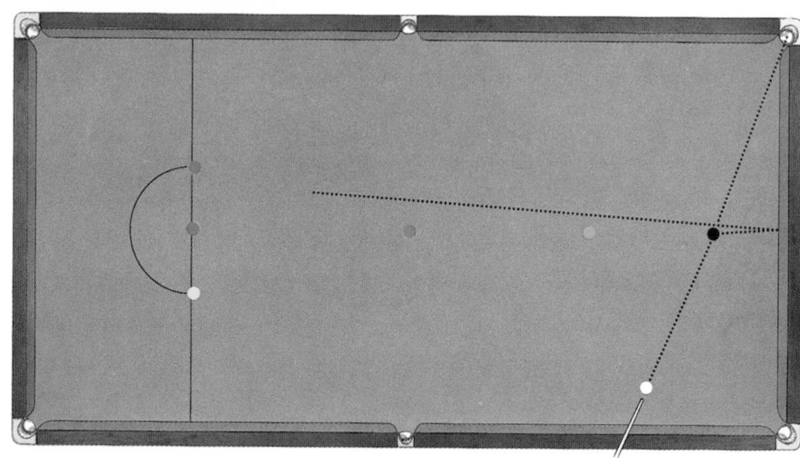

2. Davis put a lot of left-hand side on the cue-ball so that it would not hit the pink after coming off the cushion: the black went in, but position on the yellow was not perfect – it was too straight for an easy continuation of the break with the green...

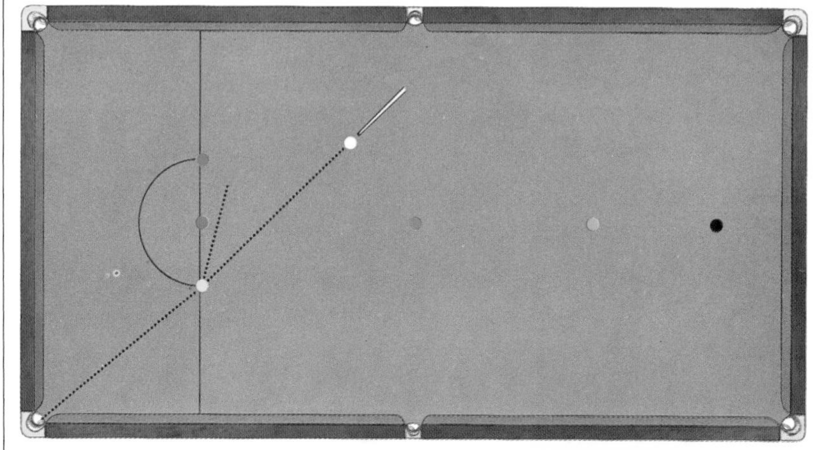

3. This time a screw-shot was called for to achieve a good position on the green, but a kiss on the brown could be disastrous. Davis managed to avoid this, but it was going to be difficult to hold position for the brown when the green was potted...

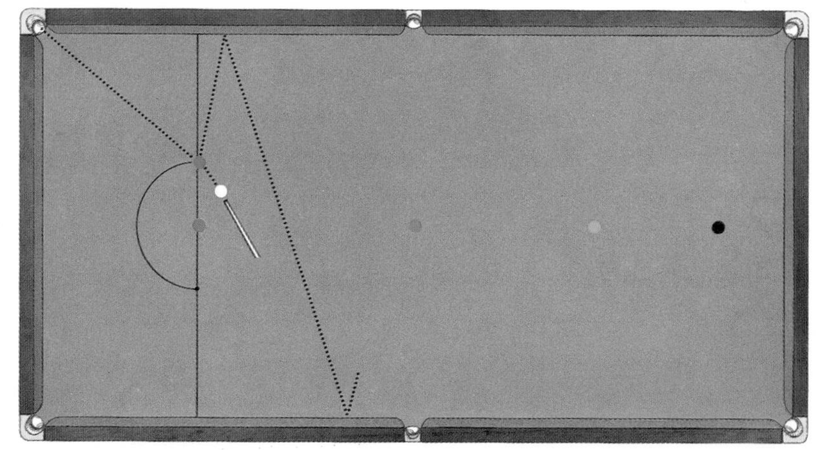

4. The problem here was to keep the cue-ball from travelling to the top of the table after the pot. Davis had to put a lot of left-hand side on the ball to hold it in the centre of the table...

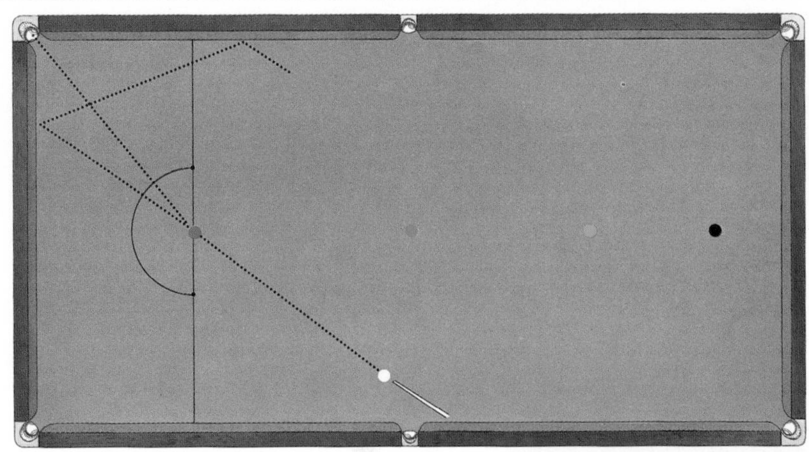

5. Davis knew well what shot he had to play, but he did not hit the cue-ball correctly and made the wrong contact with the brown. The cue-ball ended up too near the side cushion for comfort, and on an unfavourable angle for holding position on the pink after the blue...

6. A gentle shot, running the blue into the pocket would have meant no position on the pink, so he went off three cushions to get into the ideal position. Davis regarded this as his best shot of the break...

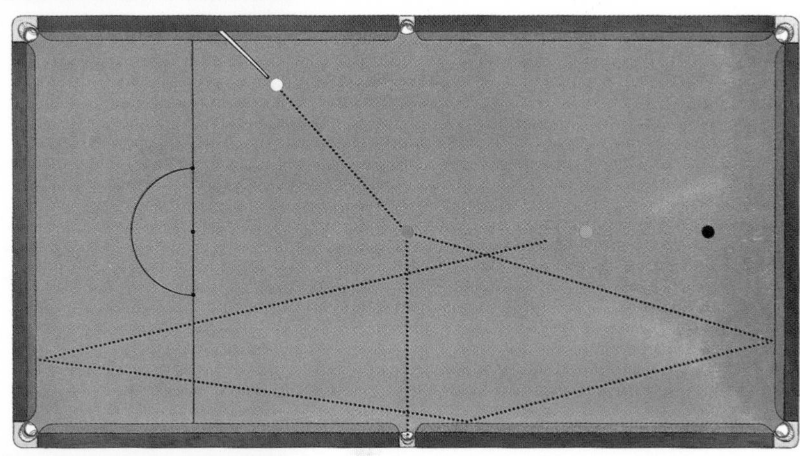

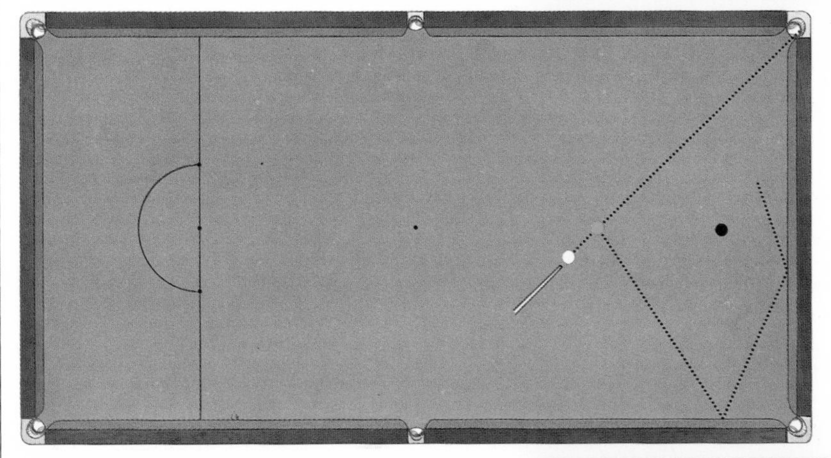

7. A lot of right-hand side was needed in order to hold the cue-ball in position for the final black...

8. One hundred and forty down, seven to go – a shot of this nature would normally be no problem to Steve Davis, but in circumstances like these the pressure is intense. However, he made no mistake: the black went down, and a piece of snooker history was made.

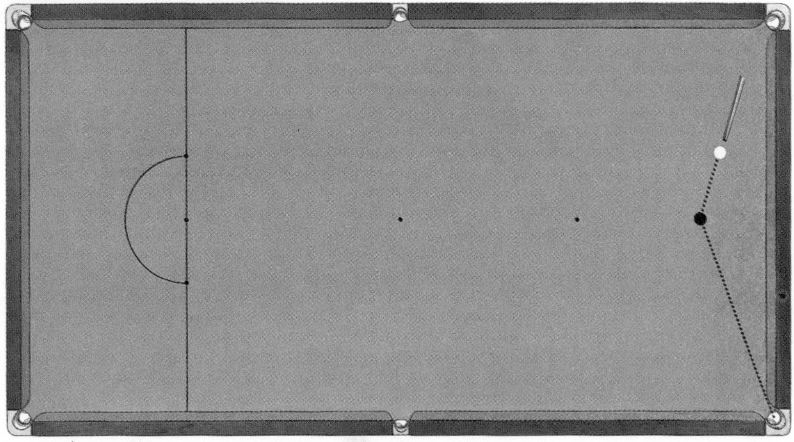

Paul Mifsud – indisputably Malta's leading player of both billiards and snooker

liards title eight times, and in 1979 he beat Britain's Norman Dagley to win the world amateur billiards title in Colombo, and thus became only the second man after Mannie Francisco to have reached the final of both the world amateur billiards and snooker championships.

Mifsud really returned to form in 1985 when he took the world amateur title in Blackpool, to become the first man to win world amateur titles at both billiards and snooker. He retained his snooker title at Invercargill, New Zealand, in 1986 by beating Welshman Kerry Jones in one of the best matches ever seen in the history of the championship.

Career highlights
- World Amateur Snooker Champion 1985, 1986
- World Amateur Billiards Champion 1979
- Maltese Amateur Snooker Champion 1967-71, 1974-76, 1978-79, 1982-83, 1985
- Maltese Amateur Billiards Champion 1968, 1970, 1972-76, 1978

Miles, Graham

The sport of snooker as a whole has a lot to thank the BBC's *Pot Black* programme for: so, as an individual, does Birmingham's Graham Miles. Invited into the 1974 programme as a late replacement for Fred Davis who withdrew because of illness, Miles went on to win the series. Furthermore, he retained the title the following year to become only the third man (after John Spencer and Eddie Charlton) to win the title twice. His 1975 victory saw him beat Reardon, Spencer, and Eddie Charlton on the way to the title – and those three were, at the time, the only previous winners of *Pot Black*.

The television coverage earned him popularity and fame. Exhibitions followed, and success bred success. Runner-up to Ray Reardon in the 1974 world professional championship, Miles was one of the best players on the professional circuit in the mid-seventies, and was ranked number five in the world in 1976. He also reached the final of that year's Benson and Hedges Masters, losing again to Reardon.

Miles has a very distinctive cueing style, but the one thing that has been lacking in his game, particularly in recent years, has been the killer instinct.

Twice Midlands amateur champion, he turned professional in 1969, but left the amateur game with few honours, and he had to wait until the 1974 *Pot Black* series for recognition.

Since those glory days of the mid-seventies, there have been very few successes. He created a championship record break, however, of 139 in the 1978 United Kingdom Professional championships in his match with Willie Thorne, but in the semi-final he was thrashed 9-1 by Mountjoy. A further *Pot Black* final appearance came that year, but yet he suffered defeat at the hands of Doug Mountjoy. The following year Mountjoy beat him again, in the final of the Pontins Professional championship at Prestatyn. Defeat in the Holsten Lager Tournament at Slough by John Spencer followed, also in 1979, and in the same year Miles reached the final of the World Team Cup, along with John Spencer and Fred Davis – only to be defeated by a Welsh team that contained his bogey-man, Doug Mountjoy, yet again.

Since the start of the eighties his only tournament victory was in the Tolly Cobbold Classic at Ipswich in 1981, when he beat Cliff Thorburn 5-1 in the final.

Away from the snooker table, however, the former diesel fitter with the Birmingham City Corporation is making a living for himself as a successful businessman, running a building business and a snooker centre.

Career highlights
- National Breaks Champion 1966
- *Pot Black* Champion 1974, 1975, 1978
- World Professional Championship (runner-up) 1974
- Benson and Hedges Masters Championship (runner-up) 1976
- Tolly Cobbold Classic Champion 1981

Mountjoy, Doug

A former miner from Ebbw Vale, Doug Mountjoy has remained consistent on the professional circuit since winning the 1977 Benson and Hedges Masters, his first professional event.

Although well-known in his native south Wales, Mountjoy, an excellent break-builder, gained national recognition in 1974. He travelled north to Prestatyn, to win the coveted Pontins Open title. He beat experienced professional John Spencer (who conceded 25 points per frame) in the final, and in doing so he became the first amateur to win a first prize of £1,000.

Having been runner-up in the Welsh amateur championship in 1966, he won the title in 1968 and again in 1976. That second victory enabled him to compete in the world amateur championships in Johannesburg. He returned from South Africa not only as champion, but having registered a record winning 11-1 margin in the final, against Malta's Paul Mifsud. Mountjoy was in devastating form throughout the championship, winning all eight of his group matches and then destroying Australian Ron Atkins and South African Silvino Francisco in the quarter- and semi-finals respectively.

He turned professional shortly after winning the world title, and he was selected as a late replacement for the 1977 Benson and Hedges Masters. To everyone's amazement he went on to win the title beating fellow Welshman Ray Reardon in the final. He then went on to reach the quarter-final of that year's world professional championships, and before the year was out he had also been a finalist in the inaugural United Kingdom Professional championship, where he lost to Patsy Fagan.

Mountjoy won the United Kingdom title the following year, and since then he has maintained his record of reaching a major final every year. His biggest moment came in 1981 when he reached the final of the world professional championship. He had started that year with an illness that left part of his face paralysed, but he recovered sufficiently to go on to reach the world final, where he came up against Steve Davis, who won his first title. But on his way to the final, in his match with Ray Reardon, Mountjoy had established a new championship record break of 145. The year ended in sadness, however, because his brother was tragically killed in a boating accident.

Mountjoy's first major win was that Pontins victory back in 1974, and since then he has earned himself a reputation as a specialist at the Prestatyn snooker week. He regained his Open title in 1976, when still an amateur, and in 1979 he won the professional title to become only the second man (after Ray Reardon) to win both titles. He won the professional title again in 1983, and reached his fifth Pontins final in the Open the following year, although this time he succumbed to fellow professional Neal Foulds.

Pot Black is another tournament at which Doug has done well. He competed in his first season as a professional and went on to reach the final, where he lost to Perrie Mans. He beat twice winner Graham Miles in 1978, and in that year's competition he became only the second man (after Eddie Charlton) to compile a century break in the tournament. A third successive final appearance followed in 1979 when he lost to Ray Reardon. He is one of only two men to have appeared in three consecutive finals; John Spencer is the other.

As an amateur Mountjoy represented Wales 16 times between 1969 and 1976, and he has since represented them in the World Team Classic as a professional, helping them to the title in 1979 and 1980. He has also added to his two Welsh amateur titles by winning the Welsh Professional title three times.

Apart from winning his fourth Welsh Professional title in 1987, Doug Mountjoy has had little to celebrate in recent years. Defeat in the final of the 1985 Benson and Hedges Masters by Cliff Thorburn, and a semi-final defeat by the same man in the 1986 Mercantile Credit Classic have been his best performances over the past two seasons. He has, however, maintained his top 16 position after picking up ranking points in all ranking tournaments in 1986-87, with the exception of the Mercantile Credit Classic. He knows full well that any slight deteriation in 1987-88 will see him replaced in the top 16 by any one of a host of youngsters.

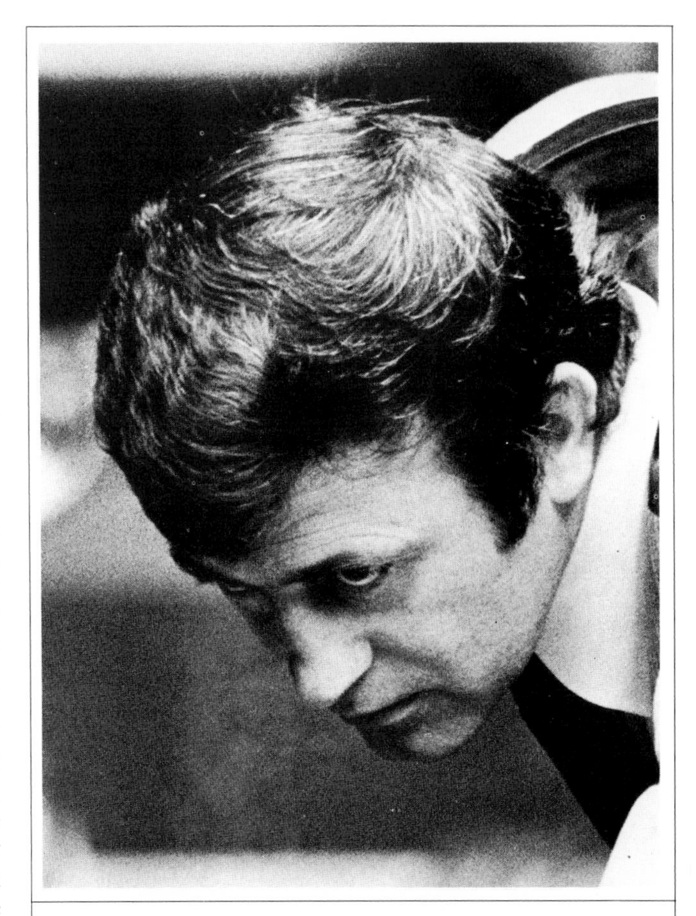

Doug Mountjoy – a consistent performer and something of a specialist at Pontins and Pot Black

Career highlights

- Benson & Hedges Masters Champion 1977
- Coral United Kingdom Professional Champion 1978
- Benson & Hedges Irish Masters Champion 1979
- World Cup winner (with Wales) 1979-80
- Welsh Professional Champion 1980, 1982, 1984, 1987
- Pontins Professional Champion 1979, 1983
- *Pot Black* Champion 1978
- World Amateur Champion 1976
- Pontins Open Champion 1974, 1976
- Welsh Amateur Champion 1968, 1976
- National Breaks Champion 1970

Tony Meo – characteristically well dressed

Graham Miles – the stance is unmistakable

N

National Breaks Competition

On 7 December 1948 the Billiards Association and Control Club announced that from the end of the 1948-49 season, it would organize a National Breaks Competition. The event was open to all billiards and snooker players over the age of 16 on January 1. The winner of the prize, in the case of both games, was the person compiling the highest certificated break during the season – in other words, the highest break that met the association's conditions.

Some famous players have won the snooker title: former world amateur champion and world professional finalist Gary Owen was the second winner – and winner again ten years later. The 1982 world amateur champion Terry Parsons won the title in 1964, and current professionals Dennis Taylor, Graham Miles, Doug Mountjoy and Mike Watterson have all won the competition.

Watterson was the last winner of the snooker title, in 1976, and, as winner the previous year, is the only person to have won the snooker competition outright in consecutive years.

With big breaks becoming a more regular occurrence, the competition was abandoned at the end of the 1975-76 season.

National Championships

See appropriate country.

National Express Women's Grand Prix

The National Express bus company invested £60,000 in women's snooker in 1984 with the introduction of their Grand Prix series. Women's snooker had been a potential growth area for some time, and the promoters felt that time was now right to launch the leading female players on the British public. Sadly, however, the public did not respond and attendance levels were very disappointing.

The series saw 16 women visit five different venues around Britain. At each venue they played a knockout tournament with each winner receiving £2,500. Points were awarded during the series, depending on how far they progressed in each competition, and there was a £5,000 snowball prize to the overall points winner. The cash incentive was enough to bring Vera Selby back into competition for the first time since winning her second world open title in 1981. But England's Mandy Fisher dominated the series. She was the overall points winner, and won two of the five legs; only once did she fail to reach the final.

The competition started at the Abertillery Sports Centre, where it received television coverage from HTV. However, that was the only television coverage the series received; at later competitions the attendances were very poor, and the idea – which was potentially a good one – fell upon stony ground.

Doug Mountjoy, in the familiar red shirt, signs autographs for some young fans

National Pairs Championship

The idea of a national pairs competition was conceived in 1969, when Watneys sponsored an event which was won by the Bolton pair of Stan Haslam and Stan Holden.

The first championships organized by the Billiards and Snooker Control Council were in 1975, and between then and 1982 the event was a sponsored one. Coral (UK) Limited sponsored it from its first year until 1980, after which Guinness sponsored it for one year, in 1981. Since then, however, it has been run by the B&SCC.

Between 250 and 350 pairs take part in the event each year and all games are the best of five frames.

National Team Championship

Although several team championships had been played since the mid-fifties, the first one to be organized by the Billiards and Snooker Control Council was in 1975.

The competition involved teams of two men in that first year and the following year, but since 1977 it has been for teams of three, each member playing two frames against one member of the opposing team. In the event of a tie a one-frame sudden-death play-off was held.

The event was unsponsored until 1979, when the tobacco company State Express – the then sponsors of the professional world team championship – stepped in, and continued to sponsor the event until 1981. The B&SCC ran the event for three more years without the aid of a sponsor, but, with the number of entries dwindling to around 120, it has not been held since 1984.

New Zealand

The New Zealand billiards championships, first held in 1908, are the second oldest national championships after the English. Surprisingly, it was another 19 years before the New Zealand Billiards and Snooker Association was formed following its inaugural meeting in 1927 at Christchurch.

Billiards had been introduced into New Zealand in the 1880s but it was not until after the first world war that snooker came to the fore. The national snooker championships were inaugurated in 1945, and the first winner was Sam Moses.

New Zealand produced two top-class players in Norman Squire and Murt O'Donoghue (the first man to compile a 147 break at snooker), but their achievements were overshadowed by those of New Zealand's greatest ever billiards and snooker player – Clark McConachy.

World professional billiards champion from 1951 until 1968, McConachy narrowly lost his title to Rex Williams. McConachy was 73 years of age at the time, Williams was 35, yet only 265 points separated the two men at the end of the match. McConachy also contested the professional snooker final on two occasions, losing to Joe Davis in 1932 and to Horace Lindrum 20 years later.

National Breaks Competition – Results (winners)

1949 W.J. Thomas (Birmingham) 95
1950 G. Owen (Great Yarmouth) 127
1951 G.M. Wright (Skegness) 114
1952 P. Houlihan (Deptford) 122
1953 M. Parkin (Sheffield) 111
1954 S.W. Walklett (Leytonstone) 134
1955 D. MacVeigh (Dagenham) 139
1956 L. Adams (Birmingham) 118
1957 T. Scott (Kidderminster) 126
1958 G.M. Cox (Dudley) 140
1959 M. Berni (Neath) 133
1960 G. Owen (Birmingham) 142
1961 M. Berni (Neath) 145
1962 W.G. Smith (Romford) 145
1963 W.J. West (Hounslow) 145
1964 T. Parsons (Penygraig) 143
1965 J. Shepherd (London) 139
1966 G. Miles (Birmingham) 139
1967 D. Thomas (Llanelli) 133
1968 C. Coulthard (Durham) 142
1969 G. Dodd (Newcastle) 138
1970 D. Mountjoy (Monmouth) 139
1971 D. Taylor (Blackburn) 136
1972 J.A. Beech (London) 137
1973 R. Pittock (Deal) 136
J.A. Beech (London) 136
1974 R. Brown (London) 143
1975 M. Watterson (Chesterfield) 144
1976 M. Watterson (Chesterfield) 146

Most wins: 2 – John Beech
2 – Mario Berni
2 – Gary Owen
2 – Mike Watterson
Highest break: 146 – Mike Watterson (1976)

National Express Women's Grand Prix – Results

Ist Leg: Abertillery Sports Centre
Sue Foster (England) 6
Georgina Aplin (England) 1
Top break: 38 Sue LeMaich
38 Georgina Aplin (twice)

2nd Leg: Armley Sports & Leisure Centre
Mandy Fisher (England) 7
Maryann McConnell (Can) 2
Top break: 40 Maryann McConnell

3rd Leg: Beechdown Squash Club
Sue LeMaich (Canada) 7
Mandy Fisher (England) 5
Top break: 62 Mandy Fisher

4th Lèg: Werrington Sports Centre, Peterborough
Sue LeMaich (Canada) 7
Mandy Fisher (England) 5
Top break: 48 Sue Foster

5th Leg: Strathallan Hotel, Birmingham
Mandy Fisher (England) 7
Maryann McConnell (Canada) 6
Top break: 44 Maryann McConnnell

Snowball points competition
Leading positions:
Ist Mandy Fisher 64 points
2nd Maryann McConnell 44 points
3rd Sue LeMaich 41 points
4th Sue Foster 39 points

National Pairs Championship – Results (finals)

1975 M. Berni & J. Selby beat
F. McCourt & G. Wood
1976 P. Medati & J. Virgo beat
D. Hughes & W. Kelly
1977 R. Bales & C. Everton beat
H. Laws & J. Pike
1978 D. Martin & D. Reed beat
H. Laws & J. Pike
1979 S. Newbury & C. Wilson beat
J. Fitzmaurice & M. Suckling
1980 H. Burns & D. French beat
T. Green & D. Grimmer
1981 R. Coles & W. Oliver beat
H. Burns & D. French
1982 J. Griffiths & Z. Lembick beat
R. Coles & W. Oliver
1983 G. Keeble & M. Smith beat
D. Hoggarth & G. Thomas
1984 P. Fryatt & A. Putnam beat
E. Hobson & A. Trigg
1985 A. Emmott & M. Unsworth beat
R. Brown & P. Remond
1986 P. Fryat & A. Durham beat
K. Owers & S. Meakin
1987 S. Brooke & P. Carney beat
G. Laney & G. Lee

National Team Championship – Results (finals)

1975 Merthyr Tydfil Ex-Servicemen's Club
beat Ashton-in-Makerfield Cricket Club
1976 Potters Club (Salford) beat
Finedon Gladstone Club (Northants)
1977 Cannock Snooker Centre
beat A.O.H. (Londonderry)
1978 Lucania (Romford)
beat Western Social Club (Middlesbrough)
1979 Western Social Club (Middlesbrough)
beat Abertysswg WMC (Wales)
1980 North Midland Snooker Centre (Worksop)
beat Abertysswg WMC (Wales)
1981 Ron Gross Snooker Club (Neasden) beat
Whitmore Reans Conservative Club (Wolverhampton)
1982 Ron Gross Snooker Club (Neasden)
beat Sutton Cricket Club (St Helens)
1983 Mackworth Snooker Club (Neath)
beat Minnesota Fats Snooker Club (Glasgow)
1984 Dawley Social Club (Shropshire)
beat Midland Snooker Centre (Hanley)

New Zealand National Amateur Snooker Championships: Results (finals)

1945 S. Moses*
1946 J. Munro*
1947 W. Thompson*
1948 L. Stout*
1949 L. Stout*
1950 L. Stout*
1951 N. Lewis*
1952 L. Stout*
1953 L. Stout*
1954 R. Franks*
1955-6 L. Stout*
1957 W. Harcourt*
1958 W. Harcourt*
1959 W. Thomas*
1960 T. Yesburg beat R. Franks
1961 R. Franks beat T. Yesburg
1962 R. Murphy beat B. Kirkness
1963 W. Harcourt beat K. Tristram
1964 T. Yesburg beat L. Glozier
1965 L. Napper beat D. Smiler
1966 L. Napper beat W. Harcourt
1967 R. Flutey beat L. Napper
1968 L. Napper beat B. Clapham
1969 L. Glozier beat L. Napper
1970 K. Tristram beat R. Flutey
1971 B. Bennett beat W. Hill
1972 N. Stockman beat S. Rota
1973 W. Hill beat K. Tristram
1974 K. Tristram beat N. Stockman
1975 K. Tristram beat L. Napper
1976 D. Kwok beat P. Mifchesuski
1977 D. Meredith beat J. Kawana
1978 D. Meredith beat L. Adams
1979 D. Meredith beat B. Kirkness
1980 D. O'Kane beat P. Mifchesuski
1981 G. Kwok beat C. Polamalu
1982 D. Kwok beat D. Allen
1983 D. Kwok beat H. Haenga
1984 G. Kwok beat S. Robertson
1985 P. de Groot beat H. Haenga
Most wins: 7 – L. Stout
* Records not kept

New Zealand's billiards and snooker 'legend' died in 1980. And, by coincidence, a new star emerged that year: a 16-year-old by the name of Dene O'Kane won the national snooker title, and three years later he broke the New Zealand snooker record break when he made a total clearance of 138 in an invitation event at the Waitomo Club, Tekuiti. This break surpassed the record of 128 made by Brian Kirkness at Christchurch in December 1977.

O'Kane was accepted as a professional in 1984 – the first New Zealander since McConachy to become a professional. Early indications are that O'Kane will enjoy a successful career.

In Brien Bennett New Zealand is fortunate to have one of the sport's great administrators. A former national champion, he represented his country in three world amateur championships. He was awarded the Queen's Service Medal (QSM) in 1984.

New Zealand not only boasts the second oldest national championship in the world, but their national billiards final of 1976 produced the only occasion of father (Herbie Robinson) and son (Russell Robinson) meeting each other in a national championship final. Herbie won.

The world amateur championship was held in New Zealand in 1986, when the Ascot Park Motor Hotel, Invercargill, played host to the tournament.

New Zealand's Brian Bennett – chairman of the International Billiards and Snooker Federation

Newbury, Steve

When Steve Newbury turned professional in 1984 the question people within the sport were asking was: Can he afford to do so? In 1983, as an amateur, he had won over £8,000 in prize-money, and was the envy of many professionals. He took three £2,000 first prizes – in the Ealing Open, the South of England Open, and the Gordon Hamilton Trophy in Glasgow. The first two came within a three-week spell.

But his decision to turn professional soon paid dividends. A 5-2 win over Bill Werbeniuk in the first round of the Jameson International guaranteed him £3,000 for reaching the next round, where he narrowly lost, 5-4, to Tony Knowles. He followed up his Jameson performance with an excellent win over Terry Griffiths in the Dulux British Open at Derby.

Newbury is, in fact, something of a bogey-man to Griffiths. But Griffiths also has a lot to thank him for – indirectly: on the way to his first Welsh amateur final in 1978, where he lost to Alwyn Lloyd, Newbury eliminated Griffiths 4-0 in the quarter-final. The latter having no chance of making the world amateur championships that year, made the decision to turn professional; less than a year later he was holder of the world professional title. Newbury had a distinguished amateur career. He turned his Welsh amateur final defeat to victory in 1980, when he gained revenge over Alwyn Lloyd; in between those two finals he won the National Pairs title with fellow Welshman Cliff Wilson. He also reached the quarter-final of the 1980 world amateur championship in Launceston, losing 5-4 to Jimmy White, the eventual winner.

At international level as an amateur, Steve played for Wales

33 times. He showed great promise in his first professional season, 1984-85, reaching the last 16 of both the Jameson International and Dulux British Open. He reached 34th place in the rankings but slipped slightly in his second season to finish in 45th place.

Despite another drop in the rankings in 1986-87, from 40th to 45th, Steve enjoyed the greatest moment of his professional career when he reached the final of the Welsh Professional championship. After beating Ray Reardon and then Terry Griffiths, he lost the final 9-7 to another seasoned campaigner, Doug Mountjoy.

Steve is not the only snooker-playing member of the Newbury family: his sister Sian reached the final of the 1980 Pontins Ladies' championship, losing to Mandy Fisher.

Career highlights
- Welsh Professional Championship (runner-up) 1987
- National Pairs Champion 1979 (with Cliff Wilson)
- Welsh Amateur Champion 1980

Newman, Tom

A true Cockney, Tom Newman was born in 1894, within the sound of Bow Bells, as Tom Pratt. He established himself as one of the best billiards players of the 1920s, appearing in every world billiards championship final between 1921 and 1930, and winning the title six times – a record which has remained unbeaten this century, although Rex Williams has equalled it.

Newman was a great break builder at billiards, and was a master of the cannon shot. His first century break at the 'three-ball game' came when he was just 11 years of age; and in the 1930-31 season he made over 30 breaks of 1,000.

Like so many players of that era he regarded snooker as the less 'serious' of the two sports, but nevertheless he made an officially recognized record snooker break of 89 in 1919, and in 1934 reached the world championship final. He met the legendary Joe Davis in that final – a predictable clash, since they were the only two contestants!

That same year he met Davis in the United Kingdom billiards final and again Newman came out second best. He met Davis in six world finals, the honours being equally distributed overall at three wins each.

Tom Newman died in 1943, just short of his 50th birthday.

Career highlights
- World Professional Billiards Champion 1921-22, 1924-27
- World Professional Billiards Championship (runner-up) 1923, 1928-30, 1934

Tom Newman – a great billiards player, but second of two to Joe Davis in the 1934 world snooker championships

News of the World Tournament

One of the leading post-war professional tournaments, the News of the World tournament used to carry annual prize-money of £1,500 – a large sum in those days. The first tournament was held at the Leicester Square Hall in 1950, with the leading snooker players of the day taking part in a round-robin competition. Joe Davis, because of his superiority, was handicapped and had to concede anything from seven to 20 points. Despite his handicaps, Davis still managed to win the first event in 1950, and he won it on two other occasions.

One notable feature of the competition was the number of high breaks, and in his match with Albert Brown in 1955 Davis equalled the world record with a break of 146. (A few weeks later, at the same venue, he bettered this record when he registered the first official maximum.)

The competition was last held in 1959, when Joe's brother Fred became the last News of the World champion. It was during this last championship that Joe Davis introduced the game of Snooker Plus.

Northern Ireland

Although Northern Ireland has only five members of the World Professional Billiards and Snooker Association, two of them, Alex Higgins and Dennis Taylor, are among the élite of professional snooker players. But they, and many snooker players in Northern Ireland, have another current Irish professional to thank for their inspiration – Jackie Rea.

Rea, a professional for nearly 40 years, has given a lot to the sport – mostly in his role as comedian and extraordinary exhibition player. But he was also a skilful match player and did much to popularize the sport in Northern Ireland. In terms of victories however, Alex Higgins has been by far Ireland's most successful professional player, with two world titles among his many honours.

The Northern Ireland Billiards Association and Control Club was founded in 1924, and three years later the inaugural national snooker championships were held – (although the national billiards championships had been first held two years earlier). Since 1935 there has been an all-Ireland championship in which the winner of the Northern Ireland title meets the winner of the Republic of Ireland title to decide the all-Ireland crown.

One of the first oustanding Northern Ireland players was Jack Bates. National snooker and billiards champion in 1947, 1948 and 1949, he turned professional and won the Irish professional title in 1951. He lost it the following year to Jackie Rea (who went on to hold the title for 20 years) and reverted to amateur status. He then went on to win the national billiards titles of the Republic of Ireland and Scotland.

News of the World Tournament – Results

1950 Winner: Joe Davis
Runner-up: Sidney Smith
Top break: 130 – Joe Davis

1951 Winner: Alec Brown
Runner-up: John Pulman
Top break: 143 – Joe Davis

1952 Winner: Sidney Smith
Runner-up: Albert Brown
Top break: 140 – Albert Brown

1953 Winner: Joe Davis
Runner-up: Jackie Rea
Top break: 132 – Joe Davis

1954 Winner: John Pulman
Runner-up: Joe Davis
Top break: 135 – Fred Davis

1955 Winner: Jackie Rea
Runner-up: Joe Davis
Top break: 146 – Joe Davis

1956 Winner: Joe Davis
Runner-up: Fred Davis
Top break: 110 – Joe Davis

1957 Winner: John Pulman
Runner-up: Fred Davis
Top break: 102 – John Pulman

1958 Winner: Fred Davis
Runner-up: John Pulman
Top break: 141 – Walter Donaldson

1959 Winner: Fred Davis
Runner-up: Joe Davis
Top break: 100 – Fred Davis

Most wins: 3 – Joe Davis

Highest break: 146 – Joe Davis (1955)

In recent years the country's leading amateur at international level has been Sammy Pavis. A former prolific goal-scorer with Irish soccer team Linfield, Pavis has appeared for Ireland on a record 30 occasions in the Home International snooker championships. In 1982 he played a part in promoting Northern Ireland from their usual last – or next to last – position in the table, as they finished a creditable third behind Wales and England.

It is, however, on the professional front that Northern Ireland are currently a major force. Not only do they have Higgins and Taylor among the top flight, but in Jack McLaughlin and Tommy Murphy they have two other players who are always capable of springing a surprise.

Both men have steadily moved up the world rankings, with Murphy enjoying slightly better success than McLaughlin. But it may not be long before they are offering a serious challenge to the country's top two professionals.

Fred Davis, winner of the last two News of the World tournaments in 1958 and 1959

One of Northern Ireland's sporting heroes – Dennis Taylor, 1985 world snooker champion

Northern Ireland Snooker Championships – Results (finals)

1927 G. Barron beat*
1928 J. Perry beat*
1929 W. Lyttle beat Capt. J. Ross
1930 J. Luney beat*
1931 J. McNally beat W. R. Mills
1932 Capt. J. Ross beat W. R. Mills
1933 J. French beat J. Chambers
1934 Capt. J. Ross beat W. Price
1935 W. Agnew beat Capt. J. Ross
1936 W. Lowe beat S. Brooks
1937 J. Chambers beat J. Blackburn
1938 J. McNally beat W. Sankon
1939 J. McNally beat S. Brooks
1940 Not held
1941 J. McNally beat A. Heron
1942 Not held
1943 Not held
1944 Not held
1945 J. McNally beat C. Downey
1946 J. McNally beat J. Rea
1947 J. Rea beat J. Bates
1948 J. Bates beat E. Haslem
1949 J. Bates beat J. Stevenson
1950 J. Bates beat J. Dickson
1951 J. Stevenson beat E. Haslem
1952 J. Stevenson beat D. Turley
1953 J. Stevenson beat J. Thompson
1954 W. Seeds beat J. Stevenson
1955 J. Stevenson beat M. Gill
1956 S. Brooks beat G. Lyttle
1957 M. Gill beat D. Anderson
1958 W. Agnew beat W. Hanna
1959 W. Hanna beat W. Seeds
1960 M. Gill beat D. Anderson
1961 D. Anderson beat M. Gill
1962 S. McMahon beat D. Anderson
1963 D. Anderson beat J. Clint
1964 P. Morgan beat M. Gill
1965 M. Gill beat S. Crothers
1966 S. Crothers beat W. Caughey
1967 D. Anderson beat S. Crothers
1968 A. Higgins beat M. Gill
1969 D. Anderson beat A. Higgins
1970 J. Clint beat N. McCann
1971 S. Crothers beat*
1972 P. Donnelly beat S. Pavis
1973 J. Clint beat S. McMahon
1974 P. Donnelly beat S. Pavis
1975 J. Clint beat S. McMahon
1976 E. Swaffield beat D. McVeigh
1977 D. McVeigh beat G. Maxwell
1978 D. McVeigh beat L. McCann
1979 R. Burke beat J. Begley
1980 S. Clarke beat D. McVeigh
1981 T. Murphy beat W. Mills
1982 S. Pavis beat K. Erwin
1983 J. McLaughlin Jnr beat J. McIntyre
1984 J. McLaughlin Jnr beat H. Morgan
1985 S. Pavis beat K. Erwin
1986 C. Sewell beat G. Campbell
1987 S. McClarey beat J. Swail

Most wins: 6 – J. McNally

All-Ireland Championship – Results

1935 S. Fenning (E) beat W. Agnew (NI)
1936 S. Fenning (E) beat W. Lowe (NI)
1937 P. O'Connor (E) beat J. Chambers (NI)
1938 J. McNally (NI) beat P. O'Connor (E)
1939 S. Fenning(E) beat J. McNally (NI)
1940 P. Merrigan (E) beat J. McNally (NI)
1941 P. Merrigan (E) beat J. McNally (NI)
1942 Not held
1943 Not held
1944 Not held
1945 J. McNally (NI) beat*
1946 J. McNally (NI) beat*
1947 J. Rea (NI) beat C. Downey (E)
1948 J. Bates (NI) beat P. Merrigan (E)
1949 J. Bates (NI) beat W. Brown (E)
1950 J. Bates (NI) beat J. Redmond (E)
1951 J. Stevenson(NI) beat P. O'Connor (E)
1952 J. Stevenson(NI) beat W. Brown (E)
1953 J. Stevenson(NI) beat S. Brooks (E)
1954 S. Fenning (E) beat W. Seeds (NI)
1955 J. Stevenson(NI) beat S. Fenning (E)
1956 W. Brown (E) beat S. Brooke (NI)
1957 M. Gill (NI) beat J. Connolly (E)
1958 J. Gibson (E) beat W. Agnew (NI)
1959 Not held
1960 Not held
1961 Not held
1962 J. Weber (E) beat S. McMahon (NI)
1963 D. Anderson (NI) beat J. Rogers (E)
1964 P. Morgan (NI) beat J. Rogers (E)
1965 M. Gill (NI) beat W. Fields (E)
1966 G. Hanway (E) beat S. Crothers (NI)
1967 P. Morgan (E) beat D. Anderson (NI)
1968 A. Higgins (NI) beat G. Hanway (E)
1969 D. Anderson (NI) beat D. Daley (E)
1970 J. Clint (NI) beat D. Sheehan (E)
1971 D. Sheehan (E) beat S. Crothers (NI)
1972 Not held
1973 Not held
1974 P. Donnelly (NI) beat P. Burke (E)
1975 Not held
1976 Not held
1977 Not held
1978 Not held
1979 E. Hughes (E) beat R. Burke (NI)
1980 D. Sheehan (E) beat S. Clarke (NI)
1981 T. Murphy (NI) beat A. Kearney (E)
1982 P. Browne (E) beat S. Pavis (NI)
1983 J. Long (E) beat J. McLaughlin Jnr (NI)
1984 Not held
1985 S. Pavis (NI) beat G. Burns (E)

Most wins: 4 – Seamus Fenning (E)
4 – J. Stevenson (NI)
(E) denotes Republic of Ireland
(NI) denotes Northern Ireland
(see also Irish Professional Championship)

* Records not kept.

Object-ball
The fifteen reds and the six colours are known as the object-balls (as opposed to the white, which is the cue-ball). They are never legally struck directly with the cue – only indirectly by the cue-ball.

See also Cue-ball

Oddities
Like all sports, snooker has enjoyed its fair share of unusual, odd and humorous moments. Here are just some of them.

☆ Lord Lonsdale, who was responsible for giving the Lonsdale Belt to boxing, was a great all-round sportsman. He was at one time the President of the Billiards Control Council, and in 1922 his horse, Royal Lancer, won the St Leger at Doncaster.

☆ Current professional Jon Wright is nicknamed 'Giro' because he used to cash his unemployment cheque to stake his next match when he was out of work.

☆ During the 1985 Australian Amateur Championship Phillip Tarrant was forced to retire from play for an hour with back trouble during his semi-final against John Gibbons. He returned after receiving treatment from a local football coach on a table in the boardroom of the Coomealla Memorial Club in New South Wales, where his match was being played.

☆ Current professional Malcolm Bradley is looking for some heavenly guidance in his latest venture: he bought the Christ the King Church in Cresswell, Derbyshire, with the intention of turning it into a snooker hall.

☆ Jim Meadowcroft was due to play Graham Miles in the 2nd round of the English Professional championship in 1987. Meadowcroft did not turn up for the match but still won a frame! Miles did turn up, but was late in arriving and thus forfeited a frame which was credited to Meadowcroft.

☆ Alex Higgins finished 3rd in a popularity poll in 1987. The poll, conducted by the London Dungeon Museum, was to see who visitors would most like to see locked in stocks and pelted with rotten fruit. The winner (easily!) was East Enders' Dirty Den, followed by the elusive gasman Sid.

☆ Playing at the Cherry Tree Hotel in St Helens in 1983, John Parrott made a break of 93 in which he potted neither a black nor a pink.

☆ In February 1981 Alex Higgins lost 11-8 to Ray Reardon in a one-day challenge match. The two men played out the 'dead' frames and in the first Higgins made a clearance of 130. He broke first in the next frame, fluked a red from the break, and proceeded to make a 141 break which meant he had made a continuous break of 271.

☆ John Spencer's and Paddy Morgan's concentration was broken during their match in the 1981 World Team Cup by… an alarm clock! Referee John Smyth had been out and purchased a new battery for his portable alarm on the morning of the match. He put the clock in his jacket pocket, and forgot about it. With a great sense of timing the alarm went off during the match.

☆ A notice inside the R & S Snooker Club in Morden, Surrey reads: 'Fire exit at rear of hall. Members only.' That's taking prejudice a bit far!

☆ In 1984, 18-year-old Steve Carr from Felling, Tyne and Wear, was granted a £40 per week enterprise allowance by the Department of Employment to allow him to play full-time snooker with a view eventually to becoming a professional. Carr, who had been unemployed since leaving school, was ordered by the Department of Employment not to *hustle* or play exhibition matches while he was receiving the allowance.

☆ In October 1947, Joe Davis was taking part in an exhibition at Truro, Cornwall, and a shot he played caused the cue-ball to hit a pocket, bounce off the table and hit the marker, Mr A. James, who was knocked unconscious. (Mr James recovered consciousness ten minutes later.)

☆ In his second-round match with Murdo McLeod in the 1982 Professional Player's Tournament, Willie Thorne made breaks of 94, 109, and 135 in consecutive frames, and yet he still lost the match 5-4.

☆ Still with Willie Thorne: he is reported to be the champion 'maximum' break maker, with over 50 to his credit in exhibition and practice matches. But he must stand unique as the only person to have made a maximum with both legs in plaster. Involved in a go-karting accident in 1982, he broke both legs below the knee, but that did not stop him from playing, and making 147s.

☆ The trophy awarded to the winner of the Lombard-RAC Rally each year is the W.J. Peall Trophy. The trophy was initially given to Peall by the Billiards Association in 1891 after he had won the 'All-in' Professional Billiards Championship on four occasions. It is not clear how the RAC got hold of the trophy, although it is known that Peall was a keen motorist.

☆ The only known instance of 'rain stopping play' in a snooker match was during the 1973 World Professional championships at the City Hall, Manchester. Rain seeped through the roof during the quarter-final match between Fred Davis and Alex Higgins, and on to the table. Play was held up while repairs were made.

☆ In October 1957 Walter Lindrum won a $100 bet from the Australian test cricketer Keith Miller when he compiled a billiards break of 50 in just 30 seconds; nothing unusual in that for a man of Lindrum's calibre except that the break was compiled on grass! Playing on the lawn of a suburban Melbourne house with six jam tins as pockets, Lindrum proved Miller wrong when he said a player's skill only depended on the surface on which he was used to playing and added: 'Even Walter Lindrum would have difficulty playing billiards on grass.' Lindrum could not resist the challenge; he duly won the match and passed his winnings on to a local charity.

☆ In 1983 Gary Miller and Stuart Alliston of Humberside took 1 hour 13 minutes to complete one frame of snooker. They used a potato as cueball.

☆ Current professional Paddy Morgan claims to be the only professional snooker player ever to have been a bus conductor in three countries: the Republic of Ireland, Australia and England.

O'Donoghue, Murt
New Zealander E.J. 'Murt' O'Donoghue has no 'career highlights' – simply because he won nothing of note. His name is, however, immortalized in snooker history, on two counts.

First, at Wellington on 2 May 1929 he is credited with making the first total clearance at snooker. He broke, potted one of

Fred Davis, the oldest player in the 1982 world professional championships, beat Dean Reynolds, the youngest, 10-7

the reds from the break (!) and then went on to clear the table.

Secondly, while playing Maurice O'Reilly on 26 September 1934 at O'Donoghue's own Sports and Billiards club at Griffiths, New South Wales, he became the first person to compile a maximum 147 break. Neither break was ratified as an official record but, nevertheless, Murt O'Donoghue is generally recognized as the first to achieve the maximum.

Born in Auckland in 1901, he spent most of his life and playing career in Australia. His only claim to fame was as above – he never won a national title, and never competed in the world championships.

O'Kane, Dene

New Zealander Dene O'Kane returned from the wilderness in 1987 when he reached the quarter-final of the world professional championship at the Crucible.

New Zealand amateur champion in 1980, when only 17, the British public had their first glimpse of him the following year when he was runner-up to Dean Reynolds in the inaugural *Junior Pot Black*. He turned professional in 1984, and in his first year he made the top 32 thanks to reaching the first round proper of the Jameson and the quarter-final of the Dulux British Open, where he lost 5-1 to Steve Davis.

By complete contrast, his second year was a disaster, and he only managed to win one game during the entire season. The 1986-87 season showed little signs of improvement – until the world championships. The man who turns to yoga and meditation to relax was certainly in the right frame of mind for the big event of the year. Feeling more relaxed than ever, possibly after joining the Winsor Management Group (which also managed Cliff Thorburn), O'Kane compiled five century breaks in the qualifying competition, including two against the much-fancied Peter Francisco in the last round before Sheffield. His 132 against Dave Gilbert and 130 against Ian Black were the two highest breaks of the entire championship.

In the first round at Sheffield he was paired against stablemate Thorburn, and when the Canadian raced to a 5-1 lead it looked as though the young New Zealander was on his way out. But the youngster won nine successive frames for a remarkable comeback.

He beat 1981 finalist Doug Mountjoy in the next round but then came up against Jimmy White in the quarter-final. O'Kane could not recover from an 8-0 deficit and went out 13-6.

Dene O'Kane has at last shown the standard he is capable of, and if he carries on the 1987-88 season where he left off then a top-16 place is a certainty in 1988.

Career highlights

World Professional Snooker Championship (quarter-final) 1987
Dulux British Open (quarter-final) 1985
New Zealand Amateur Champion 1980
Junior Pot Black (runner-up) 1981

Oldest

In reaching the final of the 1984 Yamaha Masters, Gildersome-based grandfather John Dunning became, at 56, the oldest man to reach the final of a major professional snooker tournament. Fred Davis however, is the champion of snooker longevity. He was 65 when he reached the final of the Castle Open at

Southampton in 1979. On his way to the final he beat some notable younger men, including Willie Thorne and Cliff Thorburn, before losing to Alex Higgins in the final. When Davis qualified for the competition proper at the 1984 world professional snooker championships in Sheffield, he was in his 71st year. In 1980, at 66, he had fulfilled a life-long dream by winning the world professional billiards title. He made one successful defence of the title, then in 1983 reached the final again.

Fred Davis is not, however, the oldest person to contest the world professional billiards title. That honour goes to Clark McConachy of New Zealand, who was 73 when he played the much younger Rex Williams for the title in 1968. Williams only narrowly won the title from the former champion.

The oldest person to win the world professional snooker championship is Ray Reardon, who was 45 years 6 months when he beat Perrie Mans for the title in 1978.

During the 1983 Pontins Open, Liverpool bookmaker Sid Lane compiled a break of 101 – at the age of 70; his previous century break had been 44 years earlier!

Australia's Bob Marshall reached the 1985 World Amateur Billiards final at the age of 75 – 49 years after he first won the title.

Owen, Gary

Like his younger brother Marcus, Gary Owen was outstanding as a junior and senior amateur. The first winner of the national under-16 snooker championship in 1944, he reached the final of the English amateur championship in 1950, despite the fact that he only played as a hobby at the time.

His second attempt at the English amateur title, 13 years later, saw him win the title by beating top amateur Ron Gross – three times winner of the title – in the final. That victory made him eligible to compete in the inaugural world amateur championships in Calcutta that year.

Born in Tumble, South Wales, Gary Owen spent two years in Great Yarmouth where he did his National Service. By the time the world championships came around he was living in Birmingham, where he was in the fire service. He went on to win the world title by winning all four of his matches in the round-robin competition. He retained his title in Karachi in 1966, and still remains one of only two men to have retained the title (Ray Edmonds being the other). His match with John Spencer was the deciding match; it not only clinched the title for Owen, but avenged brother Marcus's defeat by Spencer in that year's English amateur championship final.

With snooker going through a growth period in the late sixties Gary turned professional in 1968 along with Ray Reardon and John Spencer; the three of them became the first new professionals since 1951. The world professional championship reverted to a knockout-style competition in 1969, in which year Gary went all the way to the final. Here he was beaten by John Spencer, who thus made amends for his defeat in the world amateur championship three years earlier.

A brilliant potter, Gary Owen decided to emigrate in 1971 to become resident professional at a snooker club in Sydney. He rarely comes back to Britain, and the last time he came back for the world championships was in 1976 – he has never competed since the event moved to the Crucible Theatre.

John Parrott of Liverpool – one of the rising stars of English snooker. He played well in the 1985 world championships, but Ray Reardon proved too tough for him in their quarter-final match

He is still a professional player although he has now relinquished his membership of the WPBSA (unlike his brother Marcus). He competes very little at the top level, but has unsuccessfully challenged Eddie Charlton for the Australian professional title on several occasions.

Gary Owen was awarded the MBE in 1966.

Career highlights
- World Professional Snooker Championship (runner-up) 1969
- World Amateur Champion 1963, 1966
- English Amateur Champion 1963
- National Under-16 Champion 1944
- National Breaks Champion 1950, 1960

Owen, Marcus

Younger brother of Gary Owen, Marcus was born in Wales but spent much of his early snooker career in Great Yarmouth. A child prodigy at both billiards and snooker, he won national under-16 titles at both games in 1950. In 1951 he reached both finals again, but he lost the billiards final. He also reached the under-19 snooker final in 1951, but lost to Cliff Wilson.

Although Marcus turned professional over 20 years later, it was as an outstanding amateur that he will be remembered.

Between 1958 and 1973 he won the English amateur title on four occasions, a record for the championship jointly held with Pat Matthews. His four wins saw him beat such other notable amateurs as Jack Fitzmaurice, Sid Hood, Ray Edmonds and Alan Barnett. Marcus Owen appeared in one other final, in 1966, but lost to John Spencer. Had he won, he would have been eligible to play in that year's world amateur championships alongside his brother, who was the defending champion. (Gary defeated Spencer in the world final to retain his title.)

Marcus never appeared in the world amateur championships, but upon turning professional in 1974 he made an instant impact on that year's professional world championships by defeating Dennis Taylor, Maurice Parkin and his brother Gary before reaching the quarter-finals, where he played defending champion Ray Reardon. Although Reardon won 15-11 it was the toughest match he played on the way to retaining his title.

Owen still competes, and has retained his membership of the WPBSA, but the number of events he takes part in is limited these days. In fact, since that first world professional championship appearance in 1974, he has only twice appeared in the championship – in 1976, when he was eliminated in the preliminary round by Australian Lou Condo, and in 1983, when beaten, also in the preliminary round, by Scot Murdo McLeod.

Career highlights
- English Amateur Champion 1958-59, 1967, 1973
- National Under-16 Snooker Champion 1950-51
- National Under-16 Billiards Champion 1950

Padmore/Super Crystalate International

The Padmore/Super Crystalate International nearly died before it was born. The orginal sponsors, who had promised £15,000, pulled out four days before the event was due to start at the Gala Baths, West Bromwich. Fortunately, top promoter Mike Watterson stepped in and, at the last minute, got billiard and snooker traders Padmore and the manufacturers of the Super Crystalate balls to invest £5,000 in the tournament.

Eight men took part, and the eventual winner was Alex Higgins but he, like the tournament itself, had problems.

The night before his opening match he spent several hours in hospital following an ear infection which came on top of the influenza he already had. That was then followed by a six-hour drive down the M6 from Manchester to West Bromwich – a journey that would normally take an hour – because of the dreadful winter conditions.

Not suprisingly, the Padmore/Super Crystalate International was not held again.

Padmore/Super Crystalate International: Result (final)

1980 A.Higgins (Ireland) 4
P.Mans (South Africa) 2
Highest break: 106 – Willie Thorne

Parrott, John

Long before the millions of national television viewers became aware of Liverpudlian John Parrott during the 1984 Lada Classic, the Merseyside snooker-playing population knew they had a future champion in their midst. Having started to play at the age of 12, when his father first introduced him to the game, Parrott used to play in the Garston and Bootle Leagues in Liverpool – both good training grounds for the aspiring professional.

Parrott's amateur record was better than that of many others who had turned pro in the couple of years prior to him. But shrewd advisers, led by his business manager Phil Miller, encouraged him to wait for the most favourable moment before applying for professional status.

Parrott hoped to leave the amateur game with the English Amateur title to his name, but although he reached the 1983 inal, he was, surprisingly, beaten by Chesterfield's Tony Jones.

Parrott first came to national prominence in 1981, when he won the Pontins Junior Championship and recorded the highest break (97) in the inaugural *Junior Pot Black* series, which was won by current professional, and good friend of Parrott's, Dean Reynolds.

The following year he enjoyed further success at Pontins when he won the Open event, beating Ray Reardon in the final. As an amateur, he enjoyed the luxury of a 25-point start per game...and even Ray Reardon could not afford to give that away to an amateur of Parrott's stature.

Also in 1982 he became the first person ever to win the junior and senior Merseyside titles in the same year, incidentally becoming the youngest ever winner of the senior title. He also went on to win the *Junior Pot Black* title and was runner-up in the national junior championship – adding to his two runner-up positions in the boys' championship in 1979 and 1980.

At this time Parrott was attracting a lot of interest from inside the snooker world – so much so that cue manufacturers Peradon and Fletcher arranged a contract with him to endorse their goods. The contract was worth in the region of £5,000 – a substantial sum for an amateur.

A second *Junior Pot Black* title came Parrott's way, and then he was accepted into the professional ranks before the start of the 1983-84 season. He burst upon the scene as dramatically as

Steve Davis and Tony Knowles had done previously: in the Lada Classic at the Spectrum Arena, Warrington, he appeared calm and relaxed as he ousted Alex Higgins in the first round. Their match attracted a large crowd; there were scenes reminiscent of the Stretford Road End or the Anfield Kop, and for many spectators the appeal of these two popular players added a new dimension to the sport. After beating Higgins, Parrott came up against Tony Knowles in the next round. Everybody was only too conscious of what Knowles had done to Steve Davis in the 1982 World Championship. Could it happen again...but this time with Knowles on the receiving end?

It could, and it did, and the name of John Parrott was firmly established in the minds of millions. The semi-final against Steve Davis saw Parrott lose 5-4, and for the first time signs of nerves showed through. But he had done enough to prove himself a star player, and even a possible successor to the 'king' – Davis himself.

The John Parrott success story continued in 1985 when, after beating former champion John Spencer and then Kirk Stevens, he reached the quarter-final of the world championship before losing to Ray Reardon 13-12.

He picked up valuable ranking points in the first big tournament of the 1985-86 season, when he reached the semi-final of the Goya Matchroom Trophy, but this time it was Dennis Taylor who deprived him of his chance of participating in his first major final.

Following that early-season success, Parrott went out in the early stages of most other competitions, but still managed to move within one place of a top-16 ranking position. However, he achieved such a position in the top 16 the following year thanks to four points collected by reaching the semi-final of the Tennents United Kingdom Open, where his friend and rival Neal Foulds ended his chances of making a final appearance, and with two points from the world championship at Sheffield, where he was knocked out in the last 16 after a great game with Jimmy White which the Londoner won 13-11.

Terry Parsons

Career highlights

- World Professional Snooker Championship (quarter-final) 1985
- Tennents United Kingdom Open (semi-final) 1986
- Lada Classic (semi-final) 1984
- Pontins Open Champion 1982, 1986
- Pontins Junior Champion 1981
- *Junior Pot Black* 1982-83

Parsons, Terry

The third Welshman, after Doug Mountjoy and Cliff Wilson, to win the world amateur title, Terry Parsons, unlike the other two, has never applied for professional status. Born in the thirties, the postman from Trealaw in the Rhondda is an amateur in the true sense of the word. He does not play full-time, and very rarely does he venture outside his native Wales to play the game – he gets very homesick.

Parsons has been Welsh amateur champion on five occasions, the first title coming in 1961 and the last in 1984, when he beat current professional Wayne Jones in the final. In so doing he avenged his defeat of the previous year, which remains the only time he has been beaten in the final.

As an international Parsons has represented Wales 37 times, which is the second best record in the Home International championships, behind fellow Welshman Alwyn Lloyd. His greatest moment, however, came in Calgary in 1982 when he added the world amateur title to his impressive list of honours.

Playing in his first world championship, he won his qualifying group with seven wins out of eight matches; only current professional Paddy Browne beat him. In the quarter-final he disposed of Malcolm Bradley (another current professional) by five frames to nil, and in so doing, played his best snooker of the competition. The semi-finals saw him beat off the challenge from fellow Welshman Wayne Jones, and in the final he beat Canadian Jim Bear although here he had to pull himself back from 7-1 down before winning 11-8.

Attempting to retain his title in Dublin in 1984 he found himself up against the tough Indian competitor O.B. Agrawal in the final. Again he was trailing: this time he was 7-4 down, but pulled back to 7-7 and the spectators had visions of him repeating his 1982 performance. However, it was not to be, Agrawal won the last four frames to take the match 11-7.

A great friend of Terry Griffiths, the pair of them spent a great deal of time practising together in Terry's amateur days, but Parsons has no ambitions of following in his friend's footsteps. He is quite happy playing for fun, and earning his living delivering letters.

Career highlights

- World Amateur Snooker Champion 1982
- Welsh Amateur Champion 1961, 1965, 1969, 1982, 1984
- WMC & IU Champion 1970, 1973
- National Breaks Champion 1964

Plant

The plant shot is made when one red ball is played on to another red ball in order to make the second ball enter the pocket. There are rare instances when a plant consists of more than two object-balls.

In most instances of plants – also called sets – the two object-balls are touching or very nearly touching; but the more spectacular plant shot is when the two object-balls are apart.

Examples of plants are shown in the diagrams below.

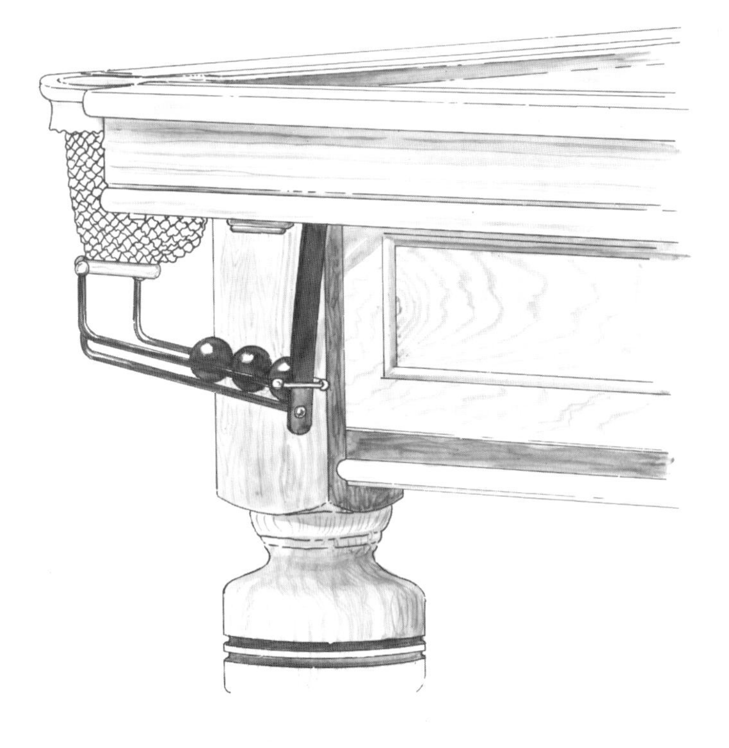

Pockets

The size of pockets is not specified by the Billiards and Snooker Control Council in their rules. The only requirement is that they must conform to the the council's official templates.

Pockets can therefore be any size but, for uniformity, tables are assembled to the specifications of the official templates.

Before a break can be ratified for record purposes, the pockets must be checked with templates to ensure that they conform to the standards.

See also Template.

Plant

An example of a plant, or 'set', involving two reds which are touching each other. The cue-ball will strike the first object ball, which will then force the other into the pocket. Provided the two reds are in a straight line with the pocket, this shot should result in a successful pot every time.

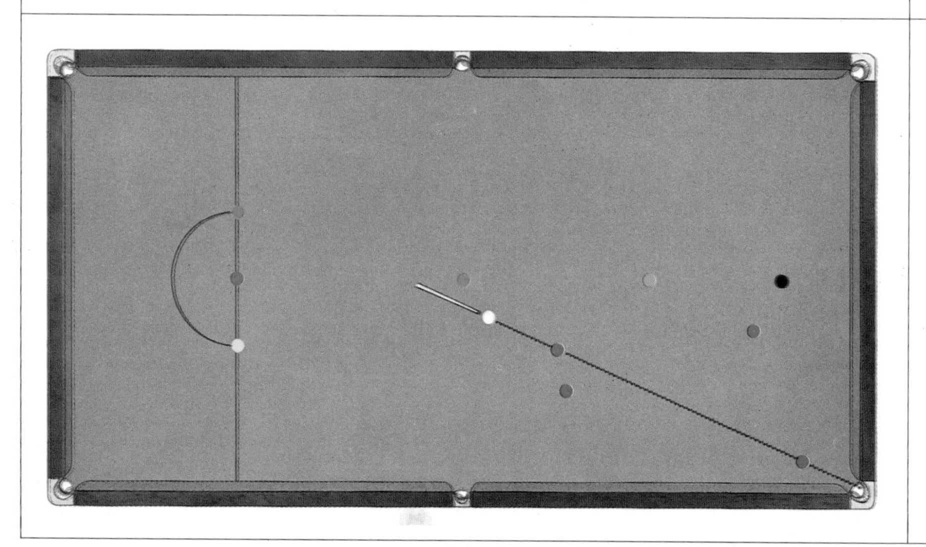

Another situation in which a plant can be successfully made, but this time there is a considerable distance between the two object-balls. The shot between the cue-ball and the first object-ball must be accurate or the second object ball will not go into the pocket.

Left – the referee's eye view of the pocket, illustrating what happens when a ball has been potted. Below: the player's eye view. The width of the pocket is 3½ inches (9cm), conforming with the rules laid down by the Billiards and Snooker Control Council.

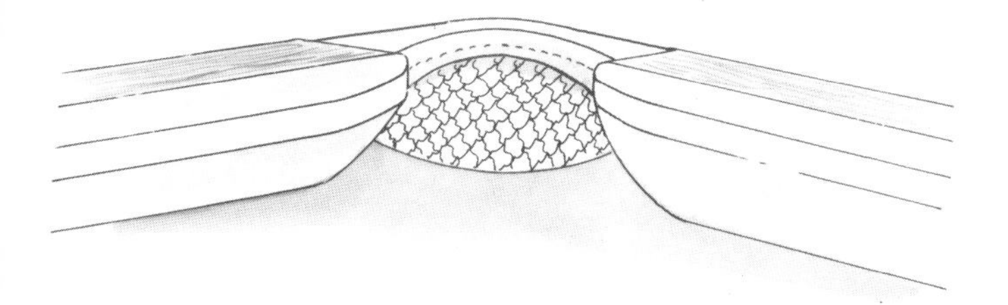

Pontins

Top-class entertainers in many fields start their careers touring the holiday camps, and snooker players also owe a large debt to that circuit.

In snooker, the contribution of the Pontin company has been immense. It has been responsible for giving the Home International Championship its current status. It has provided a useful source of income for many professionals who entertain Pontins holidaymakers during the summer months. But, perhaps more important, they organize and sponsor one of the biggest tournaments in the world.

Every spring, over 900 aspiring amateurs and professionals visit the Prestatyn Camp in North Wales for a week of snooker, at the end of which four champions emerge. There is the professional champion from one of the eight invited professionals, the open champion, the junior champion and the women's champion.

The professional and open events were first held in 1974; the junior and women's championships were not added until 1977. In 1980 over 1000 people took part, which resulted in overcrowding at Prestatyn; for this reason a second week was organized at Camber Sands. Another second week was organized at Brean Sands in 1983, when the women's world open championships were included in the week's events.

The Home International championship used to be held at the Prestatyn Camp each Autumn, until it moved to Heysham in 1986.

Many current professionals still work for Pontins during the summer season, and despite the lack of television coverage and the relatively small prize money, Pontins Spring Week still remains popular with them.

The eight invited professionals have to concede 25 points per frame to their opponents (at one time they had to concede 30), while uninvited professionals concede 21 points. Alex Higgins took good advantage of this situation in 1977. He was not invited, but competed as an uninvited professional and thus received four points per frame from his fellow pros – a situation he does not find himself in too often. Sure enough, he won the open title.

Ray Reardon is the only person to have won the professional and open titles in the same year (in 1975), while Doug Mountjoy is the only person to have won both titles twice. Tony Meo is the only person to have appeared in the junior, open and professional finals.

Former Hereford United goalkeeper David Icke had the honour of hosting Pot Black *in its final series*

Pot Black

Although the single-frame formula used by the BBC Television *Pot Black* programme is not the most suitable for deciding a match, the sport has the programmme to thank for providing a springboard from which it has become one of television's most popular sports.

In 1969, with the introduction of colour television, producer Phillip Lewis was responsible for the birth of the programme.

Snooker had been tried in the days of black and white television – unsuccessfully. But with new technology, there was an ideal opportunity to try it again.

Despite problems with lighting initially, the programme was a success, and projected the skills of such leading players as Ray Reardon and John Spencer into the nation's homes. More important the clean-cut, well-dressed, image of the players helped make it popular with female viewers. That is still part of the sport's success on television today.

Various different formulas have been tried, and the number of contestants has varied from eight in its first year, down to six, and up to its present figure of 16. The first series was conducted as a straight knockout competition, but thereafter the competition was held as a round-robin tournament with group winners meeting in the final. The 1984 and 1985 events reverted back to the old knockout system, with the last 16 survivors from the previous year's world championships being invited to take part. All matches except the final are played over one frame; the final is the best-of-three frames. As stated, the one-frame match is never satisfactory, but it remains an honour to be invited to

Pontins: Results

Prestatyn

Professional

1974 R. Reardon 10
J. Spencer 9
1975 R. Reardon 10
J. Spencer 4
1976 R. Reardon 10
F. Davis 9
1977 J. Spencer 7
J. Pulman 5
1978 R. Reardon 7
J. Spencer 2
1979 D. Mountjoy 8
G. Miles 4
1980 J. Virgo 9
R. Reardon 6
1981 T. Griffiths 9
W. Thorne 8
1982 S. Davis 9
R. Reardon 4
1983 D. Mountjoy 9
R. Reardon 7
1984 W. Thorne 9
J. Spencer 7
1985 T. Griffiths 9
J. Spencer 7
1986 T. Griffiths 9
W. Thorne 6
1987 N. Foulds 9
W. Thorne 6

Open

1974 D. Mountjoy 7 (25)
J. Spencer 4
1975 R. Reardon 7
J. Virgo 1 (25)
1976 D. Mountjoy 7 (25)
L. Pibworth 1 (25)
1977 A. Higgins 7 (4)
T. Griffiths 4 (25)
1978 S. Davis 7 (30)
T. Meo 6 (30)
1979 S. Davis 7
J. White 3 (30)
1980 W. Thorne 7
C. Wilson 3
1981 J. Hargreaves 7 (30)
C. Wilson 2
1982 J. Parrott 7 (25)
R. Reardon 4
1983 T. Griffiths 7
R. Reardon 3
1984 N. Foulds 7 (4)
D. Mountjoy 4
1985 J. Chambers (25) 7
J. Parrott 6
1986 J. Parrott 7
T. Putnam (25) 6
1987 S. Mazrocis (25) 7
B. Pinches (25) 2

(Figures in brackets indicate the number of points received per frame.)

Junior

1977 T. Meo 3
J. White 2
1978 J. White 3
J. Bennett 2
1979 D. Gilbert 3
J. Parrott 1
1980 T. Whitthread 3
J. Harrop 1
1981 J. Parrott 3
D. Tate 1
1982 P. Morgan 3
S. Ventham 0
1983 S. Ventham 3
P. Donegan 1
1984 G. Cundy 3
M. Causton 1
1985 B. Wildman 3
P. Mumford 1
1986 P. Dawkins 1
N. Martin 1
1987 R. Lawler 3
R. O'Sullivan 0

Women

1977 A. Davies 3
S. Foster 1
1978 A. Johnson 3
S. Foster 1
1979 M. Baynton 3
A. Davies 0
1980 M. Fisher 3
S. Newbury 2
1981 L. McIlrath3
J. Hanlon 0
1982 A. Davies 3
S. Foster 0
1983 S. Foster 3
G. Nakamura 1
1984 J. Dowen 3
L. Lucas 2
1985 A. Fisher 3
A. Jones 0
1986 A. Fisher 3
C. Walch 0
1987 S. Hillyard 3
C. Walch 1

Autumn Open

1976 C. Wilson 7
P. Medati 4
1977 W. Kelly 7
G. Scott 5
1978 J. White 7
S. Hood 6
1979 A. Knowles 7
D. Martin 0
1980 P. Medati 7
V. Harris 4
1981 W. Oliver 7
I. Williamson 5
1982 S. Duggan 7
K. Lownds 3
1983 R. Bales 7
G. Filtness 0
1984 B. West 7
G. Heycock 3
1985 G. Bray 7
M. Johnston-Allen 5
1986 Not held

Camber Sands 1980

Professional: A. Higgins 9
Dennis Taylor 7
Open: Dennis Taylor 7
G. Foulds 5 (30)
Junior: N. Foulds 3
J. Williams 2
Women: A. Burns 3
L. Kellerer 1

Brean Sands 1983

Professional: T. Meo 9
S. Francisco 7
Doubles: J. White and T. Meo 4
J. Spencer and J. Virgo 3
Women: (For World Open title)
S. Foster 8
M. Baynton 5

Most wins (all competitions):

Professional: 4 – Ray Reardon
Open: 2 – Steve Davis
2 – Doug Mountjoy
2 – John Parrott
Junior: no one has won more than 1 title
Women: 2 – Agnes Davies
2 – Sue Foster
2 – Allison Fisher
Highest break: 144 – Willie Thorne (1987 Open)

take part in the series, and few have refused. The sudden-death atmosphere is popular with both studio and viewing audiences.

The first programme was recorded at the BBC's Gosta Green studio in Birmingham, but now the series is recorded over three days just after Christmas at the Pebble Mill Studios in Birmingham. Viewing figures have reached 10 million for the final, and tickets for the recordings are extremely hard to obtain.

Many people have been involved in the programme's success, notably Reg Perrin, who was producer from 1971 until 1983. When Perrin took early retirement from the BBC he was replaced as producer by John G. Smith. The commentary team would not be the same without the voice of 'whispering' Ted Lowe, who has been involved with the programme since its inception.

Another man involved in nearly all programmes was Alan Weeks, who was the front man for all but two of the series; the job was latterly held by David Icke. One of snooker's great characters, Sydney Lee, was the resident referee for the series until ill health caused him to retire in 1980.

Following the success of the parent programme, a *Junior Pot Black* competition was first broadcast in 1981, and this gave the opportunity for rising stars to show their skills in front of the television cameras. The competition was limited to players up to the age of 18, and the only two winners, Dean Reynolds and John Parrott, have both since proved themselves in the professional ranks.

The programme was very popular in Australia – so much so, that they now have their own *Pot Black* style competition, the Winfield Masters, every year.

The *Pot Black* trophy was much sought after. So was the Joe Davis Trophy – a beautiful decanter – awarded to the scorer of the highest break in each series. Another cherished prize is the Personality Award. And no one who saw it will ever forget the expression on Alan Weeks's face in 1980 when he opened the envelope to reveal that the identity of the recipient was...Alan Weeks!

The popular Pot Black theme tune, Black & White Rag by Winifred Atwell, was heard in that capacity for the last time in 1986 as the axe fell on the programme after 17 years. Jimmy White emerged as the last winner and it was slightly ironic that the last black potted in the series, by White, should give him a break of 106 – only the third century in the programme's great history.

Prize Money

Snooker has, in recent years, moved into the million pound bracket: in the 1986-87 season total prize money available to the professional players was in excess of £3 million. The increased prize money has rapidly elevated snooker players to superstar status. In 1972, when Alex Higgins first won the world championship, he collected just over £400 for winning the title. In 1987 the prize was £80,000.

Amateurs have also reaped the benefits of the current explosion. Restrictions on their winnings were lifted in 1972, and two years later Doug Mountjoy, when he won the first Pontins Open, became the first amateur to win a £1,000 first prize. First prizes in excess of £3,000 are commonplace in the non-professional game, and in 1985 Steve James of Cannock collected the first £4,000 prize by a non-professional player when he won the Warner's Open at Puckpool, Isle of Wight.

Listed here are the ten biggest events (in terms of prize money) on the 1986-87 professional calendar. For comparison the first prize of the same event (or its predecessor) from the 1982-83 season is given to indicate how prize money has risen.

Event	1986-87 First prize	1986-87 Total prize money	1982-83 First prize
Embassy World Pro Championships	£80,000	£400,000	£30,000
Dulux British Open	£60,000	£300,000	£12,000 *(a)*
Rothmans Grand Prix	£55,000	£275,000	£ 5,000 *(b)*
Mercantile Credit Classic	£50,000	£250,000	£16,000 *(c)*
Benson and Hedges Masters	£51,000	£200,000	£16,000
Hofmeister World Doubles	£50,000	£200,000	£24,000
Tuborg World Cup	£32,000	£100,000	£16,500 *(d)*
BCE International	£35,000	£175,000	£22,000 *(e)*
Tennents UK Open	£60,000	£300,000	£11,000 *(f)*

(a) formerly Yamaha International Masters
(b) formerly Professional Players' Tournament
(c) formerly Lada Classic
(d) formerly State Express World Team Classic/Guinness World Cup
(e) formerly Jameson International/Goya Matchroom Trophy
(f) formerly Coral UK Open

Pro-Am Tournaments

Pro-am tournaments are essential for two reasons: first they give top-quality amateurs the opportunity to compete regularly against professionals, and second, they give the lower-ranked professionals the opportunity to compete at tournament level.

Many professionals fail to qualify for the competition proper of the major professional events and, at the same time, do not enjoy the benefit of regular exhibition work. Consequently the pro-am events, which quite often carry first prizes in the region of £2,000, are a necessary source of revenue for them.

Amateur players regularly win pro-am events, because the professionals are handicapped and some top-class amateurs are as good as, and in some cases better than the lower-ranked

Pot Black: Results (finals)

1969 R. Reardon (Wales) beat J. Spencer (England) 88-29 (one frame)

1970 J. Spencer (England) beat R. Reardon (Wales) 88-27 (one frame)

1971 J. Spencer (England) beat F. Davis (England) 61-40 (one frame)

1972 E. Charlton (Australia) beat R. Reardon (Wales) 75-43 (one frame)

1973 E. Charlton (Australia) beat R. Williams (Eng.) 93-33 (one frame)

1974 G. Miles (England) beat J. Spencer (England) 147-86 (aggregate score over two frames)

1975 G. Miles (England) beat D. Taylor (Ireland) 81-27 (one frame)

1976 J. Spencer (England) beat D. Taylor (Ireland) 69-42 (one frame)

1977 P. Mans (South Africa) beat D. Mountjoy (Wales) 90-21 (one frame)

1978 D. Mountjoy (Wales) beat G. Miles (England) 2-1 (best of three frames)

1979 R. Reardon (Wales) beat D. Mountjoy (Wales) 2-1 (best of three frames)

1980 E. Charlton (Australia) beat R. Reardon (Wales) 2-1 (best of three frames)

1981 C. Thorburn (Canada) beat J. Wych (Canada) 2-0 (best of three frames)

1982 S. Davis (England) beat E. Charlton (Australia) 2-0 (best of three frames)

1983 S. Davis (England) beat R. Reardon (Wales) 2-0 (best of three frames)

1984 T. Griffiths (Wales) beat J. Spencer (England) 2-1 (best of three frames)

1985 D. Mountjoy (Wales) beat J. White (England) 2-0 (best of three frames)

1986 J. White (England) beat K. Stevens (Canada) 2-0 (best of three frames)

Most wins: 3 – John Spencer
3 – Eddie Charlton

Most finals: 6 – Ray Reardon
6 – John Spencer

Top break: 110 – Eddie Charlton (1973)

Junior Pot Black

1981 D. Reynolds (England) beat D. O'Kane (New Zealand) 151-79 (aggregate score over two frames)

1982 J. Parrott (England) beat J. Keers (England) 156-70 (aggregate score over two frames)

1983 J. Parrott (England) beat S. Ventham (England) (aggregate score over two frames)

Highest break: 97 – John Parrott (1981)

Dennis Taylor in action at Pontins, Prestatyn

professionals. A handicap can therefore be a big burden for such a professional to have to carry.

One of the best known pro-am events is the Pontins Open, which gives the opportunity to over 500 promising amateur players to pit their skills against top-class amateurs and professionals during the Pontins Snooker Festival week at Prestatyn each spring.

The Pontins Open has been won by promising amateurs who have subsequently gone on to make the grade in the professional world: Doug Mountjoy was a double winner as an amateur, in 1974 and 1976. Steve Davis won the title in 1978 by beating Tony Meo in the final and, in 1982, the winner was current professional star, John Parrott.

Professional

Snooker no longer possesses amateurs and professionals, although the word amateur is still widely used within the sport. There are, in the eyes of the Billiards and Snooker Control Council, professionals and non-professionals.

The old professional was easily distinguishable from the amateur – he played for money. That applied to all sports that had the two classes of participants. In 1972, however, all restrictions were lifted on how much amateur players could win – hence their new title of non-professionals.

Anybody can call himself a professional snooker player, but to participate in competitions organized under the auspices of the World Professional Billiards and Snooker Assocation, one must be a member of the association. With membership already over the 120 mark, access to the association is not easy to come by. A player must have a proven track record at international level or in domestic competitions before he is even considered for membership. There is talk of the association introducing a ceiling of 128 members, with a promotion and relegation system at the end of each season whereby the leading non-professionals play the bottom-ranked professionals in a series of 'test matches'.

At the beginning of the 1985-6 season there were 128 professionals who were members of the WPBSA. England had by far the greatest number of members, with 55.

Professional Match-Play Championship

In 1952, following a dispute over terms between the professional players and the Billiards Association and Control Club, the professionals split from the association. They formed a break-away governing body and organized their own championships, known as The Professional Match-Play Championships. Only two professionals remained to contest the traditional world championships that year – Horace Lindrum and Clark McConachy.

Fred Davis and Walter Donaldson, who had met in five world championship finals, renewed their rivalry in the inaugural match-Play final in 1952. They met again in the finals of 1953 and 1954 as well – and Davis won all three.

With the decline of snooker in the fifties, the championship was not held after 1957. In 1976 however, Eddie Charlton promoted a tournament, billed as the World Professional Match-

Most of the prize money goes to the top few players

Play Championship, in Melbourne. The World Professional Billiards and Snooker Association gave their blessing, and accorded it 'world' status. Charlton beat Ray Reardon in the final and the event has not been held since.

Professional Match-Play Championship – Results

1952 F. Davis (England) 38 W. Donaldson (Scotland) 35
1953 F. Davis (England) 37 W. Donaldson (Scotland) 34
1954 F. Davis (England) 39 W. Donaldson (Scotland) 21
1955 F. Davis (England) 37 J. Pulman (England) 34
1956 F. Davis (England) 38 J. Pulman (England) 35
1957 J. Pulman (England) 39 J. Rea (Ireland) 34
1958-1975 Not held
1976 E. Charlton (Australia) 31 R. Reardon (England) 24

Professional Players' Tournament

See Rothman's Grand Prix

Professional Referees' Association

The Professional Referees' Association was formed following a meeting at the West Bromwich Conservative Club in December 1979, and it became affiliated to the World Professional Billiards and Snooker Association at the same time. Initially it was known as the Professional Billiards and Snooker Referees' Association.

Sixteen referees were founder members of the Association; the chairman was John Smyth, and the first secretary was John Street of Devon. The Association was formed in order to better the standards of professional refereeing. The constitution of the Association was amended in 1984, and technically the original Association disbanded, although it never lapsed completely.

As at the beginning of 1987 there were more than 21 members of the PRA, all of whom were Grade 'A' referees. Vera Selby was the only female member.

Professional Snooker League

The idea of a professional snooker league, launched in the 1983-84 season, was a sound one. Financially it was a disaster. Held around Britain at venues as widely separated as Inverness and St Austell, the matches were well attended. But the cost of transporting twelve leading snooker players around the country was too much for the promoters to bear without sponsorship. It is estimated that the league made a loss of around £100,000.

In the end the winner, John Virgo, received no prize money, and all players were asked to accept less appearance money than initially promised. All but one agreed.

The twelve leading players, according to the WPBSA rankings, were invited to take part in the league. Steve Davis, Terry Griffiths and Cliff Thorburn all declined the invitation. Dennis Taylor, John Virgo and Tony Meo were invited as 13th, 14th and 15th ranked players. Meo declined, and so the final place went to seasoned campaigner John Spencer.

Each game was played over ten frames, all of which had to be played. Two points were awarded for a win, with one point to each player in the event of a drawn game.

After completing seven of his scheduled eleven matches, Kirk Stevens withdrew from the league, and this caused further problems for the promoters. His results were deleted from the league, and his withdrawal meant a rearrangement of the remaining matches. By the time the final matches came around the following April, the sad state of affairs was only too well known, but the remaining players still completed their matches.

The idea of a professional league came from promoter Ken Upperton, who successfully ran a four-man pilot league in 1983. It is sad that his idea of a twelve-man league was never fully realized.

Professional Snooker League – results

Final table (points)
1 John Virgo 16
2 Dennis Taylor 15
3 Eddie Charlton 15
4 Alex Higgins 11
5 Doug Mountjoy 10
6 Tony Knowles 10
7 John Spencer 9
8 Jimmy White 8
9 Ray Reardon 7
10 Bill Werbeniuk 5
11 David Taylor 4
12 Kirk Stevens (did not complete fixtures)

Highest break: 136 – Alex Higgins (v Bill Werbeniuk)
136 – Bill Werbeniuk (v Dennis Taylor)

William Camkin (centre), billiard hall proprietor, with four of the leading professionals of the 1930s. From left to right: Walter Lindrum, Joe Davis, Tom Newman and Clark McConachy

Promoters

The role of the promoter in snooker is an important one. He is the link between the players, the sponsors, and the television companies. He also makes sure that the event runs smoothly.

The most famous of all promoters is Mike Watterson. Himself a professional player, he promoted his first snooker event in 1972 when he paired Ray Reardon with Alex Higgins in a challenge match at Stavely. Although he lost money on the venture, he was undaunted and, in 1977, he took over the promotion of the world professional championships, and arranged for them to be held in the Crucible Theatre in Sheffield. Since then Watterson has gone on to promote many more major professional tournaments.

Other famous promoters, since the boom of the 1970s, have been West Nally – the West half of the combination being well-known cricket and *Come Dancing* commentator, Peter West. They were responsible for the world championships in the early seventies, and were also the promoters who brought the Benson and Hedges Masters into snooker.

Most major professional tournaments are currently promoted by the WPBSA's own promotions company, WPBSA Promotions Ltd. It was set up in March 1983 with Mike Watterson's former right-hand man Paul Hatherell as Managing Director.

Pulman, John

When snooker went into decline in the fifties, John Pulman was one of only a handful of professionals who continued actively to pursue the sport, and he made a good living from sponsored exhibition matches and the holiday camp circuit.

It was in 1946 that the tall Devonian hit the headlines when, as an unknown, he beat Albert Brown 5-3 in the final of the English amateur championship to become the (then) youngest champion. He turned professional later that year and in his first professional tournament he won a cheque for £400 – a large sum in those days.

It was not long after he turned professional that Pulman came to be regarded as one of the sport's leading players, along with personalities such as Joe and Fred Davis and Walter Donaldson. He did not do particularly well in the world championship in his first few years as a professional, but he did reach the final of the Professional Match-Play championship – the world title in everything but name – in 1955 and 1956, although he lost to Fred Davis on both occasions. He did, however, win the title in 1957, when he beat Jackie Rea in the final.

After that, the sport suffered its decline, and Pulman's activities were restricted to exhibition and challenge matches. The world championship was re-introduced in 1964 and Pulman beat Fred Davis for the title. Thereafter it was held as a challenge competition, and he went on to make six further successful defences of the title, against Fred Davis (twice), Rex Williams (twice), Freddie van Rensburg and Eddie Charlton.

When he won the world title in 1964 he became the first former English amateur champion to go on to win the world professional title, an achievement since equalled only by Ray Reardon, John Spencer and Terry Griffiths.

When the knockout style world championship was reintroduced in 1969, Pulman suffered a shock first-round defeat at the hands of new professional John Spencer, but the following year he reached the final where he lost 37-33 to Ray Reardon. In 1977, he reached the semi-final of the championships, although

John Pulman – six times world snooker champion, and one of the few professionals to continue to develop the sport when it went into decline during the 1950s

now in his fifties, before narrowly losing 18-16 to John Spencer. Since then he has not progressed beyond the first round, and the last time he competed in the championships was in 1981 when he lost to Dave Martin in the qualifying round.

Pulman is still an active member of the professional snooker scene. He is part of the ITV commentary team and is also an experienced coach.

Career highlights
- World Professional Snooker Champion 1964-68 (challenge system)
- Professional Match-Play Champion 1957
- News of the World Champion 1954, 1957
- English Amateur Champion 1946

Push Shot

A push shot is deemed to have been made when either (**a**) the tip of the cue is making contact with the cue-ball at the same time as the cue-ball makes contact with the object-ball, or (**b**) the cue remains in contact with the cue-ball after this has commenced its forward motion. The push shot is not allowed in snooker, and is deemed a foul stroke. Under this rule, it would be impossible to play a shot when the cue-ball and an object-ball are touching. In this case the touching ball rule is applied.

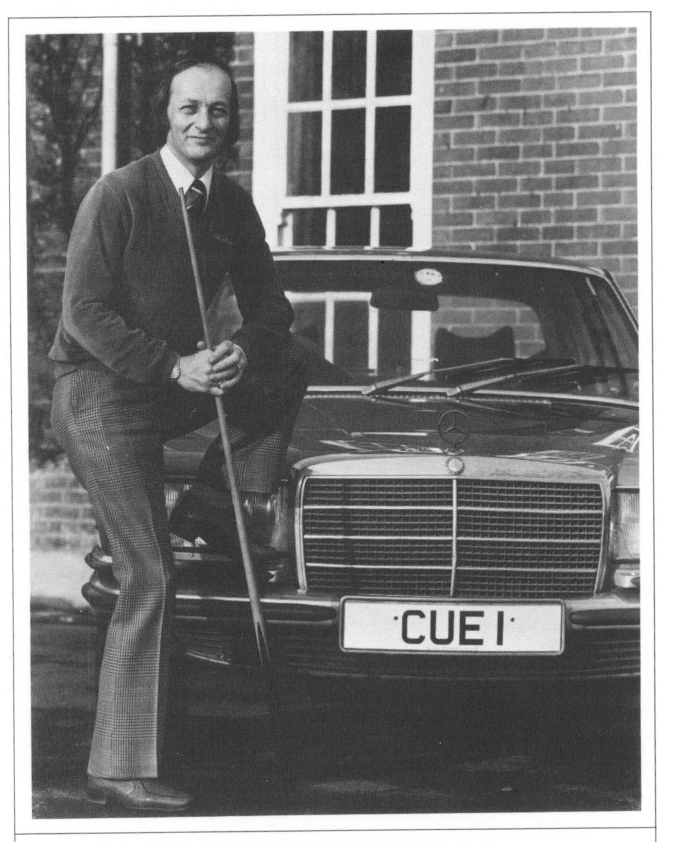

Mike Watterson: his car's registration plate once belonged to Joe Davis

Q

Qualifying Matches

Because of the increasing number of professionals, it is necessary to hold qualifying rounds for the major tournaments. Most leading competitions start with a first round of 32 players, and normally the top 16 ranked players automatically qualify for that stage of the competition, at which time they are joined by 16 pre-qualifiers. In events open to all professionals, it may be necessary to play three or more qualifying rounds before the competition proper. The ranking system is still used; players ranked 17-32 are exempt until the final qualifying round.

A place in the top 16 in the rankings is therefore a goal for all professionals, as it removes that burden of having to pre-qualify for the final stages of the major events.

One benefit of the qualifying matches is that they are normally held at a venue different from the main event, and consequently the public gets a greater chance of seeing top class snooker live. Because of their size some venues are just not suitable for major events, but the following are venues that are very popular, and widely used for pre-qualifying matches: Bradbury Hall, Chesterfield; Masters Club, Stockport; Redwood Lodge Country Club, Bristol; Romiley Forum, Stockport; and the Sheffield Snooker Centre.

Steve Davis in the Anglia Television studios, where he hosted 'The Sports Quiz' for Channel 4

Quick Scoring

Although no official records of quick scoring are kept, several players over the years have earned reputations for fast play. Current professionals Alex Higgins and Jimmy White are noted for their speed around the table, and consequently have been nicknamed The Hurricane and The Whirlwind respectively.

Of the past players, the late Warren Simpson of Australia had a reputation for his speed, as did fellow Australian Walter Lindrum. Lindrum made an official century break at billiards in 1941 in just 46 seconds. He is also credited with making an unofficial century break in 27½ seconds.

On 22 April 1923 Britain's Claude Falkiner made a billiards break of 86 in just 1 minute 20 seconds in an exhibition match at Moose Jaw, Alberta, Canada. Three years later, on 14 April 1926, he claimed another world record for fast scoring when he made a 651 break in 24 minutes in an exhibition in Shanghai.

The fastest century break at snooker is not known, but one would have to go a long way to beat the 2 minutes 45 seconds Alex Higgins took to compile a break of 122 against Patsy Fagan in the Irish professional championships.

It is impossible to compare games because of their varying length in terms of frames; but the 1982 world championship semi-final encounter between Alex Higgins and Jimmy White must rank as one of the quickest best-of-31 frame matches to go the distance. Higgins won the match 16-15 and the first eight frames took just 1 hour 50 minutes – an average of less than 14 minutes per frame.

Against the clock, Jimmy White once cleared the colours in 27. 8 seconds, but Lancastrian Shaun Berry knocked a staggering 10.2 seconds off White's time when he cleared them in 17.6 seconds at Chalkers Snooker Club, Burnley, in 1986.

Quiz Shows

Television quiz shows of all kinds are becoming increasingly popular with one of the most popular being the BBC's *A Question of Sport*. Many leading snooker players have appeared on the programme over the years, including Steve Davis (twice), Terry Griffiths (twice), Alex Higgins (twice), Tony Knowles, Ray Reardon and Dennis Taylor.

After winning the Mercantile Credit Classic in 1985, Willie Thorne announced that *A Question of Sport* was his favourite programme and it was his ambition to appear on it. Less than a month later he was invited, but could not make the date.

BBC Television tried a new quiz programme in 1984 called *Pot the Question*. The format of the quiz revolved around the game of snooker and part of the quiz involved leading professionals making attempted pots. The professionals who competed in the programme were Terry Griffiths, Alex Higgins, Tony Knowles, Jim Meadowcroft, Tony Meo, John Parrott, Ray Reardon, John Spencer, Dennis Taylor, Willie Thorne, John Virgo and Jimmy White.

In 1983 Steve Davis played the part of questionmaster on Channel 4 TV's *The Sports Quiz* – a challenging competition involving members of the public with an exceptional knowledge of sport. Davis was glad he was asking the questions and not answering them!

The next in popular quiz programmes was Central Television's 'Sporting Triangles' hosted by Nick Owen. Snooker figured prominently as one of the three major sports.

R

Rankings

The WPBSA world ranking system was first adopted in 1976. At that time it was based solely on the previous three years' performances in the world championships, and the only purpose of the rankings was to establish the seedings at the world championships (although the previous year's winner and runner-up were automatically numbers one and two seeds, irrespective of their placing in the ranking list).

Ranking points were awarded following each championship. The winner received five points, the runner up four, the losing semi-finalists three each and so on; thus the last 16 in each championship received points.

Following the 1982 world championships a new system was introduced. Two more events were designated as being ranking tournaments – the Jameson International and the Professional Players Tournament. Both these events were nominated by the WPBSA because they were open to *all* its members. The points system was adapted from the previous formula but the 1983 world championship carried double points, i.e. 10-8-6-4-2.

The ranking sytem was changed in 1985-86 to allow for 6 points for the winner of a ranking tournament down to 1 point for a loser in the last 32, plus merit points dependent on a player's position in the rankings, and his exemption status. The world championship carried a different points structure, starting with 10 points for the winner, down to 1 point for a loser in the last 32. The points accumulated from the previous two years' ranking tournaments are calculated after the world championship each year and are enforced for the following season.

The ranking tournaments in 1986-87 were: BCE International, Rothmans Grand Prix, Tennents United Kingdom Open, Mercantile Credit Classic, Dulux British Open and Embassy World Professional championship.

With the introduction of the Professional Ticket tournaments, which effectively means a promotion and relegation system for the paid ranks, points are awarded for players at the bottom of the ranking ladder, based on frames won.

World rankings

1976	1977	1978	1979
1 Ray Reardon	1 Ray Reardon (–)	1 Ray Reardon (–)	1 Ray Reardon (–)
2 Alex Higgins	2 John Spencer (+6)	2 Perrie Mans (+8)	2 Dennis Taylor (+6)
3 Eddie Charlton	3 Eddie Charlton (–)	3 Eddie Charlton (–)	3 Eddie Charlton (–)
4 Fred Davis	4 Dennis Taylor (+5)	4 John Spencer (−2)	4 John Spencer (–)
5 Graham Miles	5 Alex Higgins (−3)	5 Cliff Thorburn (+1)	5 Cliff Thorburn (–)
6 Rex Williams	6 Cliff Thorburn (+7)	6 Fred Davis (+3)	6 Fred Davis (–)
7 Perrie Mans	7 John Pulman (+8)	7 Alex Higgins (−2)	7 Perrie Mans (−5)
8 John Spencer	8 Graham Miles (−3)	8 Dennis Taylor (−4)	8 Terry Griffiths
9 Dennis Taylor	9 Fred Davis (−5)	9 Graham Miles (−1)	9 Graham Miles (–)
10 Gary Owen	10 Perrie Mans (−3)	10 John Pulman (−3)	10 John Virgo (+9)

1980	1981	1982	1983
1 Ray Reardon (–)	1 Cliff Thorburn (+1)	1 Ray Reardon (+3)	1 Steve Davis (+3)
2 Cliff Thorburn (+3)	2 Steve Davis (+12)	2 Alex Higgins (+9)	2 Ray Reardon (−1)
3 Eddie Charlton (–)	3 Terry Griffiths (+2)	3 Cliff Thorburn (−2)	3 Cliff Thorburn (–)
4 Alex Higgins (+9)	4 Ray Reardon (−3)	4 Steve Davis (−2)	4 Tony Knowles (+11)
5 Terry Griffiths (+3)	5 Dennis Taylor (+1)	5 Eddie Charlton (+3)	5 Alex Higgins (−3)
6 Dennis Taylor (−4)	6 Doug Mountjoy (+9)	6 Kirk Stevens (+4)	6 Eddie Charlton (−1)
7 Perrie Mans (–)	7 David Taylor (+2)	7 Doug Mountjoy (−1)	7 Kirk Stevens (−1)
8 Fred Davis (−2)	8 Eddie Charlton (−5)	8 David Taylor (−1)	8 Bill Werbeniuk (+1)
9 David Taylor (+6)	9 Bill Werbeniuk (+1)	9 Bill Werbeniuk (−1)	9 Terry Griffiths (+5)
10 Bill Werbeniuk (+2)	10 Kirk Stevens (+1)	10 Jimmy White (+11)	10 David Taylor (−2)

1984	1985	1986	1987
1 Steve Davis (–)	1 Steve Davis (–)	1 Steve Davis (–)	1 Steve Davis (–)
2 Tony Knowles (+2)	2 Cliff Thorburn (+1)	2 Cliff Thorburn (–)	2 Jimmy White (+3)
3 Cliff Thorburn (–)	3 Tony Knowles (−1)	3 Dennis Taylor (+1)	3 Neal Foulds (+10)
4 Kirk Stevens (+3)	4 Dennis Taylor (+7)	4 Tony Knowles (−1)	4 Cliff Thorburn (−2)
5 Ray Reardon (−3)	5 Kirk Stevens (−1)	5 Jimmy White (+2)	5 Joe Johnson (+3)
6 Eddie Charlton (−1)	6 Ray Reardon (−1)	6 Alex Higgins (+3)	6 Terry Griffiths (+4)
7 Jimmy White (+4)	7 Jimmy White (–)	7 Willie Thorne (+4)	7 Tony Knowles (−3)
8 Terry Griffiths (+1)	8 Terry Griffiths (–)	8 Joe Johnson (+8)	8 Dennis Taylor (−5)
9 Alex Higgins (−4)	9 Alex Higgins (–)	9 Kirk Stevens (−4)	9 Alex Higgins (−3)
10 Tony Meo (+5)	10 Tony Meo (–)	10 Terry Griffiths (−2)	10 Silvino Francisco (+2)

(Figures in brackets indicate places gained or lost on previous year)

Rea, Jackie

Until the emergence of Alex Higgins, Jackie Rea was Ireland's 'Mr Snooker'. He was holder of the Irish professional title continuously from 1951 until successfully challenged for the title by the young Higgins in 1972.

Rea started playing snooker in his father's pub in Dungannon when he was just nine. In 1947 he became Irish amateur champion, immediately turned professional – and before the year was out he was Irish professional champion as well! He subsequently lost his professional title to Jack Bates, but won it back from him in 1951 to start his 21-year reign as champion.

Although he was a popular member of the professional circuit in Britain in the early fifties, Rea never fared very well in the big tournaments. His world championship record was very unimpressive and his reaching the final of the Professional Match-Play Championships in 1957, when he lost to John Pulman, was a somewhat hollow performance in view of the lack of competitors. His best professional result was his winning of the 1955 News of the World tournament at the Leicester Square Hall. He beat Joe Davis into second place; two years earlier, Davis had pipped Rea for the title.

The main obstacle to success for Jackie Rea was his lack of dedication – he always treated the game as fun. As a result of that, he was one of the most sought-after players for exhibition matches in the fifties and sixties, and his great sense of humour and banter with his audiences have been well received by fans all over the British Isles. A great story-teller, Rea was one of the innovators of the 'Irish jokes'. He used to start off his routine with the following lines: 'Don't call us Irish stupid. We invented a comfortable toilet-seat until, 200 years later, some stupid Englishman went and put a hole in it!'

His reputation was enhanced in the late sixties when he was one of the early members of the *Pot Black* team.

Rea is still a member of the World Professional Billiards and Snooker Association, and now lives in Cheshire where he has been settled for many years. Nowadays his appearances at competitive matches are few and far between, and it was back in 1980 that he last competed in the world professional championships. Nevertheless, that was 31 years after he first competed.

Career highlights
- Northern Ireland Amateur Champion 1947
- News of the World Champion 1955
- Northern Ireland Professional Champion 1947-1950, 1951-1972

Reardon, Ray

When Ray Reardon turned professional in 1967 he took the gamble of leaving the security of a job in the Stoke-on-Trent constabulary. He had a wife and young family to support, and no home of their own. But in retrospect the gamble completely paid off for the affable Reardon.

Progress was slow in the beginning, but in 1970 he won his first of six world professional titles. The prize money – meagre by today's standards – was £1,250, but it enabled Reardon to put a deposit down on a small bungalow. Within a year he had earned enough to pay the mortgage off in full.

Since then, the Ray Reardon story is well known: five more world professional titles plus a host of other major honours. Reardon was born in 1932 in Tredegar, and at the age of 14 followed tradition by going down the mines. Interested in snooker at that time, Ray used to protect his hands while down the mine by wearing white gloves. The caution paid off – in 1949 he won the News of the World Amateur title at the age of 17. For winning the title he was presented with an ash cue by the late Joe Davis. That cue was to be the key to his success.

During his amateur days in Tredegar Reardon enjoyed a great rivalry with another Tredegar man, Cliff Wilson – today a fellow professional.

Ray Reardon got the better of their battles, which always attracted large crowds, and also large sums of money were invested in the outcome of their matches.

Reardon won the Welsh amateur title six years in succession between 1950 and 1955, and it was only after he left the area that Wilson won his first title.

With the Tredegar pits closing in the mid-fifties, the Reardon family moved to the Stoke-on-Trent area to continue life in the mines and Reardon got a job at the Florence Colliery. It was as a result of being buried alive for three hours in a pit accident that he decided enough was enough, and he left to become PC 184 with the Stoke-on-Trent constabulary.

He won the coveted English amateur title in 1964 – beating John Spencer in the final – and after offers of sponsorship he turned professional in 1967.

The first world title in 1970 resulted in his being in demand for exhibition matches and for the holiday camp summer circuit. Reardon has not forgotten the people who supported him in his early days as a professional, and still tries to accommodate them for exhibition matches – competitions permitting. He has a great liking for the holiday camp circuit – in particular the Pontins Festival where he has won the Pontins Professional title a record four times, and won the Open once.

He is popular wherever he plays, not only because he is entertaining and humourous, but because of his impeccable sportsmanship. A natural for television, he took part in – and won – the inaugural *Pot Black* tournament, and has appeared in every subsequent tournament with the exception of one.

It is not only for his playing skills that he has been sought after by television and radio. He was the first snooker player, in 1976, to appear on *This is Your Life* and has appeared on many 'chat-show' programmes and *A Question of Sport*. Ray was also Roy Plomley's radio guest on *Desert Island Discs* in 1979.

He was invincible during the 1970s – particularly in the world championships – but his game collapsed shortly after his 1978 world championship win over Perrie Mans. This slide coincided with the falling apart of the cue given to him by Joe Davis in 1949. It was as if Reardon had lost a limb. He struggled to get his game together, and suffered some embarrassingly early exits from major tournaments.

Between his 1978 world championship success and 1982, when he won the inaugural Professional Players' Tournament, he never won a major individual tournament – although he did twice help Wales to win the World Team Cup.

It all came right when he found a new cue – which had been standing on the rack alongside his own table in the three years or so he had been looking for a new one.

This found, things improved for Reardon and and a seventh world championship final appearance followed when he lost a great final to Alex Higgins. This was Ray's first defeat in world championship finals.

Victory in the Yamaha Masters followed the Professional Players' Tournament success. A second Welsh Professional title came his way in 1983 and he reached the final of both the Benson and Hedges Masters and the Benson and Hedges Irish Masters. In that year's world championship, against Tony

Ray Reardon, smiling as usual

Knowles, he became the first person since 1979 to compile century breaks in consecutive frames.

Reardon enjoyed a slight resurgence in his career in 1985. He reached the semi-final of the world championship before losing heavily to Steve Davis and that year he was awarded the MBE for his services to snooker. The year ended with him and partner Tony Jones reaching the final of the Hofmeister World Doubles but here they suffered defeat at the hands of that great doubles partnership of Davis and Meo.

Since then Ray, nicknamed 'Dracula' by television personality Paul Daniels, has slipped out of the top ten for the first time, and in 1986-87 he dropped dramatically from 15th to 38th place.

He has since re-married. The revival of Reardon's domestic fortunes could be matched by that of his snooker career in 1987-88.

Career highlights

World Professional Snooker Champion 1970, 1973-76
Benson & Hedges Masters Champion 1976
Yamaha International Masters Champion 1983
Professional Players' Tournament Champion 1982
Hofmeister World Doubles (runner-up) 1986
(with Tony Jones)
World Cup 1979-80 (member of winning Welsh team)
Welsh Professional Champion 1981, 1983
Pot Black Champion 1969, 1979
Pontins Professional Champion 1974-76, 1978
Pontins Open Champion 1975
English Amateur Champion 1964
Welsh Amateur Champion 1950-55

As the first snooker player to appear on BBC Radio Four's *Desert Island Discs*, it is worth looking at the eight records Ray Reardon chose to have on his desert island with him:

Ramona – The Bachelors
A Song of All Nations – The Morriston Orpheus Choir
The Blood Donor – Tony Hancock
Zorba's Dance – London Festival Orchestra
You Always Hurt the One You Love – Spike Jones and His City Slickers
Theme from 'Love Story' – Mantovani and his Orchestra
Land of My Fathers – Tredegar Orpheus Male Voice Choir
Symphony No. 5 in C Minor (Beethoven) – Chicago Symphony Orchestra

Redwood Lodge Country Club

Because of its restricted seating capacity the Redwood Lodge Country Club in Bristol is, these days, used only to stage qualifying matches for major tournaments. Even so, it is one of the most attractive and popular venues on the professional circuit.

Originally called Ashton Court Lodge, it was acquired by John Ley just after the war. Ley was a local businessman who owned a chain of cake shops at the time.

Ashton Court was a small lodge with 12 acres of land, and it stood within the grounds of Ashton Court Mansion (owned by Lord and Lady Smythe). Ley rebuilt the lodge and turned it into a very exclusive cabaret/dinner dance club in the sixties.

As the nation became more sports orientated Ley added various sports facilities: ten pin bowling, saunas, squash, and so on. John Ley sold the lodge to John Pontin, the chairman of Country Club Hotels, in 1974, and the latter added further plush sports facilities. They now have six badminton courts, seven tennis courts, indoor and outdoor swimming pools, a multi-gymnasium, saunas, and 18 snooker tables in what was formerly the ten-pin bowling alley. In addition to the sporting facilities, the lodge boasts 72 bedrooms.

It became the Redwood Lodge in 1979 after Ashton Court Mansions turned the grounds into a nature reserve. To avoid any confusion, John Pontin changed the name.

The major snooker matches are held in one of the badminton halls which can accommodate 600 spectators. As stated before, the venue is not used for the final stages of any major professional events, but hosts the qualifying rounds of the world professional championships, and hosted the qualifying stages of the inaugural Rothmans Grand Prix in 1984. It has also staged qualifying rounds of other important tournaments, such as the Jameson International and the Hofmeister World Doubles. The only tournament to hold its final stages at Redwood Lodge was the untelevised Professional Player's Tournament in 1983.

The Association of Sports Writers also uses the venue for the presentation of their annual awards, which were made for the first time in 1983.

Referee

The main duties of the referee are to be the sole judge of fair play and be responsible for the proper conduct of the game. In addition, he/she has other tasks to perform, for example, replacing potted balls on their respective spots and advising the players and marker of the score.

The referee must not give advice to players, nor answer any queries regarding the rules that players may ask.

To become a referee, an applicant has to satisfy an official examiner as to his or her knowledge of the game. Once qualified, he receives a Grade 'C' certificate, and after 12 months a Grade 'B' certificate can be applied for. This time, in addition to proving to an examiner that he has an extensive knowledge of the rules, the applicant must also satisfy him that he is capable of handling matches at the highest level. After three years as a Grade 'B' certificate holder, a referee can be nominated by a County or National association for promotion to Grade 'A' status. Only referees of proven outstanding ability are nominated.

All referees are encouraged to become members of the Billiards and Snooker Referees' Association, which exists to improve the standard of refereeing at all levels.

Senior Grade 'A' referees are eligible for membership of the Professional Referees' Association, and it is from this association's list of members (21 at the start of 1985) that officials for all major professional championships are chosen. All official examiners are Grade 'A' referees.

Former women's world champion Vera Selby is a Grade 'A' referee, and is at present the only female member of the Professional Referees' Association.

The youngest person to be appointed a certified referee was 9-year-old Warren Smith, who was granted a Grade C certificate in 1986.

Ray Reardon

Rensburg, Jimmy van

Jimmy van Rensburg was one of South Africa's top amateur players in the post-war years, together with the two Francisco brothers. He won his country's amateur snooker title on 11 occasions, and the billiards title once, and in 1976 he reached the semi-final of the world amateur snooker championship before losing to Malta's Paul Mifsud.

Because of South Africa's political limitations on his international career as an amateur, van Rensburg turned professional in 1978 along with South Africa's other leading amateurs of that time.

Although he occasionally ventures out of his home country, generally to compete in the world professional championship at the Crucible Theatre, it is in South Africa that he earns the bulk of his income from snooker. A promoter as well as a player, he promotes events in South Africa with fellow professional Perrie Mans. And it was perhaps ironic that in winning his first South African Professional title in 1984, van Rensburg should beat Mans in the final – only the second time since 1964 that Mans had lost in the championship.

The 1984 season was one of his best as a professional, as he beat Viv Blignaut to win the South African Open. In the semi-final he beat Silvino Francisco, after Francisco had eliminated Mans. Van Rensburg enjoyed his most successful world championship to date in 1984, when he had good wins over Vic Harris and Ray Edmonds in the qualifying competition before falling to fellow South African Silvino Francisco in the final stage before the competition proper.

Career highlights

- South African Professional Champion 1984
- South African Open Champion 1984
- South African Amateur Snooker Champion 1953-55, 1957, 1961-63, 1967, 1970, 1972-73
- South African Amateur Billiards Champion 1967

Reynolds, Dean

Although he beat Tommy Murphy, the defending champion, to win the national under-19 snooker title in 1981 very few people had heard of Humbersider Dean Reynolds. But before the year was out, he had become widely known up and down the country as a result of beating New Zealander Dene O'Kane in the final of the inaugural *Junior Pot Black*.

A snooker player since the age of five, when he was encouraged by his father, Reynolds turned professional shortly after winning the *Pot Black* title, yet surprisingly he had achieved very little as an amateur; in fact he had not gained any international honours.

Despite that, he fully justified his acceptance as a member of the World Professional Billiards and Snooker Association by reaching the last 16 of the following year's world championships – at the first attempt. He beat Dessie Sheehan, fellow Humbersider Ray Edmonds, and Fred Davis before going out to Silvino Francisco.

Two other good performances, in the Jameson International and Professional Players' Tournament in the 1982-83 season, saw him 19th in the rankings.

In the Jameson he had an excellent win over Willie Thorne before losing 5-0 to Steve Davis. And in the Professional Players' Tournament he beat seasoned campaigner Cliff Wilson 5-1 before losing to Eddie Charlton in the quarter-final.

Reynolds moved up the rankings and into the top 16 in 1986-87 thanks to a semi-final appearance in the Mercantile Credit

Dean Reynolds, a winner of 'Junior Pot Black', clearly enjoying himself at the world championships

Classic and a first round appearance at the Crucible, where he narrowly lost to Jimmy White.

Career highlights
- Mercantile Credit Classic (semi-final) 1987
- National Under-19 Snooker Champion 1981
- *Junior Pot Black* Champion 1981

Riley, E.J. Limited

Riley Leisure operates the largest chain of snooker clubs in the United Kingdom, controlling over 70 in all. In addition, they manufacture snooker and pool tables and a wide range of accessories at their Accrington-based factory.

The company was founded in the late 19th century when renowned 'failed' businessman E.J. Riley was about to fail for the third time. He met a Mr Kenyon, who had a reputation for buying ailing businesses cheap, making them profitable, and then selling them. On looking at Riley's sports shop idea, Kenyon liked it and decided to help Riley. Together they formed a Limited Company in the 1890s and started manufacturing bowls, billiard tables and cricket bats. At one time they were the largest manufacturer of cricket bats, and were the first to introduce the idea of autographed bats.

By 1910 they had turned most of their energies into billiard-table manufacture, and that year they made 800 tables! That figure was down to just 120 by 1979, but the recent boom has seen production rise to 25 per week. Riley tables are regarded as among the best in the world, and have been used for most major tournaments.

The company had a match-room at their Accrington factory, and opened the first one outside the factory in 1910. By the mid-twenties they had nearly 40 halls, and the current figure of over 70 halls was reached in 1982 when they paid Barry Hearn £3·1 million for 16 of his 17 Lucania Snooker Halls. Barry Hearn became a director of Rileys, which went public in 1977, and through him the company has found many leading professionals – such as Steve Davis – to endorse their goods.

One of the game's senior referees, John Williams

Roberts, John Junior

In the late-19th/early-20th century John Roberts Junior was to billiards what Joe Davis later became to snooker. He completely dominated the sport, and when he refused to compete in the then world championships, they were totally devalued.

He won the world title in April 1870 by defeating William Cook, the man who had deprived John's father of the title. He lost it to Joseph Bennett the following November, but regained it two months later with an easy victory over Bennett.

Then followed a series of meetings with Cook which saw Roberts lose three matches for the title. But in May 1875 he wrested the title from Cook, and managed to make two further successful defences against him before setting off for Australia in 1878. Cook claimed the title because Roberts was not around to defend it, but Roberts carried the tag of 'Champion of the World' with him to Australia.

With the rules of billliards not standardized at that time, Roberts vowed he would never compete in the championships again. He returned to Britain, and in February 1885 he chaired a meeting which brought into being the Billiards Association. A set of universal rules were drawn up, and two months later when Roberts and Cook met, again, for the world title, Roberts rightfully won back his crown.

He successfully defended the title once more against Bennett, but after that he never again competed in the championships – he felt 'above' them. Without John Roberts competing they seemed pointless, and for the next four years they were not held at all.

A great crowd puller, John Roberts Junior was one of the first true professionals. His name was used to endorse a wide variety of goods ranging from snooker accessories to cigars and china cups! His road-show, which he used to take around the British Isles, was very popular as it gave many people the chance to witness real billiards skills.

Not only did Roberts take his talents to Australia, but he also visited South Africa, New Zealand, the United States and India. He set up a billiard table manufacturing business in Calcutta, and it was during this time that he met Sir Neville Chamberlain, in 1885. Chamberlain, by then, had fully developed the game of snooker, and drawn up the rules of the game. Roberts brought the new game back to England with him, and although he remained loyal to billiards, he was a competent snooker player. In 1907, the year after he was supposed to have retired from competitive play because of failing eyesight, he made a snooker break of 73, which was officially recognized as a new record.

Like Joe Davis, John Roberts Junior was 'king' and, also like Davis, he was talked about long after his retirement. Billiards has struggled to find his equal since.

Career highlights
World Professional Billiards Champion 1870-71, 1875, 1877, 1885

John Roberts Junior dominated the World Professional Billiards Championships between 1870 and 1885

Roberts, John Senior

One of the first real champions, John Roberts Senior bridged the gap between the earliest competitive billiard matches in the mid-19th century and the championship game later in the 1800s. Liverpool-born Roberts became billiards champion in 1849, when he made the long journey to Brighton from his new home in Oldham, to challenge Jonathan Kentfield for the title. Kentfield had held the title since 1820, but refused to accept the challenge from Roberts; Roberts was then acknowledged as champion. He held the title until 11 February 1870, when he met William Cook at St James's Hall for the first official world billiards title. The Prince of Wales was in attendance as Cook became the first official champion. (Cook carried off the £200 first prize and at 21, was – and still is – the youngest ever winner of the title. The Roberts family honour was upheld two months later when John's son, John Jnr, beat Cook for the title.

A splendid figure of a man, in the mould of cricket's W.G. Grace, Roberts Senior was a perfect gentleman. Around the table he had a speedy manner, but that was accompanied by a great deal of skill. In those days there were no rules about balls leaving the table, and Roberts could play a shot that removed his own ball and the red ball from the table simultaneously. This would leave his opponent with just one ball on the table, and thus forced to play a no-scoring safety shot!

Like his son after him, Roberts took his skills to Australia, in 1864. John Roberts Senior was a good all-round sportsman: he was an expert fighter, and was just as good at bowls as he was at billiards.

He died in March 1893 aged 67, and was fortunate to live long enough to see his son succeed him and become a great champion.

John Roberts Senior: career highlights
Unofficial World Billiards Champion 1849-1870
World Professional Billiards Championship (runner-up) 1870

Rothmans Grand Prix

When the Rothmans Grand Prix was first contested in 1984, it carried the then biggest ever first prize in the history of the sport – £45,000. It was planned as a replacement for the Professional Players' Tournament which had started in 1982 and lasted only two years, carrying first prize money of £5,000 in 1982 and £12,500 in 1983.

The Professional Players' Tournament was established by the World Professional Billiards and Snooker Association (WPBSA) and was the first venture of their own promotion company. The idea was that revenue received by the WPBSA from television rights should be redirected back to the players via a tournament, rather than going to the Inland Revenue in taxes. In principle this was a good idea, but unfortunately, without the attraction of a big name sponsor and television coverage, the tournament did not receive the support it deserved, and was subsequently dropped from the professional calendar. It was then that Rothmans stepped in and filled the gap by announcing their £200,000 Grand Prix.

Rothmans, and the BBC, certainly got their money's worth out of the new event – which, incidentally, carried ranking points. Millions watched, and willed on the likeable Irishman, Dennis Taylor, to victory over Cliff Thorburn in the first final. It was Taylor's first major victory in 13 years as a professional. But Taylor had a more important personal reason for wanting to win – for the memory of his mother, who, sadly, had died the previous month. His sadness – and joy – was shared by television viewers all over the country. Taylor could not withhold his emotions, particularly when his son rushed forward to congratulate him.

Like so many tournaments, the Rothmans was built on shaky foundations. Its predecessor, the Professional Players' Tournament, was not a great success in 1982, its first year. Held at two different venues in the Birmingham area – the La Reserve in Sutton Coldfield, and the International Snooker Club in Aston – the event was poorly supported by the public.

Ray Reardon beat Jimmy White in the final, in which he also made a 132 clearance, to gain his first major tournament win since 1978. Even this was not the highest break of the tournament though; Willie Thorne had scored a 135 in his second round defeat by Murdo McLeod.

The event was held again in 1983 and moved to the Redwood Lodge Country Club in Bristol. The 600-seater badminton hall was regularly filled to capacity and certainly never fell as low as the three spectators that watched one match the previous year.

Steve Davis fell to Humbersider Mike Hallett, but the real hero was Joe Johnson. The likeable Yorkshireman had always showed potential, but disliked playing in front of the television cameras. The Professional Players' Tournament was an untelevised event and he went all the way to the final. Trailing 6-1 to Tony Knowles he started his comeback with a championship-equalling break of 135 before going down 9-8.

Dennis Taylor was the first winner under its new style in 1984, and the following year he lost a 19-frame thriller to Steve Davis while attempting to keep his crown. Davis led 6-1 at the end of the first session, but Taylor went into an 8-7 lead before losing the last two frames.

Twelve months later Jimmy White lined up against Rex Williams who was playing in his first major snooker final. Despite taking a 5-2 lead in the opening session, Williams eventually succumbed to his younger opponent and lost 10-6.

Results (finals)

Professional Players' Tournament

1982 Ray Reardon (Wales) 10
Jimmy White (England) 5
1983 Tony Knowles (England) 9
Joe Johnson (England) 8

Rothmans Grand Prix

1984 Dennis Taylor (Ireland) 10
Cliff Thorburn (Canada) 2
1985 Steve Davis (England) 10
Dennis Taylor (Ireland) 9
1986 Jimmy White (England) 10
Rex Williams (England) 6

Most wins: 1 – Tony Knowles
1 – Ray Reardon
1 – Dennis Taylor
1 – Steve Davis
1 – Jimmy White

Most finals: 2 – Dennis Taylor
2 – Jimmy White

Highest break: 138 – Jimmy White (1986)

Royalty and Nobility

For more than 500 years royalty and nobility have been connected with the game of billiards. The first known reference to a billiard table is in the mid-15th century, when Louis XI of France is believed to have been responsible for having the game of billiards moved from outdoors to indoors.

It was Louis XIV, however, who was instrumental in popularizing the sport in France. He took up billiards in 1694 on doctors' orders as a means of keeping fit, and became so good at the sport he was one of the country's leading players. The only man who could beat him was Monsieur de Chamillart who, in recognition of his mastery of the sport, was made Finance Minister – a bit like making Jimmy White the Foreign Secretary!

In Britain, Mary Queen of Scots enjoyed the game and when she was a state prisoner in Fotheringay Castle in 1576, she complained bitterly to Queen Elizabeth I of the cruelty of depriving her of her billiard table.

In 1605 James I ordered his joiner James Walter to build him one 'billiarde bourde'. Nearly 150 years later George II was not so keen on the sport: around 1750 he banned the playing of billiards in public places.

Table builder John Thurston had several Royal patrons. The first was King George IV, who enjoyed the game, as did his wife, Queen Caroline. Thurston also supplied tables to Queen Victoria. She had a replacement table installed at Buckingham Palace (the first one to be installed at the Palace was in 1836), one at Windsor Castle, and one at Osborne House. Queen Victoria received the first set of rubberized cushions, installed by Thurstons at Windsor Castle on 15 October 1845.

Napoleon III of France was another famous billiard-player. He tried to introduce the sport into Russia in 1855 when he presented Czar Alexander II with a table as a coronation gift.

The first billiards player to give a 'Royal Command Performance' at Buckingham Palace was the famous one-armed player Arthur Goundrill, in 1921. He was soon followed by Walter Lindrum, Tom Reece and Clark McConachy who all gave such performances at the Palace.

Dennis Taylor, winner of the first Rothmans Grand Prix – he had waited 13 years for a major professional win

Rules of Snooker

The rules of snooker as drawn up by the game's inventor, Sir Neville Chamberlain, were officially recognized by the Billiards Association and Control Council (BACC) in 1906.

The following explains how the game is played:

☆ Snooker is played on a standard English billiard table. The approximate playing area is 12′×6′.

☆ A total of 22 balls are used: the cue-ball (white), and 21 object balls – 15 reds, together with yellow, green, brown, blue, pink and black balls (one of each, referred to as the 'colours').

☆ Each red ball has a points value of one when potted and the colours have the following values:

yellow	2
green	3
brown	4
blue	5
pink	6
black	7

☆ At the commencement of the frame the balls are placed in position as shown in the diagram. The cue-ball may be placed anywhere within the 'D' along which the yellow, green and brown balls stand. The position of the cue-ball at the commencement of the frame is the choice of the player taking the first shot – known as the 'break-off.'

☆ The first player has to propel the cue-ball towards the pyramid of reds. And, after hitting at least one of them, it is in his or her interest to disturb them as little as possible and then return the cue-ball to the baulk area. The baulk area is that part of the table between the baulk line and the bottom of the table.

☆ To develop a break, a red ball must first be potted – that is, it must enter the pocket before any other ball does so. Once a red has been potted the player who played the shot may, if he wishes, extend the break by potting one of the colours, which he must nominate if it is not obvious which one he is aiming for. Once a colour has been potted another red must be potted before the break can continue, and so on in the sequence red-colour-red-colour-red...

☆ The red balls, once potted, remain in the pockets, but the coloured balls are returned to the table and placed on the appropriate spot. If their own spot is not available they are placed on the nearest available spot of the highest value. If no spot is available the colour shall be placed as near as possible to its own spot between that spot and the nearest part of the top cushion.

As soon as all the reds have been potted, the colours are potted in ascending order of their points value. This time they are not returned to the table.

☆ At the end of the frame (i.e. when the last ball, the black, has been potted) the player with the most points is the winner. If both players are level then the black ball is respotted. The players toss to decide who strikes first, and play re-starts with the cue-ball being played from the 'D' again. The first person to pot the black ball receives seven points and is the frame winner.

☆ A player does not have to pot a ball, or attempt to pot a ball, with every shot. If he feels that no ball is in a good enough position to be potted, or that it is just impossible, to pot any legal ball, he may play the cue-ball towards the object-ball and leave the cue-ball in such a position that his opponent faces a difficult shot. If the cue-ball rests in such a position that there is not a direct route from the cue-ball to any part of an object ball, he is deemed to be snookered.

☆ All breaks come to an end when a player fails to pot a ball or a foul stroke is played. The next shot is then played from where the cue-ball comes to rest or from the 'D' should the cue-ball have entered the pocket.

☆ If the white does enter the pocket this is a foul stroke and penalty points are awarded against the offending player.

☆ There are many ways that foul strokes and penalties may occur. The most common forms of foul strokes are as follows:

White entering pocket Commonly referred to as 'in-off': if, at any time, the white enters the pocket, this is a foul. If it enters the pocket when the object-ball is a red then a four-point penalty is incurred. If the object ball is a colour then the penalty value is the value of the colour. (Subject to a minimum penalty of four points.)

Hitting the wrong ball If the cue-ball fails to hit the correct object-ball then the shot is deemed to be a foul. If the intended object-ball is a red then the penalty points are equivalent to the points value of the coloured ball incorrectly hit – subject to the four-point minimum.

Similarly, if the object-ball is a colour and the cue-ball hits a red ball or an incorrect coloured ball first, then the penalty is the value of the coloured ball that was 'on' or the coloured ball it hit if a higher value – again with a four-point minimum.

Failing to hit any ball Similar to the above. A four point penalty is awarded if the object ball is a red, and the points value of the colour if the object ball was a coloured ball.

There are many other forms of a foul or penalty shot, as already mentioned. For example:

1 A player not having at least one foot on the ground when playing a shot.
2 A ball leaving the table
3 A player causing the cue-ball to jump over another ball
4 A shot played before a ball comes to rest.
...and many more

Remember, all foul strokes have a *minimum penalty of four points*.

See also Baulk, Break, Cue-ball, Foul, Frame, Free ball, Game, Object-ball, Push-shot, Snookered, Spotting, Touching ball.

The full guide to the rules of snooker, can be obtained from the Billiards and Snooker Control Council, Coronet House, Queen Street, Leeds, West Yorkshire LS1 2TN.

S

Scoring

In the game of snooker, every ball legally potted is worth one point; and once a red ball has been potted the successful player may pot a coloured ball if he so wishes. He is then credited with the value of the ball. The values of the colours are as follows:

yellow	2
green	3
brown	4
blue	5
pink	6
black	7

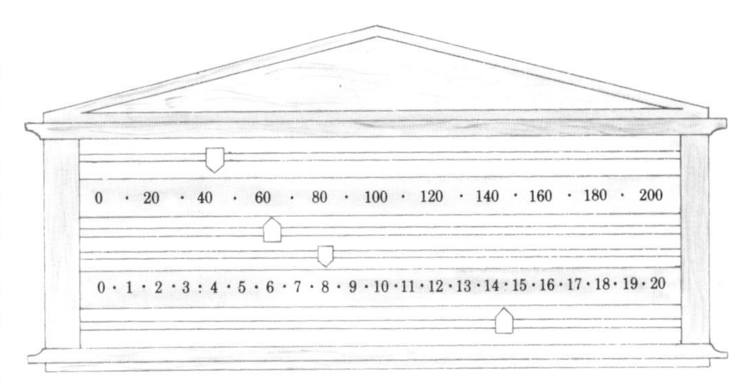

Above: a typical club-room scoreboard with sliding pointers

After a colour has been potted, in order to continue the break the striker must pot another red, and then another colour, and so on. The break continues until a ball is not potted, or a foul shot is played. At that stage, the relevant points are added to the player's score.

At the end of the frame the player with the most points is the winner. In the event of a tie the black ball is re-spotted, and when it is potted, or a foul shot is played, a further seven points are added to the appropriate player's score, and this will decide the frame winner.

Scotland

Although professional billiards was played in Scotland in the late 19th century, the country had to wait 60 years, until the emergence of Walter Donaldson, for a true world-class player.

Donaldson was capable of holding his own alongside the greats like Joe and Fred Davis, Clark McConachy and Horace Lindrum, and in 1947 he brought the country its first world snooker title when he beat Fred Davis 82-63 in the final. His confrontations with Davis were legendary in the early fifties and, while Davis dominated their meetings, Donaldson managed to wrest the title from him for a second time in 1950.

After Donaldson the professional scene in Scotland was virtually non-existent: until 1979, when leading amateur Eddie Sinclair turned professional, the country only possessed one other professional player – Chris Ross. When Sinclair turned professional, the opportunity arose to revive the defunct Scottish professional championship, which Donaldson used to dominate. Then in April 1981, seven new Scottish players were

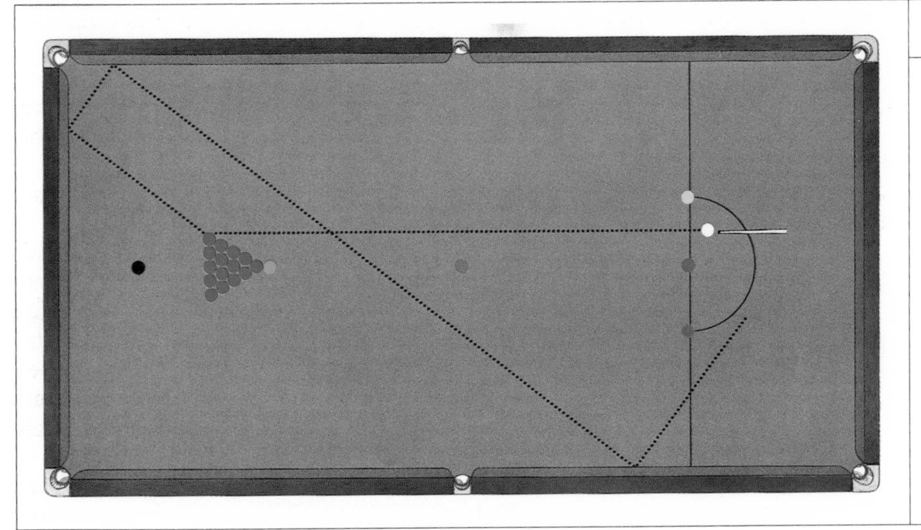

Rules

At the beginning of a frame the balls must be set up as shown, with the colours on their spots and the reds forming a pyramid behind the pink. The dotted line illustrates a typical break-off, showing how the white returns to the relative safety of the baulk area without having dislodged too many reds from the pack.

Scottish Amateur Snooker Championships – Results (finals)

1946 J. Levey beat N. McGowan
1947 J. Levey beat T. Gray
1948 I. Wexelstein beat R. Walls
1949 W. Ramage beat P. Spence
1950 W. Ramage beat R. McKendrick
1951 A. Wilson beat A. Wishart
1952 D. Emerson beat P. Spence
1953 P. Spence beat H. Thompson
1954 D. Edmond beat P. Spence
1955 L. U. Demarco beat P. Spence
1956 W. Barry beat R. McKendrick
1957 T. Paul beat H. Thompson
1958 J. Phillips beat J. Ferguson
1959 J. Phillips beat E. Sinclair
1960 E. Sinclair beat A. Kennedy
1961 J. Phillips beat L. U. Demarco
1962 A. Kennedy beat L. U. Demarco
1963 E. Sinclair beat D. Miller
1964 J. Phillips beat E. Sinclair
1965 L. U. Demarco beat P. Spence
1966 J. Phillips beat E. Sinclair
1967 E. Sinclair beat L. U. Demarco
1968 E. Sinclair beat J. Zonfrillo
1969 A. Kennedy beat L. U. Demarco
1970 D. Sneddon beat M. McLeod
1971 J. Phillips beat D. Miller
1972 D. Sneddon beat L. U. Demarco
1973 E. Sinclair beat J. Zonfrillo
1974 D. Sneddon beat E. Sinclair
1975 E. Sinclair beat J. Phillips
1976 E. Sinclair beat D. Sneddon
1977 R. Miller beat E. McLaughlin
1978 J. Donnelly beat E. McLaughlin
1979 S. Nivison beat I. Wallace
1980 M. Gibson beat E. McLaughlin
1981 R. Lane beat J. Rea
1982 P. Kippie beat K. Baird
1983 G. Carnegie beat J. Rea
1984 S. Hendry beat D. Sneddon
1985 S. Hendry beat J. McNellan
1986 S. Muir beat D. Campbell
1987 S. Nivison beat B. Kelly
Most wins: 7 – Eddie Sinclair
Most finals: 11 – Eddie Sinclair

Scottish Open

1961 J. Phillips beat T. Paul
1962 L. U. Demarco beat T. Paul
1963 A. Kennedy beat T. Paul
1964 A. Kennedy beat W. Kelly
1965-1971 Not held
1972 D. Sneddon beat L. U. Demarco
1973 D. Sneddon beat W. McKerron
1974 W. McKerron beat E. McLaughlin
1975 E. Sinclair beat M. McLeod
1976 J. Phillips beat T. Kelly
1977 R. Cadman beat J. Donnelly
1978 M. Gibson beat W. McKerron
1979 J. Phillips beat E. Sinclair
1980 E. McLaughlin beat W. McKerron
1981 J. McNellan beat J. Zonfrillo
1982 J. Allan beat J. Zonfrillo
1983 M. Gibson beat J. Laidlaw
1984 not known
1985 J. McNellan beat J. Allan
1986 J. Allan beat not known
1987 E. Henderson beat J. Kemp

Most wins: 3 – J. Phillips
Most finals: 4 – W. McKerron

accepted *en bloc* as members of the World Professional Billiards and Snooker Association. This move brought the number of Scottish professionals up to nine, which meant that the championship could be organized as a proper knockout competition.

In 1982 Jim Donnelly became the first Scot to reach the competition proper of the world championship at Sheffield. Scotland enjoyed its best ever period in recent professional snooker at the 1987 championship when Murdo Mcleod became the first Scot ever to win a match at the Crucible. But this achievement was soon overshadowed by that of wonderboy Stephen Hendry, who had come within sight of the title when he lost a classic quarter-final to defending champion Joe Johnson by 13 frames to 12.

Scotland was the first of the home countries to break away from the Billiards Association and Control Club and form its own billiards championships, which it did in 1925. Yet surprisingly they did not institute their official amateur snooker championships until after the war, although an unofficial championship was held in 1931.

It was a Scot who became the first amateur to make a maximum 147 break in a tournament – in 1982, when Jim McNellan did so at the Cue Club in Glasgow; but unfortunately it was not recognized as a record amateur break. Ewan Henderson, however, established a new Scottish amateur championship record break of 133 during the 1986 competition.

The professional season of snooker in Britain traditionally starts in Scotland, with eight leading of the leading professionals contesting the Langs Scottish Masters tournament in September each year.

See also Scottish Professional Championships

Scottish Masters

see Langs Scottish Masters

Scottish Professional Championships

The Scottish Professional Championship dates back to pre-war days when Walter Donaldson used to take on, and invariably beat, challengers for the title. After the war, the so-called Championships fell into disuse because of the lack of Scottish professionals.

Eddie Sinclair – Scotland's top player over the last 20 years

In 1979, however, Eddie Sinclair turned professional and met 'Anglo' Chris Ross in a challenge match for the title. The idea was revived by Scottish amateur (later professional) Bert Demarco. Six more Scots joined the professional ranks in 1981, making it possible to organize a new eight-man knockout competition. Ian Black beat Matt Gibson 11-7 in that first final.

The following year, at the Glen Pavilion, Dunfermline, the event was sponsored by Tartan Bitter and the Daily Record. Eddie Sinclair, the last winner of the old challenge system and Scotland's most consistent player of the previous 20 years, beat defending champion Ian Black in the final to win the £1,000 first prize.

In 1983 the tournament was down to seven entrants; it was played at the Students' Union at Glasgow University, and it provided yet another new winner – Murdo McLeod.

At one point McLeod was trailing Sinclair 8-4 in the final, but he went on to win 11-9. The 1983 event was promoted without the aid of sponsors, but even so it carried £5,000 total prize money. More important for McLeod than the victory, however, was the remaining place he had earned himself in the Scottish Masters, and a plum match with Steve Davis.

The championship was moved from its early-season slot in the calendar in 1984-85 to a later in the season. Murdo McLeod retained his title but a year later he and his fellow professionals were no match for the outstanding 17-year-old Stephen Hendry, who won the title at the first attempt in 1986.

Scottish Professional Championships – Results

1981 I. Black 11 M. Gibson 7
1982 E. Sinclair 11 I. Black 7
1983 M. McLeod 11 E. Sinclair 9
1984 Not held
1985 M. McLeod 11 E. Sinclair 2
1986 S. Hendry 10 M. Gibson 5
1987 S. Hendry 10 J. Donnelly 7

Most wins: 2 – Murdo McLeod
2 – Stephen Hendry

Most finals: 3 – Eddie Sinclair

Highest break: 106 – Murdo McLeod (1983)

Screw
See Shots

The youngest Scottish professional champion, Stephen Hendry, who was only 17 years 3 months when he beat Matt Gibson to win the title in 1986

Season

Neither the Billiards and Snooker Control Council nor the World Professional Billiards and Snooker Association lay down any specific dates at which the snooker season must start and finish. In the UK, however, it is generally regarded as starting in September and ending in May. But nowadays, most clubs organize summer tournaments, which mean it has become an all-year round sport. Many top-class professionals play most of the year because, after the end of the season in Britain, they fly off to the Far East, Australia, New Zealand, Canada, Spain and other far-flung destinations to compete in tournaments.

The 1986-87 season in Britain started on 7 September with the qualifying matches for the BCE International. The first major final, the Scottish Masters, was contested on 21 September. The season ended on 4 May with the final of the world professional championship at the Crucible Theatre.

Seeding

The principle of seeding in snooker, as in any sport, is to provide the final stages of a competition with the better players. Most major events use the World Professional Billiards and Snooker Association's rankings as a guideline to establish the seeded players, although some events give preference to their defending champion by making him the number one seed, the other players following in ranking order.

The following is a hypothetical draw for round one of a championship involving the top 16 WPBSA seeded players at the start of the 1986-87 season:

Steve Davis (1) v Rex Williams (16)
Joe Johnson (8) v Kirk Stevens (9)
Jimmy White (5) v Silvino Francisco (12)
Tony Knowles (4) v Neal Foulds (13)
Dennis Taylor (3) v Doug Mountjoy (14)
Alex Higgins (6) v Tony Meo (11)
Willie Thorne (7) v Terry Griffiths (10)
Cliff Thorburn (2) v Ray Reardon (15)
(Figures in brackets indicate seeding)

The winner of game one would play the winner of game two in the next round, and so on. It can be seen that, if all matches went according to form, the 1, 2, 3 and 4 seeds would reach the semi-finals, and the 1 and 2 seeds would progress to the final.

It is rare for seedings to work out like that, because – fortunately – the elements of chance and fortune play a role.

Vera Selby – not only a champion snooker player, but a grade 'A' referee and television commentator as well

Selby, Vera

With five national ladies' snooker titles and eight billiards titles to her credit, Vera Selby's record is second only to Maureen Baynton's. But unlike Maureen, Vera has won the ladies' world title – twice. What makes Vera Selby's record all the more remarkable is the fact that she did not take up playing either sport until 1968 when she was 37 years old; and within two

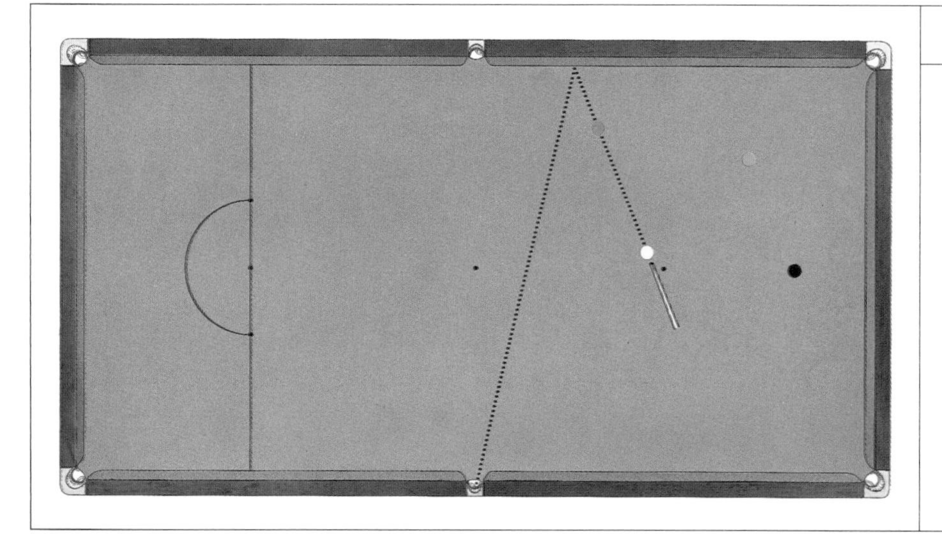

Shots

An example of a successful double. Although shots such as this are popular among spectators and club players, professional snooker players avoid performing them because they are too risky.

How right-hand side affects the angle at which the cue-ball will leave the cushion. The inset diagram shows where the cue should strike the white in order to impart right-hand side spin.

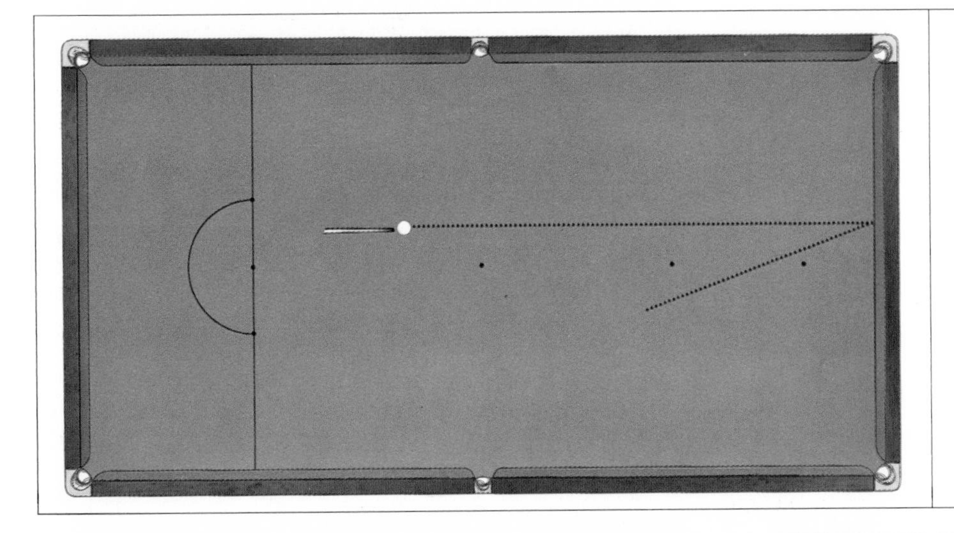

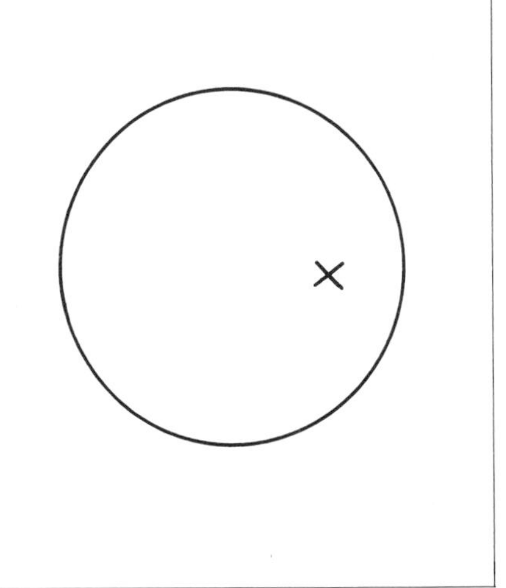

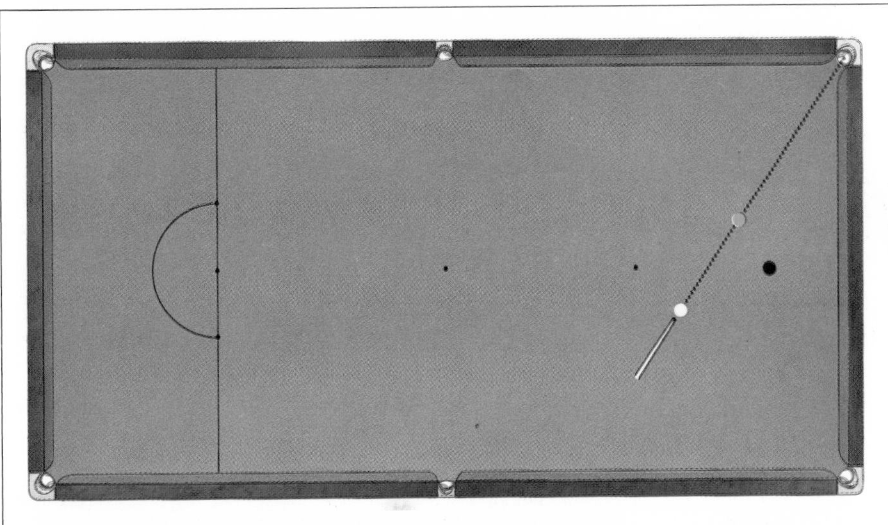

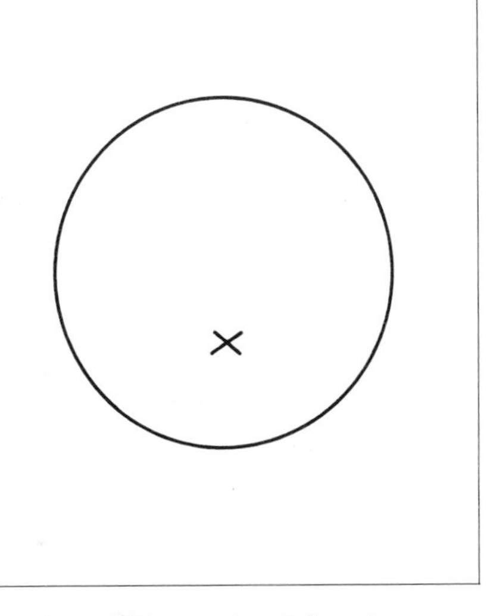

Above: *this stun shot will pot the pink and leave the cue-ball precisely in the position that the pink previously occupied. It will then be in position to pot the black. The inset diagram shows where the cue must strike the white.*

Below: an expert screw shot which pots the pink and brings the white back for the black, instead of following the pink. Inset, the cue-ball must be struck lower down than for a stun shot, to impart back-spin.

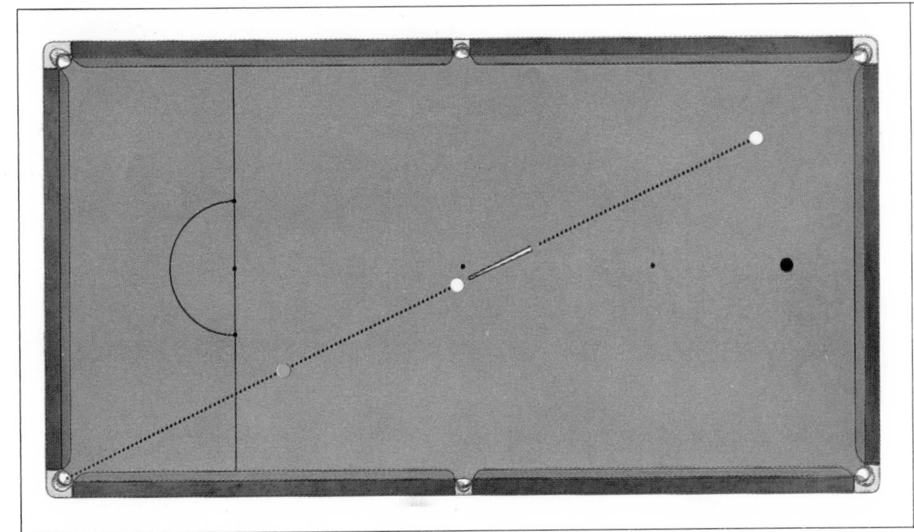

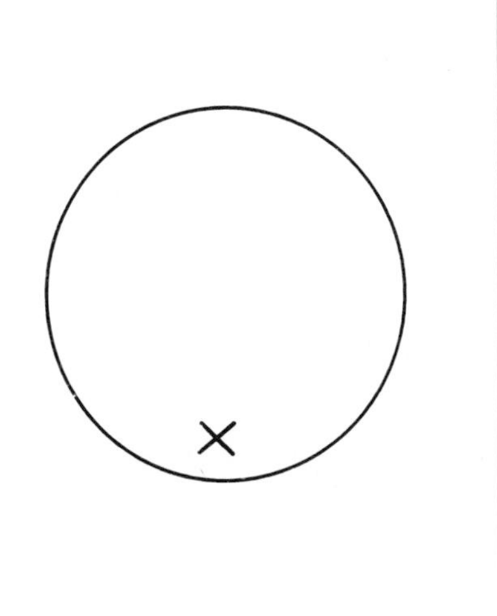

title – twice. What makes Vera Selby's record all that more remarkable is the fact that she did not take up playing either sport until 1968 when she was 37 years old; and within two years she had won her first national (billiards) title.

Vera won the world snooker championship in Middlesbrough in 1976, when the ladies' championship was run in conjunction with the men's. The next world championships were held in 1980, but Vera failed to retain her title, losing to Ann Johnson in the quarter-final. The following year she regained it at Thorness Bay, defeating Mandy Fisher 3-0 in the final and taking the £2,000 first prize.

Her winning of the world title was rewarded by her being voted the Newcastle City Sports Council's Personality of the Year – not bad for a 51-year-old. Vera plays in a male-dominated league in the Gateshead area, and it was significant that as she got better, the number of clubs that refused admission to women increased!

Vera is also a Grade 'A' referee and was the first woman to officiate in tournaments involving the leading male professionals. She also summarized for the BBC during their coverage of the 1982 world professional championships and in 1987 she became the first lady to be appointed an official examiner of Billiards and Snooker referees.

Career highlights
World Open Champion 1976, 1981
National Women's Snooker Champion 1972-75, 1979
National Women's Billiards Champion 1970-74, 1976-78

Shots

The art of controlling the cue-ball is the secret of successful snooker. The ability to apply side, screw and stun to the cue-ball successfully turn an ordinary club player into a good-quality player. The following is a guide as to how these shots should be played, and what effect they have.

Side is achieved, as its name implies, by striking the cue-ball to the right or left of its centre. When this is done, the ball is sent into a spinning motion, and the spin will affect the angle at which the cue-ball leaves the object-ball, or cushion, after striking it. Right-hand side will cause the cue-ball to take a wider angle to the right, and left-hand side will cause it to take a wider angle to the left. When right-hand side is applied to the cue-ball and it makes contact with the right-hand side of the object-ball, this is known as running side.

When the object-ball is hit on the left hand side by a cue-ball with right-hand side on it, this is known as check side.

Screw: striking the cue-ball as near the bottom as possible will cause it to go into a reverse spinning motion, and, after striking the object-ball, this will propel it backwards in the direction from which it came.

The **stun** shot is used to make the cue-ball stop immediately after it has made contact with the object-ball. One has to strike the cue-ball below its centre, but not so low as to put screw to it.

One of the most spectacular of shots (when it works), the **double** is rarely used by the professional player, unless he is left with no alternative. A double is achieved when the object-ball is pocketed after rebounding off one, or more, cushions.

Simpson, Warren

Australian Warren Simpson turned professional in the early 1960s, and up to the time of his death in 1980 he had to cope with two giant obstacles in his life. One was the diabetes from which he had suffered since an early age. The other was Eddie Charlton. Had it not been for Charlton's presence, Simpson would have been his country's top snooker player of the sixties and seventies. Simpson had to play second-fiddle to Charlton, but he did have two moments of glory.

The first was in 1968 when he won the Australian professional title for the second time. He had won the title in 1963, but the following year Charlton won it for the first time and, apart from defeat by Simpson in the 1968 final, retained it until 1984. But Simpson's greatest moment came two years later when the world professional championships were held in Australia: he beat Gary Owen, John Pulman and Perrie Mans in his round-robin group to qualify for a semi-final meeting with Charlton. Charlton was clear favourite to reach the final, but against all the odds Simpson beat his fellow Australian for the second time in his professional career, and thus set himself up to meet John Spencer in the final. But he was no match for the Englishman, who went on to win.

Simpson never recaptured that form, ill-health playing a large part in the decline of his fortunes. After losing 15-11 to Ray Reardon in the second round of the 1975 world championships he never competed in them again.

An accurate potter, one of the features of Simpson's game was his speed around the table. He was also a great gambler and loved playing money matches, mostly at his beloved City Tattersalls Club in Sydney. Just before he died at Towoon Bay, New South Wales, he was honoured with a special presentation at City Tatts.

Career highlights
World Professional Snooker Championship (runner-up) 1970
Australian Professional Snooker Champion 1963, 1968
Australian Open Champion 1954, 1957
Australian Amateur Snooker Champion 1953, 1957

Willie Smith – a billiards man with little regard for snooker, he nevertheless reached two world finals

Smith, Willie

Willie Smith is immortalized as the man against whom Joe Davis recorded the first official 147 break in 1955. But in his own right Smith was a top-class player, and earned a great deal of respect.

It was with the ordinary working man that Darlington-born Smith identified; he was the original 'People's Champion', a title which has come down to Alex Higgins today. He did not restrict his playing to the exclusive London billiard halls, but took his game to the working men's clubs where his skills could be witnessed by far more people. As important a snooker centre as Thurston's was, it could accommodate only 172 at that time.

A natural cueman, Smith became a professional in 1901 at the age of 15; he lost his amateur status after receiving the sum of 10s 6d. (52½p) for taking part in a match.

It was at billiards that Smith excelled, however. He entered only two world professional billiards championships – and won them both. The second, in 1923, saw him beat the legendary Tom Newman.

Smith had an outstanding season in 1928-29. He registered the highest billiards break of his career (2,743) against Newman, and during the season he made 15 breaks of 1,000 or more.

As snooker became popular he commented that the public would never stand for it! But, going along with his fellow professionals, he started playing seriously and went on to reach two snooker world finals, losing to Joe Davis on each occasion.

In the light of his lack of love for snooker, it was perhaps a touch ironic that Willie Smith should be involved in the first snooker match to be televised when part of his match with Horace Lindrum was screened in April 1937.

Smith died at his Leeds home in June 1982 at the age of 96. He remained very active in his latter years, and was still driving a car well into his nineties, and not just to the corner shop – he once drove as far as Cornwall on holiday.

He spent the post-war years playing exhibition matches, and was playing well into his seventies when he was still capable of billiard breaks of 500 and snooker breaks in excess of 70.

Two years before his death he was asked whether his views on snooker had changed in 50 years. His reply: 'They should change the rules – all of them...'

Right to the very end, Willie Smith remained a devoted billiards man.

Career highlights

- World Professional Snooker Championship (runner-up) 1933, 1935
- World Professional Billiards Champion 1920, 1923

Smyth, John

In 1978, Dublin-born John Smyth became the first full-time snooker referee. At that year's annual general meeting of the Billiards and Snooker Control Council at the London Polytechnic, Smyth asked the meeting if he could call himself a professional referee. Nobody could see any reason why not, and that is what he became.

His action eventually led to the formation of the Professional Referees' Association, and he subsequently dedicated himself to the sport full-time, giving up his job as a tube-train driver with London Transport.

Now living in London, John Smyth is one of the sport's leading referees. Although he started officiating only in 1968, he became a Grade 'A' referee just four years later and has since officiated at every major professional event, including the world championship.

One of snooker's leading, and most respected, referees, John Smyth

Snooker Origins

The exact origins of the game of snooker, like those of billiards, are not known. Billiards was played as long ago as the 14th century, but snooker is a relatively new variation.

One theory as to how billiards got its name arises from a story involving a London pawnbroker named William Kew – known as Bill. On rainy days he would remove the three balls that were the emblem of his trade from outside his shop, and bring them indoors to protect them. When bored through lack of customers he would place the balls on the floor and push them about with his yard-stick – hence the expression Bill-Yard.

Between the 14th and 17th centuries a form of billiards not dissimilar to croquet was played outdoors, but it is Louis XI of France who is credited with first playing the game indoors, and on a table. The first public billiard room in Great Britain – the Piazza, Covent Garden – opened in the early part of the 19th century, and it was not long before many people were playing.

The sport of billiards was a popular pastime with army officers, and it was with one of them, Neville Bowes Chamberlain (later General Sir Neville Chamberlain – no relation to the Prime Minister), that the game of snooker is said to have started. In 1875, while with the Devonshires at Jubbulpore, India, he and his fellow officers, getting increasingly bored with billiards, began to introduce extra balls into the standard game in an attempt to vary the game. They went on to devise new games, including the forerunner of snooker, a game called pyramids, which was played with a white ball and 15 reds. To these, the other colours were added, one at a time, until the present day quota of 22 was reached.

It was during one of his billiard sessions with the newly added colours, that Chamberlain called one of his fellow officers a 'snooker' after the latter had failed to pot a relatively easy coloured ball. The term was the name given to new recruits at the Royal Military Academy in Woolwich. His opponent taking offence at this, Chamberlain was quick to point out that they were all 'snookers' when it came to this new game. He added, therefore, that the game itself should be called snooker.

Snooker was not played outside India for ten years, and it was only in 1880, when Chamberlain was posted to Ootacamund, Nilgris, in southern India, that it was seen outside Jubbulpore. It was at the Ooty Club that Sir Neville drew up the first rules of snooker and posted them in the billiard room there.

The new game came to England in 1885 when a leading billiard player of the era, John Roberts, visited Calcutta to coach the Maharajah of Cooch Behar. The Maharajah was a friend of Sir Neville's, and he and Roberts were introduced. Roberts later returned to England with the new sport.

Billiards remained the more popular of the two sports in Britain until the 1940s, since when snooker has gradually overtaken it in popularity. Snooker has now gathered such a following that it is one of Britain's largest spectator and participant sports, and its popularity is still increasing. It is not only in

Snookered

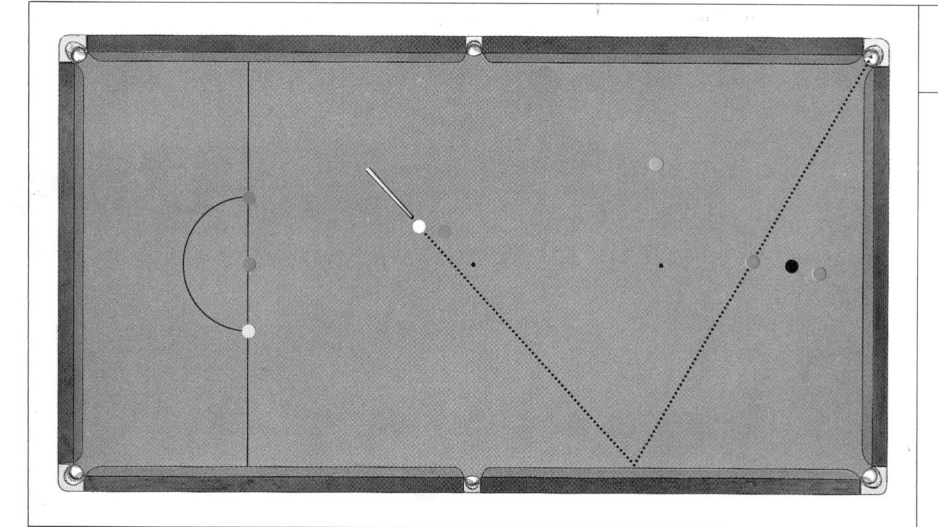

A typical snooker; the dotted line shows the easiest way of getting out of it. The more adventurous player may attempt the pot, but a miss could leave his opponent in a good position to finish the frame.

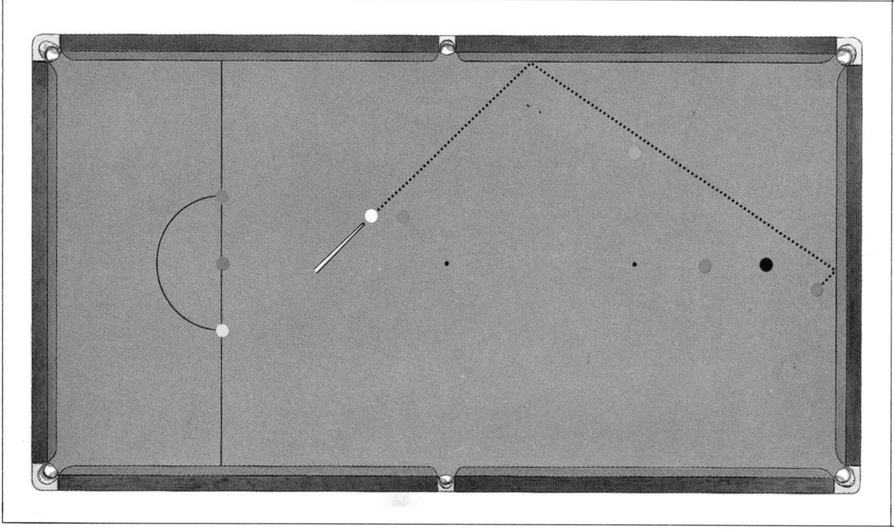

The same snooker, showing how the more experienced player would go about getting out of it – no chance of scoring, but his opponent is unlikely to be left 'on', and may even be snookered himself.

Britain that it has captured the imagination: thanks to television coverage it has become a major pastime in Canada and Australia. The Far East and Europe are other growth areas.

Snooker Plus

Snooker plus was the idea of Joe Davis and was first seen during the News of the World tournament at Burroughes Hall on 26 October 1959. Davis felt that leading players needed a further goal once the magical 147 break had been achieved, and the introduction of two new coloured balls to the game provided the opportunity to make those bigger breaks. The two new balls were orange (worth eight points) and purple (worth ten points). Consequently it was possible to make a break of 210. Most players felt the making of a 147 break was hard enough – to extend the maximum beyond that point was even harder.

The diagram shows the position of the balls on the table in a game of snooker plus, with the orange ball being spotted midway between the blue and pink. The purple was spotted midway between the brown and blue.

As a result of the high-value purple ball being spotted so far up the table, the making of a maximum 210 break would have required tremendous skill and control; it is hardly surprising that there were no recorded instances of a maximum break.

The Billiards Association and Control Club included the rules of snooker plus in their handbook for the first time in the 1965-66 season. Appropriately, Davis was the first player to compile a century break at snooker plus, doing so against his brother Fred at the 'unveiling' of the new game in 1959, when he compiled a 108 break. The highest recorded break is one of 156 by Irishman Jackie Rea.

Snooker Scene

Snooker Scene is the sport's best known and longest established magazine. Published monthly by sole proprietors Everton's News Agency, the editor is professional player Clive Everton.

The first edition appeared in April 1972, and the main story in that edition was the winning of the world professional title by a little-known youngster, Alex Higgins.

Snooker Scene was born out of the amalgamation of *Billiards and Snooker* and *World Snooker*. Everton had been editor of the former since 1966, and left in the seventies to start the new magazine. In 1972, following discussions with the B&SCC, the two magazines merged to form *Snooker Scene*.

Clive Everton's assistant editor is Janice Hale, and one of the features of *Snooker Scene* is her *Day-by-Day* diary.

Snookered

The cue-ball is snookered when it is impossible to make a direct stroke in a straight line to any part of every ball that is 'on'. This

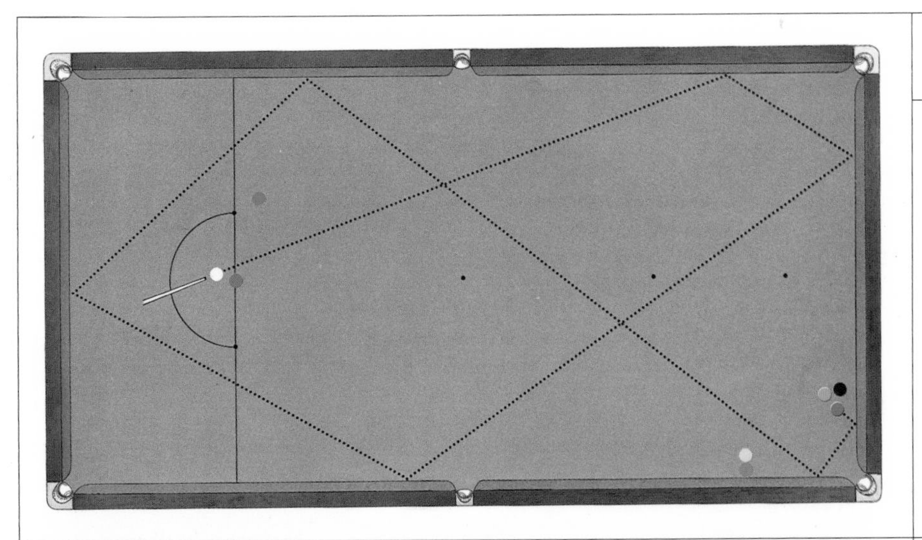

Snookered

There is virtually no such thing as the 'impossible' snooker, as demonstrated here. The player unfortunate enough to find himself in this situation will have to go off no fewer than seven cushions – and play the ball with plenty of side.

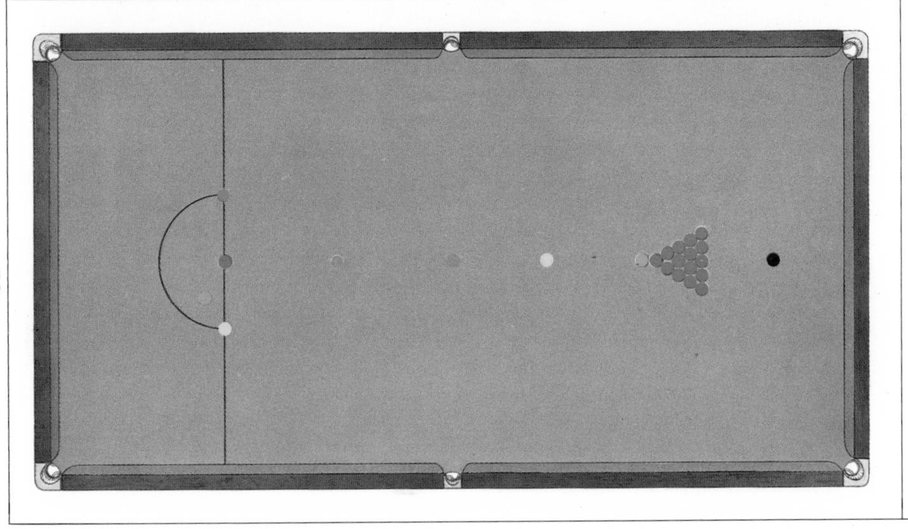

Snooker Plus

Position of the balls at the start of a game of snooker plus. Due to the distance between the purple and the pack of reds, it is more difficult to build a break around a sequence of red-purple-red shots than with the black in conventional snooker.

situation almost always arises when a ball or balls that are 'not on' obstruct the cue ball. But it is possible to be snookered by the cushion as well as by other balls – see diagram on page 123.

Getting out of snookers is often not as difficult as it looks, particularly to the experienced player. But there is much more to it than just making sure the cue-ball hits the object-ball after a snooker. The art of getting out of snookers is making sure, after you have hit – or even missed – the object-ball, that your opponent is not left in an advantageous position. (But note that a deliberate miss constitutes a foul stroke; *see also* Foul.)

The diagrams give examples of how to get out of snookers.

South Africa

The South African Billiards and Snooker Association was formed in 1915 and is one of the oldest in the world. The association started organizing its national billiards championships in 1920, and snooker championships from 1937.

The popularity of the sports in South Africa dates back to the early part of the 20th century, when the legendary John Roberts Junior toured the country. Despite its early beginnings, it is only since the mid-sixties that the country has produced players of world quality. Perrie Mans – South African professional champion from 1965 to 1984 (with the exception of 1979-80), and son of Peter Mans, South Africa's first professional snooker champion – became the first and only South African to reach the professional world championship final when he lost to Ray Reardon in 1978. As Mans spends more time in his home country these days, he has been succeeded as his country's number one on the international stage by Silvino Francisco, who has rapidly developed into one of the world's leading players.

Francisco has a good snooker-playing pedigree – his brother Mannie was a runner-up in the world amateur championship; and Mannie's son was one of eight South Africans who were members of the World Professional Billiards and Snooker Association in 1985.

South Africa has staged three world amateur championship finals – the 1929 and 1936 billiards finals, and the 1976 snooker final. The latter was held in Johannesburg, and was won by Doug Mountjoy. The country has, however, had one world champion – Allan Prior, who won the 1927 world amateur billiards championship. And in Gerry Povall they had a one-time holder of the official amateur world record snooker break – 105, made in 1956.

The suggestion that a world amateur billiards championship should be held was made by a South African, Arthur Walker, and it is for the Arthur Walker Trophy that the world championships are contested today.

In 1965 the world professional snooker championships were held in South Africa – the first time they had been played outside England. Rex Williams challenged defending champion John Pulman, and they played 47 matches around the country. Pulman retained his title but, shortly after the championship, Williams became the second man after Joe Davis to make an official 147 break. He achieved this while playing against Mannie Francisco in Cape Town.

Snooker in South Africa has, like other sports, been affected by the political situation, and because they could not compete at international level many of the leading amateurs turned professional in 1978. But for many of them it was too late to break into the sport at the highest level. Even so, the country had a leading player in Perrie Mans, who turned professional in the 1960s and reigned supreme for nearly 20 years. His domination

South Africa's only world professional championship finalist, Perrie Mans – seen here in action against Ray Reardon in the 1978 final, which Reardon won

South Africa – Results (winners)

South African professional champions
1948-1950 Peter Mans
1950-1965 Freddie van Rensburg
1965-1979 Perrie Mans
1979-1980 Derek Mienie
1980-1984 Perrie Mans
1984 Jimmy van Rensburg
1985 Silvino Francisco
1986 Silvino Francisco

South African amateur champions
1937 A. Prior
1938 A.H. Ashby
1939 A. Prior
1940-1945 Not held
1946 F. Walker
1947 Not held
1948 F. Walker
1949 E. Kerr
1950 T.G. Rees
1951 T.G. Rees
1952 T.G. Rees
1953 J. van Rensburg
1954 J. van Rensburg
1955 J. van Rensburg
1956 F. Walker
1957 J. van Rensburg
1958 R. Walker
1959 M. Francisco
1960 Perrie Mans
1961 J. van Rensburg
1962 J. van Rensburg
1963 J. van Rensburg
1964 M. Francisco
1965 M. Francisco
1966 M. Francisco
1967 J. van Rensburg
1968 S. Francisco
1969 S. Francisco
1970 J. van Rensburg
1971 M. Francisco
1972 J. van Rensburg
1973 J. van Rensburg
1974 S. Francisco
1975 M. Francisco
1976 Not held
1977 S. Francisco
1978 J. van Niekerk
1979 F. Ellis
1980 F. Ellis
1981 P. Francisco
1982 P. Francisco
1983 P. Francisco
1986 S. Francisco

Most wins: 11 – Jimmy van Rensburg

of the South African professional championships was broken in 1979 when he lost the title to Derek Mienie.

The championships fell into disuse in 1981, but were revived in 1984, when seasoned campaigner Jimmy van Rensburg beat Mans 10-7 in the final at the MOTHS Club in Johannesburg. Unfortunately for the organizers, the championships did not receive the usual £1,000-per-entrant grant from the World Professional Billiards and Snooker Association because many of the entrants were recognized as professionals only in South Africa.

On the national amateur front, Jimmy van Rensburg has been the most successful snooker player, winning 11 titles.

South Africa has twice figured in amateur snooker test matches. The first was in 1965, when Mannie Francisco and Jimmy van Rensburg took part in a three-test series against

South Africa boasts two players in the world's top 20 – nephew and uncle, Peter (left) and Silvino Francisco

England, represented by Ray Reardon and Jonathan Barron. The series was played in Cape Town, Durban and Johannesburg, and England won 2-1. The same three cities were chosen for the next three-test series in 1975. This time South Africa, represented by Silvino and Mannie Francisco and Mike Hines, took on a British Isles team consisting of Alwyn Lloyd and Ray Edmonds. The British Isles won the series 1-0 with two matches drawn.

Spain

The opening of two snooker halls on the Costa del Sol, one in 1983 and the other in 1984, gives some indication that the sport is now spreading beyond its traditional Commonwealth bases. The sport has not traditionally been played by the Spaniards, but all that is now changing as a result of the building of the two snooker centres at Fuengirola and Torremolinos.

The idea to introduce snooker into southern Spain came from Stockport businessmen Joe Parkinson and Ian Lennox. With 12,000 British subjects resident in the Marbella area, they saw a need for a snooker hall, and consequently set up their Stockport-based enterprise, *Snooker España*.

That first tournament saw twelve invited British players take part, four of whom – Tony Knowles, Dennis Taylor, Joe Johnson and Mark Wildman – were seeded to the final stages. The opening matches were played at the Fuengirola and Torremolinos Snooker Centres, but at the quarter-final stage, the tournament moved to the Las Palmeras Hotel in Torremolinos. there was seating for 380 people, and the matches were watched by capacity crowds.

Dennis Taylor beat Grimsby's Mike Hallett in the best-of-nine frame final, and the top break of the tournament was made by Joe Johnson with a 105.

John Spencer, the first player to win the world title using a two-piece cue, enjoying himself at the Crucible

Spectrum Arena

The Spectrum Arena, Warrington, is one of the leading concert theatres, sporting venues, and exhibition centres in the north-west of England. Owned by the Warrington and Runcorn Development Corporation, it was opened in November 1981, and is situated within the Birchwood New Town development on the outskirts of Warrington.

The maximum seating capacity of 1,900 makes the Spectrum Arena a popular venue – particularly with snooker and basketball fans. It is the home of the FSO Cars/Manchester United basketball team that plays in the National Basketball League. But snooker and basketball are just two of the many sports played here: there are also four squash courts, roller skating, indoor tennis, badminton, karate, ju-jitsu, indoor bowls... even popmobility. Besides these there are facilities for circuit training, and a comprehensive health suite containing an impressive array of saunas and sun-beds.

As a theatre the Spectrum is gaining in popularity and now attracts big name stars. Because of its size, it can also attract, and accommodate, big bands like James Last.

Competitive snooker first came to the Spectrum in 1983, when it staged the second playing of the Lada Classic. The previous year had seen Steve Davis register the first televised 147 break, but the Spectrum was not as fortunate in 1983. The audience did, however, see Davis win the title as he beat Bill Werbeniuk – playing in his first major final – by 9 frames to 5.

Davis retained his title in 1984 when he beat fellow Londoner Tony Meo 9-8 in a close final. But the 1984 competition belonged to one man – John Parrott. From nearby Liverpool, Parrott eliminated such notable stars as Alex Higgins and Tony Knowles before being eliminated in the semi-final by Davis. The scenes at Parrott's match with Higgins were reminiscent of a soccer match between Liverpool and Manchester United. both players were encouraged by fervent supporters.

Lada withdrew from snooker sponsorship in 1984, but the replacement tournament, the Mercantile Credit Classic, was also staged at the Spectrum.

Sadly the facilities have been lost to snooker as a result of its closure in 1986.

Spencer, John

Since winning his third world professional title in 1977, John Spencer's only major successes have been winning the Wilson's Classic – forerunner of the Lada Classic – in January 1980, the Winfield Australian Masters the same year, and being a member of the England team that won the World Team Cup in 1981.

That is, however, a poor reflection on the snooker career of John Spencer. The old breed of snooker follower – he who has followed the sport since its rebirth in the late sixties – will testify that John Spencer was one of the best. He was certainly one of the most lethal long potters of the ball, and his ability to play the deep screw shot left many a spectator, and opponent, in awe.

Spencer, who came from Radcliffe, Lancashire, started playing at the age of 15, and within a year of first holding a cue was compiling century breaks. But in 1953, two years after taking up snooker, he was called up for national service. He then stopped playing, and it was not until 1963 that he took it up seriously again. He entered the English amateur championship for the first time in the 1963-64 season and went all the way to the final where he lost to a man with whom he was to share many tense battles over the years – Ray Reardon. He lost in the following year's final to Pat Houlihan but in his third successive final, in 1966, he beat Marcus Owen. Spencer travelled to Karachi as one of England's representatives for that year's world amateur championships, but he finished runner-up to Gary Owen.

Spencer's days as an amateur came to an end in 1968 when he, Gary Owen and Ray Reardon became the first new professionals since 1951. John was 33 years of age at the time, but he enjoyed every minute of playing the holiday camp circuit, and travelling over 50,000 miles a year to perform exhibitions at £14 per night.

The world professional championship was revived as a knockout tournament in 1969 and Spencer gained revenge over Gary Owen by beating him 37-24 in the final, which was played at London's Victoria Hall. He lost his crown to Reardon in 1970, but regained it later that year when the championship was held in Australia. Fully expected to retain it in 1972, he lost to a little-known player, who had had to come through the qualifying rounds, in the final. That little-known player was Alex Higgins. Spencer's third title came in 1977, when he won the first championship to be held at Sheffield's Crucible Theatre. There he beat Cliff Thorburn 25-21 to become the first champion to win the title using a two-piece cue.

In between his first and last world titles, Spencer had become the first winner of the prestigious Benson and Hedges Masters tournament, beating Ray Reardon 9-8 in the final in 1975. He had also appeared in five *Pot Black* finals and won three of them. He has since appeared in one more *Pot Black* final, losing to Terry Griffiths in 1984.

In 1979 Spencer became the first player to compile a maximum 147 break in tournament play, and nearly recorded the first televised maximum at the same time. He was playing Cliff Thorburn in the quarter-final of the Holsten Lager tournament at Slough (which Spencer went on to win). It was never ratified as an official break because the pockets of the table did not conform to the official templates. To add to his misfortune, the television crew covering the event were at lunch because of a work-to-rule, and the cameras were not rolling at the time of his historic break. By a further irony, the Holsten was one of the few competitions that did not carry a special prize for a 147 break.

Spencer's career nearly came to an end in 1984 when he contracted a disease that caused double vision. He did not play at all between May and August but, thankfully, the ailment has been stemmed, although he needs constant medication to keep it under control.

The eye trouble was part of the reason for Spencer's decline and his drop from 20th to 34th in the rankings, but he showed true fighting spirit in the 1986-87 season and hauled himself back into the top 32 and into 28th place in the rankings. That upward trend was largely thanks to a great performance in the Dulux British Open, when, after fine wins over Tony Meo and Dave Martin, Spencer found himself in the quarter-final. Up against Jimmy White he trailed 3-2 in the best-of-9. Needing six snookers to win the sixth frame, Spencer forced White to make errors and thus levelled the match. However, it was all in vain as White eventually won 5-3. Spencer collected £9,000 for that day's work – the biggest cheque of his 20-year professional career.

One of the game's great characters, John Spencer treats the game as fun, but he also knows how and when to play it seriously. His vast experience is much sought after and his broad Mancunian/Lancastrian accent can regularly be heard in his role as a television summarizer.

Career highlights

- World Professional Snooker Champion 1969, 1971, 1977
- Benson & Hedges Masters Champion 1975
- Benson & Hedges Irish Masters Champion 1978
- Wilsons Classic Champion 1980
- Winfield Australian Masters Champion 1980
- Holsten Lager Tournament Champion 1979
- World Cup 1981 (member of winning England team)
- *Pot Black* Champion 1970-71, 1976
- Pontins Professional Champion 1977
- English Amateur Champion 1966

Sponsors

Like all sports, snooker is dependent upon sponsorship. Fortunately, because of its extensive television coverage, it has relatively little difficulty in attracting major sponsors. As one

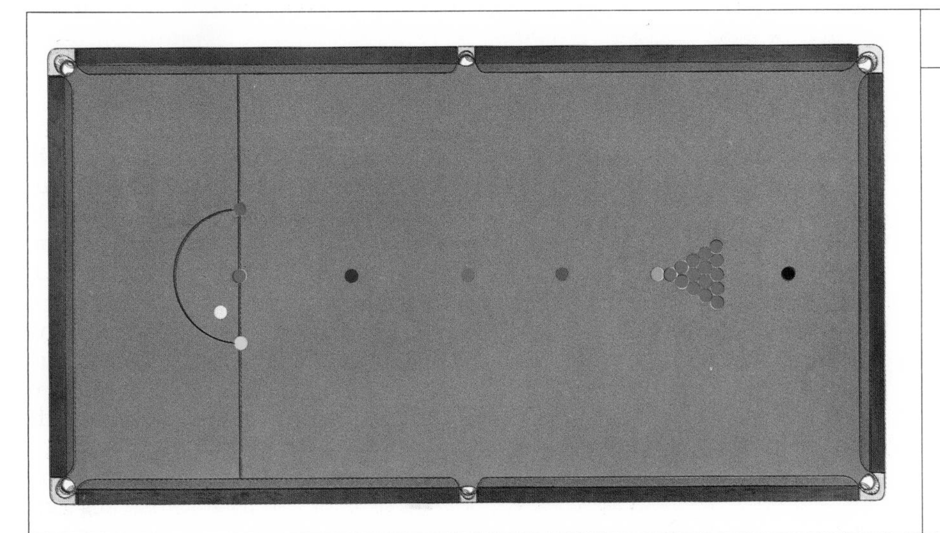

Spotting

Position of the balls at the beginning of a frame. The cue-ball may be placed anywhere within the 'D'. The coloured balls, if potted after a red, are returned to their positions as shown in the illustration.

John Spencer – world champion in 1977

sponsor pulls out, others queue up to step in. This was demonstrated in 1984 when Lada, State Express and Yamaha Organs withdrew their sponsorship. They were readily replaced by Mercantile Credit, Dulux and Guinness respectively.

The upsurge of snooker in the late sixties originally attracted sponsors' interest, and tobacco company John Player and Son sponsored the revived world professional championship in 1969. They were joined as sponsors in those early days of the modern game by brewers Watneys and whisky distillers Haig.

Today, sponsors who have little or no connection with the leisure industry have become major sponsors of professional events – finance house Mercantile Credit and ICI Paints Division (with the Dulux Open) – are two examples.

The longest surviving of current sponsors are tobacco company Gallahers, who sponsor the Benson and Hedges Masters and the Benson and Hedges Irish Masters. Gallahers first became involved in snooker sponsorship in 1971 with their Park Drive £2000 tournaments.

A major televised snooker event would cost a sponsor somewhere in the region of £350,000 – that is, £250,000 in prize money and the remainder in promotional costs.

The sponsors of major professional events in 1986-87 were:

BCE International – BCE Tables Ltd (Billiard table manufacturers)

Langs Scottish Masters – Lang Brothers Limited (Distillers)

Rothmans Grand Prix – Rothmans of Pall Mall Limited (Cigarette manufacturers)

Tennents UK Open – Bass Brewing (Brewers)

Hofmeister World Doubles – John Smith Brewery Limited

Mercantile Credit Classic – Mercantile Credit Co. Limited (Finance company)

Benson and Hedges Masters – Gallaher Limited (Cigarette manufacturers)

Embassy World Professional Championship – Imperial Tobacco Limited (Cigarette manufacturers)

Dulux British Open – Imperial Chemical Industries plc – Paints Division (Paint manufacturers)

Tolly Cobbold English Professional Championship – Tollemache and Cobbold Breweries Limited (Brewers)

Spotting

Each of the six colours has a designated spot upon which it must be placed at the commencement of a frame. It should also be replaced to that spot once it has been potted.

Once all the reds have been potted, and the colours are potted in their correct order (yellow-green-brown-blue-pink-black), they are not returned to their spots, unless potted in the course of a foul shot.

If a colour has to be re-spotted and its own spot is not available, then it is placed on the highest-value spot available.

If it cannot be placed on any spot, because they are all occupied, then it must be placed as near its own spot as possible between its own spot and the top cushion.

In 1919 a rule was introduced in an effort to cut down on the number of drawn frames. It was ruled that in the event of a tie the black should be re-spotted. The players would toss to decide who played first, and the frame would then continue until the black was potted – or a foul shot was made. This rule remains in force today.

Sri Lanka

The Billiards Association and Control Council of Sri Lanka (or Ceylon as it was then known) was formed in 1948. And mention of billiards or snooker in Sri Lanka brings the name of one man to mind – Mohammed Lafir. A national hero, Lafir was synonymous with both games in his country, and in winning the world amateur billiards championship in Bombay in 1973 he became the first Sri Lankan to win a world title in any sport. Six years earlier Lafir had been runner-up to Britain's Leslie Driffield in the championship which was held at the Samudra Hotel, Colombo.

The world amateur billiards championships returned to Sri Lanka in 1979 when, again, they were held in Colombo. This time Lafir could only reach the semi-finals.

National snooker champion 18 times and billiards champion on 16 occasions, Mohammed Lafir regularly played in India, mainly because he had outplayed all opposition in his home country.

Surprisingly, he did not fare as well at snooker internationally as he did at billiards – probably because he was not used to the cold climates in which the world snooker championships were often held. (When they were held in Dublin in 1974, Lafir used to wear a woollen sweater under his shirt and waistcoat!)

Lafir's death, at the age of 53 in 1981, stunned Sri Lanka – their one world-class sporting hero was gone.

Sri Lanka National Snooker Championship – Results (finals)

1948 M.J.M. Lafir beat E.A. Jayasundera
1949 M.M. Faiz beat K. Rabel
1950 M.J.M. Lafir beat J.D. Perera
1951 M.S.A. Hassan beat T.M. Ambrose
1952 M.J.M. Lafir beat N.D. Ismail
1953 M.J.M. Lafir beat N.D. Ismail
1954 M.J.M. Lafir beat P.R.E. Seneviratne
1955 M.J.M. Lafir beat T.G. Kirshna
1956 M.J.M. Lafir beat M.H.M. Mujahid
1957 M.J.M. Lafir beat P.R.E. Seneviratne
1958 M.J.M. Lafir beat T.A. Selvaraj
1959 M.J.M. Lafir beat T.A. Selvaraj
1960 M.J.M. Lafir beat M.H.M. Mujahid
1961 M.J.M. Lafir beat M.H.M. Mujahid
1962 M.J.M. Lafir beat M.S.M. Faeez
1963 M.J.M. Izzath beat M.T.M. Jiffry
1964 M.J.M. Lafir beat M. Izzath
1965 M.J.M. Lafir*
1966 M.J.M. Lafir beat N.J. Rahim
1967 N.J. Rahim beat N.A. Rahim
1968 Not held
1969 M.J.M. Lafir beat M. Faeez
1970 N.J. Rahim beat M.J.M. Lafir
1971 Not held
1972 N.J. Rahim beat M.J.M. Lafir
1973 M.J.M. Lafir beat M. Izzath
1974 Not held
1975 N.A. Rahim*
1976 M.S.U. Mohideen beat J. Boteju
1977 M.S.U. Mohideen beat J. Boteju
1978 N.A. Rahim beat J.W.H. Boteju
1979 Not held
1980 Not held
1981 J.W.H. Boteju beat K. Jayasekera
1982 J.A. Wahid beat J.W.H. Boteju
1983 J.W.H. Boteju*
1984 H.K. Sirisoma beat M. Setupathy
1985 J.W.H. Boteju*

Most wins: 18 – Mohammed Lafir

* Records not kept.

State Express World Team Classic

See Tuborg World Cup

Stevens, Kirk

Born in Toronto, Kirk Stevens started his snooker-playing at the Golden Cue Centre in the city in 1968 when he was just ten years of age. Two years later – with his first century break to his name – he had the audacity to challenge his hero, Cliff Thorburn, to a challenge match for two dollars. Thorburn could not resist; he won, and the young Stevens produced two filthy dollar notes from his pocket in order to honour his debt.

He got his two dollars back – and much more – when he beat Thorburn in the final of the Canadian professional championship in 1979. The year before, Stevens turned professional after losing to Cliff Wilson in the semi-final of the world amateur championships in Malta.

A great happy-go-lucky personality, his flamboyance was like a breath of fresh air to the professional scene – and his bright white suits, breaking with the tradition of the black evening suits, made him distinguishable.

Stevens first appeared in the world championships in 1979 and reached the competition proper before he lost to Fred Davis. The following year he became the youngest-ever semi-finalist when he lost narrowly, 16-13, to Alex Higgins. Even so, he set the championships alight on the first day with a break of 136 in his match against Graham Miles. Had he not missed the final black he would have gained a new championship record.

The match against Higgins was the first of many semi-final appearances over the next five years for the young Canadian, but unfortunately he could never get over that last hurdle, and had to wait until 1985 for his first major individual final. He had, however, appeared in the final of the State Express World Team Cup twice – when Canada lost to Wales in 1980, and in 1982 when he helped his country to victory over England.

He lost to David Taylor in the semi-final of the 1981 Yamaha Masters, and in 1982 he lost heavily, 9-3, to Tony Knowles in the semi-final of the Jameson International. Defeat by fellow Canadian Bill Werbeniuk followed in the 1983 Lada Classic semi-final, and in 1984 he reached three 'semis' – losing them all by small margins. Steve Davis beat him 5-4 in the Tolly Cobbold Classic, Jimmy White beat him 18-16 in the world championships in one of the all-time classic matches, and White beat him in the last four of the Benson and Hedges Masters, by six frames to four. But this last defeat had its compensation for Stevens – a televised 147 break. He was still hoping for his first major final appearance at that time, but would never have exchanged that 147 for a place in the final – it was the pinnacle of his career.

Those semi-final appearances in the 1983-84 season helped move him up the rankings to the number four position – a position he consolidated the following season. A one-time great attacking player, he has now slowed down and concentrates on the safety element of his game. The change in style paid dividends for Stevens, as he went on to reach that elusive first major final in 1985, when he met South African Silvino Francisco in the final of the Dulux British Open at Derby.

A great semi-final victory over Steve Davis – avenging a 9-2 drubbing in the semi-final of the Coral United Kingdom Open at Preston a couple of months earlier – saw Kirk go into the final as favourite, but he was slightly hindered by a painful shoulder. He let Francisco gallop away with the opening frames and, although Stevens pulled back to 9-8 at one stage, the South African went on to win 12-9.

Stevens has had his problems, both on and off the snooker table, since his appearance in the British Open, but it happily looks as though his troubles are behind him and he should start enjoying success again.

Career highlights
- World Professional Snooker Championship (semi-final) 1980, 1984
- Dulux British Open (runner-up) 1985
- BCE Belgian Classic (runner-up) 1986
- World Cup 1982 (member of winning Canadian team)
- Canadian Professional Champion 1981, 1983

Kirk Stevens – The Entertainer...

Street, John

The first secretary of the Professional Referees' Association (founded in 1979), Devonian John Street is one of the most popular referees on the circuit. He is not a full-time referee, but dovetails his duties with those of insurance agent with the Pearl Insurance in Exeter, and he is also responsible for the promoting of several events in his home county.

Street has never lived away from his native Devon, apart from during the war when he spent four years as an evacuee in Bishop Auckland. Born in Exmouth he now lives in Exeter, and has been a prominent figure on the local billiards and snooker scene since the late fifties/early sixties.

It was only as a result of contracting tuberculosis at the age of 17 that he took up snooker. He was a keen table-tennis player at the time, but had to give up that sport for something less strenuous. He became as good at snooker as he had been at table-tennis and was, in the 1960s, reckoned to be one of the best ten players in the Exeter area.

He took to refereeing in 1960, and became a Grade 'A' referee in 1968. His first major final was that of the 1979 English amateur championship between Jimmy White and Dave Martin at Helston. Since then he has officiated at all major professional events.

The world professional championship is as important to the referees as it is to the players, and Street always looks forward to officiating at the Crucible. His first world final was the 1980 classic between Cliff Thorburn and Alex Higgins, which the Canadian won.

Stun

See Shots

Swerve

The swerve shot is normally employed to get out of a snooker, and is an alternative to bouncing the cue-ball off one or more cushions. Although the swerve shot looks dramatic when it works, it is difficult to position the cue-ball with accuracy after it has made contact with the object-ball.

To play the swerve shot one has to strike the cue-ball in a downwards motion on either the top right or top left side.

One of the greatest exponents of the swerve shot was Australian billiards champion Walter Lindrum.

T

Table

The shape and design of the billiard table has altered very little since the middle of the 19th century. At that time, the last innovation – vulcanized rubber cushions – was added, and apart from occasional slight refinements the table has been much the same since.

Early tables were made entirely of wood and covered with a coarse green cloth.

The colour green was chosen because the game was originally played outdoors on grass. When brought indoors, and played on a table, the green cloth was used so as to make the playing surface look like grass.

One of the first specialist billiard table manufacturers was John Thurston, and it was he, in 1826, who introduced the slate bed as a replacement for the wooden one. Within 15 years, all tables had slate beds. The table design had to be altered to cope with the extra weight of the slate, and consequently, the modern eight-leg table was developed.

The other major development around that time was the introduction of the rubber cushion in 1835. The cushions were originally made of felt, and it was only after several attempts to find a new material (including hair, swan skin and other substances) had all ended in failure, that rubber was introduced.

The measurements of the table, as shown in the diagram below, were drawn up and approved by the Billiards Association in 1892.

Tables used in major competitions are not, as many people believe, transported in one piece, but assembled by experts at the appropriate venue. The job is a specialist one, requiring an eye for absolute accuracy. It also needs a fair amount of muscle – the five slates on each table are up to 5cm (2 inches) thick and each one weighs around 200kg (4cwt).

The specifications of the pockets have changed little over the years, although their design has changed.

See also Pockets

One of the pioneers of billiard table manufacture, John Thurston

Below: the dimensions and plan of the standard table as used in both billiards and snooker.

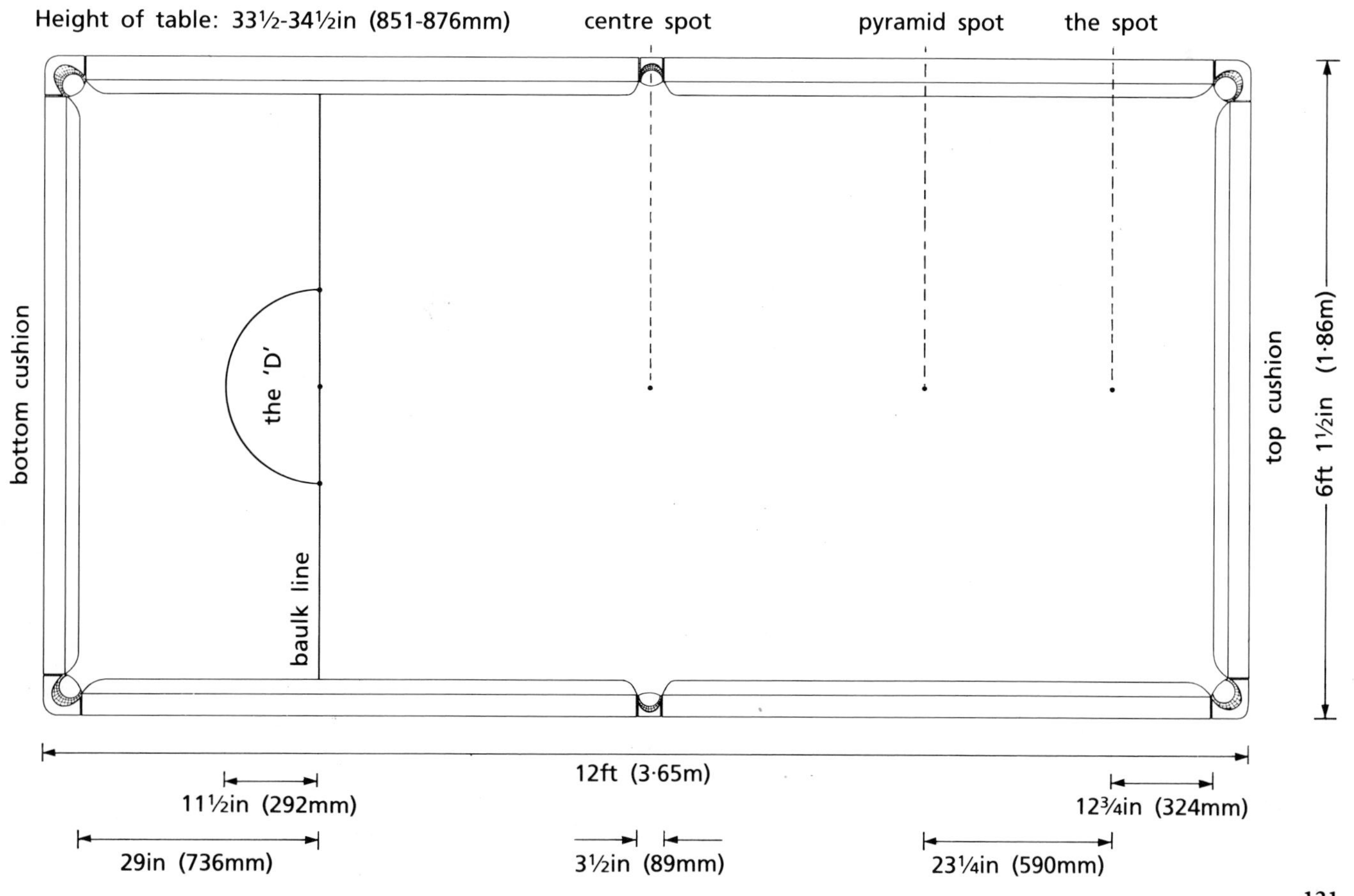

Taylor, David

A professional since the late sixties, David Taylor is one of the many top-class snooker players to have emerged from the Manchester area. To be precise, he hails from Bowden in Cheshire, and started playing snooker at the age of 14. He earned a reputation for himself as a leading amateur in the 'tough school' around Manchester, and in 1968 he reached the double pinnacle of his amateur career.

First he beat Colin Ross 11-8 in the final of the English amateur championship, and later in the year he went to Sydney as England's representative in the world amateur championships. He returned as world champion, having beaten Australian Max Williams 8-7 in a tense final.

Upon his return to England, Taylor turned professional, but he found the going tough. He achieved very little early success, and even changed jobs so as to give himself more time to play snooker – but still the wins did not materialize. In the mid-seventies his luck began to change when he was asked to join the holiday camp circuit. A friendly and popular character, he thrilled crowds with his exhibition play at the various camps.

His first success as a professional came in 1978, when he reached the final of the Coral United Kingdom championship. This was David Taylor's first major final as a professional, and despite losing 15-9 to Doug Mountjoy, he had already proved his ability by beating defending champion Patsy Fagan and fellow Manchester-based players John Virgo and Alex Higgins on the way to the final.

The 1980s saw a marked improvement in Taylor's game. In 1980, for the first time, he was ranked in the WPBSA's top ten, and that year he reached the semi-final of the world championships. After beating Ray Reardon 13-11 in their quarter-final, he lost to eventual champion Cliff Thorburn in the semi-final.

His best season to date followed in 1981. He reached the final of the new Yamaha Organs Trophy, and lost only after pushing Steve Davis hard in the final. Later that year he joined forces with Davis in the England team that won the world team cup; he also made a reappearance on the popular BBC *Pot Black* series after an absence of ten years. At the end of that season Taylor was ranked number seven in the world. Although he slipped one place in 1982, he remained in the top ten thanks to an excellent performance in the Jameson International, where he lost in the final to fellow Lancastrian Tony Knowles, who was winning his first major title. But it was his quarter-final match against Steve Davis that gave Taylor the most pleasure. Beaten 5-1 by Davis at the same stage of the competition the previous season, he avenged that defeat with a famous 5-3 win, and that was after Davis had twice held the lead.

David Taylor has slipped down in the rankings since then, but is playing well and is still capable of coming back to win that elusive first professional championship. In the meantime, the 'Silver Fox' – so called because of his conspicuous mane of white hair – will continue to make a healthy living from the sport because he remains one of the most popular men on the exhibition circuit.

Career highlights

- Coral United Kingdom Professional Championship (runner-up) 1978
- Jameson International (runner-up) 1982
- Yamaha International Masters (runner-up) 1981
- World Cup 1981 (member of winning England team)
- World Amateur Champion 1968
- English Amateur Champion 1968

David Taylor, the 'Silver Fox' – always in demand for exhibitions, but big wins have so far eluded him

Taylor, Dennis

If any man deserved to win his first major tournament in the 1984-85 season then that man was Dennis Taylor. A professional for 12 years, Dennis had been a 'nearly' man all those years – coming close to his first major title, but not quite making it at the final hurdle. In those 12 years he has made an immense contribution to the sport through his wit and humour, which have made him one of the most sought after players for exhibition matches.

It all came together for Taylor, however, in the 1984 Rothmans Grand Prix at the Hexagon Theatre, Reading, where he beat his great friend Cliff Thorburn 10-2 to clinch his first major honour.

Taylor is a great family man, and the nation shared his joy while his young son shared the glory in front of the television cameras. On that occasion, Taylor could not hide his own – mixed – emotions: shortly before the event, his mother died suddenly, back home at Coalisland in County Tyrone. But despite that, Taylor, trooper that he is, insisted on giving the audience their money's worth by providing one of his special exhibitions after the final with Thorburn.

All that, as great a moment as it was for Taylor, was well and truly eclipsed in the 1985 world championships at the Crucible Theatre. A beaten finalist once before, and losing semi-finalist on three occasions, Taylor reached the final to meet hot favourite Steve Davis. With many armchair fans willing him to win he clawed his way back from 8-0 down to twice draw level with Davis. But each time he levelled the score, Davis pulled away again. He drew level for a third time at 17-17 with just one frame to play. It was a nervous affair that lasted 68 minutes but it was Dennis Taylor who potted the final black – eventually – to win the cherished world crown.

The friendly Irishman is one of the most popular players on the circuit, and despite living in Lancashire since 1966 has not lost that Irish brogue. He started playing at the age of nine, and by the time he was 14 was the local senior champion. He came to England as a 17-year-old and lived with relatives in Darwen, near Blackburn, Lancashire. Two years later he was the national under-19 billiards champion. He gained one England cap in the 1971-72 season before turning professional in November 1972. Even in those early days as a professional he was making a name for himself as an exhibition player.

Taylor first appeared in the world championships in 1973 and played Cliff Thorburn. The Canadian won on that occasion but Taylor took his revenge in the 1984 Rothmans Grand Prix.

The first time the snooker public were made aware of Dennis Taylor was in the 1974 Canadian Open. He reached the final after beating Alex Higgins in the semi-final, but lost at the last hurdle – to Cliff Thorburn again. Taylor had, however, amazed the Canadian fans with some high-scoring snooker in practice matches for the event.

In 1975 the Irishman reached the semi-final of the world championships, losing to Eddie Charlton, and two years later he reached the same stage again. Once more though, it was Thorburn who put the jinx on him and ended his chance of reaching the final. Two years further on, 1979, and Taylor was in the semi-final once more, and this time he overcame John Virgo.

The final was against new professional Terry Griffiths. On paper Dennis should have been clear favourite, but Griffiths had stunned everybody with his fine play during the championships and it was Griffiths who won the title at his first attempt.

Since then Taylor has made one further semi-final appearance, in 1984, losing to Steve Davis. And it was Davis who inflicted an embarrassing 9-0 defeat on Taylor in the final of the 1981 Jameson International.

Ranked number two in the world in 1979, Taylor went on to win his first Irish Professional title the following year by taking the crown from Alex Higgins. He made successful defences against Higgins and Patsy Fagan before winning the first of the new-style knockout championships in 1982.

He caused quite a stir at the 1983 Benson and Hedges Irish Masters when he appeared wearing his new 'Joe 90' spectacles, which were designed by former optical instrument maker Jack Karnehm. The spectacles caused Dennis to come in for some friendly banter, notably from John Spencer, but they certainly helped him to improve his game.

The Association of Snooker Writers' Personality of the Year in 1984, Taylor gave notice that a big victory was not far away when he was runner-up in the inaugural professional snooker league that year.

After winning the world title, the best Dennis could achieve the following season was a share of the World Team Cup; he then beat his fellow Irishman Alex Higgins to win their national title. He was again a member of the Irish team that won the World Cup in 1987, but returned to individual winning ways by beating Higgins in the Benson & Hedges Masters at Wembley.

Career highlights

- Winfield Australian Masters Champion 1986
- World Professional Snooker Champion 1985
- Rothmans Grand Prix Champion 1984
- Benson & Hedges Masters Champion 1987
- World Cup 1985-87 (member of winning All-Ireland team)
- Irish Professional Champion 1982, 1985-87
- Pontins Open Champion 1980
- National Under-19 Billiards Champion 1968
- National Breaks Champion 1971

Television

If there has ever been a marriage of convenience in sport, it is that between television and snooker. Snooker might have been tailor-made for television – colour television, that is – and the game is now the most popular television sport in Britain, with over 75 days' coverage on network television per annum. One important factor in its popularity is the large female viewing audience – estimated at 55% of the total.

While snooker has been good for television, by the same token, television has been good for snooker, and has helped to introduce a new breed of superstars into the world of sport in recent years.

The televising of snooker started way back in 1937, when Sydney Lee gave a demonstration of the sport from the BBC's old Alexandra Palace studios. Shortly afterwards, on 14 April that year, the first actual match was seen when Horace Lindrum played Willie Smith.

In those days the BBC were experimenting with all sports, but with transmission being only in black and white, the idea never caught on. However, the sport was not neglected altogether: the popular midweek sports programme *Sportsview*, introduced by Peter Dimmock, used to feature Joe Davis trying to compile a big break during the programme each week.

Following the introduction of colour television in Britain in 1967, a Birmingham-based BBC producer, Phillip Lewis, realized that snooker might now have a new appeal, and it was from his idea that the *Pot Black* programme was born. The new pre-recorded programme introduced the British public – many of whom still regarded the billiard-hall as a den of iniquity – to the true skills of snooker, and at the same time put over the clean-cut image of the sport. *Pot Black* ended in 1986 but it still showed a top-class field right up to the end.

Despite the popularity of *Pot Black*, snooker was slow to develop as a television sport. There had been regional BBC and local ITV coverage of events, but it was not until the 1978 world professional championships that the BBC extended their coverage to any great extent. That year they covered the championships in their entirety for the first time, although up to the final only late-night highlights were shown. But since then the 17 days at the Crucible have become an established part of television sport.

To cover a snooker tournament on television might seem, on the face of it, an easy operation – but it is far from being so. Normally from two to four cameras are needed to cover each table, and it is vital that the producer selects the right camera angle for each shot. Over 200 people are involved in the recording of the world championships each year. And in order for 100 hours of play to be shown, over 300 hours have to be recorded, complete with commentaries.

One of the early problems with television coverage of snooker was the lighting. The traditional shade over the table had to be removed to make way for special lighting, and initially this caused glare and reflection off the balls. Another constant problem was bursting bulbs, which damaged many a good cloth. The lighting problem has now been resolved thanks to sophisticated lighting systems, and many players now prefer playing under the television lights rather than the traditional lighting.

The commentary teams of both the BBC and ITV provide expert and often humorous coverage of the sport, with such notables as Jack Karnehm, Clive Everton, Rex Williams and John Pulman behind the microphones. But the daddy of them all is 'whispering' Ted Lowe.

Lowe started his broadcasting career as the 'stats man' to Raymond Glendenning, who used to cover snooker matches for BBC radio. One day in September 1954, Glendenning was

Dennis Taylor, 1985 world champion, at the table...and a view of the table through those famous spectacles

taken ill and Lowe took over the microphone – and from that day to this he has remained the voice of snooker.

Until the 1978 world championships, his was the only voice heard on BBC coverage of the sport. But to help out with the increased coverage of those championships the services of Jack Karnehm and Clive Everton were recruited.

Snooker currently attracts a lot of sponsorship money, but even so, it remains a relatively cheap sport for sponsors. For example, the 1985 Dulux Open received nine days' television coverage, and cost the sponsors £250,000. Compared to other methods of advertising, this is an extremely reasonable sum for the amount of exposure given to the company name.

The Dulux is also a good example to illustrate the power of television over the organization of a sport. To produce a tournament on that scale entails enormous costs. For example, it costs more to film before 2.00 p.m. and/or after midnight; so, to keep the costs down, ITV insisted on changing the start time from 1.00 p.m. to 2.00 p.m., and also, to make sure the day's play finished before midnight, had the number of frames per match reduced in the second round to the best of nine, whereas the first – untelevised – round of the competition had been the best of eleven!

Undoubtedly the greatest moment so far in televised snooker is Steve Davis's 147 break in the Lada Classic at Oldham in 1982. Captured by the Granada TV cameras, it was the first maximum to be seen on television.

ITV – via Thames Television – were also involved in a bizarre incident which took place during their coverage of the Holsten Lager Tournament at Slough in 1979. John Spencer, in his match with Cliff Thorburn, made a 147 break which would have been the first to be seen on television – except that the camera crew were away at lunch due to a union ruling, and consequently the cameras were not rolling when Spencer compiled his break.

Television coverage has done much for snooker as both a participant and a spectator sport since the coverage of the world championships in 1978. Snooker has repaid the television companies in kind with coverage of the sport regularly figuring high in the viewing ratings.

Template

If any single argument has raged longer than any other in snooker, it has been concerning the pockets.

The world body – the Billiards and Snooker Control Council – does not lay down specific measurements of pockets. It merely states that they should: 'conform to templates authorized by the Council'. But for many years the official templates were not felt to fulfil the necessary requirements.

The first templates – which should really be described as gauges – were designed in the late 19th century. In an effort to standardize tables, the governing body asked leading manufacturers to submit templates. That they did, and the ones submitted by George Wright were accepted in 1892. These templates, however, did not take into account the undercut – the part of the cushion between the bed of the table and the top of the cushion – that is cut away.

As the diagrams show, the undercut is all-important, because the amount of the undercut determines how easy or difficult a pocket may be. The first template that took undercut into account was designed by former professional Herbert Holt, but these templates were never used.

In the mid 1970s it was agreed that new templates ought to be designed and produced with this problem in mind. And the current templates, designed by Norman Clare, and taking into account a suggestion by Clive Everton, were adopted by the B&SCC in 1980.

Four templates constitute a set – two for the top and bottom pockets and two for the middle pockets. Each pocket is tested for correct width and drop, and also for correct undercut.

All manufacturers, and many county and national associations have sets of the templates – there are 144 sets spread around the world... there is even a set in Brazil!

Holders of sets of templates are, from time to time, called

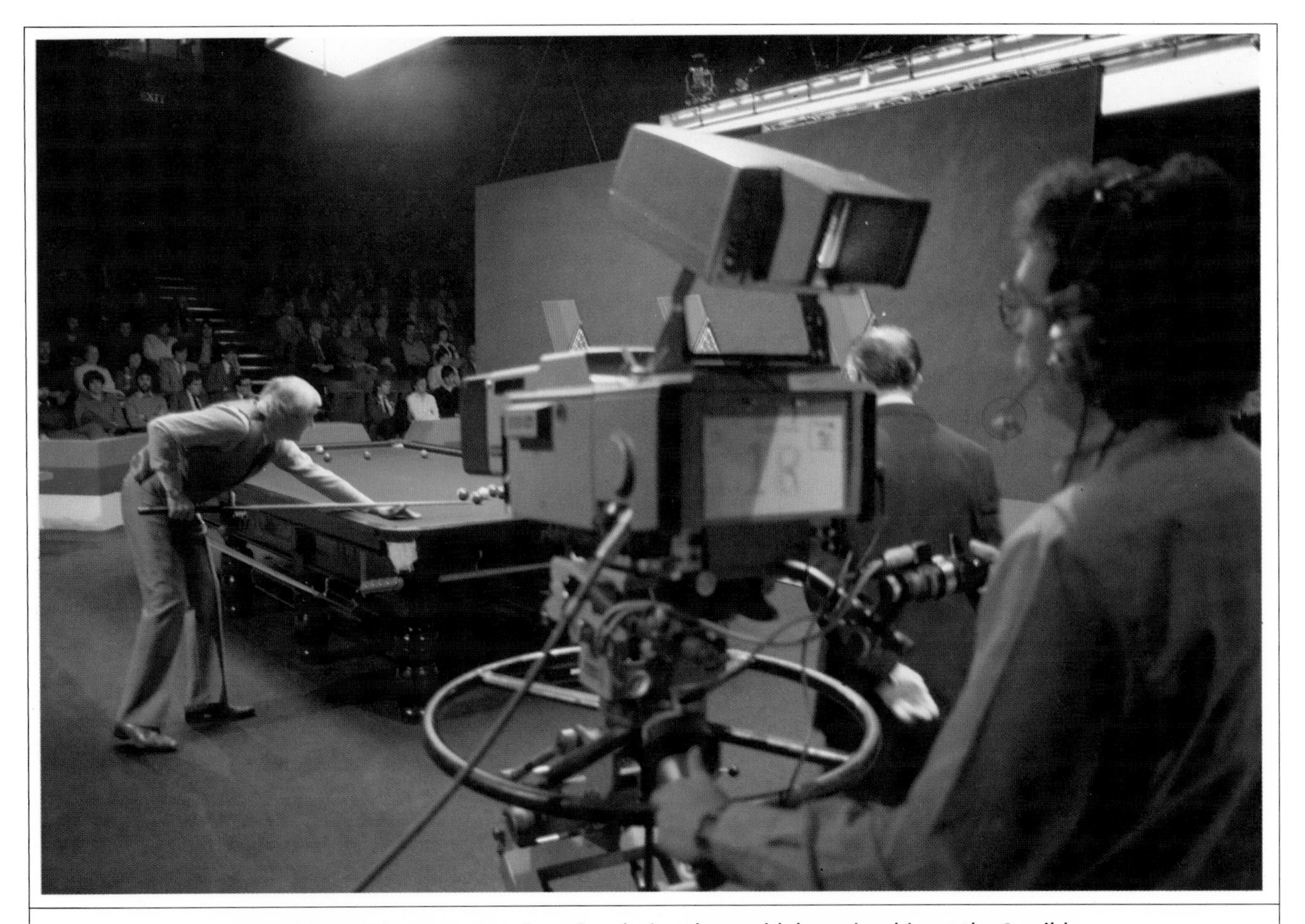

One of the BBC's cameramen in action during the world championships at the Crucible

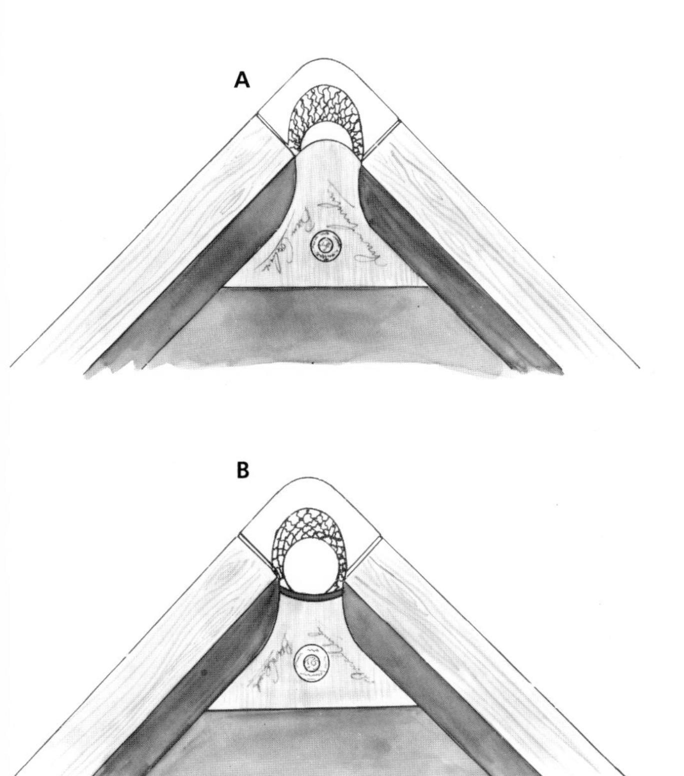

Templates: the template in diagram A checks the correct ***width*** *at the top of the cushion and that the pocket does not narrow after the point of fall; that in diagram B checks the* ***undercut*** *of the corner pocket, and also that the slate bed has been correctly cut (this is known as the fall). When the template is removed the ball should be able to stand on the concave line, hanging over the pocket, but without falling in. The templates in diagrams C and D are similar to those in A and B respectively, but are for checking the middle pockets.*

Behind the scenes – not how television viewers normally see David Vine

upon to check pockets in case a record break needs ratifying.

For all major amateur championships and tournaments the tables are constructed to the dimensions of the templates and are confirmed as complying with them before the event starts. All record breaks made on the table can then be quickly and automatically ratified.

On the other hand, should, for example, a new world amateur record break be made on a club table in the middle of the country, the pockets would have to be tested before the record could be ratified.

Responsibility for ensuring that tables conform to the templates rests in the very experienced and capable hands of the table fitters at the time of a table's assembly.

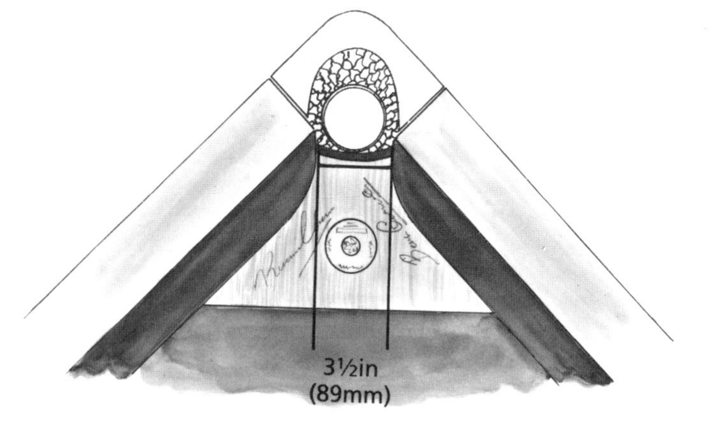

Templates: the diagram above shows the point at which pockets are 3½ inches wide. The two diagrams on the facing page show the effects different undercuts can have on a pocket. The upper diagram shows a cushion that has not been cut away at the point where the widest part of the ball makes contact with it, so that the effective width of the opening does not exceed 3½ inches. The one below shows a pocket with greater undercut: in this case the widest part of the ball makes contact with the cushion at a point where the opening is approximately 3¾ inches wide – enough to make the pocket considerably easier.

Tennents United Kingdom Open

Formerly known as the United Kingdom Professional Championship, the tournament used to be open only to players who held current UK passports. Its title changed in 1984 however, to the United Kingdom Open. Being an open tournament it carries world ranking points.

Sponsored by Coral Racing since 1978, it was sponsored the previous year – its first year – by the manufacturer of Super Crystallate balls.

In its eight-year history, the tournament has been responsible for putting many players on the snooker map. The first winner, Patsy Fagan, registered the biggest win of his professional career when he took the title. David Taylor, in 1978, reached his first major final in ten years as a professional. It provided John Virgo with his first major professional win, and it did the same for Steve Davis.

The first championship was held in December, and was not well supported. Nevertheless, the final had television coverage. Patsy Fagan won the first final against Doug Mountjoy.

With the new sponsors – Coral's – and a change of venue to the pleasant surroundings of the Preston Guildhall, the 1978 competition was a far bigger success all round. The spectators and players also warmed to the increase in the size of matches from the best of nine frames to the best of 17; Doug Mountjoy beat David Taylor in the final.

The 1979 final saw John Virgo win his first major prize as a professional when he beat the reigning world champion Terry Griffiths in a final which went the full distance – one of three UK championship finals to do so.

Television coverage was up to eight days by 1980, and the viewing audience were treated to the skills of 'newcomer' Steve Davis. Not only did he win his first major title but he did so by destroying his opponents: he beat Terry Griffiths 9-0 in the semi-final, and Alex Higgins 16-6 in the final.

Davis retained his title in 1981, and again he whitewashed his opponent. This time it was Jimmy White – in the semi-final. And once again, the final was an easy affair as he beat Terry Griffiths 16-3. Griffiths, however, gained revenge in 1982 when he beat Davis in the quarter-final before going on to beat Alex Higgins in a classic final. Higgins led 15-13 with just three frames to go, and Griffiths won all three to snatch the title.

Alex Higgins had one of his best ever wins in beating Davis in 1983, but the Englishman has won every championship since then, and his victory over Neal Foulds in the 1986 final took his career prize winnings past the £1 million mark.

That 1986 triumph of Davis's was the first year for the event's new sponsors, Tennents Lager.

Tennents United Kingdom Open – Results (finals)

1977 P. Fagan (Ireland) 12 – D. Mountjoy (Wales) 9
1978 D. Mountjoy (Wales) 15 – D. Taylor (England) 9
1979 J. Virgo (England) 14 – T. Griffiths (Wales) 13
1980 S. Davis (England) 16 – A. Higgins (Ireland) 6
1981 S. Davis (England) 16 – T. Griffiths (Wales) 3
1982 T. Griffiths (Wales) 16 – A. Higgins (Ireland) 15
1983 A. Higgins (Ireland) 16 – S. Davis (England) 15
1984 S. Davis (England) 16 – A. Higgins (Ireland) 8
1985 S. Davis (England) 16 – W. Thorne (England) 14
1986 S. Davis (England) 16 – N. Foulds (England) 7

Most wins: 5 – Steve Davis
Most finals: 6 – Steve Davis
Highest break: 140 – Willie Thorne (1985)

Thailand

Snooker has been played in Thailand for many years, but in a country that thrives on gambling, the main focus of attention had always been on individual money matches. That changed in

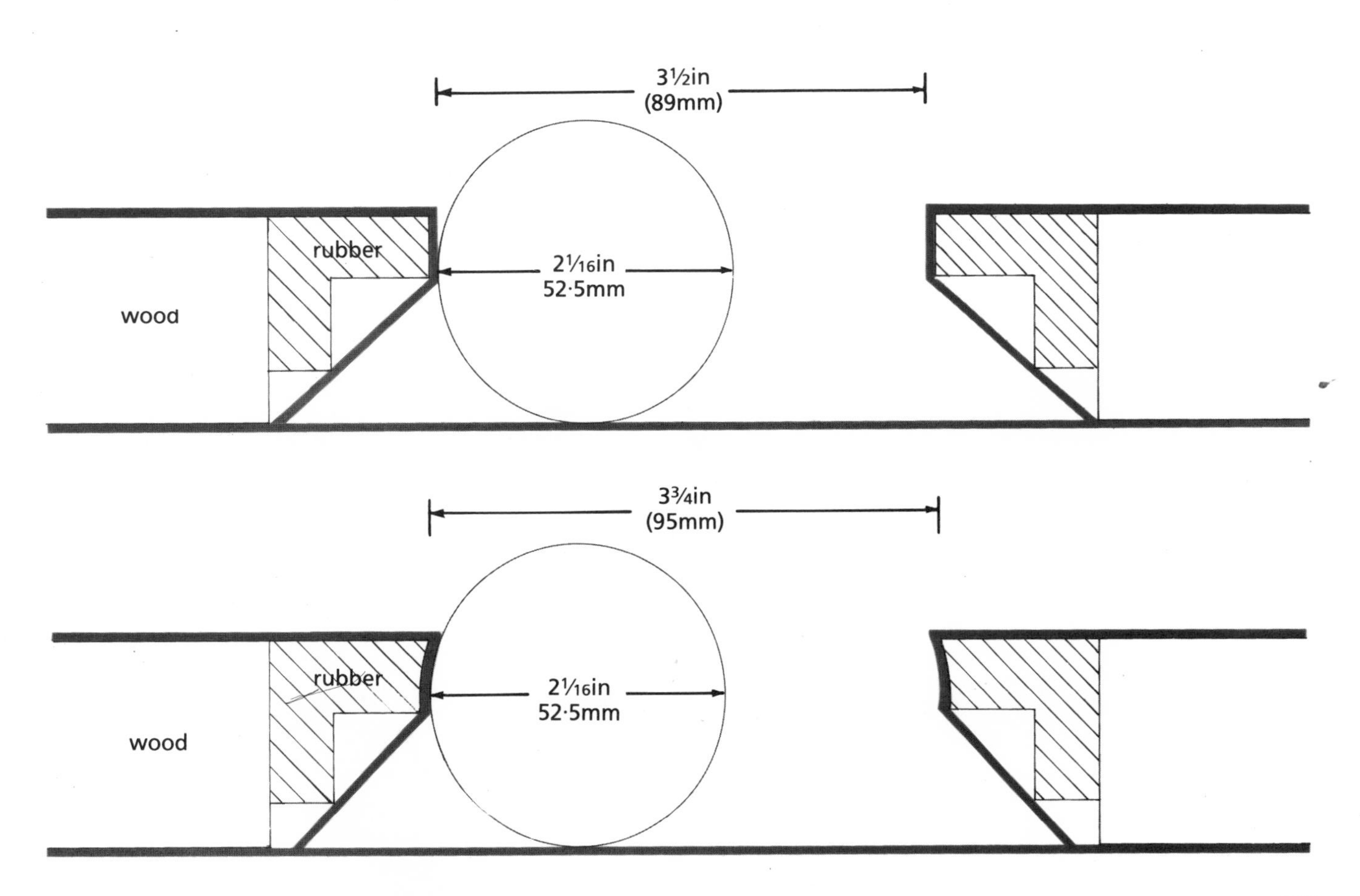

1982, with the formation of the Thailand Association, whose aim was to organize the sport at a competitive level.

They received an enormous boost later that year when Barry Hearn took his two players – Steve Davis and Tony Meo – to the country to play exhibitions, and to participate in the country's first major tournament. Having seen BBC recordings of leading tournaments, the Thai people were no strangers to the sport; when the four-man tournament involving Davis, Meo and local players Saengthong and Tanyuthitham was televised, it attracted a viewing audience of 10 million – and the population of Thailand is only 43 million. Later that year, in Calgary, Vichien Saengthong became Thailand's first representative in the world amateur snooker championships.

So popular was the Barry Hearn visit that the players were invited back in 1983, and this time Terry Griffiths and Doug Mountjoy joined Davis and Meo. Two six-man tournaments were organized, and both were won by Tony Meo: in the final of the Bangkok Golden Cue he beat Davis 2-1, and in the final of the Channel 7 TV Masters (a *Pot Black* style tournament) he beat Griffiths 2-1.

Thailand national champions	
1982 V. Saengthong	1985 V. Saengthong
1983 V. Saengthong	1986 J. Wattana
1984 V. Saengthong	

Cliff Thorburn, concentrating hard

Thorburn, Cliff

Upon the death of George Chenier in 1970, Cliff Thorburn, from Victoria, British Columbia, took over the crown as Canada's leading snooker player, even though he had only been playing for just over a year. But at that time, he had never tested his skills against the best players in the world: the one-time dish-washer was more used to the cut and thrust of the money matches and the hustling. Then in 1971 John Spencer visited Canada and played Thorburn in three exhibition matches around the country. Spencer, one of the world's leading players at that time, won all three matches, but Thorburn proved a worthwhile opponent for him.

Having won the Canadian and North American titles, Cliff Thorburn made his way to England for his first world professional championships in 1973, having shortly before turned professional. His very first opponent was Dennis Taylor. Thorburn won that encounter 9-8, but was narrowly beaten 16-15 in the next round by Rex Williams.

But Thorburn had made the breakthrough, and had proved to himself and to the rest of the snooker world that he was a man to

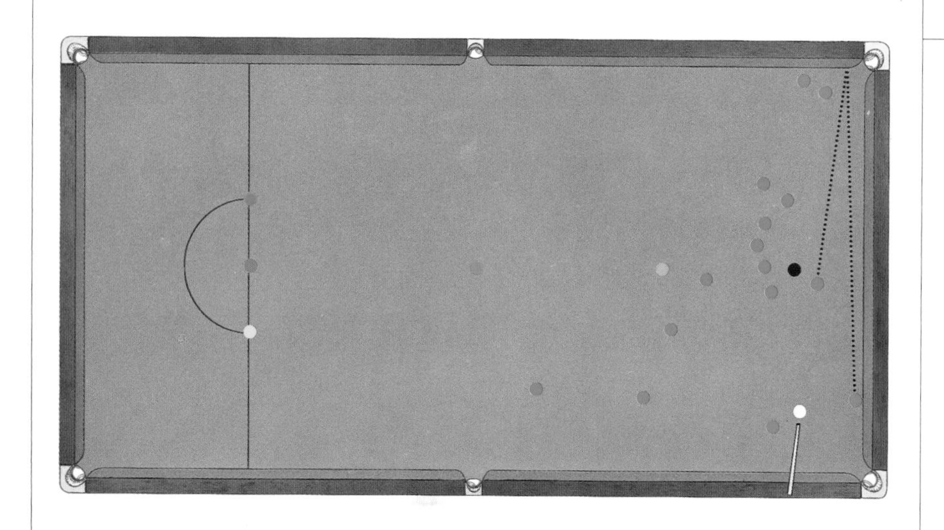

Thorburn

How Cliff Thorburn fluked the first red on the way to his world championship 147: the intended shot was to pot the red in the corner pocket as indicated. It missed, rolled along the bottom cushion and knocked another red into the opposite pocket. A lucky start – but the rest of the break was all concentration and skill.

be taken seriously. The following year he won the first Canadian Open when he beat Dennis Taylor, yet again, in the final. He won the Canadian Open a record four times during its seven-year life.

The next big breakthrough for the very popular and much respected Canadian came in 1977, when he reached the world championship final and nearly lifted the title. He lost 25-21 to John Spencer, but with wins over Rex Williams, Eddie Charlton and Dennis Taylor, his place in the final was hard-earned.

The following year Thorburn was runner-up to Alex Higgins in the Benson and Hedges Masters, but in 1980 his finest hour came when he did become the first overseas player since 1952 to lift the world crown: he beat Alex Higgins 18-16 in a classic confrontation. After this match Alex called Cliff a 'grinder'.

That same year Cliff Thorburn was responsible for the formation of the Canadian Professional Association, which has subsequently provided the sport with many more top class Canadian Professionals. Before 1980 was out, the strong Canadian trio of Thorburn, Kirk Stevens and Bill Werbeniuk had reached the final of the State Express World Team Cup, but there they lost to Wales.

1981 saw Thorburn reach the world number one position according to the rankings. He could not, however, retain his world title, losing 16-10 to Steve Davis in the semi-final. Apart from winning the BBC *Pot Black* title by beating fellow Canadian Jim Wych in the final, his only other notable successes in 1981 were runner-up position in both the Scottish Masters and the Tolly Cobbold Classic.

Having to commmute from Canada, Thorburn cut down his tournament appearances in 1982. A first-round defeat by Jimmy White in the world championships did him no good, but he did help Canada to a memorable 4-2 victory over England in the final of the World Team Classic.

The following season heralded the revival of Cliff Thorburn and he has remained one of the toughest competitors in the world ever since. He started 1983 with the Benson and Hedges Masters title, achieving victory over Ray Reardon in the final, and soon afterwards he set the snooker world alight with the first maximum break in the history of the world championships. He had compiled many maximums in his career, but mostly on the 'generous' Canadian tables; now he made history with his 147 in the match against Terry Griffiths. Up against the handicap of a runny nose during the break, he had that one bit of luck that is normally required: it came on the first red, when he missed the intended pocket. The red ball moved along the bottom cushion, and knocked in another red (see diagram), and the rest is history.

The championships were also memorable because of the length of Thorburn's matches. His meeting with Griffiths finished at 3.51 a.m. after 6 hours 25 minutes play; his 13-12 win over Kirk Stevens in the quarter-final lasted 6 hours 11 minutes and finished at 2.12 a.m., and his semi-final win over Tony Knowles lasted 4 hours 45 minutes. It was hardly surprising that when Thorburn lined up to play Steve Davis in the final he was physically and mentally shattered, and consequently the title went to Davis, who won easily 18-6.

Thorburn followed his world championship final appearance with victory in the Australian Winfield Masters, and was runner up, to Davis again, in the Jameson International.

Based in Britain once again, he became the most consistent player during the 1984-85 season. Runner-up in the Rothmans Grand Prix to his great friend Dennis Taylor, he was also beaten finalist (with Willie Thorne) in the Hofmeister World Doubles championship, losing to Alex Higgins and Jimmy White. A third runner-up position followed when he lost to another great friend, his doubles partner Willie Thorne, in the final of the Mercantile Credit Classic.

After finishing runner-up in three finals, Thorburn erased the 'bridesmaid's' tag when he beat Doug Mountjoy for first prize in the Benson and Hedges Masters for the second time.

The 1984-85 season was not one of undiluted success for Thorburn. It also brought about personal tragedy when his manager, Darryl McKerrow, was accidentally killed while on a hunting expedition in Manitoba. This loss affected Thorburn more than it showed, and his Benson and Hedges victory was dedicated to his ex-manager and former friend. His new mentor Robert Winsor has helped pull him through his moments of grief and thankfully his snooker has not been affected.

Thorburn's style of play is methodical, calculated and cool. He rarely gets ruffled, and is a credit to the sport. His sportsmanship, his services to snooker, and his being an unofficial ambassador for Canada resulted in his being presented with the Order of Canada (OBC) in 1984.

Career highlights

- World Professional Snooker Champion 1980
- Goya Matchroom Trophy Champion 1985
- Benson & Hedges Masters Champion 1983, 1985-86
- Langs Scottish Masters Champion 1985, 1986
- World Cup 1980, 1982 (member of winning Canadian team)
- Winfield Australian Masters Champion 1983
- Canadian Professional Champion 1984-87
- *Pot Black* Champion 1981
- Canadian Open Champion 1974, 1978-80
- North American Champion 1971-72

Willie Thorne relaxing at home

Thorne, Willie

When Willie Thorne reached his first major individual final in 1985 the list of spectators in the large crowd was like a *Who's Who* in Sport. In the audience for the confrontation with Cliff Thorburn in the final of the Mercantile Credit Classic at the Spectrum Arena, were Leicester City footballer Gary Lineker, Liverpool captain Phil Neal, Olympic gold medallist Tessa Sanderson, and European boxing champion Tony Sibson. They were all there because they enjoy the sport. They were also there because of their friendship with Willie Thorne. Sibson and Lineker in particular are great friends because, like Thorne, they are based in Leicester. Lineker is his best friend and a regular practice partner at Thorne's snooker centre in Charles Street, Leicester, and he is capable of scoring 60-70 breaks, which helps keep Thorne on his toes.

After many years of trying, and much devotion, he got that first title under his belt; but one regret was having to beat another great friend, Cliff Thorburn, in the final. Thorburn was his partner when they reached the world doubles final in 1984, and it was with a touch of irony that just before the Mercantile event, Thorburn had been staying at Thorne's house in Oadby while he was looking for a home of his own in the area.

Thorne started playing snooker at the Anstey Conservative Club near Leicester when he was 13, and four years later he made his international debut. He won the national under-16 billiards championship in 1970, and the following year went on to win the first of three successive under-19 titles. Runner-up in the under-16 snooker final in 1969, he won it the following year, and in 1973 added the under-19 snooker title to his already impressive list of junior honours. He nearly won the senior amateur championship in 1975, but lost to Sid Hood in the final. Later that year he took part in the Canadian Open, and he lost in the semi-finals to John Pulman. But he left his mark on the event, beating John Spencer 9-7 in the quarter-final.

He turned professional in 1976 and when he was invited to compete in that year's *Pot Black* competition he was, at 21, the youngest-ever competitor in the event. Thorne's first win as a professional was in the 1980 Pontins Open. He beat fellow-professional Cliff Wilson in the final, and beat Steve Davis on the way there. The following year he reached the professional final, and led Terry Griffiths 5-1 before going down 9-8.

His best-ever world championship came in 1982, when he reached the quarter-final. Before losing to Alex Higgins he managed to make a break of 143 – his highest in tournament play, and the second-highest ever in the world championships at the time. The remainder of 1982 was not the best times for the former tic-tac man, bookie's runner and photographic model: he broke both legs below the knee in a go-karting accident during the summer and was forced to withdraw from the Jameson International. He continued to play snooker despite his injuries, and in a practice match registered a maximum 147 break – the only man to have done so with both legs in plaster!

Thorne claims to have made more maximums, in either practice or exhibition play, than any other player. He registered the 34th of his career while practising for the 1984 Winfield Australian Masters. The first came at Osborne's Club, Leicester, when he was 22; it was against Brian Cakebread.

Ranked 18th in the world in 1983-84, he moved into the illustrious top 16 in 1984-85. Being in the top 16 meant that he did not have to qualify for tournaments; this proved to be a great weight off his shoulders, and his game improved. With Cliff Thorburn he reached the 1984 world doubles final, only to lose to Alex Higgins and Jimmy White. Also in 1984 he won the Pontins professional title that had eluded him three years earlier, beating John Spencer in the final.

All that was the build-up to his first big one – the Mercantile. His victory in the final saw him take the £40,000 first prize, plus £4,000 for the highest break. Although the title was something special, he also cherishes his semi-final win over Steve Davis: in a titanic struggle, he beat Davis 9-8. Thorne broke down and wept afterwards, when it dawned on him what he had done. A teetotaller, he allowed himself a glass of champagne that night.

Since his first major success in the 1985 Mercantile, Willie has had to endure the 'bridesmaid' tag, finishing runner-up in the Scottish Masters, UK Open, British Open and Benson & Hedges Irish Masters two years in succession. Despite his lack of success, he has maintained his place in the top 16.

Career highlights

- Mercantile Credit Classic Champion 1985
- Matchroom Trophy Champion 1986
- Pontins Professional Champion 1984
- Pontins Open Champion 1980
- National Under-19 Snooker Champion 1973
- National Under-19 Billiards Champion 1971-73
- National Under-16 Snooker Champion 1970
- National Under-16 Billiards Champion 1970

Thurston's

The name of Thurston's has been synonymous with the games of billiards and snooker for over 150 years. Having originally set his company up in Newcastle Street, Strand, London in 1799 as furniture makers, John Thurston changed his operation in 1814 to that of specialist billiard table manufacturer. At the same time the firm moved to new premises at nearby Catherine Street. The company was responsible for the design and specifications of the modern table: the specifications in force today are those of the Thurston tables accepted by the Billiards Association in the late 19th century.

It was Thurston, during the last century, who designed the current slate bed and the rubber cushions. He was also responsible for the adoption of a larger size ball, similar to the type used today. He started to give away 2-inch diameter balls with each of his tables in 1830; until then the balls used in billiards had been somewhat smaller.

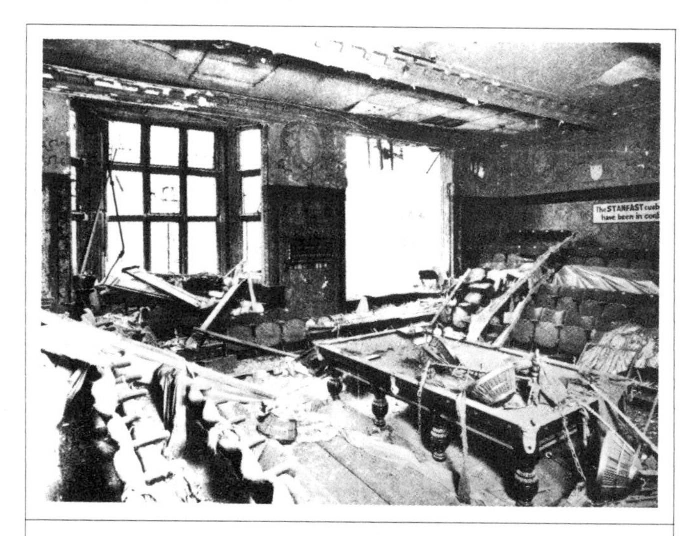

The scene at Thurston's Hall, Leicester Square, after it was hit by a German bomb in October 1940

The original Thurston's billiard hall in Catherine Street, in the year 1839

John Thurston was such a craftsman and innovator that the company received five Royal Warrants, and at the Great Exhibition of 1851 received the supreme gold medal. Sadly, John Thurston himself was not alive to receive the award – he died the previous year. The company employed many great craftsmen, a notable one being table assembler Francis Carey, who saw 60 years service with the company from 1839 to 1899.

In 1963 the company joined forces with another leading manufacturer – E. A. Clare and Son Ltd of Liverpool. Clare's had been in existence since 1912. In 1968 the Birmingham firm of Thos. Padmore and Sons (established 1830) joined the group to form the Clare-Padmore-Thurston Group. The group also manufactures bowling-green bowls.

With snooker gaining in popularity and output of tables increasing every year, Thurston's opened a new 1,100 square metre (12,000 square foot) factory at Camden, North London, in 1983, at a cost of £500,000.

Thurston's have given more to the game than just their tables – they gave it one of the best-known billiard halls. Built on a site in Leicester Square, London, and opened in 1901, Thurston's Hall staged all major billiards and snooker tournaments. Such famous pre-war tournaments as the Daily Mail, Empire News, Sporting Record and News of the World tournaments were held there. The first world amateur billiards championship (known then as the Empire Championships) were held at Thurston's in 1926.

Many famous breaks were scored at Thurston's, none more famous than Walter Lindrum's world record billiards break of 4,137 in 1932. Walter's nephew Horace Lindrum established a then record snooker break of 136 at the hall in 1935.

One of the most famous personalities at Thurston's Hall was referee Charlie Chambers, and the highlight of each year was at Christmas when the leading players would put on a gala show that attracted all the leading showbusiness and sports stars of the era; all proceeds went to Charlie.

In January 1940 an exhibition containing some of the finest billiards and snooker memorabilia was opened within the hall. But on 31 October that year the hall was destroyed when a bomb fell in the south-west corner of Leicester Square, and most of the cherished items from the exhibition were lost. Fortunately, part of a table sold to Queen Victoria in 1838 was saved. By coincidence, another famous sporting venue, Wimbledon, was hit by a bomb that same day.

The site in Leicester Square was redeveloped, and the hall reopened in 1947 under different management. Officially it was known as the Leicester Square Hall, but from then until its closure in 1955 it was still affectionately known as Thurston's.

Tolly Cobbold Classic

Founded in 1723, Suffolk brewers Tolly Cobbold have been involved in professional snooker sponsorship in the Ipswich area since 1979. Moving with the present trend, they have abandoned their very popular eight-man tournament, which was played for the last time in 1984. The company has moved into snooker on a larger scale, becoming sponsors of the reborn English professional championship – last contested in 1981.

The Classic was born in 1979 following the success of a four man tournament at the Ipswich Corn Exchange the previous year. They had the support of Anglia Television, and the round-robin formula, involving two four-man groups, made the tournament a popular one.

The Corn Exchange was the venue for the first championship, and has been for every subsequent competition. Group winners Alex Higgins and Ray Reardon fought out the best-of-nine frame final in 1979. Higgins won 5-4, then retained his title in 1980 with another 5-4 victory in the final. This time he beat fellow Irishman Dennis Taylor. Graham Miles was the surprise 5-1 winner over Cliff Thorburn in the 1981 final – the last year the round-robin format was used.

In 1982 a straightforward knockout competition, but still involving eight players, was adopted. Steve Davis was the new champion, winning the first of three successive 'Classics.' He beat Dennis Taylor, who was appearing in his second final, 8-3 in the new extended best-of-17 frame final.

When Davis won the title for the second time, in 1983, it cost the Anglia Television company a few extra pounds in overtime. His final with Terry Griffiths was a best-of-13 affair, to be played in one session. The match finished at 1.50 a.m. – and cameramen at that time had to be paid at double rate.

Davis completed his hat-trick of wins in 1984 when he beat Tony Knowles 8-2 in the final. He made the final only after a nervous semi-final meeting with Kirk Stevens. With the players level at 4-4 the match hinged on the last frame: it came down to the final black, and after a dozen shots by both players, it was Stevens who made the mistake that let Davis in. Prize money for the winner was only £7,000, but Steve Davis has always been prepared to support the tournament.

As the sport said goodbye to the Tolly Cobbold Classic in 1984 it was only too pleased to welcome the sponsors' new venture – the Tolly Cobbold English Professional Championship.

Tolly Cobbold Classic – Results (finals)

1979 A. Higgins (Ireland) 5
R. Reardon (Wales) 4
1980 A. Higgins (Ireland) 5
D. Taylor (Ireland) 4
1981 G. Miles (England) 5
C. Thorburn (Canada) 1
1982 S. Davis (England) 8
D.Taylor (Ireland) 3
1983 S. Davis (England) 7
T. Griffiths (Wales) 5
1984 S. Davis (England) 8
T. Knowles (England) 2
Most wins: 3 – Steve Davis
Most finals: 3 – Steve Davis
Highest break: 119 – Terry Griffiths (1980)

Touching Ball

If the cue-ball comes to rest touching an object-ball the referee will declare it a 'touching ball'. In this case the striker *must not* play the cue-ball towards that object-ball, otherwise he will be deemed to have played a push shot, which is a foul.

The rules were changed following a meeting of the Control Council on 14 January 1927: it ruled that a player could play away from a touching ball without incurring a penalty for a miss if the cue-ball contacts no other object-ball.

Trick Shots

Trick shots are widely identified with the game of snooker. Not only do they allow players to perform shots that would normally be illegal within a game, but they provide spectacular entertainment. Consequently most players who perform exhibition matches carry out trick-shots at the end of their night's play. Most professionals have shots that they have designed and perfected themselves. Joe Davis was one of the pioneers of the trick shot, and Sydney Lee was also an expert at them.

Two well-tried trick shots are illustrated opposite and below.

Tuborg World Cup

When British American Tobacco pulled out of sponsoring the World Cup, known as the State Express World Cup and then later the State Express World Team Classic, it looked as though the event was going to disappear from the professional calendar. The competition has, however, stayed alive thanks to a succession of three different sponsors in the three years since then.

Brewers Guinness were first to offer assistance, followed by Car Care Plan and, in 1987, Tuborg Lager.

During BAT's tenure as sponsors the format changed very little. Six teams would play in two groups, and the top two in each group went on to play in semi-finals and a final. When new sponsors took over it bacame a straight knockout competition involving eight teams. The winning country is now permitted to enter two teams the following year.

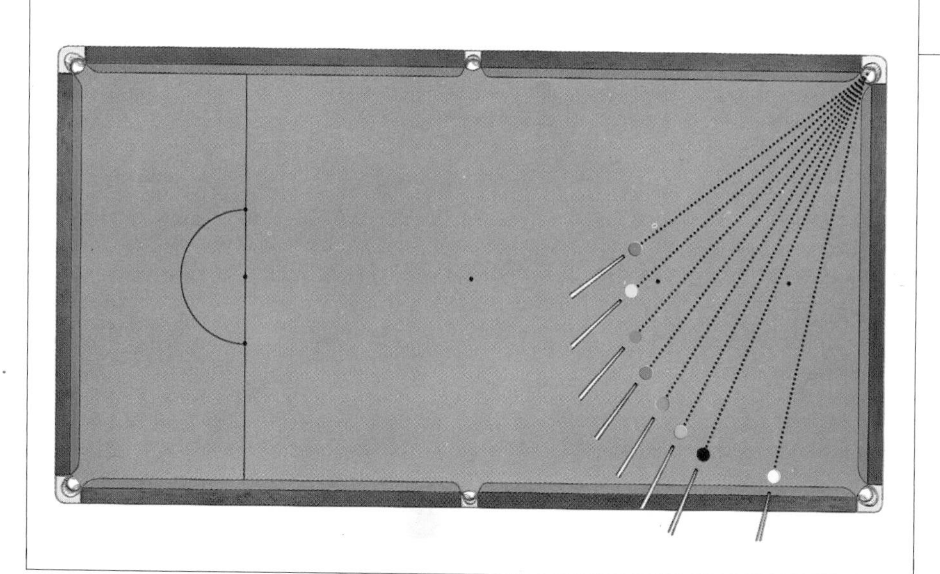

Trick shots

The 'machine gun shot', one of the most widely used of all trick shots. After striking the white towards the pocket, the idea is to strike each of the other balls – rapidly – so as to get them into the pocket before the white, which rolls gently in afterwards.

Tuborg World Cup

1979 Wales (Griffiths/Mountjoy/Reardon) 14
England (F. Davis/Miles/Spencer) 3
1980 Wales (Griffiths/Mountjoy/Reardon) 8
Canada (Stevens/Thorburn/Werbeniuk) 5
1981 England (S. Davis/Spencer/Taylor) 4
Wales (Griffiths/Mountjoy/Reardon) 3
1982 Canada (Stevens/Thorburn/Werbeniuk) 4
England (S. Davis/Knowles/White) 2
1983 England (S. Davis/Knowles/Meo) 4
Wales (Griffiths/Mountjoy/Reardon) 2
1985 All Ireland (Higgins/Hughes/Taylor) 9
England 'A' (S. Davis/Knowles/Meo) 7
1986 Ireland 'A' (Higgins/Hughes/Taylor) 9
Canada (Stevens/Thorburn/Werbeniuk) 7
1987 Ireland 'A' (Higgins/Hughes/Taylor) 9
Canada (Stevens/Thorburn/Werbeniuk) 2

Most wins (team): 3 – All-Ireland/Ireland 'A'
Most wins (individual): 3 – Alex Higgins, Eugene Hughes, Dennis Taylor (all Ireland)
Most finals (team): 5 – England (one as England 'A')
Most finals (individual): 4 – Terry Griffiths, Doug Mountjoy, Ray Reardon (all Wales)
4 – Kirk Stevens, Cliff Thorburn, Bill Werbeniuk (all Canada)
Highest break: 127 – Terry Griffiths (1981)

Wales, represented by Ray Reardon, Terry Griffiths and Doug Mountjoy, easily beat England 14-3 in the first final. They retained the title the following year, this time beating Canada in the final.

The Welsh trio of Reardon, Griffiths and Mountjoy have made up the Welsh team in all eight competitions held to date, while Canada have been represented by Cliff Thorburn, Kirk Stevens and Bill Werbeniuk in all eight. Fred Davis led England in the 1979 and 1980 competitions, but a new-look team consisting of Steve Davis, David Taylor and John Spencer lifted the trophy for the first time in 1981.

The experienced Canadians beat a young England team consisting of Steve Davis, Tony Knowles and Jimmy White to win the trophy in 1982. England beat Wales to win the last of the State Express sponsored events in 1983, skippered once again by Steve Davis.

The Irish trio of Alex Higgins, Dennis Taylor and Eugene Hughes won the first event under the sponsorship of Guinness. They beat the strong England 'A' team of Davis, Meo and Knowles after coming from behind. The Irish team retained the title in 1986 and made it a hat-trick of wins the following year.

In addition to the Welsh and Canadian trios who have represented their countries in every competition, the following individuals have also competed in all eight tournaments: Alex Higgins, Dennis Taylor and Eddie Charlton. But a unique appearance record is that of Irishman Patsy Fagan; he has appeared in the competition five times – and with four different teams, namely, Ireland, Ireland 'B', Republic of Ireland, and the Rest of the World!

Undefeated

Without any shadow of a doubt Joe Davis's unbeaten record in the world professional championships must rank as one of the greatest of all snooker feats. Even though his number of opponents was as low as one for two of the championships, his record of playing in – and winning – every world championship between 1927 and 1946 is unequalled in the snooker world.

Altogether Davis played 34 games in the championship, winning them all with an average score of 25 frames to 15.

In more recent world championships Ray Reardon's record is second to none. Between losing to Rex Williams in the quarter-final in 1972, and losing to John Spencer, also in the quarter-final, in 1977, Reardon did not lose a game in the championships. He played and won 17 games, and won the title four times.

Considering how the number of competitors in the world championships has risen from 27, when Reardon won the title in 1976, to around 100, Steve Davis's performance of winning the title in successive years is, perhaps, even more remarkable.

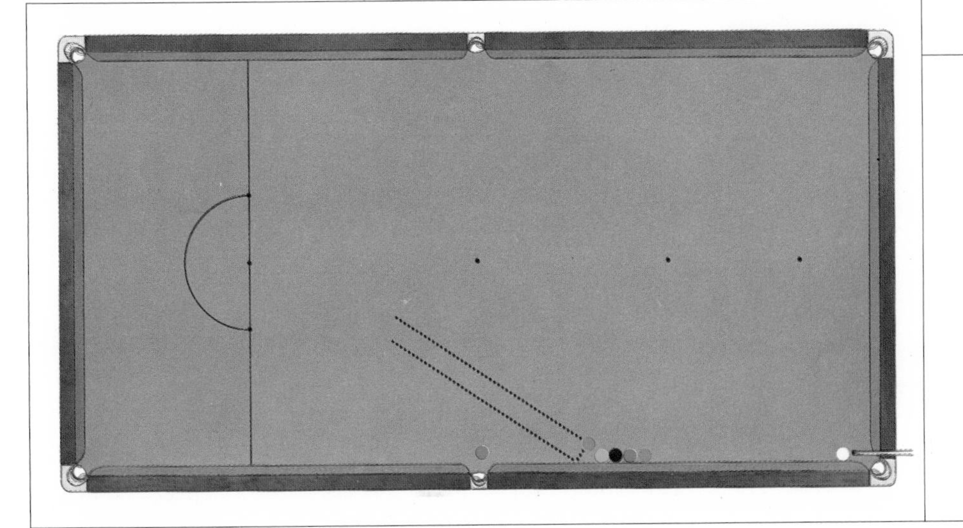

Trick shots

The 'alternative pot black' trick shot: how to pot the black ball when this is least expected. The cue-ball strikes the first object-ball; the last ball in the line strikes the ball that is slightly away from the cushion; those two balls disappear up the table (dotted lines) while the black continues along the cushion to go in-off the ball over the middle pocket.

United States of America

When Jim Rempe competed in the 1987 world professional championship he became the first competitor from the United States in the tournament's 60-year history.

Rempe beat Martin Smith 10-9 and in doing so recorded the first century break of the 1987 championship. He also beat John Rea before Stephen Hendry shattered his dream of becoming the first American world champion.

The exploits of Rempe could just be the start of an invasion of players from the United States, which is seen as yet another tremendous potential growth area for the sport.

Steve Davis and top American pool player Steve Mizarek took part in a £50,000 Fiat-Snooker/Pool challenge in St. Moritz in 1987. Mizarek won the three-game event, but more importantly, it attracted great interest on television in the United States. As a result of the interest shown in snooker there, Barry Hearn arranged for Davis and Jimmy White to play exhibition matches in the United States later in the year.

If the Americans take to the game as they do to most other sports, it cannot be long before there is a United States snooker champion of the world.

Steve Davis shakes hands with the victorious Tony Knowles after the biggest upset in recent snooker

Upsets

As the gap between the top and bottom rungs of the professional snooker ladder narrows, the number of upsets that can be truly regarded as shocks reduces. But snooker, like all sports, has produced its shocks over the years, and without doubt the biggest upset of modern times was in the 1982 world professional championships at the Crucible Theatre.

Steve Davis, the defending champion, was up against a newcomer from Bolton, Tony Knowles. Knowles had been a professional for only two years, and he had a good track record; but beating Davis at that time was regarded as a feat in itself. To beat him 10-1 was nothing short of outstanding.

Davis was also the subject of another upset when he lost 5-2 to youngster Mike Hallett in the 1983 Professional Players' Tournament.

The most remarkable sequence of upsets strung together by one player in a single tournament must have been that by Doug Mountjoy in the 1977 Benson and Hedges Masters. Mountjoy, a professional for only a couple of months, only came into the tournament as a late replacement, and then proceeded to beat four former world champions – John Pulman, Fred Davis, Alex Higgins and Ray Reardon – to win the title.

Eddie Charlton was the subject of one of the biggest upsets in the world championships prior to Steve Davis's defeat by Knowles. The 1970 championships were staged in Charlton's native Australia, and he was one of the favourites for the title. He reached the semi-final, but was beaten by fellow Australian Warren Simpson. That was only the second time Charlton had been beaten by an Australian on level terms, and it was 1980 before the same thing happened again.

Doug Mountjoy, perpetrator of an astonishing string of upsets in the 1977 Benson and Hedges Masters

Virgo, John

After being consistently ranked in the top 16 of the World Professional Billiards and Snooker Association's rankings, the bearded John Virgo lost his all-important top-16 placing in 1984. It came at a time when, ironically, he had become one of the most sought-after members of the professional circuit for exhibitions. His popularity stems from the 'cabaret' act he performs. His act, in which he impersonates his fellow professionals, was first seen on television during the 1982 world championships, and since then he has always been in demand.

The big events have eluded Virgo since he turned professional in July 1976, and it is ironic that when he recovered something like his old form to win the new Professional Snooker League in 1984, not only did it carry no ranking points, but it did not carry any prize-money either!

Originally from Rochdale, but now living down south in Guildford, John learnt his snooker in the tough schooling area of Manchester – notably at Potters Club in Salford. In 1962 he was National Under-16 champion, and three years later he won the Under-19 championship.

The remainder of his amateur career saw him win many north-west competitions, and between 1971 and 1976 he gained international honours, representing England 15 times. In 1975 he reached the final of the Pontins Open but, despite receiving 25 points per frame from Ray Reardon, he lost 7-1.

The year before he turned professional he won, with Paul Medati, the National Pairs title. In the all-Manchester final, they beat the pairing of Billy Kelly and Dennis Hughes. Virgo also came close to reaching the English Amateur final that year, but he lost in the northern final to Roy Andrewartha. Two nights before his defeat by Andrewartha he had compiled his first maximum 147 break; his opponent – Andrewartha.

Virgo's first couple of years as a professional were a struggle, but in 1979 it came right. First he beat Willie Thorne, Cliff Thorburn and Bill Werbeniuk to reach the world championship semi-final, where he lost to Dennis Taylor. And then, after a move down south to join Henry West's stable, he lifted the Coral United Kingdom title at Preston. With good victories over Tony Meo and Steve Davis, and an avenging win over Dennis Taylor in the semi-final, he earned himself a meeting with the then world champion, Terry Griffiths.

He beat Griffiths in the final, but not before he had given his supporters – and himself – a few heart-stopping moments. Leading 11-7 at the start of the final session, and only needing three frames for victory, he was 20 minutes late in arriving. Under the rules he was penalized two frames; that made it 11-9. Griffiths then won the first two frames of the session to level the score at 11-all. But Virgo managed to come back eventually to win 14-13, and thus take his first major professional title.

Serious play from snooker's joker – John Virgo

The 1979-80 season ended with Virgo winning the Pontins Professional title, beating Ray Reardon 9-6 in the final and thus avenging his defeat in the Open final five years earlier. On the way to the final he also beat Steve Davis.

From then until 1984 – apart from finishing runner-up, with John Spencer, in the Pontins Doubles Championship at Brean Sands in 1983 – John Virgo had very little to shout about, as he struggled to find his old form. The new professional snooker league in the 1983-84 season saw him emerge as its winner but, sadly for him, there was no pot of gold at the end of it. It was, nevertheless, a creditable win, as he was playing alongside ten other top ranked players. Throughout the tournament he only lost one match – to Eddie Charlton – and he was the last man to lose his 100% record. Going into his final match against Tony Knowles, at Kelham Hall, Newark, Virgo was lying in third place in the league, but knew that a win would make him champion. He nervously beat Knowles 6-4 to clinch the title by just one point from Dennis Taylor and Eddie Charlton.

Virgo regained some of his lost form towards the end of 1984 when he beat his former doubles partner Cliff Thorburn 5-0 in the first round of the Jameson International. And in the Mercantile Credit Classic at the beginning of 1985 he reached his first quarter-final since the 1982 Coral UK Championship when he met and lost to Thorburn's new doubles partner, Willie Thorne.

Being out of the top 16 means John has to work harder to qualify for the ranking tournaments, but he enjoyed his best result for a long time in 1987 when he beat Steve Davis in the 4th round of the Dulux British Open – the first time he has beaten Davis since he did so on his way to winning the 1979 Coral United Kingdom title.

The three ranking points from the Dulux helped Virgo maintain his number 19 ranking and, as the 'Mike Yarwood of the snooker world' tries to get back into the top 16, he will no doubt continue to keep the customers satisfied with his cabaret act.

Career highlights

- World Professional Snooker Championship (semi-final) 1979
- Coral United Kingdom Professional Champion 1979
- Pontins Professional Champion 1980
- Professional Snooker League winner 1984
- National Pairs Champion 1976 (with Paul Medati)
- National Under-16 Snooker Champion 1962
- National Under-19 Snooker Champion 1965

Wales

In producing three world amateur champions, and winning the Home International series on nine occasions, Wales has proved itself the foremost producer of amateur players since 1970. Add to their amateur record the professional records of Ray Reardon, Terry Griffiths and Doug Mountjoy, and nobody can dispute that Wales is one of the world's outstanding snooker-playing nations.

Many prominent Welsh amateurs have emerged in the post-war era. First there were Ray Reardon and Cliff Wilson. Twenty-two years after winning his first Welsh national title, Wilson

John Virgo in another hat – impersonating Dennis Taylor during the interval

won the world amateur title. Reardon and Wilson were followed by Mario Berni and the Owen brothers, Marcus and Gary, in the sixties, while the seventies saw the emergence of Doug Mountjoy – world amateur champion in 1976 – Terry Griffiths, Alwyn Lloyd, Des May and Geoff Thomas. In the eighties Terry Parsons took a third world amateur title for Wales when he won in 1982 – and this was 21 years after *he* first won the Welsh title!

Wales also has a strong crop of new professionals in Steve Newbury, Colin Roscoe, Tony Chappell and Wayne Jones, and with them the future of Welsh snooker looks healthy for several years to come.

The Welsh amateur snooker championships date back to 1930, when the first winner was the great Welsh player of the day, Tom Jones. The billiards championship started ten years earlier and was won by Horace Coles who, in 1935, became the first Welsh-born world billiards champion – although he represented England at the time.

Tom Jones won the first seven Welsh snooker titles, after which it was not until the emergence of a young Tredegar player – Ray Reardon – in 1950 that the championships were so dominated by a single player.

Reardon won the title six years in succession from 1950 to 1955, and would surely have won more had he not 'emigrated' to Stoke-on-Trent in the mid-fifties. Tredegar was lucky to have two outstanding snooker players in those days, for Cliff Wilson also hailed from the town. Their rivalry split the town – a situation not dissimilar to the rivalry between Everton and Liverpool soccer clubs.

As Reardon joined the professional ranks in the late sixties, Wilson left the game altogether until the seventies. And in 1978, by coincidence, Tredegar claimed both world amateur and professional champions as Reardon and Wilson won the respective titles.

Ray Reardon has undoubtedly been the country's most successful player overall, with six national titles, one English amateur title, and six professional world titles as well as numerous others to his credit. Reardon has also won the Welsh professional championship, which is the oldest national professional championship in the world. It was first held in 1922 and won by J.S. Nicholls, but it then fell into disuse until revived in 1977. It has since been a well supported event, and is one of the few national professional titles to have been contested without interruption between 1977 and 1987.

The record of Wales in the Home International championship is only equalled by that of England, but in recent years, when competition has got tougher, Wales has dominated the championships.

Had it not been for Wales there would have been no Home International championships in the first place. It was their idea to have an official international match against England to commemorate the investiture of Prince Charles as the Prince of Wales in 1969, and in June of that year England beat Wales 10-8 at Port Talbot.

Wales possesses the most capped player in the whole of the Home International championships in Alwyn Lloyd, who has represented his country 47 times since 1969 and has never had the desire to turn professional. The same is true of another of their outstanding amateurs, Terry Parsons. A postman from Penygraig, he was world amateur champion in 1982 and beaten finalist in Dublin two years later.

Wales has an abundance of snooker talent – and the fact that men of the calibre of Lloyd and Parsons are prepared to retain their amateur status, gives some indication as to the country's strength in depth.

Warners Open

Three years after Pontins started their Snooker Festival in 1974, Warner Holidays did the same at their Sinah Warren Holiday Camp on Hayling Island, near Portsmouth. The first Warners Open was not well supported, with just 27 entrants contesting the £250 first prize. A 17-year-old amateur, Tony Meo, beat professional Doug Mountjoy (who was conceding 21 points) in the final. Another young aspirant in the first championships was Steve Davis, but he was knocked out in the first round by the experienced Ron Gross.

The number of competitors rose to 64 in the second year when John Spencer took the £250 first prize by beating fellow-Lancastrian, talented amateur Tony Knowles in the final. The first prize rose dramatically in 1979 to £1,750, and the popularity of the event rose in proportion. This time the final was contested by two amateurs – Tony Meo and Jimmy White – whose paths have crossed many times in their amateur and professional days.

Steve Davis, in 1980, was the first – and only – professional to win the title when he beat local south-coast player Brian Watson in the final. After Davis's victory, the event was scrapped because it became too large for the Sinah Warren Camp to

Welsh Amateur Snooker Championships (finalists)

1930 T. Jones*
1931 T. Jones*
1932 T. Jones*
1933 T. Jones*
1934 T. Jones*
1935 T. Jones*
1936 T. Jones*
1937 G. Howells*
1938 B. Gravenor*
1939 W.E. James*
1940-1946 Not held
1947 T. Jones beat R. Smith
1948 R. Smith beat A.J. Ford
1949 A.J. Ford beat C. Coles
1950 R. Reardon beat A.J. Ford
1951 R. Reardon beat R. Smith
1952 R. Reardon beat A.J. Ford
1953 R. Reardon beat A. Kemp
1954 R. Reardon beat A.J. Ford
1955 R. Reardon beat A.J. Ford
1956 C. Wilson beat V. Wilkins
1957 R.D. Meredith beat M. Williams
1958 A. Kemp beat R.D. Meredith
1959 J.R. Price beat M.L. Berni
1960 L. Luker beat A. Kemp
1961 T. Parsons beat J.R. Price
1962 A.J. Ford beat M.L. Berni
1963 R.D. Meredith beat J.R. Price
1964 M.L. Berni beat A.J. Ford
1965 T. Parsons beat A.J. Ford
1966 L.L. O'Neill beat D. Mountjoy
1967 L.L. O'Neill beat K. Weed
1968 D. Mountjoy beat J. Terry
1969 T. Parsons beat J.T. Prosser
1970 D.T. May beat G. Thomas
1971 D.T. May beat R.W. Oriel
1972 G. Thomas beat T. Griffiths
1973 A. Lloyd beat G. Thomas
1974 A. Lloyd beat G. Thomas
1975 T. Griffiths beat G. Thomas
1976 D. Mountjoy beat A. Lloyd
1977 C. Wilson beat D. Thomas
1978 A. Lloyd beat S. Newbury
1979 C. Wilson beat G. Thomas
1980 S. Newbury beat A. Lloyd
1981 C. Roscoe beat E. Richards
1982 T. Parsons beat M. Berni
1983 W. Jones beat T. Parsons
1984 T. Parsons beat W. Jones
1985 M. Bennet beat D. John
1986 K. Jones beat J. Griffiths
1987 D. Morgan beat J. Herbert
Most wins: 8-Tom Jones
Highest break: 123 – Tony Chappel (1980)

*Records not kept.

handle. It returned in 1983, however, due to the efforts of Doug Gordon of the Havant-based promotions company, Pegasus Promotions. His efforts were well rewarded with a record 96 entries. This success guaranteed the Warners Open a place in the 1984 fixture list, and also led to Warners sponsoring a second event in 1984 – the Warners Pro-Am.

Alwyn Lloyd – the most capped Welsh player

The Pro-Am was taken off the calender in 1985 and made way for an amateur-only Isle of White Festival at Warners new holiday centre at Puckpool, near Ryde. The festival retained the 'Open' title, and carried a £3,000 first prize unprecedented for an amateur-only event. It also included the Warners Ladies Bowl, and the world junior championships.

Warners Open – Results (finals)

1977 A. Meo (21) beat D. Mountjoy 5-4
1978 J. Spencer beat A. Knowles (21) 7-4
1979 A. Meo (21) beat J. White (21 5-2
1980 S. Davis beat B. Watson (21) 5-1
1981 Not held
1982 Not held
1983 N. Foulds (18) beat D. Fowler (18) 4-0
1984 M. Smith (18) beat W. Thorne 4-3
1985 S. James beat D. Roe 4-2
1986 M. Clark beat G. Keeble 5-2
(Figures in brackets indicate start received per frame)
Most wins: 2 Tony Meo
Highest break: 119 Tony Chappel (1984)

Junior championship
1985 W. Rendle beat B. Morgan 4-1
1986 A. Fisher beat W. Rendle 4-2

Women's bowl
1985 A. Fisher beat S. Hillyard 3-1
1986 A. Fisher beat S. Hillyard 4-0

Watterson, Mike

When the Association of Snooker Writers presented Mike Watterson with their 'Services to Snooker' award at their Gala Night in 1983, they were recognizing the giant contribution he had made to snooker – a contribution acknowledged by most people within the sport.

Mike Watterson has come a long way since his days as a car salesman with the Sheffield-based Vauxhall dealers, Bentley Brothers. (He holds the distinction of being one of the first people in the country to sell the Vauxhall Viva when it was introduced in 1963.)

A successful businessman, he has always been interested in snooker as a player and was a notable amateur. He first entered a billiard hall when he was 14, but got a 'clip round the ear' from his father for doing so. Surprisingly, his next visit to a billiard hall was 13 years later. He started playing in the Chesterfield League for the Angel Hotel, and in 1971 reached the semi-final of the Derbyshire championships; the following year he won the title. He subsequently went on to gain international honours for England in 1979 and 1980. But his greatest success as an amateur came in 1979, when he won the prestigious CIU championships.

Watterson's first venture into promotion was in 1972, when he promoted a match between Ray Reardon and Alex Higgins at Staveley. He soon established himself in his new field, and it was because of his efforts that the world championships were saved from threatened oblivion.

The 1976 championships, held in Middlesborough and Manchester, were a near disaster for the (then new) sponsors, Embassy. But Watterson convinced them that he could make the championships work, and the following year he proved himself correct when he took the tournament to the plush new setting of the Crucible Theatre in Sheffield. Since then the Crucible has been the permanent home of the world championships. It was in fact Watterson's wife Carol who was responsible for that venue being chosen... it was after she had been to the theatre to watch a play that she suggested to him the possibility of staging a major snooker event there.

After those initial world championships, Watterson went on to promote the World Team Cup, the Jameson International, and many other championships and tournaments. He also tried his hand at bowls and darts, and was responsible for promoting the inaugural Embassy World Professional Darts Champion hip in Nottingham in 1978.

As a player Mike Watterson has been ranked among the top 40, and he was accepted as a professional in 1981. Big wins have so far eluded him, but he claimed two major scalps in 1983 when he beat Tony Meo and Alex Higgins. He beat Meo 5-3 in the intermediate round of the Jameson International before losing 5-0 to Steve Davis in the next round. And in the first round of the Professional Players' Tournament at Bristol he beat Alex Higgins 5-2.

One of the crowning achievements in a snooker player's career is to make that elusive 147 break. Watterson had gone 15 years without making one until 1984 when, within the space of three days, he made two of them.

Snooker's most successful promoter, he also tried his hand at soccer in 1983-84. First he became chairman of Derby County, but resigned in July that year because of the increasing amount of crowd trouble at the Baseball Ground. He then became vice-chairman of his home-town team Chesterfield, but only stayed until November when he resigned again.

Career highlights
National Breaks Champion 1975-76
WMC & IU Champion 1979

One of the most popular players on the professional circuit, Terry Griffiths – the second Welshman after Ray Reardon to win the world title

Welsh Professional Championships

Although the first contest for the title of leading Welsh professional dates back to the 1920s when J.S. Nicholls beat W. Davies, there were no subsequent contests for the title for over 50 years. In those days the leading players preferred to play money-matches rather than championship matches.

The 'championship' was reborn in 1977 when the only two Welsh professionals – Ray Reardon and Doug Mountjoy – met at Caerphilly for the title. The contest attracted a lot of attention, and was sponsored by William Hill bookmakers. BBC Wales covered the event, which Reardon won 12-8.

One of the early televised events, it was not without its problems, notably with the lighting. One of the powerful overhead lights used by the BBC exploded and burnt the cloth.

It is perhaps surprising in view of the attention that match attracted, that the first official Welsh professional Championships were not instituted until 1980. Under the sponsorship of cider manufacturers H.P. Bulmer & Co., the Woodpecker Welsh Professional Championships were then born. The Ebbw Vale Leisure Centre was the venue for the first championship, and it was the venue for all championships up to 1984.

Doug Mountjoy became the first champion, beating Ray Reardon in the final of the four-man competition. Reardon won his first title in 1981 when he beat his old adversary Cliff Wilson in the final. Wilson eliminated defending champion Mountjoy in the semi-final.

For the first time, in 1982 eight men took part. The final was a classic which saw Doug Mountjoy regain his title. His opponent was Terry Griffiths, and it was Griffiths who took an early 2-0 lead. Mountjoy caught him and from then on there was never more than one frame between the two players. Mountjoy eventually won 9-8. Reardon took the title again in 1983 when he defeated Mountjoy 9-1. But in 1984 Mountjoy won the title for the third time with a 9-3 win over Cliff Wilson. Wilson picked up the biggest cheque of his professional career – £3,200. Just as significantly for Wilson, he beat Ray Reardon in the semi-final – the first time he had beaten Reardon since their amateur days in Tredegar in the fifties. Even though the competition developed into an eight-man tournament the same four men – Reardon, Mountjoy, Griffiths and Wilson – contested every semi-final between 1980 and 1986, when Wayne Jones beat Reardon to spoil the sequence.

Welsh Professional Championships – Results

1980 D. Mountjoy 9 R. Reardon 6
1981 R. Reardon 9 C. Wilson 6
1982 D. Mountjoy 9 T. Griffiths 8
1983 R. Reardon 9 D. Mountjoy l
1984 D. Mountjoy 9 C. Wilson 3
1985 T. Griffiths 9 D. Mountjoy 4
1986 T. Griffiths 9 D. Mountjoy 3
1987 D. Mountjoy 9 S. Newbury 7
Most wins: 4 – Doug Mountjoy
Most finals: 6 – Doug Mountjoy
Highest break: 127 – Terry Griffiths (1980)

Wembley Conference Centre

Just as Wembley is the biggest soccer venue in England, the Conference Centre at Wembley is the biggest snooker venue. And it is at the Conference Centre that snooker's largest ever crowd for one session has been gathered. That was in 1983, when 2,876 spectators witnessed the Benson and Hedges first-round match between Alex Higgins and Bill Werbeniuk.

Owned by Wembley Stadiums Limited, it was built in 1977, and it was the next step for the company after the stadium, and the Wembley Arena. Used mainly for exhibitions, it was first chosen as a snooker venue in 1977 when boxing promoter Mike Barrett ventured into the sport to promote the Dry Blackthorn Cup. A one-day tournament, it received television coverage and was won by reigning United Kingdom champion, Patsy Fagan.

The Benson and Hedges Masters moved to Wembley in 1978, and it has been staged at the Centre ever since.

Wembley was fortunate enough to share one of the sport's magic moments when, in 1984, Kirk Stevens registered a maximum 147 break in the Masters, playing against Jimmy White – the eventual winner of the tournament.

Werbeniuk, Bill

Who was the first man to split his trousers during a live television snooker broadcast? Which snooker player was allowed to set £2,000 worth of lager against his income as a tax-deductible item? Which snooker player lives in a mobile home? And who

Cliff Wilson and Ray Reardon with referee John Smyth, before the start of the 1981 Welsh Professional final

is the heaviest professional snooker player? The answer to all those questions is, of course, Canadian Bill Werbeniuk.

'Big Bill' is continually in the limelight for his activities both on and off the table. Born in Winnipeg, he started playing snooker in 1956 at the age of nine. He became a professional in 1973 and celebrated by completing the double consisting of the Canadian professional championship and North American championship that year. British audiences saw him for the first time the following year when he arrived for the world professional championship and he has been a popular figure on the professional scene in Britain ever since.

Werbeniuk is readily identifiable by his massive 20-stone frame (although not always exactly 20 stone – it fluctuates) and has now made his home in Britain, living in the Worksop area. That is he is based in the Worksop area – he 'lives' wherever his next tournament or exhibition takes him because he lives in a luxuriously fitted out old bus that he purchased.

The lager is a life-saver to Bill Werbeniuk: he suffers from a disease known as familial benign essential tremor, which causes his right hand to shake, and the only cure he has found for it is to drink large quantities of lager. Because of this, and the fact that he needed a cure in order to carry on his profession, the Inland Revenue ruled in 1981 that he could write off £2,000 of his income against tax.

Werbeniuk reached the quarter-final of the world championship in 1978, losing to Ray Reardon. In 1979 he enjoyed one of his best years. He reached the quarter final stage of the world championships again, losing to John Virgo; but on the way he had beaten number four seed John Spencer and also equalled Rex Williams's 14-year-old world championship record break of 142.

In 1980 Werbeniuk had moved into 10th place in the world professional rankings, and that year, together with Kirk Stevens and Cliff Thorburn, he reached his first major final, as Canada played Wales in the final of the World Team Cup. Canada lost in the final, but the competition was quite an eventful one, because it was then that his trousers split – in front of the television cameras – and he wasn't wearing underpants at the time either!

The incident happened when Canada was playing England, during Werbeniuk's match with David Taylor, and after an appeal was made for needle and cotton, he had to leave the arena for 15 minutes for the necessary repairs to be made. Canadian captain Cliff Thorburn took the opportunity to make a few comments like: 'This is really a needle match', and 'I was hoping Bill was going to sew it up for us!'

Another quarter-final place came Werbeniuk's way in the 1981 world championship but, yet again, he could not overcome that hurdle. This time he lost 13-10 to Ray Reardon. His first major honour came in 1982 when he helped Canada win the World Team Classic, by beating the strong English trio of Steve Davis, Tony Knowles and Jimmy White in the final. Werbeniuk played an important role in Canada's victory, only losing one game throughout the whole tournament, and that was his very first, against Doug Mountjoy. His 2-1 win over Davis in the final was a vital one for the Canadians who went on to win the final 4-2.

The following year saw Werbeniuk enjoy his best-ever season. In the Lada Classic at Warrington, after wins over Alex Higgins, Doug Mountjoy and Kirk Stevens, he reached his first final, where he came up against Steve Davis. He could not match his previous results, however, and lost to Davis in the

In his first two seasons as a professional, Yorkshire's Barry West moved up the world rankings to number 29

Mark Wildman, who represented England ten times in the Home International championships between 1970 and 1975

final by 9 frames to 5. Werbeniuk's Lada success was followed by his best world championship performance when, yet again, he reached the quarter-final. Playing Alex Higgins, he came as near as he has been to getting into the semi-final. He narrowly lost by 13 frames to 11.

But 1983 was far from over for the Canadian. In the summer he finished runner-up to team-mate Cliff Thorburn in the Winfield Australian Masters, and very nearly scooped the jackpot for a 147 break. Having taken 14 reds and 13 blacks, he missed the next black, which, ironically, was not all that difficult. To crown a memorable year, Werbeniuk was recognized as the Personality of the Year by the Snooker Writers' Association.

Since then, 'Big Bill' has slid down the rankings and out of the top 32, and has not even shown signs of coming close to winning any of the big tournaments. His slump reached a low when he failed to qualify for the final stages of the 1987 world championship at the Crucible.

Career highlights

- Lada Classic (runner-up) 1983
- Winfield Australian Masters (runner-up) 1983
- World Cup 1982 (member of winning Canadian team)
- North American Champion 1973-76
- Canadian Amateur Champion 1973

West, Barry

A professional since 1985, Yorkshireman Barry West jumped straight to number 30 in the world rankings at the end of his first season as a result of reaching the quarter-final of the Coral UK Open. Steve Davis brought him down to earth with a 9-1

Jimmy White

defeat, but West continued to show good form and reached the 4th round of the Mercantile Credit Classic.

He picked up ranking points in four of the six ranking events in 1986-87, including one for reaching the televised stage of the world championship. Having beaten John Spencer in the last qualifying round to reach the Crucible, he then met another former champion, Ray Reardon, but did not show any confidence and lost 10-5 to the Welshman.

Career highlights
Coral United Kingdom Open (quarter-final) 1985
Pontins Open Champion 1984

White, Jimmy

A great natural player, Jimmy White – the Whirlwind – was hailed as the greatest thing to hit snooker since Alex Higgins when he turned professional shortly after winning the 1980 world amateur championship. Success was gradual for the man Cliff Thorburn described as the world's best potter, but White developed into one of the sport's most consistent money winners.

He was introduced to snooker by his father as an 11-year-old. Within a year he had made his first century break, and by the time he was 15 he had compiled over 50 centuries. Zans Billiard Hall in Tooting was his regular haunt, and he spent more hours there than he did at the nearby Ernest Bevin comprehensive school. The headmaster, Mr Beattie, fully appreciated Jimmy's skills and realized that whatever he said it would not stop the youngster from attending Zans. Shrewdly, he did a deal with White whereby the boy was allowed to take the afternoons off from school to play snooker, providing he stayed for lessons in the mornings! Mr Beattie realized that Jimmy White had more chance of succeeding as a snooker player than he did academically.

White's first manager was Tooting taxi-driver Bob Davis, who also managed Jimmy's Ernest Bevin schoolmate, Tony Meo. The pair of them became too good for Davis to handle and they both teamed up with Henry West, who was then managing another of snooker's hottest properties, Patsy Fagan.

White first attracted national attention in 1977 when he beat Dave Bonney of St Helens in the final of the national under-16 snooker championship. Two years later he was selected for the London team that won the Inter Counties championship. Only 17 at the time, he became the youngest person ever to play for London. That same year he had also, at 16 years 11 months, become the youngest winner of the English amateur championship when he beat Dave Martin in the final at Helston, Cornwall. Not only did White beat Martin 13-10, but he compiled a 130 break which, unfortunately, was not ratified as a championship record because of oversized pockets.

White made the long voyage to Tasmania for the world amateur championships in 1980. But the trip was worthwhile because he returned as champion after beating Ron Atkins of Australia in the final. In winning the world crown he became another 'youngest' – he was just 18 years 191 days at the time.

And on his way back from Tasmania, White stopped off in India and won their national snooker title!

He turned professional upon returning to England, and became the youngest winner of a professional tournament at 19 years 4 months when he won the 1981 Scottish Masters, beating Cliff Thorburn in the final. He followed that up a few weeks later with victory in the Northern Ireland Classic, this time beating Steve Davis in the final.

Jimmy White, thoughtfully chalking his cue

Having beaten Steve Davis in the Northern Ireland Classic White's confidence was sky-high, and before their semi-final clash in the Coral United Kingdom championship that December he said: 'I am not convinced Steve is that far out on his own, as a lot of people believe, and I aim to prove my point in our semi-final showdown.' He couldn't have got it more wrong in the event: Davis gained revenge by winning 9-0.

Davis had inflicted defeat upon White in the first round of his world championship debut earlier in 1981, but in 1984 the two of them were engaged in one of the best world finals ever seen. White trailed 6-1 at the end of the first session and then 12-4 at the end of the second. He pulled back to 11-13 at the end of the third session and in the fourth only trailed by one frame at 16-15, before allowing Davis to win three successive frames to take the title by 18 frames to 16.

Prior to 1984 his best world championship performance had been in 1982, when he reached the semi-final. Once again he was involved in an epic, this time with Alex Higgins, and once again he threw away a lead to lose. With three frames to go, White was leading by two frames, but he allowed Higgins in to win those last three to go on to the final.

White teamed up with Higgins for the world doubles championship in 1984 and they ended the two-year run of Davis and Meo to win the title, beating the partnership of Thorburn and Thorne in the final. This made amends for Jimmy White, as he had been a beaten finalist, with Tony Knowles, in 1983.

This doubles success followed his biggest individual professional success when he won the Benson and Hedges Masters earlier in the year, beating Terry Griffiths in the final. Prior to that his best results in major individual tournaments was to finish runner-up to Ray Reardon in both the Professional Player's Tournament in 1982 and in the 1983 Yamaha International Masters. White won his first Benson and Hedges Irish Masters title in 1985 when he beat his doubles partner Alex Higgins in the final at Goffs.

The last two seasons have been one success after the other for White. His joining the Barry Hearn stable has been an influencing factor on recent successes, and he and his Matchroom colleagues have remained the most consistent performers in the sport.

The world title still eludes Jimmy White. The stumbling block in three of the last four world championships has been Steve Davis, the only man ranked higher than White. If he can overcome that obstacle, the title could be his for the taking.

Career highlights

- World Professional Snooker Championship (runner-up) 1984
- Mercantile Credit Classic Champion 1986
- Rothmans Grand Prix Champion 1986
- Dulux British Open Champion 1987
- Benson & Hedges Masters Champion 1984
- Benson & Hedges Irish Masters Champion 1985-86
- Langs Scottish Masters Champion 1981
- Hofmeister World Doubles Champion 1984 (with Alex Higgins)
- World Amateur Champion 1980
- English Amateur Champion 1979
- Indian Amateur Champion 1980
- National Under-16 Snooker Champion 1977
- Pontins Open Champion 1978
- Pontins Doubles Champion 1983 (with Tony Meo)
- Pontins Junior Champion 1978

Wildman, Mark

It is primarily as a billiards player that Mark Wildman is best known, but he was a junior champion at both billiards and snooker in the fifties, and he holds the distinction of becoming, in 1960, the first person to make a snooker century break on television.

Wildman's biggest handicap over the years has been his inconsistency. This may in part be due to the fact that while attempting to carve out a billiards and snooker career, he was, at the same time, attempting to build a successful business career with the finance house United Dominions Trust (UDT). Now committed to billiards and snooker full-time there has been a notable improvement in his game, and his taking the world professional billiards title in 1984 appeared to confirm this.

A member of the ITV commentary team, his many hours in the commentary box may also have contributed to the improvement in his snooker. He used to have little confidence in his snooker play – he made too many mistakes, as he said. But after watching the leading professionals for hour after hour from his commentary position, he realized that they made mistakes as well. That realization boosted Wildman's confidence and he went on to make 1984 a memorable year by reaching the semi-final of the Lada Classic at Warrington. After coming through the qualifying rounds he beat John Virgo 5-2, Silvino Francisco 5-1 and Eddie Charlton 5-4 before meeting Tony Meo in the semi-final. He held Meo at 3-3 in the best-of-nine frame match before losing 5-3.

It was as a junior that Wildman first hit the headlines. He won five junior titles in 1952-1953, and in the 1962-63 season won the highly rated Working Men's Club & Institute Union (CIU) snooker championship. He represented England in the Home International championship ten times between 1970 and 1975, and one of his best wins in the series was in 1973-74 when he beat future world amateur champion Doug Mountjoy 2-1.

Mark (his real name is Markham) turned professional in the 1979-80 season, but had to wait until two weeks before his 47th birthday, in 1983, for his first major professional title. This was in the United Kingdom billiards championship. The following year, in his third final (he had previously lost to Fred Davis and Rex Williams), he won the world billiards title, beating Eddie Charlton by just 33 points in the closest final since 1871 (when William Cook beat John Roberts Junior by 1,000 points to 985).

Career highlights

- World Professional Billiards Champion 1984
- United Kingdom Professional Billiards Champion 1983
- Lada Classic (semi-final) 1984
- English Amateur Billiards Champion 1968
- WMC & IU Snooker Champion 1963
- National Under-19 Snooker Champion 1954
- National Under-19 Billiards Champion 1953-54
- National Under-16 Snooker Champion 1952
- National Under-16 Billiards Champion 1952

Williams, John

One of snooker's senior referees, John Williams gave up a secure job as an Executive Officer with the Department of Employment in 1981 to become a full-time snooker referee.

A referee since 1971, he has officiated at several world championship finals, the first being that between Ray Reardon and Perrie Mans in 1978. It was a bizarre incident in the 1973 championships, however, that launched his refereeing career.

The sport received little television coverage in those days, but once the media heard that rain had stopped play during the Alex Higgins-Fred Davis quarter-final they rolled up to the Manchester City Halls to record the incident. Suddenly the little-known Williams was a television personality.

Williams was suspended for a while in 1982 by the World Professional Billiards and Snooker Referees' Association following a brief skirmish with the law. He was reinstated in time to officiate at the 1983 world championships at Sheffield.

The regular referee on BBC television's *Pot Black* series, he took over the role from Sydney Lee in 1981, when Lee had to withdraw through ill-health.

A native of Wrexham, North Wales, John Williams now lives in the Shrewsbury area, and is regularly involved with the organizing of the Pontins May Festival each year as well as officiating at the event.

Williams, Rex

His playing record reads as follows:- world professional billiards champion, world snooker finalist, national junior billiards and snooker champion, English amateur snooker champion, and United Kingdom billiards champion. Clearly, Rex Williams is one of the sport's great all-rounders.

Away from the table he has made as great a contribution to billiards and snooker as he has on it. He was largely responsible for the re-introduction of the world professional snooker championships, albeit as a challenge competition, in 1964. And he was responsible for re-forming the defunct Professional Billiard Players' Association (later the World Professional Billiards and Snooker Association). He has contributed a great deal to both

Rex Williams – not only a fine billiards and snooker player, but also an innovator, administrator and TV commentator

sports via the WPBSA, whom he has served as chairman for over ten years.

Rex at one time had a cue manufacturing business, which is now in the capable hands of his brother Ken; Rex concentrates on the lucrative pool and snooker table manufacturing business which he runs from his Brierley Hill, West Midlands factory. The company – Rex Williams Leisure – was set up in 1975 and manufactures its own tables for hire to pubs and clubs up and down the country. It has over 1,000 pool tables, and 100 snooker tables out on hire.

Rex Williams learnt a lot of his playing skills from Joe Davis, and was an outstanding player as a junior. He won the under-16 billiards and snooker titles twice each, and won both titles in the under-19 age group as well. In 1951 he won the English amateur snooker championship at the age of 17 to become the youngest winner of the title (a distinction which he held until Jimmy White took it from him in 1979). Not only did he win the title, but he destroyed all opposition in the process, and dropped only five frames throughout the entire competition.

Williams turned professional before he was 18, but it was at a time when the professional sport started its decline. Had he not turned professional there is little doubt he would have dominated the amateur scene for many years. He maintained his contacts with the sport via his cue manufacturing business, serving the amateur game, which did not decline in the same way as the professional game.

Determined to bring the professional sport back to life, he was largely responsible for the re-introduction of the world professional snooker championships in 1964, when Fred Davis challenged John Pulman for the title. Between then and 1968 the title was contested on a challenge system, and Williams twice challenged Pulman for the title, losing on each occasion.

During his match with Pulman for the title in 1965, Williams created a new world championship record break of 142, which stood until 1981, when it was beaten by Doug Mountjoy's 145. He made another big break in 1965, when he became only the second man – after Joe Davis – to register an official maximum 147 break. This came about during a match against Mannie Francisco at the Princes Hotel, Newlands, Cape Town on 22 November.

Thanks to Williams, again, the game's professional body was resurrected in 1969, and consequently the world championships reverted to the knockout format. Despite his efforts in making the championships a success, Williams has never appeared in a world final since 1969. The nearest he came was in reaching the semi-finals in 1969, 1972 and 1974 when John Spencer, Alex Higgins and Graham Miles respectively ended his chances. He has, however, appeared in several world professional billiards finals and, yet again, he was responsible for the championship being re-instituted in 1968. Like the snooker championship it was held on a challenge system, and Australian Clark McConachy had held the title unchallenged since 1951. Williams travelled to Australia, thanks to the sponsorship of Scotch whisky distillers John Haig, to challenge – and narrowly beat – McConachy.

Williams made four more successful defences of his world title, then in 1980 he lost to Fred Davis, who successfully challenged him to take his first world billiards title. Later that year the competition was restored to the knockout format. Rex Williams became champion again in 1982 when he beat Mark Wildman in the final; he retained his title in 1983, gaining revenge over Davis in the final, but during the tournament he became surrounded by controversy, which resulted in his resigning as chairman of the WPBSA. Following an incident during a practice session before his match with Ray Edmonds, which resulted in the match starting late, Williams was fined £500 by the WPBSA. He resigned his position in protest, but, after receiving many requests to return, he was re-instated.

Williams did not defend his world billiards title in 1984, but decided to concentrate on snooker instead. Although he did not win any major titles in 1984, he managed to register the highest breaks in the Lada Classic (143) and the world professionals championships (138).

Williams is still showing younger players a thing or two, and in 1985-86 he climbed into the top 16 after a semi-final place in the Mercantile Credit Classic. He moved up the rankings even further the following season, largely due to reaching the Rothmans Grand Prix final, which he lost to the much younger Jimmy White.

In another capacity, Rex Williams is involved with the sport as a summarizer with the ITV commentary team, which he joined on a three-year contract in 1984, after six years with the BBC. In the rare intervals when he is not involved in billiards and snooker Rex is a keen bird-watcher.

Career highlights
- World Professional Snooker Championship (runner-up) 1964-65
- World Professional Billiards Champion 1968-80 (challenge system), 1982-83
- Rothmans Grand Prix (runner-up) 1986
- United Kingdom Professional Billiards Champion 1979, 1981
- English Amateur Snooker Champion 1951
- National Under-19 Snooker Champion 1951
- National Under-19 Billiards Champion 1949-50
- National Under-16 Billiards Champion 1948-49
- National Under-16 Snooker Champion 1948-49

Wilson, Cliff

In Cliff Wilson the game of snooker has one of its great characters. He is always in demand for exhibition matches, where his personality and rapport with spectators make for an amusing and entertaining evening. He is also a great potter, and with the pressure of tournament play off him he can regularly put together century breaks in exhibition surroundings.

Disillusioned with the sport, Wilson left the game in 1957 and was out of it for 15 years. Had this not been the case, and had he not suffered from the bad eyesight which still plagues him, there is no telling what heights he might have reached within the professional game. Like Ray Reardon, Wilson hailed from Tredegar, South Wales, and in 1951 he came close to his first national title when he lost to Rex Williams in the national under-19 snooker final. He did manage to win the title the following year when he beat Marcus Owen in the final, he beat Owen to retain the title a year later.

It was his clashes with Reardon that attracted so much attention in Tredegar, and when the pair of them met, whether in a local league match or in a major competition, the venue would be packed to capacity. Reardon generally had the upper hand, and dominated the Welsh championships in the fifties, although Wilson gained some compensation by defeating Reardon in the semi-final of the English amateur championship in 1954 before losing to Geoff Thompson in the final.

After Reardon 'defected' to Stoke-on-Trent, Wilson won his first Welsh title, in 1956. But it was then that disillusionment set in, and he stopped playing. He was coaxed back into the sport by a local club team whom he agreed to help out: the bug got him once more, and it was not long before he was playing to his former high standard. In 1973 he won the first of his ten international caps and in 1977 he won his second Welsh title.

Being national champion he was eligible for the world amateur championships (which had not been introduced when he had last won the title). He travelled to Malta the following year and easily won his qualifying group, taking all eight games. In the knock-out stage of the competition he beat Paul Mifsud 5-0, Kirk Stevens 8-2 and in the final he beat Joe Johnson 11-5.

He resisted the temptation to turn professional, and in 1979 won his third Welsh amateur title as well as winning the national pairs championship with fellow Welshman and current professional, Steve Newbury.

By this time Cliff Wilson was earning good money as an amateur, both from in prizes and from his many exhibitions, but he made the decision to turn professional, and was accepted as a member of the WPBSA. Since turning professional his best performance to date has been in the 1982 Jameson International, when he reached the last eight, having beaten Doug Mountjoy and Jimmy White in the process. His biggest payday however, came in 1984, when he reached the final of the Welsh professional championship for the second time in his career. Again he filled the runner-up position, but on his way to collecting the biggest cheque of his professional career – £3,200 – he beat Ray Reardon for the first time since their amateur days.

Cliff Wilson lives in Caldicot, in a house overlooking the Severn Bridge, and not far from the motorway network which carries him all over the country to give exhibitions. One of his favourite parts of the country is Southport, and that area of the Fylde coast, because there he can – time permitting – indulge in his favourite pastime of deep-sea fishing.

Career highlights
- Welsh Professional Championship (runner-up) 1981, 1984
- World Amateur Snooker Champion 1978
- Welsh Amateur Champion 1956, 1977, 1979
- National Pairs Champion 1979 (with Steve Newbury)
- Pontins Open Champion 1976
- National Under-16 Snooker Champion 1952-53

Wilsons Classic

See Mercantile Credit Classic

Winfield Australian Masters

First held in 1979, the Winfield Australian Masters is a televised event run on similar lines to BBC television's former *Pot Black* series, except that it is sponsored by Rothmans (Winfield is one of their brand names in Australia).

Originally the tournament had a sprint (single-frame) format, but in 1983 the number of frames per game was increased to five in the first round and 13 in the final. The series used to be recorded in the studios of Channel 10 television. In 1984 however, the event moved out of the studios for the first time, and was played at the Paramatta Leagues Club in Sydney. It moved back to the television studios for the final stages. One of the most popular members of the Winfield Masters team is referee Ron Tscherne, brother-in-law of the late Warren Simpson.

Winfield Australian Masters – Results (finals)

1979* I. Anderson (Australia) beat P. Mans (South Africa)
1980* J. Spencer (England) beat D. Taylor (Ireland)
1981* T. Meo (England) beat J. Spencer (England)
1982* S. Davis (England) beat E. Charlton (Australia)
1983 C. Thorburn (Canada) 7 B. Werbeniuk (Canada) 3
1984 T. Knowles (England) 7 J. Virgo (England) 3
1985 T. Meo (England) beat J. Campbell (Australia) 7-2
1986 D. Taylor (Ireland) 3 S. Davis (England) 2
1987 S. Hendry (Scotland) beat M. Hallett (England) 371-226 over 5 frames
*Prior to 1983 the result was decided on the aggregate score over three frames
Most wins: 2 – Tony Meo
Most finals: 2 – John Spencer, Tony Meo
Highest break: 134 – Tony Meo (1985)

Women's Snooker

Women have played both billiards and snooker since the early days of the sports, but they have struggled to break through the barrier of male domination.

Although the Sex Discrimination Act did very little to help the women's cause as far as entry into men-only emporiums was concerned (it did not apply to private members clubs), more and more clubs are gradually opening their doors to women. But there are still a lot that refuse to do so.

It is only since the mid-seventies that the women's game has taken off, despite the fact that the Women's Billiards and Snooker Association was formed as long ago as 1931. (It was only known as the Women's Billiards Association at that time.)

The first meeting of the Women's Billiards Association was at the Women's Automobile and Sports Association in Buckingham Palace Road on 20 May 1931. Eleven delegates from London, the Home Counties, Birmingham and Bournemouth attended. They voted Mrs Longworth their first chair.

The inaugural national billiards championships were organized that year, and two years later the first national snooker championships were held. Those first championships were amateur events, and the following year the first women's national professional championships were organized. The first winner, Ruth Harrison, was the outstanding female player of the era; she won the professional title every year from 1934 to 1940, and also won the professional billiards title twice.

The professional game suffered in the post war years, and the last professional championships were held in 1950. The amateur championships survived and the outstanding competitor of the post war era has been Maureen Barrett-Baynton. Winner of the national title for the first time in 1954, she won the title eight times in all – the last time being in 1968. She is still a prominent part of the female snooker scene.

In the seventies the women's association became dormant until one man – virtually single-handedly – gave it the 'kiss-of-life.' That man was London amateur snooker player, Wally West. He became chairman of the association and did much to put the women's game on the map. He was responsible for organizing the Guinness World Open championship at Hayling Island in 1980. The 1980 world open was not a new venture. A similar tournament was run in 1976 in Middlesbrough and ran concurrently with the men's world championships. The sponsors of both events were Embassy.

Lesley McIlrath of Australia won the 1980 world open, and she won a cheque for £700 – the biggest ever prize in women's snooker at the time. The following year Vera Selby, a Newcastle Art Lecturer, won the £2,000 first prize that went with the title.

Since the rebirth of the sport in the eighties, the leading British player has been Mandy Fisher. One time secretary of the WPBSA she won over £14,000 in prize money during the 1983-84 season – a figure bettered by only 16 of her male counterparts; this in no way reflects the comparative skills of the two sexes. As Mandy herself says: 'We don't want to compare ourselves with the men. We've got our own game.'

Women's snooker possesses its own personalities. Sue Foster, scorer of the first 50 break in the world championships (1983), was vying with Mandy Fisher for the British number one tag when she surprisingly announced her retirement in 1984. There are a number of up-and-coming young women taking to the sport. Teenager Allison Fisher is one of the world's leading players. There are even younger girls as well: Stacey Hillyard at 15 became the first female to score a century break in tournament play, and has proved she can upset the best players; and there is Lynette Horsburgh of Blackpool who at the age of 10 reached the third round of the 1984 world amateur championships. Enjoying the benefits of coaching from Steve Davis's

Allison Fisher, the leading player in the women's game, seen outside the Crucible Theatre

Women's Snooker – Results (finals)

World open championship

1976 Vera Selby (England)
1977 Not held
1978 Not held
1979 Not held
1980 Lesley McIlrath (Australia)
1981 Vera Selby (England)
1982 Not held
1983 Sue Foster (England)
1984 Not held
1985 Not held
1986 Allison Fisher (England)

Most wins: 2 – Vera Selby

World amateur championship

1984 Stacey Hillyard (England)
1985 Allison Fisher (England)

National amateur championship

1933 Margaret Quinn
1934 Ella Morris
1935 Molly Hill
1936 Vera Seals
1937 Mrs Morland-Smith
1938 Ella Morris
1939 Agnes Morris
1940-1946 Not held
1947 Mrs M. Knight
1948 Joan Adcock
1949 Rosemary Davies
1950 Pat Holden
1951 Rosemary Davies
1952 Rosemary Davies
1953 Rita Holmes
1954 Maureen Barrett
1955 Maureen Barrett
1956 Maureen Barrett
1957 Rita Holmes
1958 Rita Holmes
1959 Mrs D. Thompson
1960 Muriel Hazeldine
1961 Maureen Barrett
1962 Maureen Barrett
1963 Rita Holmes
1964 Maureen Baynton (née Barrett)
1965 Mrs S. Jeffries
1966 Maureen Baynton (née Barrett)
1967 Mrs H. Futo
1968 Maureen Baynton (née Barrett)
1969 Mrs R. Craven
1970 Muriel Hazeldine
1971 Muriel Hazeldine
1972 Vera Selby
1973 Vera Selby
1974 Vera Selby
1975 Vera Selby
1976 Ann Johnson
1977 Ann Johnson
1978 Agnes Davies (née Morris)
1979 Vera Selby
1980 Sue Foster
1981 Not held
1982 Sue Foster
1983 Sue Foster
1984 Not held
1985 Stacey Hillyard

Most wins 8 – Maureen Baynton (née Barrett)

National professional championship

1934 Ruth Harrison
1935 Ruth Harrison
1936 Ruth Harrison
1937 Ruth Harrison
1938 Ruth Harrison
1939 Ruth Harrison
1940 Ruth Harrison
1941-1947 Not held
1948 Ruth Harrison
1949 Agnes Morris
1950 Thelma Carpenter
Not held since 1950

Most wins 8 – Ruth Harrison

and John Parrott's mentor Frank Callan, she is definitely a star of the future.

Apart from Britain, Canada and Australia are the two other strongholds of women's snooker. Australia, in Lesley McIlrath, produced the 1980 world open champion. McIlrath and Fran Lovis have been outstanding champions in their home country. Lovis won the Australian title for the sixth time in 1984. In Sue LeMaich, Maryann McConnell and Natalie Stelmach, Canada has three of the world's leading players.

Although the first century break by a woman in tournament play came only in 1985, Stelmach is reported to be the first woman to have made a century break in practice. What is certain, however, is that she was the first woman to register a half-century break in tournament play when she made a 56 break on her way to winning the 1981 Canadian title.

Sue LeMaich had an outstanding series in the National Express Grand Prix in 1984, winning two of the finals. She, like Stelmach, is a renowned century-maker in practice. She has scored over ten centuries including a 126, which is the highest known break by a woman. Maryann McConnell is likened to fellow Canadian Cliff Thorburn – to use Alex Higgins's phrase, she is a 'grinder'.

Women's snooker received a boost in 1983 when Barry Hearn arranged a mixed doubles challenge match to be shown by ITV on the day of the 1983 FA Cup Final.

Sponsored by British Rail and known as the British Rail Inter-City Mixed Doubles title, it saw Tony Meo and Julie Islip beat Steve Davis and Mandy Fisher. It was the first, and so far the only, attempt at such a venture by ITV. But, nevertheless, it did ladies' snooker no harm.

The following year the newly formed promotional company LSI (Ladies Snooker International) was formed. They took many of the leading players under their wing contractually, and were instrumental in arranging a £60,000 sponsorship deal with National Express for the introduction of a Grand Prix series. The series was won by Mandy Fisher.

The new governing body – the World Ladies Billiards and Snooker Association – was formed in July 1981. In 1984 they established a clear distinction between amateur and professional snooker players, and have set down guidelines for acceptance into the professional ranks, just as in the men's sport.

The women's game underwent further changes from 1 January 1986 when the governing body dropped all distinctions between amateur and professional players as the game went open.

Working Men's Club and Institute Union Championships

The Working Men's Club and Institute Union Championships (commonly known as the CIU championships) are the second most prestigious amateur snooker championships after the English amateur. They date back to the 1907-08 season, when the team billiards event was held. The individual billiards competition followed in 1919-20, team snooker in 1925-26 and individual snooker in 1928-29.

The CIU, which is a limited company, dates back to 14 June 1862 and has the Reverend Henry Solly to thank for its beginnings. It was the Reverend Solly who devised the idea of the working men's club and, as its name implies, it was somewhere for the working man to go for recreation after his hard day's work. Solly gained support from many notable people of that era, who gave him financial assistance.

There are over 4,000 clubs affiliated to the CIU at present, and any member of those clubs is eligible to compete in the championships. He may also enter the national angling, golf, cribbage and darts championships organised by the CIU.

The billiards and snooker championships are played on a regional basis until the semi-final and final stages, when neutral venues are chosen. Approximately 500 entrants compete in the individual snooker competition, and 50 take part in the billiards event. For the team competition, around 300 participate in the snooker championship, and 20-30 in the billiards.

Co-ordination of the championships is the responsibility of Peter Miller, the Recreation Secretary, who works from his London headquarters.

The CIU does not accept sponsorship of their championships, but each of the four competitions carries a cash prize of £500 to each winner.

Over the years, many notable players have won CIU Individual titles. Steve Davis was the snooker champion in 1977-78 and runner-up to Norman Dagley in the billiards championship that same season. Ray Reardon appeared in two snooker finals, winning one of them, in 1964-65, and in 1967 he was the scorer of the first century break (103) in the team snooker competition.

Working Men's Club and Institute Union Championships – Results (winners)

Individual Snooker

1928-29 J.J. Ashley (Kingston WM)
1929-30 J.J. Ashley (Kingston WM)
1930-31 J.J. Ashley (Kingston WM)
1931-32 H.C. Ramsey (Clapton Park)
1932-33 E. Rooks (Leeds Anglers)
1933-34 D. Heathcote (Tudhoe & Spennymoor)
1934-35 D. Chapman (Plumstead Radical)
1935-36 D. Chapman (Plumstead Radical)
1936-37 D. Hindmarch (Edmund House)
1937-38 D. Chapman (Plumstead Radical)
1938-39 C. Jacques (Kettering Midland Band)
1939-40 T.H. Jones (Hatcham Liberal)
1940-41 T.H. Jones (Hatcham Liberal)
1941-42 T.H. Jones (Hatcham Liberal)
1942-43 T.H. Jones (Hatcham Liberal)
1943-44 R. Radford (Moorthorpe Empire)
1944-45 S. Jones (Smethwick Ex-Services)
1945-46 T.H. Jones (Hayes WM)
1946-47 H. Wood (Cross Flatts Rec)
1947-48 T.H. Jones (Hayes WM)
1948-49 Not held
1949-50 K. Wilson (Leeds Free Gardners)
1950-51 T.H. Jones (Hayes WM)
1951-52 J. Taylor (Skellow Grange)
1952-53 T. Graham (Spennymoor WM)
1953-54 T. Graham (Spennymoor WM)
1954-55 D. Robertson (Newport Dist)
1955-56 B. Simpson (Unsworth WM)
1956-57 J.O. Graham (Spennymoor WM)
1957-58 S. Haslam (Sale Excelsior)
1958-59 M. Chapman (Tyseley WM)
1959-60 D. Robertson (Newport Dist)
1960-61 L. Taylor (Carcroft Village)
1961-62 D. May (Abertysswg WM)
1962-63 M. Wildman (Mildmay)
1963-64 J. Dunning (Morley WM)
1964-65 R. Reardon (Cheadle Social)
1965-66 G. Thompson (Leics Railway)
1966-67 A. Kemp (Ynyshir District)
1967-68 W. Smith (Belvedere WM)
1968-69 G. Thompson (Leics Railway)
1969-70 T. Parsons (Penygraig Labour)
1970-71 R. Edmonds (Skegness WM)
1971-72 R. Edmonds (Skegness WM)
1972-73 T. Parsons (Penygraig Labour)
1973-74 J. Beech (Belvedere WM)
1974-75 J. Fitzmaurice (Tyseley WM)
1975-76 A. Lloyd (Abertysswg WM)
1976-77 W. Kelly (Abbey Hey WM)
1977-78 S. Davis (Plumstead Common)
1978-79 M. Watterson (Grassmoor WM)
1979-80 G. Cripsey (Skegness WM)
1980-81 E. Richards (Seaview Labour)
1981-82 S. Duggan (Thurnscoe)
1982-83 S. Duggan (Thurnscoe)
1983-84 E. Richards (Seaview Labour)
1984-85 T. Parsons (Penygraig Labour)
1985-86 K. Owers (Fleetwood West End)
1986-87 J. Birch (Newport WMC)
Most wins: 7 – Tom Jones
Highest break: 131 – John Prosser (Heolgerigh Rec) 1975

Team Snooker

1925-26 Deritend Liberal
1926-27 Deritend Liberal
1927-28 Kingston WM 'A'
1928-29 Mount Pleasant United
1929-30 Mildmay Radical 'A'
1930-31 Kingston WM
1931-32 Tyseley WM
1932-33 Fiveways WM
1933-34 Kettering Midland Band
1934-35 Swawthorne Lane WM
1935-36 Kettering Midland Band
1936-37 Tudhoe & Spennymoor
1937-38 Tudhoe & Spennymoor
1938-39 Hatcham Liberal
1939-40 Kettering Midland Band
1940-41 Moorthorpe Empire
1941-42 Smethwick Ex-Servicemen
1942-43 Smethwick Ex-Servicemen
1943-44 Abbey Hey WM
1944-45 Kingston WM
1945-46 Not held
1946-47 Kettering Midland Band
1947-48 Kettering Midland Band
1948-49 Abbey Hey WM
1949-50 Smethwick Ex-Servicemen
1950-51 Carcroft Village
1951-52 Stocksbridge & District
1952-53 Tyseley WM
1953-54 Tyseley WM
1954-55 Unsworth WM
1955-56 Smethwick Ex-Servicemen
1956-57 Tyseley WM
1957-58 Morley WM 'A'
1958-59 Sale Excelsior
1959-60 Morley WM
1960-61 Bolton North Ward Reform
1961-62 Doncaster Liberal
1962-63 Derby Ward Labour
1963-64 Morley WM
1964-65 Tyseley WM
1965-66 Morley WM
1966-67 Abertysswg WM
1967-68 Abbey Hey WM
1968-69 Athersley Social
1969-70 Abertysswg WM
1970-71 Abertysswg WM
1971-72 North Evington
1972-73 North Evington
1973-74 Ferryhill & District 'A'
1974-75 Abbey Hey WM
1975-76 North Ormsby Institute
1976-77 Portsmouth Radical
1977-78 Western Social
1978-79 North Ormsby Institute
1979-80 North Orsmby Institute
1980-81 Tyseley WM
1981-82 Cobridge Coronation 'A'
1982-83 Fleetwood West End Social
1983-84 E. Birmingham Trades & Lab. 'A'
1984-85 Penygraig Labour
1985-86 East Birmingham Trades 'A'

Most wins: 6 – Tyseley WM
Highest break: 129 – Andy Marson (East Birmingham Trades & Labour Club) 1984

Promoter and current professional Mike Watterson won the snooker title in 1978-79.

The first century break in the individual snooker competition (104) was made by Ivor Bird of the New Hirst and District Club in 1964.

World Amateur Championships

In comparison to the world amateur billiards championship, which was born in 1926, the world amateur snooker championships are relatively young. They were started in 1963 by the Billiards Association, although the idea had been discussed in the early fifties.

It was three years before the second championships were held, and they have been held every two years since. The 1985 championships in England, however, were the first of an annual competition.

When the world amateur championships were first contested at Calcutta in 1963, just five players from four countries took part. They were Gary Owen (England), Frank Harris (Australia), Mohammed Lafir (Ceylon), Wilson Jones and T. Monteiro (both India). Owen became the first world champion, a title he retained in 1966. Since then only Ray Edmonds (also of England) has successfully defended his title. Terry Parsons, in 1984, came close to doing so but was beaten in the final by O.B. (Omprakash) Agrawal of India. Agrawal became the first man who was neither an Englishman nor a Welshman to win the title.

In contrast with the 1963 championships, the 1984 event saw 41 entrants from 22 countries, including the United States, Mauritius, Belgium, Sweden and Iceland – all represented for the first time.

The host nation used to be responsible for stating how many representatives (one or two) from each competing country may take part. In addition, the host nation and the nation of the defending champion were both allowed one other entrant. From 1986, however, when the championships were held in New Zealand, the International Billiards and Snooker Federation allowed two representatives from each nation to compete. Entry has always been via a player's national championships, but in recent years many British champions have forgone the chance to compete in the world championships, preferring instead to turn professional immediately.

Jimmy White, youngest-ever winner of the world amateur title, seen here with the trophy in 1980

Of all the winners of the title, none has gone on to win the world professional title, but three men have come close. Gary Owen, Doug Mountjoy and Jimmy White have all reached the professional final, after having taken the amateur title. On the other side of the coin, in reverse, John Spencer is the only world amateur runner-up who has gone on to win the professional title.

Jimmy White, when he won the title in 1980 at the age of 18 years 191 days, became the youngest-ever winner.

The 1984 championships were notable for several records. First, the championship record break of 127 fell when Malta's Tony Drago compiled a 132. Drago also made championship history when he made successive century breaks in one match. Another 'centurion' was Stephen Hendry of Scotland. At the age of 15 years, he was not only the youngest person to make a century break in the championships, but also the youngest-ever competitor in them.

World Professional Billiards and Snooker Association

The first full season in which the World Professional Billiards and Snooker Association (WPBSA) was in existence its annual turnover was approximately £20. Today it is about £5 million.

The WPBSA was formed in May 1968 as a result of the Professional Billiards Players Association re-naming, and re-forming, itself into the professional governing body. Mike Green was the association's first secretary, and membership was just eight; at the beginning of 1986 the membership was over 120.

The WPBSA, now a limited company, was formed to organize all professional events, and to act as the disciplinary body for its members. Although the world governing body for snooker is the Billiards and Snooker Control Council (B&SCC), professional players do not come under their jurisdiction, and do not even have to be members of the B&SCC.

In 1983 the association formed a wholly-owned subsidiary, WPBSA Promotions Limited, to promote professional tournaments. With vast sums of money passing through each year, the association is keen to direct some of this money back to the players. They used to sponsor the Professional Players' Tournament (replaced by the Rothmans Grand Prix) and from the 1984-85 season sponsored the various national professional championships to the tune of £1,000 per entrant. They also sponsored the English Amateur championships in 1985.

The WPBSA took over the Snooker Writers' Awards in 1985 and their first player of the year was Irishman Dennis Taylor. Joe Johnson and Steve Davis shared the award in 1986.

Mike Green, after many years' hard work for the association, took early retirement in 1984 and was succeeded as secretary by Martin Blake, who is based at the new headquarters in Bristol. For further details contact Martin Blake, Secretary, WPBSA Ltd., 27 Oakfield Road, Bristol BS8 2AT.

World Amateur Championships – Results

1963 Calcutta, India
Gary Owen (England) beat Frank Harris (Australia)
Top break: 71 – Gary Owen
(nb: tournament played on league basis)

1966 Karachi, Pakistan
Gary Owen (England) beat John Spencer (England)
Top break: 118 – Gary Owen
(nb: tournament played on league basis)

1968 Sydney, Australia
David Taylor (England) 8
Max Williams (Australia) 7
Top break: 96 – David Taylor

1970 Edinburgh, Scotland
Jonathan Barron (England) 11
Sid Hood (England) 7
Top break: 65 – Jack Rogers

1972 Cardiff, Wales
Ray Edmonds (England) 11
Manny Francisco (S. Africa) 10
Top break: 101 – Ray Edmonds

1974 Dublin, Ireland
Ray Edmonds (England) 11
Geoff Thomas (Wales) 9
Top break: 104 – Alwyn Lloyd

1976 Johannesburg, South Africa
Doug Mountjoy (Wales) 11
Paul Mifsud (Malta) 1
Top break: 107 – Doug Mountjoy

1978 Malta
Cliff Wilson (Wales) 11
Joe Johnson (England) 5
Top break: 101 – Joe Johnson

1980 Launceston, Australia
Jimmy White (England) 11
Ron Atkins (Australia) 2
Top break: 128 – Eugene Hughes

1982 Calgary, Canada
Terry Parsons (Wales) 11
Jim Bear (Canada) 8
Top break: 103 – Terry Parsons

1984 Dublin, Ireland
O.B. Agrawal (India) 11
Terry Parsons (Wales) 7
Top break: 132 – Tony Drago

1985 Blackpool, England
Paul Mifsud (Malta)
Dilwyn John (Wales)
Top break 115 – T. Whitthread

1986 Invercargil, New Zealand
Paul Mifsud (Malta) 11
Kerry Jones (Wales) 9
Top break 118 – G. Miller

Most wins: 2 Gary Owen (England)
2 Ray Edmonds (England)
2 Paul Mifsud (Malta)
Most appearances: 6 Paul Mifsud (Malta)
Most by British player: 4 Alwyn Lloyd (Wales)
4 Bert Demarco (Scotland)

Championship record breaks (progression)
71 Gary Owen (England) 1963
118 Gary Owen (England) 1966
128 Eugene Hughes (Ireland) 1980
132 Tony Drago (Malta) 1984

Lightning fast around the table, Malta's Tony Drago, now a professional, holds the record for the highest break (132) in the World Amateur Championships

World Professional Snooker Championships

It was only natural that snooker, after gaining in popularity in the 1920s, should one day have its own professional world championship – after all the professional billiards championship had been contested since 1870. But getting the governing body of the time, the Billiards Association and Control Council (BACC), to stage such a championship was not an easy task.

Tom Dennis, a professional from Nottingham, originally approached the BACC in 1924, but they thought the time was not right. Snooker, they felt, was not popular enough. Dennis disagreed, as did Joe Davis and a friend of his, Bill Camkin. It was Davis and Camkin who put pressure on the BACC a couple of years later, and that body eventually agreed to stage the first Professional Championship of Snooker's Pool in the 1926-27 season. It was a season-long tournament; the first world championship game was between Melbourne Inman and Tom Newman at Thurston's Hall, played between 26 November and 6 December 1926. Inman won 8-5.

The final, which Davis won, was held at one of Camkin's Billiard Halls in Birmingham, and started on 9 May 1927. Davis received a first prize of £6 10s 0d (£6·50) together with the trophy that is contested in current championships. The trophy, now insured for more than £2,000, was the property of the Billiards and Snooker Control Council who, as the BACC, bought it for £19 in 1927. Stan Brooke, chairman of the B&SCC, handed it over to Rex Williams, chairman of the WPBSA, shortly before the start of the 1986 world championships, thus giving the professional body ownership of the trophy for the first time.

Ten players contested that first championship, but over the next eight years the figure declined, and in 1931 and 1934 just two competitors took part. Participation levels picked up in the mid-thirties, however, when Thurston's became the regular home of the final.

The championship remained a season-long event with each match lasting anything between three and seven days, and Joe Davis proved himself invincible, winning all of the 14 finals up to 1940. When the championship resumed after the war, in 1946, Davis won the title for the fifteenth and last time. For a few years the popularity of the event grew but eventually it became devalued, and victories were hollow. Davis was still playing, although not in championship play, and was beating men who were claiming to be 'world champions'.

In 1952, following a dispute between the BACC and the professionals over terms, a split in the snooker world occurred, with the professionals forming a breakaway governing body. They ran their own championships, called the Professional Match-Play Championships. They were the world championships in everything but name. Just two men remained to contest the official championships after the split – Australian Horace Lindrum and New Zealander Clark McConachy. Lindrum won, and thus became the first overseas winner of the title.

This was the last world championship until 1964, although the match-play championship continued until 1957. The rift between the professionals and the BACC healed and, thanks largely to the efforts of Rex Williams, the championships were revived in 1964 – on a challenge basis. John Pulman, the last winner of the match-play title, met a challenge from Fred Davis for the crown. Pulman won, and went on to defend his title successfully on six further occasions.

In the 1968-69 season the championship reverted to a knock-out system as a result of new players joining the professional ranks. Eight men contested the revived championships, which were the first to be sponsored – by John Player & Son – since the early fifties when the *Empire News* sponsored the event for a couple of years. The championships, again, were a season-long event.

The 1973 championship was an important one. It was the first to attract a field in excess of 20, was the first to have the entire play condensed into a fortnight, and the first to have its latter stages covered by the BBC television cameras. Three years later current sponsors Embassy began their sponsorship of the tournament, and in 1977 the final piece in the world championship jigsaw was put into place when the event moved to its current plush surroundings at the Crucible Theatre, Sheffield. Credit for this goes to promoter Mike Watterson's wife, who suggested the Crucible as a possible venue for the championships after she had visited the theatre to see a play one night.

In 1978 the BBC covered the event daily for the first time, thus putting the Embassy World Championships on a par in the sporting world with such major events as Wimbledon, the FA Cup Final and the British Open golf championship. Since then the cameras have brought some memorable world championship moments into the nation's homes: there was Steve Davis's magical first win; there was Alex Higgins's emotional victory in 1982; there was Cliff Thorburn's historic 147 break. And more recently, in 1985 there has been perhaps the greatest final of all, in which Dennis Taylor beat Steve Davis to win a truly epic contest. And there have been many more humorous, exciting and tense moments.

Prize money has increased considerably since Joe Davis's first win in 1927 – the 1987 winner Steve Davis received £79,993·50 more than his namesake. But Steve had to emerge from a field of 115 to win his title. Joe had just nine to beat!

Some world championship milestones

1926 The first-ever game in the world championships, between Melbourne Inman and Tom Newman, gets under way at Thurston's Hall on 29 November. Seven days later Inman wins 8-5.

1927 Joe Davis beats Tom Dennis 20-11 in the first final, played during May, in Birmingham.

1932 Clark McConachy (New Zealand) becomes the first overseas player to compete in the championships.

1935 Joe Davis registers first-ever century break (110) in the championships, in his semi-final with Tom Newman.

1935 Con Stanbury becomes first Canadian to compete in the championships.

1936 Horace Lindrum becomes the first Australian to compete in the championships

1952 Horace Lindrum becomes first overseas winner of the title – beating another overseas player, Clark McConachy, in the final.

1972 The 1972 championship started in one season – 1970-71 (March) – and finished in the next – 1971-72 (February).

1973 First championships to be condensed into a fortnight's play. Also first championship to be covered by BBC TV.

1977 John Spencer is first winner of the title using a two-piece cue. Also first championship to be staged at Sheffield's Crucible Theatre.

1978 Championships receive daily TV coverage for first time.

1983 Cliff Thorburn registers first maximum 147 break in the championship.

1984 Steve Davis becomes first player to successfully defend his title at the Crucible Theatre.

1985 Number of entrants (103) exceeds 100 for the first time.

Progressive championship record breaks
(Since first century break)
110 – Joe Davis (1935)
113 – Fred Davis (1939)
136 – Joe Davis (1946)
142 – Rex Williams (1965)
142 – Bill Werbeniuk (1979)
145 – Doug Mountjoy (1981)
147 – Cliff Thorburn (1983)

World championship final venues
1927-28 Camkin's Hall, Birmingham
1929 Lounge Billiard Hall, Nottingham
1930 Thurston's Hall, London
1931 Lounge Billiard Hall, Nottingham
1932 Thurston's Hall, London
1933 Joe Davis Billiards Centre, Chesterfield
1934 Lounge Billiard Hall, Nottingham and Central Hall, Kettering
1935-40 Thurston's Hall, London
1941-45 Not held
1946 Horticultural Hall, London
1947-49 Leicester Square Hall, London
1950-51 Tower Circus, Blackpool
1952 Houldsworth Hall, Manchester
1953-63 Not held
1964-65 Burroughes Hall, London
1966 Played in South Africa
1966 St George's Hall, Liverpool
1967 Not held
1968 Co-operative Hall, Bolton
1969-70 Victoria Hall, London
1971 Sydney, Australia (held November, 1970)
1972 Selly Park British Legion, Birmingham
1973 City Exhibition Hall, Manchester
1974 Belle Vue, Manchester
1975 Nunawading Basketball Centre, Melbourne, Australia
1976 Wythenshawe Forum, Manchester
1977-87 Crucible Theatre, Sheffield

Prize money
Joe Davis received £6.50 out of a prize fund of just £55 for winning the first title title in 1927. By 1959 total prize money was up to £1,000 but, when the championships were revived as a knockout competition in the 1968-69 season, the total prize money had only risen to £3,500. Since then the first alone has risen to £80,000.

Total prize money, and first prize money, since 1974, when current sponsors Embassy commenced their sponsorship of the championships, has been as follows:

Year	*Total Prize money*	*First Prize*
1976	£ 15,300	£ 6,000
1977	£ 17,000	£ 6,000
1978	£ 24,000	£ 7,500
1979	£ 35,000	£10,000
1980	£ 60,000	£15,000
1981	£ 75,000	£20,000
1982	£106,000	£25,000
1983	£130,000	£30,000
1984	£200,000	£44,000
1985	£300,000	£60,000
1986	£350,000	£70,000
1987	£400,000	£80,000

Number of competitors
The total number of competitors in the world championships has risen dramatically over the past six years.
A year-by-year comparison of the number of competitors:

1927	10	1937	9	1952	2	1978	28
1928	7	1938	10	1969	8	1979	35
1929	5	1939	15	1970	9	1980	49
1930	6	1940	9	1971	9	1981	44
1931	2	1946	14	1972	16	1982	67
1932	3	1947	19	1973	23	1983	74
1933	5	1948	15	1974	31	1984	94
1934	2	1949	11	1975	27	1985	103
1935	5	1950	15	1976	27	1986	112
1936	12	1951	10	1977	24	1987	115

Longest reign as champion – Joe Davis (1927-46)
Shortest reign as champion – Ray Reardon (Apr-Nov 1970)
Most titles (pre-1968) – 15 Joe Davis
Most titles (post-1968) – 6 Ray Reardon
Most finals without winning title – 4 Tom Dennis (1927-29-30-31)
Biggest winning margin (final) – 45 frames (Lindrum 94 McConachy 49 1952)

Closest finals
There have been four finals separated by just one frame
1940 Joe Davis beat Fred Davis 37-36
1965 John Pulman beat Fred Davis 37-36 (challenge system)
1975 Ray Reardon beat Eddie Charlton 18-17
1985 Dennis Taylor beat Steve Davis 18-17

Finalists who have had to play through the qualifying rounds
1972 Alex Higgins (winner)
1977 Cliff Thorburn (runner-up)
1978 Perrie Mans (runner-up)
1979 Terry Griffiths (winner)

Whitewash
There has been one instance of a whitewash in the competition proper: in 1974 John Pulman beat Sydney Lee 8-0 in the first round. There have, however, been 22 other instances of whitewashes in the qualifying rounds. The full list is:
1974 John Pulman beat Jack Karnehm 8-0
John Pulman beat Sydney Lee 8-0
1977 David Taylor beat David Greaves 11-0
Dennis Taylor beat Jack Karnehm 11-0
Cliff Thorburn beat Chris Ross 11-0
1978 Roy Andrewartha beat Jack Karnehm 9-0
1979 Rex Williams beat Maurice Parkin 9-0
Kirk Stevens beat John Pulman 9-0
1980 Steve Davis beat Paddy Morgan 9-0
1981 Tony Knowles beat Chris Ross 9-0
1982 Silvino Francisco beat Chris Ross 9-0
1983 Rex Williams beat Mike Darrington 10-0
Tony Meo beat Vic Harris 10-0
Joe Johnson beat Paul Watchorn 10-0
1984 John Parrott beat Perrie Mans 10-0
Ray Edmonds beat David Greaves 10-0
1985 Danny Fowler beat John Hargreaves 10-0
Danny Fowler beat Jim Donnelly 10-0
1986 Sakchai Simngam beat Bernard Bennett 10-0
Ray Edmonds beat Billy Kelly 10-0
1987 Billy Kelly beat Bernard Bennett 10-0
Jon Wright beat Mark Wildman 10-0
Tony Jones beat Jimmy van Rensburg 10-0

The Embassy World Professional Snooker Championship final is the climax of the snooker calendar: the match lasts two days and is a harsh test of mental and physical endurance as well as of snooker skill

Roll of Honour – World Championship Records of the 13 World Champions

	No of championships	Years	Titles	Finals	Matches played	Won	Lost	Percentage success
Davis, Joe	15	1927-46	15	15	34	34	0	100.00
Davis, Steve	9	1979-87	4	6	38	33	5	86.84
Reardon, Ray	19	1969-87	6	7	55	42	13	76.36
Donaldson, Walter	9	1933-51	2	5	23	16	7	69.57
Johnson, Joe	8	1980-87	1	2	19	13	6	68.42
Higgins, Alex	16	1972-87	2	4	44	30	14	68.18
Griffiths, Terry	9	1979-87	1	1	24	16	8	66.67
Thorburn, Cliff	15	1973-87	1	3	40	26	14	65.00
Lindrum, Horace	7	1936-52	1	4	16	10	6	62.50
Spencer, John	18	1969-87	3	4	43	26	17	60.47
Taylor, Dennis	15	1973-87	1	2	35	21	14	60.00
Pulman, John	26	1947-83	7	8	43	23	20	53.49
Davis, Fred	31	1937-87	3	9	60	32	28	53.33

World Professional Snooker Championships – Results

1927

Round One
T. Carpenter beat N. Butler 8-3
M. Inman beat T. Newman 8-5

Round Two
T. Carpenter beat M. Inman 8-3
A. Cope beat A. Mann 8-6
J. Davis beat J. Brady 10-5
T.A. Dennis beat F. Lawrence 8-7

Semi-finals
J. Davis beat A. Cope 16-7
T.A. Dennis beat T. Carpenter 12-10

Final
J. Davis beat T.A. Dennis 20-11

1928

Round One
A. Mann beat A. Cope 14-9
T. Newman beat F. Smith 12-6

Round Two
F. Lawrence beat A. Mann 12-11
T. Newman beat T.A. Dennis 12-5

Round Three
F. Lawrence beat T. Newman 12-7

Final
J. Davis beat F. Lawrence 16-13

1929

Round One
F. Lawrence beat A. Mann 13-12

Semi-finals
J. Davis beat F. Lawrence 13-10
T.A. Dennis beat K. Prince 14-6

Final
J. Davis beat T.A. Dennis 19-14

1930

Round One
N. Butler beat T. Newman 13-11
F. Lawrence beat A. Mann 13-11

Semi-finals
J. Davis beat F. Lawrence 13-2
T.A. Dennis beat N. Butler 13-11

Final
J. Davis beat T.A. Dennis 25-12

1931

Final
J. Davis beat T.A. Dennis 25-21

1932

Round One
C. McConachy beat T.A. Dennis 13-11

Final
J. Davis beat C. McConachy 30-19

1933

Round One
W. Donaldson beat W. Leigh 13-11

Semi-finals
J. Davis beat W. Donaldson 13-1
W. Smith beat T.A. Dennis 16-9

Final
J. Davis beat W. Smith 25-18

1934

Final
J. Davis beat T. Newman 25-23

1935

Round One
W. Smith beat C. Stanbury 13-12

Semi-finals
J. Davis beat T. Newman 15-10
W. Smith beat A. Mann 13-4

Final
J. Davis beat W. Smith 25-20

1936

Round One
J. Davis beat T. Newman 29-2
H. Lindrum beat H. Terry 20-11
C. O'Donnell beat S. Lee 16-15
W. Smith beat S. Smith 16-15
C. Stanbury beat A. Mann 22-9

Round Two
Alec Brown beat C. Stanbury 16-15
J. Davis beat W. Smith 2-9
H. Lindrum beat C. O'Donnell 19-6
(O'Donnell retired)
S. Newman bye

Semi-finals
J. Davis beat Alec Brown 21-10
H. Lindrum beat S. Newman 29-2

Final
J. Davis beat H. Lindrum 34-27

1937

Round One
W.A. Withers beat F. Davis 17-14

Round Two
J. Davis beat W.A. Withers 30-1
H. Lindrum beat S. Lee 20-11
S. Smith beat Alec Brown 18-13
W. Smith beat T. Newman 16-15

Semi-finals
J. Davis beat S. Smith 18-13
H. Lindrum beat W. Smith 20-11

Final
J. Davis beat H. Lindrum 32-29

1938

Qualifying Round One
H. Holt beat C.W. Read 21-10

Qualifying Round Two
F. Davis beat H. Holt 23-8

Round One
F. Davis beat Alec Brown 14-6
(Brown retired ill)
J. Davis beat S. Lee 24-7
S. Smith beat C. Stanbury 27-4
W. Smith beat T. Newman 16-15

Semi-finals
J. Davis beat W. Smith 24-7
S. Smith beat F. Davis 18-13

Final
J. Davis beat S. Smith 37-24

1939

Qualifying Round One
W. Donaldson beat H. Holt 18-13
H.W. Laws beat S. Newman 19-12

Qualifying Round Two
W. Donaldson beat H.W. Laws 18-13

Round One
F. Davis beat C. Stanbury 19-12
W. Donaldson beat C. Falkiner 21-10
T. Newman beat A. Mann 19-12
S. Smith beat S. Lee 21-10

Round Two
Alec Brown beat H. Lindrum 17-14
F. Davis beat T. Newman 20-11
J. Davis beat W. Smith 19-12
S. Smith beat W. Donaldson 16-15

Semi-finals
J. Davis beat F. Davis 17-14
S. Smith beat Alec Brown 20-11

Final
J. Davis beat S. Smith 43-30

1940

Qualifying Round One
H. Holt beat C. Stanbury 18-13

Round One
F. Davis beat S. Lee 20-11
J. Davis beat Alec Brown 20-11
W. Donaldson beat H. Holt 24-7
S. Smith beat T. Newman 22-9

Semi-finals
F. Davis beat S. Smith 17-14
J. Davis beat W. Donaldson 22-9

Final
J. Davis beat F. Davis 37-36

1941-1945 Not held

1946

Qualifying Round One
K. Kennerley beat F. Lawrence 22-9
S. Newman beat W. Leigh 16-15
C. Stanbury beat J. Barrie 18-13

Qualifying Round Two
K. Kennerley beat T. Reece 8-2
(Reece retired)
S. Newman beat C. Stanbury 17-14

Qualifying Round Three
S. Newman beat K. Kennerley 21-10

Round One
F. Davis beat Alec Brown 24-7
J. Davis beat W. Donaldson 21-10
H. Lindrum beat H. Holt 17-14
S. Newman beat S. Lee 19-12

Semi-finals
J. Davis beat S. Newman 21-10
H. Lindrum beat F. Davis 16-12

Final
J. Davis beat H. Lindrum 78-67

Ray Reardon (six times champion) and John Spencer (three) share a joke before one of their many meetings

1947

Qualifying Round One
Albert Brown beat J. Pulman 21-14
K. Kennerley beat C. Stanbury 23-12
S. Lee beat J. Lees 19-16
W. Leigh beat H.F. Francis 19-16
E. Newman beat H. holt w.o.
Qualifying Round Two
J. Barrie beat F. Lawrence 25-10
Albert Brown beat E. Newman 28-7
K. Kennerley beat A. Mann 23-12
W. Leigh beat S. Lee 25-10
Qualifying Round Three
Albert Brown beat J. Barrie 24-11
K. Kennerley beat W. Leigh 21-14
Qualifying Round Four
Albert Brown beat K. Kennerley 21-14

Round One
F. Davis beat C. McConachy 53-20
W. Donaldson beat S. Newman 46-25
H. Lindrum beat Albert Brown 39-34
S. Smith beat Alec Brown 43-28

Semi-finals
F. Davis beat S. Smith 39-32
W. Donaldson beat H. Lindrum 39-32

Final
W. Donaldson beat F. Davis 82-63

1948

Qualifying Round One
J. Barrie beat H.F. Francis 19-16
W. Leigh beat H. Holt 18-17
J. Pulman beat S. Lee w.o.
C. Stanbury beat E. Newman 26-9
Qualifying Round Two
W. Leigh beat J. Barrie 21-14
J. Pulman beat C. Stanbury 19-16
Qualifying Round Three
J. Pulman beat W. Leigh 18-17

Round One
Albert Brown beat S. Smith 36-35
F. Davis beat Alec Brown 43-28
W. Donaldson beat K. Kennerley 46-25
C. McConachy beat J. Pulman 42-29

Semi-finals
F. Davis beat C. McConachy 43-28
W. Donaldson beat Albert Brown 40-31

Final
F. Davis beat W. Donaldson 84-61

1949

Qualifying Round One
C. Stanbury beat H.F. Francis 18-17
Qualifying Round Two
C. Stanbury beat J. Rea 18-17
Qualifying Round Three
C. Stanbury beat H. Holt 18-17

Round One
F. Davis beat K. Kennerley 50-21
W. Donaldson beat C. Stanbury 58-13
J. Pulman beat Albert Brown 42-29
S. Smith beat Alec Brown 41-30

Semi-finals
F. Davis beat S. Smith 42-29
W. Donaldson beat J. Pulman 49-22

Final
F. Davis beat W. Donaldson 80-65

1950

Qualifying Round One
H. Holt beat H.W. Laws 26-9
K. Kennerley beat J. Barrie 21-14
S. Lee beat C. Stanbury 20-15
W. Smith beat W.A. Withers 28-7

Qualifying Round Two
K. Kennerley beat W. Smith 22-13
S. Lee beat H. Holt 16-8

Qualifying Round Three
K. Kennerley beat S. Lee 21-14

Round One
Albert Brown beat J. Pulman 37-34
G. Chenier beat P. Mans 37-34
F. Davis beat Alec Brown 44-27
W. Donaldson beat K. Kennerley 42-29

Semi-finals
F. Davis beat G. Chenier 43-28
W. Donaldson beat Albert Brown 37-34

Final
W. Donaldson beat F. Davis 51-46

1951

Qualifying Round One
J. Barrie beat S. Lee 23-12

Qualifying Round Two
J. Barrie beat H.W. Laws 28-7

Round One
F. Davis beat J. Barrie 42-29
W. Donaldson beat K. Kennerley 41-30
H. Lindrum beat Albert Brown 43-28
J. Pulman beat S. Smith 38-33

Semi-finals
F. Davis beat J. Pulman 22-14
W. Donaldson beat H. Lindrum 41-30

Final
F. Davis beat W. Donaldson 58-39

1952

Final
H. Lindrum beat C. McConachy 94-49

1953-63 Not Held

Between 1964 and 1968 Championship was held on a challenge basis.

1964

J. Pulman beat F. Davis 19-16

J. Pulman beat R. Williams 40-33

1965

J. Pulman beat F. Davis 37-36

J. Pulman beat R. Williams 25-22
(Series of matches in South Africa)

J. Pulman beat F. van Rensburg 39-12

1966

J. Pulman beat F. Davis 5-2

1968

J. Pulman beat E. Charlton 39-34

1969

Round One
F. Davis beat R. Reardon 25-24
G. Owen beat J. Rea 25-17
J. Spencer beat J. Pulman 25-18
R. Williams beat B. Bennett 25-4

Semi-finals
G. Owen beat F. Davis 37-24
J. Spencer beat R. Williams 37-12

Final
J. Spencer beat G. Owen 37-24

1970

Round One
David Taylor beat B. Bennett 11-8

Round Two
G. Owen beat R. Williams 31-11
J. Pulman beat David Taylor 31-20
R. Reardon beat F. Davis 31-26
J. Spencer beat J. Rea 31-15

Semi-finals
J. Pulman beat G. Owen 37-12
R. Reardon beat J. Spencer 37-33

Final
R. Reardon beat J. Pulman 37-33

1971 (Played November 1970)

Round-robin results
E. Charlton beat P. Mans 26-11
E. Charlton beat G. Owen 23-14
E. Charlton beat N. Squire 27-10
P. Morgan beat W. Simpson 21-16
G. Owen beat P. Morgan 26-11
G. Owen beat N. Squire 19-18
J. Pulman beat P. Morgan 25-12
J. Pulman beat N. Squire 26-11
R. Reardon beat E. Charlton 21-16
R. Reardon beat P. Mans 22-15
R. Reardon beat J. Spencer 21-16
R. Reardon v P. Morgan – not played
W. Simpson beat P. Mans 19-18
W. Simpson beat G. Owen 19-18
W. Simpson beat J. Pulman 21-16
J. Spencer beat P. Mans 20-17
J. Spencer beat J. Pulman 23-14
J. Spencer beat N. Squire 27-10

Players	Pld	W	For	Agst	Pts
1. Charlton	4	3	92	56	6
2. Spencer	4	3	86	62	6
3. Reardon	3	3	64	47	6
4. Simpson	4	3	75	73	6
5. Pulman	4	2	81	67	4
6. Owen	4	2	77	71	4
7. Morgan	3	1	44	67	2
8. Mans	4	0	61	87	0
9. Squire	4	0	49	99	0

Semi-finals
W. Simpson beat E.Charlton 27-22
J. Spencer beat R.Reardon 34-15

Final
J. Spencer beat W.Simpson 37-29

1972

Qualifying Round One
J. Dunning beat P. Houlihan 11-10
A. Higgins beat R. Gross 15-6
G. Miles beat B. Bennett 15-6
M. Parkin beat G. Thompson 11-10
Qualifying Round Two
J. Dunning beat G. Miles 11-5
A. Higgins beat M. Parkin 11-3

Round One
A. Higgins beat J. Rea 19-11
J. Pulman beat J. Dunning 19-7
Round Two
E. Charlton beat David Taylor 31-25
A. Higgins beat J. Pulman 31-23
J. Spencer beat F. Davis 31-21
R. Williams beat R. Reardon 25-23

Semi-finals
A. Higgins beat R. Williams 31-30
J. Spencer beat E. Charlton 37-32

Final
A. Higgins beat J. Spencer 37-32

1973

Round One
D. Greaves beat B. Bennett 9-8
P. Houlihan beat J. Rea 9-2
P. Mans beat R. Gross 9-2
G. Miles beat G. Thompson 9-5
W. Simpson beat M. Parkin 9-3
David Taylor beat J. Dunning 9-4
C. Thorburn beat Dennis Taylor 9-8
Round Two
E. Charlton beat P. Mans 16-8
F. Davis beat D. Greaves 16-1
A. Higgins beat P. Houlihan 16-3
G. Miles beat J. Pulman 16-10
G. Owen beat W. Simpson 16-14
R. Reardon beat J. Meadowcroft 16-10
J. Spencer beat David Taylor 16-5
R. Williams beat C. Thorburn 16-15
Round Three
E. Charlton beat G. Miles 16-6
A. Higgins beat F. Davis 16-14
R. Reardon beat G. Owen 16-6
J. Spencer beat R.Williams 16-7

Semi-finals
E. Charlton beat A. Higgins 23-9
R. Reardon beat J. Spencer 23-22

Final
R. Reardon beat E. Charlton 38-32

1974

Qualifying Round
J. Dunning beat D. Greaves 8-2
J. Meadowcroft beat P. Houlihan 8-5
M. Owen beat Dennis Taylor 8-1
J. Pulman beat J. Karnehm 8-0
W. Simpson beat J. Rea 8-3
David Taylor beat R. Gross 8-7
C. Thorburn beat A. McDonald 8-3
Round One
B. Bennett beat W. Simpson 8-2
J. Dunning beat David Taylor 8-6
P. Mans beat I. Anderson 8-1
J. Meadowcroft beat K. Kennerley 8-5
P. Morgan beat C. Thorburn 8-4
M. Owen beat M. Parkin 8-5
J. Pulman beat S. Lee 8-0
B. Werbeniuk beat G. Thompson 8-3
Round Two
F. Davis beat B. Werbeniuk 15-5
J. Dunning beat E. Charlton 15-13
A. Higgins beat B. Bennett 15-4
P. Mans beat J. Spencer 15-13
G. Miles beat P. Morgan 15-7
M. Owen beat G. Owen 15-8
R. Reardon beat J. Meadowcroft 15-3
R. Williams beat J. Pulman 15-12

Round Three
F. Davis beat A. Higgins 15-14
G. Miles beat J. Dunning 15-13
R. Reardon beat M. Owen 15-11
R. Williams beat P. Mans 15-4

Semi-finals
G. Miles beat R. Williams 15-7
R. Reardon beat F. Davis 15-3

Final
R. Reardon beat G. Miles 22-12

1975

Qualifying Round
L. Condo beat M. Parkin 15-8
D. Greaves beat J. Charlton 15-14
P. Tarrant beat B. Bennett 15-8

Round One
I. Anderson beat L. Condo 15-8
G. Owen beat D. Greaves 15-3
J. Pulman beat P. Tarrant 15-5
W. Simpson beat R. Mares 15-5
David Taylor beat R. King 15-8
Dennis Taylor beat P. Mans 15-12
C. Thorburn beat P. Morgan 15-6
B. Werbeniuk beat J. Meadowcroft 15-9
Round Two
E. Charlton beat B. Werbeniuk 15-11
A. Higgins beat David Taylor 15-2
G. Owen beat J. Dunning 15-8
R. Reardon beat W. Simpson 15-11
J. Spencer beat J. Pulman 15-10
Dennis Taylor beat F. Davis 15-14
C. Thorburn beat G. Miles 15-2
R. Williams beat I. Anderson 15-4

Round Three
E. Charlton beat C. Thorburn 19-12
A. Higgins beat R. Williams 19-12
R. Reardon beat J. Spencer 19-17
Dennis Taylor beat G. Owen 19-9

Semi-finals
E. Charlton beat Dennis Taylor 19-12
R. Reardon beat A. Higgins 19-14

Final
R. Reardon beat E. Charlton 31-30

Doug Mountjoy and Steve Davis line up in front of the trophy before the 1981 final

1976

Qualifying Round One
L. Condo beat M. Owen 8-6
D. Greaves beat J. Charlton 8-5
R. Gross beat M. Parkin 8-5
J. Meadowcroft beat D. Wheelwright 8-1
J. Rea beat I. Anderson 8-5

Qualifying Round Two
J. Meadowcroft beat R. Gross 8-4
J. Rea beat B. Bennett 8-5
David Taylor beat D. Greaves 8-1
W. Thorne beat L. Condo 8-3

Qualifying Round Three
J. Meadowcroft beat W. Thorne 8-5
David Taylor beat J. Rea 8-7

Round One
E. Charlton beat J. Pulman 15-9
F. Davis beat B. Werbeniuk 15-12
A. Higgins beat C. Thorburn 15-14
P. Mans beat G. Miles 15-10
J. Meadowcroft beat R. Williams 15-7
R. Reardon beat J. Dunning 15-7
J. Spencer beat David Taylor 15-5
Dennis Taylor beat G. Owen 15-9

Round Two
E. Charlton beat F. Davis 15-13
A. Higgins beat J. Spencer 15-14
P. Mans beat J. Meadowcroft 15-8
R. Reardon beat Dennis Taylor 15-2

Semi-finals
A. Higgins beat E. Charlton 20-18
R. Reardon beat P. Mans 20-10

Final
R. Reardon beat A. Higgins 27-16

1977

Qualifying Round One
J. Virgo beat R. Andrewartha 11-1

Qualifying Round Two
P. Fagan beat J. Meadowcroft 11-9
D. Mountjoy beat J. Rea 11-9
J. Pulman beat M. Parkin w.o.
David Taylor beat D. Greaves 11-0
Dennis Taylor beat J. Karnehm 11-0
C. Thorburn beat C. Ross 11-0
W. Thorne beat B. Bennett 11-4
J. Virgo beat J. Dunning 11-6

Round One
E. Charlton beat David Taylor 13-5
G. Miles beat W. Thorne 13-4
D. Mountjoy beat A. Higgins 13-12
J. Pulman beat F. Davis 13-12
R. Reardon beat P. Fagan 13-7
J. Spencer beat J. Virgo 13-9
Dennis Taylor beat P. Mans 13-11
C. Thorburn beat R. Williams 13-6

Round Two
J. Pulman beat G. Miles 13-10
J. Spencer beat R. Reardon 13-6
Dennis Taylor beat D. Mountjoy 13-11
C. Thorburn beat E. Charlton 13-12

Semi-finals
J. Spencer beat J. Pulman 18-16
C. Thorburn beat Dennis Taylor 18-16

Final
J. Spencer beat C. Thorburn 25-21

1978

Qualifying Round One
R. Andrewartha beat J. Karnehm 9-0
J. Barrie beat D. Greaves 9-3
P. Houlihan beat C. Ross 9-1
M. Parkin beat B. Bennett 9-4

Qualifying Round Two
F. Davis beat J. Virgo 9-8
P. Fagan beat J. Dunning 9-5
P. Houlihan beat J. Meadowcroft 9-6
P. Mans beat J. Barrie 9-6
D. Mountjoy beat R. Andrewartha 9-3
David Taylor beat P. Morgan 9-7
W. Thorne beat R. Williams 9-3
B. Werbeniuk beat M. Parkin 9-2

Round one
E. Charlton beat W. Thorne 13-12
F. Davis beat Dennis Taylor 13-9
P. Fagan beat A. Higgins 13-12
P. Mans beat J. Spencer 13-8
G. Miles beat David Taylor 13-10
R. Reardon beat D. Mountjoy 13-9
C. Thorburn beat P. Houlihan 13-8
B. Werbeniuk beat J. Pulman 13-4

Round Two
E. Charlton beat C. Thorburn 13-12
F. Davis beat P. Fagan 13-10
P. Mans beat G. Miles 13-7
R. Reardon beat B. Werbeniuk 13-6

Semi-finals
P. Mans beat F. Davis 18-16
R. Reardon beat E. Charlton 18-14

Final
R. Reardon beat P. Mans 25-18

1979

Qualifying Round One
R. Andrewartha beat R. Edmonds 9-8
S. Davis beat I. Anderson 9-1
J. Dunning beat J. Rea 9-5
T. Griffiths beat B. Bennett 9-2
P. Houlihan beat J. Barrie 9-5
J. Meadowcroft beat J. van Rensburg 9-7
D. Mountjoy beat D. Mienie 9-1
K. Stevens beat R. Amdor 9-1
W. Thorne beat J. Charlton 9-3
J. Virgo beat M. Parkin 9-0
R. Williams beat D. Greaves 9-2

Qualifying Round Two
S. Davis beat P. Fagan 9-2
T. Griffiths beat J. Meadowcroft 9-6
G. Miles beat R. Williams 9-5
D. Mountjoy beat P. Houlihan 9-6
K. Stevens beat J. Pulman 9-0
David Taylor beat J. Dunning 9-8
J. Virgo beat W. Thorne 9-8
B. Werbeniuk beat R. Andrewartha 9-2

Round One
E. Charlton beat D. Mountjoy 13-6
F. Davis beat K. Stevens 13-8
T. Griffiths beat P. Mans 13-8
A. Higgins beat David Taylor 13-5
R. Reardon beat G. Miles 13-8
Dennis Taylor beat S. Davis 13-11
J. Virgo beat C. Thorburn 13-10
B. Werbeniuk beat J. Spencer 13-11

Round Two
E. Charlton beat F. Davis 13-4
T. Griffiths beat A. Higgins 13-12
Dennis Taylor beat R. Reardon 13-8
J. Virgo beat B. Werbeniuk 13-9

Semi-finals
T. Griffiths beat E. Charlton 19-17
Dennis Taylor beat J. Virgo 19-12

Final
T. Griffiths beat Dennis Taylor 24-16

1980

Qualifying Group 1
J. Rea beat B. Bennett 9-1
W. Thorne beat K. Robitaille 9-4
W. Thorne beat J. Rea 9-1

Qualifying Group 2:
S. Davis beat C. Ross 9-3
P. Morgan beat P. Thornley 9-4
S. Davis beat P. Morgan 9-0

Qualifying Group 3:
M. Hallett beat K. Kennerley 9-2
K. Stevens beat D. Greaves 9-3
K. Stevens beat M. Hallett 9-3

Qualifying Group 4:
J. Johnson beat R. Andrewartha 9-5
P. Houlihan beat J. Johnson 9-6
T. Meo beat J. van Rensburg 9-1
T. Meo beat P. Houlihan 9-1

Qualifying Group 5:
R. Amdor beat B. Mikkelsen 9-7
R. Williams beat R. Amdor 9-4
J. Wych beat J. Bear 9-5
J. Wych beat R. Williams 9-7

Qualifying Group 6:
F. Jonik beat M. Wildman 9-7
C. Wilson beat F. Jonik 9-6

Qualifying Group 7:
R. Edmonds beat M. Parkin 9-2
S. Hood beat J. Dunning 9-7
R. Edmonds beat S. Hood 9-6

Qualifying Group 8:
E. Sinclair beat M. Morra 9-5
E. Sinclair beat D. Mienie 9-7
J. Meadowcroft beat E. Sinclair 9-1

Round One
S. Davis beat P. Fagan 10-6
A. Higgins beat T. Meo 10-9
D. Mountjoy beat C. Wilson 10-6
K. Stevens beat G. Miles 10-3
David Taylor beat R. Edmonds 10-3
J. Virgo beat J. Meadowcroft 10-2
B. Werbeniuk beat W. Thorne 10-9
J. Wych beat J. Pulman 10-5

Round Two
E. Charlton beat J. Virgo 13-12
S. Davis beat T. Griffiths 13-10
A. Higgins beat P. Mans 13-6
R. Reardon beat B. Werbeniuk 13-6
K. Stevens beat J. Spencer 13-8
David Taylor beat F. Davis 13-5
C. Thorburn beat D. Mountjoy 13-10
J. Wych beat Dennis Taylor 13-10

Round Three
A. Higgins beat S. Davis 13-9
K. Stevens beat E. Charlton 13-7
David Taylor beat R. Reardon 13-11
C. Thorburn beat J. Wych 13-6

Semi-finals
A. Higgins beat K. Stevens 16-13
C. Thorburn beat David Taylor 16-7

Final
C. Thorburn beat A. Higgins 18-16

1981

Qualifying Group 1:
D. Greaves beat M. Parkin 9-5
W. Thorne beat M. Morra 9-5
W. Thorne beat D. Greaves 9-3

Qualifying Group 2:
J. White beat B. Mikkelsen 9-4
J. White beat J. Meadowcroft 9-8

Qualifying Group 3:
R. Edmonds beat M. Wildman 9-3
R. Williams beat S. Hood 9-4
R. Edmonds beat R. Williams 9-7

Qualifying Group 4:
M. Hallett beat F. Jonik 9-1
T. Meo beat J. Johnson 9-8
T. Meo beat M. Hallett 9-4

Qualifying Group 5:
J. Dunning beat B. Bennett 9-6
J. Dunning beat P. Fagan 9-7

Qualifying Group 6:
D. Martin beat I. Anderson 9-3
D. Martin beat J. Pulman 9-2

Qualifying Group 7
E. Sinclair beat P. Morgan 9-8
C. Wilson beat R. Andrewartha 9-4
C. Wilson beat E. Sinclair 9-4

Qualifying Group 8:
T. Knowles beat C. Ross 7-0
(Ross retired)
T. Knowles beat J. Wych 9-3

Round One
S. Davis beat J. White 10-8
T. Meo beat J. Virgo 10-6
G. Miles beat T. Knowles 10-8
D. Mountjoy beat W. Thorne 10-6
K. Stevens beat J. Dunning 10-4
J. Spencer beat R. Edmonds 10-9
David Taylor beat C. Wilson 10-6
B. Werbeniuk beat D. Martin 10-4

Round Two
S. Davis beat A. Higgins 13-8
T. Griffiths beat T. Meo 13-6
R. Reardon beat J. Spencer 13-11
David Taylor beat F. Davis 13-3
Dennis Taylor beat K. Stevens 13-11
C. Thorburn beat G. Miles 13-2
B. Werbeniuk beat P. Mans 13-5

Round Three
S. Davis beat T. Griffiths 13-9
D. Mountjoy beat Dennis Taylor 13-8
R. Reardon beat B. Werbeniuk 13-10
C. Thorburn beat David Taylor 13-6

Semi-finals
S. Davis beat C. Thorburn 16-10
D. Mountjoy beat R. Reardon 16-10

Final S. Davis beat D. Mountjoy 18-12

1982

Qualifying Group 1:
John Bear beat F. Jonik 9-4
John Bear beat J. Wych 9-4

Qualifying Group 2:
D. Hughes beat C. Everton 9-4
T. Meo beat D. Hughes 9-4

Qualifying Group 3:
D. Reynolds beat D. Sheehan 9-5
D. Reynolds beat R. Edmonds 9-6

Qualifying Group 4:
E. Hughes beat D. Mienie w.o.
T. Knowles beat E. Hughes 9-7

Qualifying Group 5:
M. Wildman beat G. Foulds 9-8
J. White beat M. Wildman 9-4

Qualifying Group 6:
C. Roscoe beat B. Mikkelsen 9-6
W. Thorne beat C. Roscoe 9-1

Qualifying Group 7:
P. Medati beat J. Phillips 9-3
C. Wilson beat P. Medati 9-5

Qualifying Group 8:
P. Houlihan beat I. Anderson 9-5
D. Martin beat P. Houlihan 9-3

Qualifying Group 9:
M. McLeod beat E. McLaughlin 9-8
J. Dunning beat M. McLeod 9-4

Qualifying Group 10
M. Watterson beat B. Demarco 9-6
J. Meadowcroft beat M. Watterson 9-7

Qualifying Group 11
D. French beat B. Bennett 9-3
P. Fagan beat D. French 9-6

Qualifying Group 12:
I. Black beat M. Parkin 9-6
R. Williams beat I. Black 9-2

Qualifying Group 13
J. Johnson beat V. Harris 9-4
M. Hallett beat J. Johnson 9-8

Qualifying Group 14
J. Donnelly beat M. Gibson 9-8
E. Sinclair beat B. Kelly 9-8
J. Donnelly beat E. Sinclair 9-8

Qualifying Group 15:
S. Francisco beat C. Ross 9-0
P. Morgan beat D. Greaves 9-2
S. Francisco beat P. Morgan 9-1

Qualifying Group 16:
J. Fitzmaurice beat J. Pulman w.o.
M. Morra beat T. Murphy 9-5
J. Fitzmaurice beat M. Morra 9-7

Round One
E. Charlton beat C. Wilson 10-5
P. Fagan beat David Taylor 10-9
S. Francisco beat Dennis Taylor 10-7
A. Higgins beat J. Meadowcroft 10-5
T. Knowles beat S. Davis 10-1
P. Mans beat T. Meo 10-8
G. Miles beat D. Martin 10-5
D. Mountjoy beat R. Williams 10-3
R. Reardon beat J. Donnelly 10-5
D. Reynolds beat F. Davis 10-7
J. Spencer beat J. Dunning 10-4
K. Stevens beat J. Fitzmaurice 10-4
W. Thorne beat T. Griffiths 10-6
J. Virgo beat M. Hallett 10-4
B. Werbeniuk beat J. Bear 10-7
J. White beat C. Thorburn 10-4

Round Two
E. Charlton beat B. Werbeniuk 13-5
S. Francisco beat D. Reynolds 13-8
A. Higgins beat D. Mountjoy 13-12
T. Knowles beat G. Miles 13-7
R. Reardon beat J. Virgo 13-8
K. Stevens beat P. Fagan 13-7
W. Thorne beat J. Spencer 13-5
J. White beat P. Mans 13-6

Round Three
E. Charlton beat T. Knowles 13-11
A. Higgins beat W. Thorne 13-10
R. Reardon beat S. Francisco 13-8
J. White beat K. Stevens 13-9

Semi-finals
R. Reardon beat E. Charlton 16-11
A. Higgins beat J. White 16-15

Final
A. Higgins beat R. Reardon 18-15

1983

Qualifying Group 1:
B. Kelly beat B. Demarco 10-4
S. Francisco beat B. Kelly 10-5

Qualifying Group 2:
P. Morgan beat P. Burke 10-9
G. Miles beat P. Morgan 10-6

Qualifying Group 3
T. Murphy beat P. Houlihan 10-9
J. Virgo beat T. Murphy 10-8

Qualifying Group 4:
R. Williams beat M. Darrington 10-0
R. Williams beat F. Davis 10-1

Qualifying Group 5:
M. Wildman beat B. Harris 10-7
M. Wildman beat J. Wych w.o.

Qualifying Group 6:
R. Edmonds beat F. Jonik 10-4
D. Reynolds beat R. Edmonds 10-6

Qualifying Group 7:
M. Fisher beat P. Fagan 10-8
E. McLaughlin beat D. Greaves 10-7
M. Fisher beat E. McLaughlin 10-9

Qualifying Group 8
G. Foulds beat M. Gibson 10-6
T. Meo beat V. Harris 10-0
T. Meo beat G. Foulds 10-4

Qualifying Group 9:
I. Black beat M. Morra 10-9
P. Medati beat J. Bear 10-7
I. Black beat P. Medati 10-4

Qualifying Group 10:
J. Johnson beat P. Watchorn 10-0
C. Wilson beat C. Everton 10-1
C. Wilson beat J. Johnson 10-8

Qualifying Group 11:
M. McLeod beat M. Owen 10-5
D. Martin beat M. Parkin 10-1
D. Martin bet M. McLeod 10-7

Qualifying Group 12:
G. Cripsey beat D. Hughes 10-2
J. Meadowcroft beat B. Bennett 10-3
J. Meadowcroft beat G. Cripsey 10-6

Qualifying Group 13:
J. Campbell beat M. Watterson 10-6
J. Donnelly beat D. Sheehan 10-6
J. Campbell beat J. Donnelly 10-2

Qualifying Group 14:
L. Dodd beat J. Dunning w.o.
I. Williamson beat D. French 10-8
L. Dodd beat I. Williamson 10-9

Qualifying Group 15
M. Hallett beat R. Andrewartha 10-7
W. King beat I. Anderson 10-6
M. Hallett beat W. King 10-6

Qualifying Group 16
E. Hughes beat J. Fitzmaurice 10-7
E. Sinclair beat C. Roscoe 10-2
E. Hughes beat E. Sinclair 10-8

Round One
E. Charlton beat L. Dodd 10-7
S. Davis beat R. Williams 10-4
T. Griffiths beat M. Wildman 10-8
A. Higgins beat D. Reynolds 10-4
T. Knowles beat G. Miles 10-3
P. Mans beat I. Black 10-3
T. Meo beat J. White 10-8
D. Mountjoy beat C. Wilson 10-2
R. Reardon beat E. Hughes 10-7
J. Spencer beat M. Hallett 10-7
K. Stevens beat M. Fisher 10-2
David Taylor beat J. Meadowcroft 10-2
Dennis Taylor beat S. Francisco 10-9
C. Thorburn beat J. Campbell 10-5
W. Thorne beat J. Virgo 10-3
B. Werbeniuk beat D. Martin 10-4

Round Two
E. Charlton beat J. Spencer 13-11
S. Davis beat Dennis Taylor 13-11
A. Higgins beat W. Thorne 13-8
T. Knowles beat R. Reardon 13-12
T. Meo beat D. Mountjoy 13-11
K. Stevens beat P. Mans 13-3
C. Thorburn beat T. Griffiths 13-12
B. Werbeniuk beat David Taylor 13-10

Round Three
S. Davis beat E. Charlton 13-5
A. Higgins beat B. Werbeniuk 13-11
T. Knowles beat T. Meo 13-9
C. Thorburn beat K. Stevens 13-12

Semi-finals
S. Davis beat A. Higgins 16-5
C. Thorburn beat T. Knowles 16-15

Final
S. Davis beat C. Thorburn 18-6

1984

Qualifying Group 1:
J. Parrott beat D. Hughes 10-3
J. Parrott beat C. Everton 10-2
J. Parrott beat P. Mans 10-0

Qualifying Group 2:
B. Mikkelsen beat P. Medati 10-8
B. Mikkelsen beat F. Jonik 10-9
W. Thorne beat B. Mikkelsen 10-3

Qualifying Group 3:
M. Morra beat G. Foulds 10-2
T. Murphy beat J. Fitzmaurice 10-8
M. Morra beat T. Murphy 10-5
M. Morra beat D. Reynolds 10-7

Qualifying Group 4:
P. Mifsud beat E. Hughes 10-5
W. Sanderson beat P. Morgan 10-8
P. Mifsud beat W. Sanderson 10-5
P. Mifsud beat C. Wilson 10-8

Qualifying Group 5:
R. Edmonds beat D. Greaves 10-0
J. van Rensburg beat V. Harris 10-7
J. van Rensburg beat R. Edmonds 10-9
S. Francisco beat J. van Rensburg 10-3

Qualifying Group 6:
M. Hines beat I. Black 10-5
I. Williamson beat P. Houlihan 10-5
I. Williamson beat M. Hines 10-6
G. Miles beat I. Williamson 10-6

Qualifying Group 7:
M. Fisher beat P. Thornley 10-8
M. Gibson beat G. Rigitano 10-7
M. Gibson beat M. Fisher 10-7
J. Johnson beat M. Gibson 10-3

Qualifying Group 8:
R. Andrewartha beat John Bear w.o.
E. McLaughlin beat J. Hargreaves 10-5
R. Andrewartha beat E. McLaughlin 10-8
R. Andrewartha beat M. Wildman 10-9

Qualifying Group 9:
G. Scott beat L. Heywood 10-7
J. Wych beat G. Ganim, Jnr 10-1
J. Wych beat G. Scott 10-6
J. Wych beat P. Fagan 10-3

Qualifying Group 10:
P. Browne beat S. Duggan 10-9
C. Roscoe beat B. Demarco 10-7
P. Browne beat C. Roscoe 10-4
E. Sinclair beat P. Browne 10-1

Qualifying Group 11:
G. Cripsey beat M. Parkin 10-4
M. Gauvreau beat J. Campbell 10-7
M. Gauvreau beat G. Cripsey 10-1
M. Gauvreau beat M. McLeod 10-6

Qualifying Group 12:
I. Anderson beat G. Watson 10-4
J. Donnelly beat P. Watchorn 10-7
J. Donnelly beat I. Anderson 10-6
F. Davis beat J. Donnelly 10-5

Qualifying Group 13:
W. King beat T. Jones 10-9
M. Watterson beat B. Bennett 10-5
W. King beat M. Watterson 10-8
W. King beat D. Martin 10-8

Qualifying Group 14:
J. Caggianello beat M. Darrington 10-7
B. Oliver beat J. Dunning 10-3
B. Oliver beat J. Caggianello 10-7
R. Williams beat B. Oliver 10-8

Qualifying Group 15:
L. Dodd beat J. Giannaros 10-1
N. Foulds beat D. French 10-5
N. Foulds beat L. Dodd 10-4
N. Foulds beat J. Meadowcroft 10-2

Qualifying Group 16:
P. Burke beat B. Kelly 10-7
B. Harris beat D. Sheehan 10-3
P. Burke beat B. Harris 10-4
M. Hallett beat P. Burke 10-5

Round One
E. Charlton beat R. Andrewartha 10-4
S. Davis beat W. King 10-3
N. Foulds beat A. Higgins 10-9
S. Francisco beat T. Meo 10-5
T. Griffiths beat P. Mifsud 10-2
D. Mountjoy beat M. Hallett 10-4
J. Parrott beat T. Knowles 10-7
R. Reardon beat J. Wych 10-7
J. Spencer beat G. Miles 10-3
K. Stevens beat E. Sinclair 10-1
David Taylor beat M. Gauvreau 10-5
Dennis Taylor beat J. Johnson 10-1
C. Thorburn beat M. Morra 10-3
W. Thorne beat J. Virgo 10-9
B. Werbeniuk beat F. Davis 10-4
J. White beat R. Williams 10-6

Round Two
S. Davis beat J. Spencer 13-5
T. Griffiths beat B. Werbeniuk 13-5
D. Mountjoy beat N. Foulds 13-6
R. Reardon beat S. Francisco 13-8
K. Stevens beat David Taylor 13-10
Dennis Taylor beat J. Parrott 13-11
C. Thorburn beat W. Thorne 13-11
J. White beat E. Charlton 13-7

Round Three
S. Davis beat T. Griffiths 13-10
K. Stevens beat R. Reardon 13-2
Dennis Taylor beat D. Mountjoy 13-8
J. White beat C. Thorburn 13-8

Semi-finals
S. Davis beat Dennis Taylor 16-9
J. White beat K. Stevens 16-14

Final
S. Davis beat J. White 18-16

1985

Qualifying Group 1
G. Rigitano beat D. Sheehan 10-9
G. Rigitano beat B. Harris 10-4
G. Rigitano beat B. Kelly 10-6
G. Rigitano beat M. Fisher 10-2
N. Foulds beat G. Rigitano 10-8

Qualifying Group 2
D. O'Kane beat J. McLaughlin w. o.
D. O'Kane beat V. Harris 10-5
D. O'Kane beat F. Jonik 10-5
D. O'Kane beat L. Dodd 10-7
D. O'Kane beat D. Martin 10-8

Qualifying Group 3
S. Longworth beat J. Giannaros 10-1
S. Longworth beat G. Cripsey 10-8
J. van Rensburg beat S. Longworth 10-7
M. Gauvreau beat J. van Rensburg 10-9
D. Reynolds beat M. Gauvreau 10-1

Qualifying Group 4
R. Chaperon beat R. Bales 10-7
R. Chaperon beat L. Heywood 10-1
R. Chaperon beat P. Morgan 10-3
F. Davis beat R. Chaperon 10-9
R. Williams beat F. Davis 10-6

Qualifying Group 5
D. Hughes beat D. French 10-5
S. Newbury beat D. Hughes 10-9
S. Newbury beat P. Burke 10-3
S. Newbury beat G. Scott 10-2
E. Hughes beat S. Newbury 10-6

Qualifying Group 6
M. Hines beat T. Chappel 10-8
M. Hines beat P. Watchorn 10-4
M. Gibson beat M. Hines 10-7
P. Fagan beat M. Gibson 10-8
P. Fagan beat C. Wilson 10-9

Qualifying Group 7
D. Fowler beat J. Hargreaves 10-0
D. Fowler beat G. Watson w. o.
D. Fowler beat J. Caggianello w. o.
D. Fowler beat J. Donnelly 10-0
J. Parrott beat D. Fowler 10-2

Qualifying Group 8
R. Foldvari beat P. Thornley w. o.
R. Foldvari beat B. Oliver 10-3
R. Edmonds beat R. Foldvari 10-3
R. Edmonds beat M. Wildman 10-7

Qualifying Group 9
D. Chalmers beat D. Greaves 10-3
D. Chalmers beat E. McLaughlin 10-9
D. Chalmers beat I. Black 10-4
M. Hallett beat D. Chalmers 10-1

Qualifying Group 10
G. Foulds beat M. Parkin 10-6
G. Foulds beat C. Everton 10-2
G. Foulds beat C. Roscoe 10-7
J. Johnson beat G. Foulds 10-6

Qualifying Group 11
P. Medati beat B. Bennett 10-4
P. Medati beat I. Williamson 10-8
P. Medati beat W. King 10-9
S. Francisco beat P. Medati 10-7

Qualifying Group 12
I. Anderson beat A. Kearney 10-8
P. Browne beat I. Anderson 10-5
M. Morra beat P. Browne 10-6
J. Campbell beat M. Morra 10-9

Qualifying Group 13
W. Jones beat John Rea 10-3
W. Jones beat J. Dunning 10-6
W. Jones beat M. Watterson 10-5
W. Jones beat G. Miles 10-8

Qualifying Group 14
M. Bradley beat D. Mienie 10-4
M. Bradley beat B. Mikkelsen 10-9
J. Wych beat M. Bradley 10-7
J. Virgo beat J. Wych 10-4

Qualifying Group 15
P. Francisco beat B. Demarco 10-4
P. Francisco beat T. Murphy 10-4
P. Francisco beat J. Meadowcroft 10-5
M. McLeod beat P. Francisco 10-7

Qualifying Group 16
T. Jones beat M. Darrington 10-2
T. Jones beat S. Duggan 10-8
T. Jones beat J. Fitzmaurice 10-4
T. Jones beat E. Sinclair 10-2

Round One:
E. Charlton beat J. Campbell 10-3
S. Davis beat N. Foulds 10-8
P. Fagan beat W. Thorne 10-6
T. Griffiths beat R. Williams 10-3
A. Higgins beat D. Reynolds 10-4
T. Knowles beat T. Jones 10-8
T. Meo beat J. Virgo 10-6
D. Mountjoy beat M. McLeod 10-5
J. Parrott beat J. Spencer 10-3
R. Reardon beat E. Hughes 10-9
K. Stevens beat R. Edmonds 10-8
David Taylor beat D. O'Kane 10-4
Dennis Taylor beat S. Francisco 10-2
C. Thorburn beat M. Hallett 10-8
B. Werbeniuk beat J. Johnson 10-8
J. White beat W. Jones 10-4

Round Two
S. Davis beat David Taylor 13-4
T. Griffiths beat A. Higgins 13-7
T. Knowles beat D. Mountjoy 13-6
J. Parrott beat K. Stevens 13-6
R. Reardon beat P. Fagan 13-9
Dennis Taylor beat E. Charlton 13-6
C. Thorburn beat B. Werbeniuk 13-3
J. White beat T. Meo 13-11

Round Three
S. Davis beat T. Griffiths 13-6
T. Knowles beat J. White 13-10
R. Reardon beat J. Parrott 13-12
Dennis Taylor beat C. Thorburn 13-5

Semi-Finals
S. Davis beat R. Reardon 16-5
Dennis Taylor beat T. Knowles 16-5

Final
Dennis Taylor beat S. Davis 18-17

1986

Qualifying Round 1:
D. Gilbert beat R. Bales 10-7
O. Agrawal beat D. Hughes 10-6
A. Kearney beat G. Wilkinson 10-5
B. Oliver beat J. O'Boye 10-8
D. Sheehan beat P. Houlihan 10-7
M. Gibson beat G. Jenkins 10-4
S. Simngam beat B. Bennett 10-0
J. Bear beat P. Burke 10-8
T. Drago beat G. Cripsey 10-4
M. Smith beat D. Greaves 10-4
B. West beat J. Giannaros w.o.
P. Thornley beat D. Mienie 10-3
R. Grace beat M. Parkin 10-8
S. Hendry beat B. Demarco 10-7
P. Watchorn beat J. Rempe w.o.
B. Mikkelsen beat J. Hargreaves 10-7
M. Darrington beat W. Sanderson w.o.

Qualifying Round 2:
J. Wych beat T. Chappel 10-6
S. Duggan beat M. Fisher 10-3
T. Jones beat V. Harris 10-7
D. Gilbert beat M. Bradley 10-7
S. Newbury beat O. Agrawal 10-5
I. Black beat B. Harris 10-8
G. Scott beat A. Kearney 10-8
D. Fowler beat B. Oliver 10-8
C. Roscoe beat G. Foulds 10-3
W. King beat D. Sheehan 10-4
M. Gibson beat M. Morra 10-9
P. Medati beat S. Simngam 10-9
R. Chaperon beat F. Jonik 10-8
M. Gauvreau beat J. Bear 10-5
F. Davis beat D. Chalmers 10-6
P. Francisco beat T. Drago 10-4
B. West beat J. Dunning 10-3
W. Jones beat R. Grace 10-3
S. Longworth beat P. Watchorn 10-7
M. Watterson beat B. Mikkelsen 10-2
L. Dodd beat J. Fitzmaurice 10-6
M. Darrington beat J. Meadowcroft 10-6
John Rea beat E. McLaughlin 10-6
J. Donnelly beat M. Smith 10-6
S. Hendry beat P. Browne 10-9
E. Sinclair beat P. Morgan 10-8
T. Murphy beat J. McLaughlin 10-7
P. Thornley beat P. Fagan 10-7
G. Miles beat C. Everton 10-3
R. Foldvari beat G. Rigitano 10-6
R. Edmonds beat B. Kelly 10-0
J. van Rensburg beat I. Williamson 10-9

Qualifying Round 3:
S. Hendry beat W. Jones 10-8
B. West beat J. Donnelly 10-5
T. Murphy beat P. Thornley 10-3
J. Wych beat S. Duggan 10-5
D. Gilbert beat T. Jones 10-7
S. Newbury beat I. Black 10-2
D. Fowler beat G. Scott 10-7
W. King beat C. Roscoe 10-5
P. Medati beat M. Gibson 10-6
M. Gauvreau beat R. Chaperon 10-8
P. Francisco beat F. Davis 10-1
J. van Rensburg beat E. Sinclair 10-2
S. Longworth beat John Rea 10-4
R. Foldvari beat G. Miles 10-7
L. Dodd beat M. Watterson 10-1
R. Edmonds beat M. Darrington 10-5

Qualifying Round 4:
M. Hallett beat J. Wych 10-7
D. Martin beat D. Gilbert 10-5
J. Spencer beat S. Newbury 10-7
D. Fowler beat M. McLeod 10-6
D. Reynolds beat W. King 10-7
C. Wilson beat P. Medati 10-6
R. Williams beat M. Gauvreau 10-3
N. Foulds beat P. Francisco 10-9
B. Werbeniuk beat B. West 10-8
E. Hughes beat T. Murphy 10-7
S. Hendry beat D. O'Kane 10-9
J. Campbell beat J. van Rensburg 10-6
J. Virgo beat S. Longworth 10-8
J. Parrott beat R. Foldvari 10-6
P. Mans beat L. Dodd 10-7
R. Edmonds beat M. Wildman 10-9

Round One
M. Hallett beat Dennis Taylor 10-6
J. Johnson beat D. Martin 10-3
A. Higgins beat J. Spencer 10-7
T. Griffiths beat D. Fowler 10-2
K. Stevens beat D. Reynolds 10-6
E. Charlton beat C. Wilson 10-6
S. Francisco beat R. Williams 10-4
T. Knowles beat N. Foulds 10-9
C. Thorburn beat B. Werbeniuk 10-5
E. Hughes beat David Taylor 10-7
W. Thorne beat S. Hendry 10-8
J. Campbell beat R. Reardon 10-8
J. White beat J. Virgo 10-7
J. Parrott beat T. Meo 10-4
D. Mountjoy beat P. Mans 10-3
S. Davis beat R. Edmonds 10-4

Round Two
J. Johnson beat M. Hallett 13-6
T. Griffiths beat A. Higgins 13-12
C. Thorburn beat E. Hughes 13-6
W. Thorne beat J. Campbell 13-9
J. White beat J. Parrott 13-8
S. Davis beat D. Mountjoy 13-5
K. Stevens beat E. Charlton 13-12
T. Knowles beat S. Francisco 13-10

Quarter-finals
J. Johnson beat T. Griffiths 13-12
T. Knowles beat K. Stevens 13-9
C. Thorburn beat W. Thorne 13-6
S. Davis beat J. White 13-5

Semi-finals
J. Johnson beat T. Knowles 16-8
S. Davis beat C. Thorburn 16-12

Final
J. Johnson beat S. Davis 18-12

Snooker's most sought-after trophy, the World Professional Championship trophy

1987

Qualifying Round 1:
G. Foulds beat P. Watchorn 10-6
D. Hughes beat M. Parkin 10-5
C. Roscoe beat T. Whitthread 10-2
M. Morra beat P. Gibson 10-6
S. James beat M. Watterson 10-2
G. Jenkins beat R. Grace 10-9
D. Greaves beat P. Thornley 10-6
M. Darrington beat B. Demarco 10-6
J. Rempe beat M. Smith 10-9
K. Owers beat M. Fisher 10-5
M. Bennett beat J. Hargreaves 10-6
B. Kelly beat B. Bennett 10-0
J. Meadowcroft beat D. Mienie 10-3
B. Oliver beat P. Burke 10-5
N. Gilbert beat D. Sheehan 10-6
J. Fitzmaurice beat C. Everton 10-2
J. Dunning beat J. Caggianello 10-7
J. Wright beat P. Houlihan 10-4
J. Bear beat J. Rea 10-5
G. Rigitano beat P. Morgan 4-0 (retd.)
D. Chalmers beat E. McLaughlin w.o.
D. Roe beat O.B. Agrawal w.o.
T. Kearney beat F. Jonik w.o.
B. Boswell beat S. Simngam w.o.

Qualifying Round 2:
S. Newbury beat L. Dodd 10-7
B. Oliver beat P. Fagan 10-2
M. Gauvreau beat J. Bear 10-3
R. Edmonds beat S. James 10-1
J. Spencer beat R. Bales 10-3
S. Duggan beat C. Roscoe 10-7
G. Scott beat J. Dunning 10-7
G. Rigitano beat V. Harris 10-6
R. Chaperon beat J. Fitzmaurice 10-2
M. Bradley beat M. Rowswell 10-6
T. Murphy beat G. Jenkins 10-4
D. O'Kane beat D. Gilbert 10-2
M. Gibson beat B. Kelly 10-9
W. Jones beat J. Donnelly 10-3
W. King beat D. Roe 10-4
K. Owers beat F. Davis 10-5
M. Wildman beat R. Foldvari 10-5
J. Wright beat P. Browne 10-6
J. O'Boye beat N. Gilbert 10-5
G. Miles beat D. Greaves 10-7
S. Hendry beat M. Darrington 10-7
J. van Rensburg beat J. McLaughlin 10-6
G. Cripsey beat J. Meadowcroft 10-9
I. Black beat I. Williamson 10-8
M. Bennett beat B. Mikkelsen 10-4
J. Rempe beat J. Rea 10-9
T. Chappel beat M. Morra 10-8
P. Medati beat T. Kearney 10-8
D. Fowler beat G. Foulds 10-6
E. Sinclair beat T. Drago 10-9
T. Jones beat D. Chalmers 10-1
B. Harris beat D. Hughes 10-2

Qualifying Round 3:
D. Fowler beat B. Harris 10-6
T. Chappel beat S. Duggan 10-3
T. Jones beat J. van Rensburg 10-0
P. Medati beat M. Gauvreau 10-3
G. Cripsey beat M. Gibson 10-4
R. Edmonds beat E. Sinclair 10-6
J. Wright beat M. Wildman 10-0
M. Bennett beat W. Jones 10-3
W. King beat K. Owers 10-4
D. O'Kane beat I. Black 10-2
S. Newbury beat G. Rigitano 10-4
S. Hendry beat J. Rempe 10-4
B. Oliver beat G. Scott 10-5
J. Spencer beat R. Chaperon 10-4
T. Murphy beat G. Miles 10-7
M. Bradley beat J. O'Boye 10-7

Qualifying Round 4:
J. Parrott beat D. Fowler 10-3
J. Campbell beat T. Chappel 10-6
J. Virgo beat T. Jones 10-9
E. Hughes beat P. Medati 10-2
D. Taylor beat G. Cripsey 10-7
M. McLeod beat R. Edmonds 10-7
J. Wright beat C. Wilson 10-4
M. Bennett beat B. Werbeniuk 10-8
W. King beat E. Charlton 10-4
D. O'Kane beat P. Francisco 10-5
M. Hallett beat S. Newbury 10-4
S. Hendry beat D. Martin 10-6
D. Reynolds beat B. Oliver 10-7
B. West beat J. Spencer 10-5
S. Longworth beat T. Murphy 10-2
J. Wych beat M. Bradley 10-7

First Round
S. Davis beat W. King 10-7
J. Johnson beat E. Hughes 10-9
R. Reardon beat B. West 10-5
M. McLeod beat R. Williams 10-5
T. Griffiths beat J. Wych 10-4
S. Hendry beat W. Thorne 10-7
S. Longworth beat K. Stevens 10-4
A. Higgins beat J. Wright 10-6
M. Hallett beat T. Knowles 10-6
J. White beat D. Reynolds 10-8
J. Parrott beat T. Meo 10-8
S. Francisco beat J. Campbell 10-3
N. Foulds beat J. Virgo 10-4
D. Mountjoy beat David Taylor 10-5
Dennis Taylor beat M. Bennett 10-4
D. O'Kane beat C. Thorburn 10-5

Second Round
J. Johnson beat M. McLeod 13-7
S. Davis beat R. Reardon 13-4
T. Griffiths beat A. Higgins 13-10
S. Hendry beat S. Longworth 13-7
J. White beat J. Parrott 13-11
M. Hallett beat S. Francisco 13-9
N. Foulds beat Dennis Taylor 13-10
D. O'Kane beat D. Mountjoy 13-5

Quarter-finals
J. Johnson beat S. Hendry 13-12
J. White beat D. O'Kane 13-6
S. Davis beat T. Griffiths 13-5
N. Foulds beat M. Hallett 13-9

Semi-finals
J. Johnson beat N. Foulds 16-9
S. Davis beat J. White 16-11

Final
S. Davis beat J. Johnson 18-14

Yamaha International Masters

See Dulux British Open

Youngest

Jimmy White is the youngest person to have won a snooker world championship. When he won the world amateur title at Launceston in 1980, White was just 18 years and 191 days old.

The youngest winner of the world professional title was Alex Higgins. When he beat John Spencer to win his first title in 1972, Higgins was 22 years 345 days old.

Stephen Hendry became the youngest-ever qualifier for the world amateur championships at the age of 15. When he won the 1986 Scottish Professional Championship in 1986, Stephen Hendry became the youngest-ever winner of a national professional championship, at just 17 years of age.

Gareth Thomas won his opening frame on his debut in the St Helens league in 1983. Gareth was just 11 at the time.

The youngest league player in Britain was Michael Procter Junior: he was 9 years 7 months old when he made his debut in the Oldham and District Sunday School League.

A 9-year-old girl, Lynette Horsburgh, registered a break of 40 in the opening frame of the final of the under-13 open championship at the Commonwealth Sporting Club, Blackpool, in 1984. Coached by Frank Callan, mentor of Steve Davis and John Parrott, she eventually lost the final to 13-year-old Darren Gowers of Rochdale.

Dave Grimwood, in 1986, bacame the youngest winner of the National Under-16 Championship. He was 13 years and 4 months at the time.

Ten-year-old Ronnie O'Sullivan made a century break at the Barking Snooker Centre in November 1986. He is believed to be the youngest ever century breaker.

The youngest female to be granted a referee's certificate was Charlotte Hall from Devizes, Wiltshire. She was 16 years and 9 months old when she received her certificate in 1984.

Stephen Woodley of South Shields became the youngest person in Britain to receive assistance from the Manpower Services Enterprise Allowance scheme. On his 18th birthday in

1983, he started to receive the £40-per-week allowance to manufacture undersized slate billiard tables and accessories.

When Jimmy White won the Scottish Masters at Kelvin Hall, Glasgow, in 1981, at the age of 19 years 4 months, he became the youngest player to win a professional tournament. White also holds the distinction of being the first player under the age of 15 to have compiled 50 century breaks.

Jimmy White is also the youngest-ever winner of the English amateur championship – he was just 16 years 11 months when he beat Dave Martin for the title in 1979.

In compiling a 106 break in the semi-finals of the One Frame Tournament at Southend in 1985, Sean Cote, at 13, became the youngest person to make a century break in a tournament.

Zimbabwe

Formerly Southern Rhodesia, Zimbabwe has been an independent member of the Commonwealth only since 1980. The country joined the International Billiards and Snooker Federation shortly after gaining its independence, although the game has been played there since the early fifties. The first national championships were held in 1967.

Snooker, like other aspects of the country, is still not fully developed, but several British players have visited Zimbabwe in recent years and the game is starting to grow. It is currently played strictly at amateur level, but there are hopes that the country's leading player, Alex Thompson, may one day be considered for professional status. Thompson was national champion for the first two years of the championships – 1981 and 1982; he was, however, succeeded by an Australian as national champion in 1983 when Jim Daly beat him 6-4 in the final at the Queen's Sports Club, Bulawayo, to take the title.

British amateurs Mike Darrington and George Wood visited Zimbabwe in 1981 to compete in the first Zimbabwe Open; Darrington won the inaugural title. John Parrott, visiting the country with Neal Foulds, won it the following year, then retained the title in 1983 when he returned as a professional with Joe Johnson, who made a tournament record break of 140.

1984
Zimbabwe National Championships
SNOOKER and BILLIARDS
Individual and Inter-Provincial events
AT THE
Legion Club, Mutare
MAIN TABLE
M.O.T.H. Club, Mutare
SUBSIDIARY TABLE
Monday Aug. 6th - Sunday Aug. 12th inc.

When you're **BROWNED** off
Feeling **BLUE**
Looking **GREEN**
Seeing **RED**
and all appears **BLACK** as thunder
MAKE A BREAK
regain that **GOLDEN** feeling and be in the **PINK**
by consulting the Big **WHITE** Chief
at
CENTRAL PHARMACY
69 Main Street
MUTARE
Telephone 64209

50c

Programme from the Zimbabwe National Championships